The Business of TV Production

The Business of TV Production provides an insider's view of television production from initial concept to developing, creating and airing the final program. It outlines the main functions of each of the players involved and the key stages of the production process.

Covering all genres of television – drama and comedy, documentary and current affairs, infotainment and reality TV – it deals with the business side of production and provides context for all aspects of the operation and the challenges of each genre, such as funding, sourcing a creative team, and marketing and distribution.

This book is for all students taking courses in television production and for those in the industry wanting to upgrade their skills.

Craig Collie is a freelance producer and consultant. He has been working in the television industry since 1969, both in production and network management. He has designed the television production curriculums at Queensland University of Technology, and been executive in charge of student production at the Australian Film Television and Radio School (AFTRS).

The Business of TV Production

Craig Collie

CAMBRIDGE
UNIVERSITY PRESS

CAMBRIDGE UNIVERSITY PRESS
Cambridge, New York, Melbourne, Madrid, Cape Town, Singapore, São Paulo

Cambridge University Press
477 Williamstown Road, Port Melbourne, Vic 3207, Australia

Published in the United States of America by Cambridge University Press, New York

www.cambridge.org
Information on this title: www.cambridge.org/9780521682381

First published 2007

Printed in Australia by Ligare Pty Ltd

A catalogue record for this publication is available from the British Library

National Library of Australia Cataloguing in Publication data

Collie, Craig
The Business of TV Production
Includes index.
ISBN -13   978-0-52168-238-1 paperback
ISBN -10   0-52168-238-X paperback
1. Television broadcasting.   I. Title.
384.55065

ISBN-13   978-0-52168-238-1 paperback
ISBN-10   0-52168-238-X paperback

Contents

Preface

The business of television production is all about creative management and the management of creativity. At its heart lie the conventional canons of good management – financial control, people management, inputs, legal oversight and so on – but overlying this is a need for considerable flexibility. No matter how much market research is done, no-one has any real idea whether a television program will work or not. And production costs are equally unreliable, subject to weather disruption, sulking actors and members of the public who have lost interest in being on camera. It is possibly the only manufacturing industry that conventionally puts a contingency into its production budget.

On the other side of the television coin is the management of the creative process. Sometimes the people are brilliantly and erratically creative, sometimes they are the only people in the world with any regard for their ability. They can be dishonest, backstabbing egomaniacs. Or they can be cool, calm and collected professionals who know exactly how to carry out their craft in a way that adds immeasurably to the quality of the program. They can be the source of lifelong friendships.

The television industry is an industry of paradoxes. Television programs are made, for the most part, for networks that are extraordinarily risk averse, when their own interest is best served by taking risk, and whose commissioning executives often seem to make decisions based on anything but the quality of the program proposal.

So why do people expose themselves to this degree of uncertainty and randomness? Why have I done so for over thirty-five years? Because it is perversely rewarding and because the challenge of steering a production through all the pitfalls that lie in waiting calls on all your accumulated wisdom and experience. You learn how to anticipate many of the traps and to negotiate your way around them. You take a pride in your professionalism.

This book is designed to give the reader an insight into the process of converting a curious idea into an immensely satisfying and, hopefully, successful television program. It is written from the point of view of the producer, the poor fool charged with steering the ship of production through to its destination, and it is an insider's view. The story of the business of television production is the story of the producer. It's as simple as that.

Most tertiary courses in media, communications, film and television – call them what you will – focus on teaching the creative crafts of production: camerawork, editing and, everyone's aim in the business it seems, directing. I'm not convinced that these areas can be taught to any great extent beyond basic operational skills, and these are often glossed over in favour of more time spent on aesthetics and analysis. With increasing demand for these courses to have greater connection to industry, there is a growing interest in the business side of television production. At the least, this side lends itself to the processes of teaching, although even then it has its limits. There are basic operations and basic knowledge to learn, but ultimately even the business side of television is about judgement and instinct. That cannot be taught. It is partly already there (or not, as the case may be) and partly accumulated through experience. This book is, first and foremost, a textbook at the tertiary education level, but I hope it would serve a useful purpose as well as a primer for those already in the industry who want to upgrade their skills to try their hand at producing.

There are three main aspects to the book, covering the three sets of skills required in the business of production. First, it is about people management and, through the leadership of the production team, maintaining an editorial and creative focus in all the contributing craft skills that are woven into a finished television program. These skills are common to any television production anywhere in the world, the universal qualities required of a television producer. The second aspect is how to determine and obtain the necessary resources to ensure the best possible program will be made for the funds available to it. The most crucial resource is, of course, money. This knowledge is specific to the country in which the program is being made. An Australian production needs to know what resources are available and how they are used in Australia, how the conventions of production work in Australia, and what the industry structure and culture is that prevails in Australia. The third aspect is knowing the steps along the production path from concept to delivery, what the role of each step is, and how it might be modified for the specific needs of each production. A triumvirate of people, resources and process.

This book is not a checklist of the things to do to take a production down some standard pathway. That would be a misrepresentation of the way the profession of production operates. There is no prescription for making a television program. Every program is different. Every production within a particular genre is different from the other productions in that genre, but not as different as from the productions in other genres. There are conventions that are generally useful to follow or adapt as long as they serve the particular needs of the program. Where they don't, the production process should be amended so it does suit those needs. Each production pathway is planned with a mix of experience and judgement. The guiding principle is: know what is generally done, then do what will work best for the program.

If there's no one way to make a television program, it's important that a book such as this doesn't reflect the experience of just one producer. This is not about my approach to television production, although elements of that are inevitably part of it. I have endeavoured to bring together a consensus of experiences of various participants in the industry with a wide range of approaches. I have tried to weave this aggregated experience through the common narrative of production.

I'd like to particularly note and to thank Sue Murray (Fandango Australia) and Ian Collie (Essential Viewing), who read and gave critical feedback on selected chapters, Peter Herbert (AFTRS) and John Eastway (Eastway Communication), with whom I had several discussions about what being a producer is all about, and for the insights into their particular areas of experience and expertise (in no particular order): Peter Abbott (Freehand Group), Paddy Conroy and Bob Donoghue (Ovation), Fiona Gilroy and Erika Honey (SBS Marketing), Peter George (producer), Paul Vincent (SBS), Tina Braham and Chris Spry (The Lab), David Vadiveloo (producer), David Goldie (Goldie Media), Ben Cunningham (Austar), Fiona Crago (Beyond Distribution), John Russell (Essential Viewing), and no doubt others I have accidentally overlooked. There are a number of publications whose views I have incorporated into the body of the book. They are listed at the end of chapters. There are also the people I have worked with over the last thirty-five years who have contributed to my growing understanding of the production process and, of course, my family and my wife, Jan, whose support and encouragement have made the task that much easier. Lastly, my thanks to Alan McKee of Queensland University of Technology for suggesting me to Cambridge University Press to write this book, to Cambridge University Press and Jill Henry for their faith, hopefully not misplaced, that I could, and to the editor, Carolyn Pike, for ironing out the bumps and making the book better than it was when I first wrote it.

Diagrams and tables

Abbreviations

The following abbreviations are used either in this book or in the television industry generally.

ABA	Australian Broadcasting Authority
ABC	American Broadcasting Company; Australian Broadcasting Commission/Corporation
ABN	Australian Business Number
ACCC	Australian Competition and Consumer Commission
ACMA	Australian Communications and Media Authority
ACN	Australian Company Number
AD	assistant director
ADR	automatic dialogue replacement
A&E	Arts and Entertainment
AFC	Australian Film Commission
AFL	Australian Football League
AFTRS	Australian Film Television and Radio School
AIDC	Australian International Documentary Conference
AMCOS	Australasian Mechanical Copyright Owners' Society Ltd
AP	associate producer
APRA	Australasian Performing Rights Association Ltd
APS	Australian Public Service
ARC	aspect ratio converter
ASDA	Australian Screen Directors Association
ASDACS	Australian Screen Directors Authorship Collecting Society
ASIC	Australian Securities and Investments Commission
ASTRA	Australian Subscription Television and Radio Association
ATA	Admission Temporaire/Temporary Admission
ATF	Asia Television Forum
ATMOSS	Australian Trade Marks Online Search System
ATO	Australian Taxation Office
ATPA	Actors Television Programs Agreement
ATRRA	Australian Television Repeats and Residuals Agreement

ATSC	Advanced Television Standards Committee
AT&T	American Telephone and Telegraph Company
AustLII	Australasian Legal Information Institute
AV	adult violence (classification)
AWA	Amalgamated Wireless Australasia
AWG	Australian Writers' Guild
AWGACS	Australian Writers' Guild Authorship Collecting Society Ltd
BBC	British Broadcasting Corporation
BITC	burnt-in timecode
BNF	basic negotiated fee
BRACS	Broadcasting for Remote Aboriginal Communities Scheme
BSB	British Satellite Broadcasting
C	children (classification)
©	copyright
CAL	Copyright Agency Ltd
CBS	Columbia Broadcasting System
CD-R	compact disk – recordable
CGI	computer-generated imagery
CNN	Cable News Network
CNNN	The Chaser Non-stop News Network
COFDM	Coded Orthogonal Frequency Division Multiplex
CPB	Corporation for Public Broadcasting
CSI	Crime Scene Investigation
CSIRO	Commonwealth Scientific and Industrial Research Organisation
Cth	Commonwealth (of Australia)
CTVA	Commercial Television Australia
CU	close-up
D	day
DA	director's assistant
DAT	digital audio tape
DCable	digital cable
DCITA	Department of Communications, Information Technology and the Arts
DIY	do-it-yourself
DOP	director of photography
dpi	dots per inch
DSat	digital satellite
DTH	direct-to-home
DTT	digital terrestrial television
DV	digital videotape
DVB	digital video broadcasting
DVB–H	digital video broadcasting – hand-held
DVB–T	digital video broadcasting – terrestrial
DV camera	digital video camera
DVD	digital versatile disk
DVE	digital vision effects
DVR	digital video recorder
EDL	edit decision list

EFT	electronic funds transfer
EMI	Electrical and Musical Industries
E&O	errors and omissions (insurance)
EP	executive producer
EPG	Electronic Program Guide
ESPN	Entertainment and Sports Programming Network
Ext.	exterior
FACTS	Federation of Australian Commercial Television Stations
FBT	fringe benefits tax
FCC	Federal Communications Commission
FCP	Final Cut Pro
FFC	Film Finance Corporation Australia Ltd
FLIC	Film-Licensed Investment Company
FPI	film producers' indemnity
FTA	free-to-air
FTO	Film and Television Office (NSW)
FX	effects
G	general (classification)
GDI	General Development Investment
GE	General Electric
GST	goods and services tax
HA	high angle
HBO	Home Box Office
HCA	High Court of Australia
HDTV	high-definition television
HOD	head of department
HUT	households using television
IBA	Independent Broadcasting Authority
IDFA	Amsterdam International Documentary Film Festival
IFB	interruptible foldback (or feedback)
Int.	interior
ITA	Independent Television Authority
ITV	Independent Television
iTV	interactive television
JPEG	Joint Photographic Experts Group
KKR	Kohlberg Kravis Roberts & Co.
LA	low angle
LoI	letter of interest
L-VIS	Live Video Insertion System
M	mature (classification)
MA	mature audience (classification)
MD	mini-disk
M&E	music and effects (sound track)
MEAA	Media, Entertainment and Arts Alliance
MGM	Metro Goldwyn Meyer
MHz	megahertz
MMDS	Multichannel Multipoint Distribution Service
MOU	memorandum of understanding

MPEG	Motion Picture Experts Group
MPPA	Motion Picture Production Award
MS	mid-shot
MTV	Music Television
MYOB	Mind Your Own Business
N	night
NBC	National Broadcasting Company
NGO	non-government organisation
NHK	Nippon Hoso Kyokai (Japan Broadcasting Corporation)
NITV	National Indigenous Television Ltd
NTFO	Northern Territory Film Office
NTSC	National Television Systems Committee
NVOD	near video on demand
OB	outside broadcast
OCG	Office of the Children's Guardian (NSW)
OFLC	Office of Film and Literature Classification
OH&S	occupational health and safety
OMF	open media framework
ORS	Office of State Revenue (NSW)
OzTAM	Australian Television Audience Measurement
P	preschool children (classification)
PA	producer's assistant; public address
PAL	phase alternating line
PAN R	pan right
PAYG	pay as you go
PBL	Publishing and Broadcasting Ltd
PBS	Public Broadcasting Service
PC	personal computer
PDF	portable document format
PFTC	Pacific Film and Television Commission
PG	parental guidance recommended
PIA	Production and Investment Agreement
PILA	Production Investment and Licence Agreement
PLA	Production and Licence Agreement
PMG	Postmaster-General
POC	proof of concept
POV	point of view
PPCA	Phonographic Performance Company of Australia
PPV	pay per view
PUT	people using television
PVI	Princeton Video Images
PVR	personal video recorder
RCA	Radio Corporation of America
R&D	research and development
ROW	rest of the world (sales)
SAFC	South Australian Film Corporation
SBS	Special Broadcasting Service
SDTV	standard-definition digital television

SECAM	Sequential Couleur à Memoire (Sequential Colour with Memory)
SFX	special effects
SingTel	Singapore Telecommunications
SMS	short messaging service
SOT	sound off tape
SPAA	Screen Producers' Association of Australia
STS	Simplified Tax System
TA	travel allowance
TARP	target audience rating point
TBS	Turner Broadcasting Service
Telco	telecommunications company
TEN	The Entertainment Network
TFN	Tax File Number
TIFF	Tagged Image File Format
TP	technical producer
Tx	transmission
UHF	ultra-high frequency
UTS	University of Technology, Sydney
VCR	video cassette recorder
VEA	Video Education Australasia Pty Ltd
VFX	visual effects
VHF	very high frequency
VI$COPY	Visual Arts Copyright Collecting Society
V/O	voice-over (picture)
VoIP	Voice over Internet Protocol
VOD	video on demand
VR	virtual reality
VSB	Vestigial Sideband Broadcasting
V/T	videotape
WS	wide shot
Z/I	zoom in
Z/O	zoom out
2D	two-dimensional
2S	two-shot
3D	three-dimensional

Part A

**Opiate of the people:
the television industry**

Chapter 1

Origins and growth of a global medium

At 3 pm on 2 November 1936, the British Broadcasting Corporation (BBC) commenced the world's first public 'high-definition' television service with a speech by Britain's Postmaster-General. The program included a five-minute newsreel from British Movietone, Adele Dixon's performance of a song written especially for the occasion, some Chinese jugglers, and Buck and Bubbles, a pair of African American comedy dancers. An hour later the program was broadcast again on a different system. The BBC had installed two incompatible systems, which were to transmit alternately. Within a few months, it would scrap one of them.

Waiting in a BBC corridor was John Logie Baird, a dishevelled Scotsman expecting to be honoured in the opening ceremony, but instead being snubbed by the grandees who participated. Baird, after whom Australia's annual television awards – the Logies – are named, is now regarded widely as the inventor of television or at least the father of television. In fact, he was neither. Evangelical and obstinate, he pursued a dead end in the development of a technology that now owes nothing to the systems he designed.

From this inauspicious beginning developed the most powerful medium of the second half of the twentieth century. Now, in a new millennium, it's not yet clear whether television is going through a period of adjustment or showing the first signs of slow decline. Either way, it draws from and sustains the popular ethos on a mass scale that no other cultural industry has yet been able to approach.

Television is the product of a haphazard series of developments that culminated in that bizarre double act of 1936 and then got shelved while its players were engulfed in war. When it re-emerged after the war, it was in a world so changed that all bets were off. The race would start again.

Table 1.1: Timeline of global development of television technologies.

Year	Mechanical (analogue TV)	Electronic (analogue TV)	Digital TV
1884	Invention of Nipkow disc		
1897		Invention of cathode ray tube (Braun)	
1907		1st patent for TV system (Rosing, USSR)	
1923	Baird's 1st patent	Zworykin patent (US), Westinghouse drops out	
1925	Public demonstration of Baird system		
1926			
1927	Public demonstration of Bell system (US) Baird transmits London to Glasgow and New York	1st TV broadcast (Grabovsky, USSR)	
1928	18 experimental TV stations licensed in US		
1931		UK patent for EMI (RCA/Zworykin system)	
1934		Public demonstration (Farnsworth)	
1935	1st TV service (Germany)		
	Selsdon Committee recommends BBC adopt 2 broadcast systems (Baird & Marconi EMI)		
1936	1st 'high-definition' TV service (UK)		
1937	Baird system abandoned by BBC	1st test broadcasts in US (NBC-RCA)	
1939		1st TV service in US	
1940			Development of digital signal (Shannon, US)

1951	Colour transmission starts in US
1955	Commercial TV starts in UK
1956	Ampex Corp. demonstrates V/T recording
1960	1st TV broadcast in Australia (TCN-9)
1970	1st all-transistor TV receiver (Sony, Japan)
1972	FCC curbs US network power
	US cable TV allowed into major markets
1982	1st cable channel in Europe (Sky)
1995	Pay TV starts in Australia
1998	Digital services start in US and UK
	Digital TV starts in Australia
2001	BSkyB switch-off of analogue satellite

1.1   John Logie Baird and the race to broadcast

Mechanical and electronic scanning

Television wasn't invented. It developed as a succession of technical advances through two different approaches to the problem of scanning subject matter – one mechanical, the other electronic. In the analogue television system, the camera scans light reflected from the subject and converts it to electrical impulses of varying strengths for transmission to a receiver. The scanning approach that ultimately prevailed was electronic, but unfortunately for John Logie Baird he backed the wrong horse.

The first scanning devices

There was an expectation that image transmission would be possible – George du Maurier's 1878 *Punch* cartoon of a 'telephonoscope', a two-way visual system with parents in London speaking to their daughter in Ceylon, anticipated that – but no-one was sure then how the technology would achieve it. Soon after, two German inventions provided a basis for both mechanical and electronic scanning. In 1884, Paul Nipkow devised a spirally perforated disc with twenty-four small holes through which a strong light was reflected onto a photosensitive selenium cell. Rotation of the Nipkow disc scanned the subject and broke the image into small pieces. The stage was set for competing approaches to television when, thirteen years later, the cathode ray tube was invented by Karl Braun.

The first electronic TV systems

In 1907, Boris Rosing applied for a Russian patent for a television system using a cathode ray tube as receiver. Unaware of the Russian patent, A. A. Campbell-Swinton described his proposed television in *Nature* (1908). Campbell-Swinton replaced the scanning disc with an electronic Braun tube. The image on a photosensitive plate would be bombarded with sweeping electrons and transmitted as electrical impulses. At the receiver, these impulses were to be converted back to a picture on a fluorescent screen. The Scotsman, Campbell-Swinton, never put his system into practice, but the Russian demonstrated his in 1911, producing a distinct image of luminous bands.

Baird's early designs

John Logie Baird was regarded as an 'oddball'. He already had several dubious enterprises under his belt – 'undersocks' that warmed in winter and cooled in summer, chutney and jams from Trinidad, a glass razor, and resin soap – when he began experimenting with the Nipkow disc, even though it had been overtaken by then by the work of Rosing and Campbell-Swinton. Baird was a shy man, with a sense of showmanship, a competitive streak and a passionate belief in the practicality of television. He was not satisfied with just designing a system, he strived for a working model, but reputedly not good with his hands he had to hire people to build his sets for him. After some rudimentary models, Baird moved to

London. Constantly short of money, he seldom ate and never bought new clothes. He was paid, however, for a public demonstration at Selfridge's Department Store, where his images were described as 'faint and often blurred'. Baird's early efforts, then producing only about thirty lines of definition, were elsewhere described as 'a device which only sends shadows' and 'a mere smudge'. His demonstrations promoted an initial public interest in television, but while his mechanical system was struggling, across the Atlantic significant progress was being made with both mechanical and electronic scanners.

Zworykin's all-electric system

A former pupil of Rosing, Vladimir Zworykin had migrated to America in 1919 and four years later filed a US patent for an all-electric television system consisting of a camera tube with photoelectric plate and cathode ray tube receiver. Zworykin built a working system for his employers at Westinghouse Electric, but they were unimpressed and assigned him to other work. Soon after, in Russia in 1926, another former pupil of Rosing, Boris Grabovsky, claimed the first electronic broadcast in Tashkent using Rosing tubes.

Early US mechanical scanning systems

These activities were either unknown to Baird or ignored by him, but he was aware of developments in the United States with mechanical scanners. The American Telephone and Telegraph Co. (AT&T) gave a public demonstration in 1927 of its Bell Laboratories' apparatus using a Nipkow disc. Two broadcasts were received in New York City and watched by an invited audience of business executives, bankers and newspaper editors. One, by wire from Washington DC, included a speech by then Secretary of Commerce, Herbert Hoover, the world's first televised politician. The other was by radio from Whippany in New Jersey and featured comedian A. Dolan. By the next year, eighteen experimental television stations had been licensed in the United States, all using mechanical scanners. A race had started with Britain to be the first country to set up a continuing television service.

Philo T. Farnsworth

What Baird would not have known was that the Radio Corporation of America (RCA) was then secretly testing Zworykin's 'iconoscope', a Braun tube camera that stored the image before scanning, thus requiring much less light on the subject. What also probably escaped Baird's attention at the time was the application in San Francisco by Philo T. Farnsworth for a patent for a camera tube with a photoelectric plate. Farnsworth was twenty-one years old from a poor Idaho farming family, and an avid reader of popular science. By 1929, he and Harry Lubcke had built a television system with all-electric scanning and a synchronising pulse generator. There were no mechanical parts.

Baird takes on the BBC

By then, Baird was absorbed in his competition with Americans who were in his sights. He transmitted pictures of himself, first from London to Glasgow and then from London to New York. Baird's business partner, Captain Oliver Hutchinson, often wrote letters to public officials making demands based on development progress that hadn't happened. They made announcements to the press that were untrue, but drove up share prices in Baird Television Ltd, and they kept cancelling promised demonstrations to Post Office engineers for fourteen months. A great self-publicist, Baird staged many public demonstrations of his system, but night-time test broadcasts from a BBC aerial were stopped by the network's executives. Behind this act was hostility by BBC engineers, who could see limits to the mechanical system. On the other hand, Britain's Post Office engineers were more supportive and pressured the BBC to allow Baird to continue to experiment from the station. With Baird orchestrating outrage in the British popular press and the Postmaster-General (PMG) threatening to issue him with a broadcast licence (Britain had no other radio licensee at that time), the BBC relented and allowed test broadcasts to resume in 1929 during the hours radio was not on air.

Limitations of mechanical scanning

The first live transmission of the Epsom Derby, in 1931, was made with a single camera on the winning post. However, a Baird engineer at the time said, 'You wouldn't be able to tell one horse from another or one jockey from another, but you could at least tell they were horses'. As with mechanical scanning generally, the Baird system was plagued with limitations. In addition to camera immobility, studio recording required on-camera performers to work in a very small, extremely overlit space and there was a distracting flicker in the broadcast picture.

Baird's ill-fated trip to the United States

The space and lighting problems made televised dance programs a fiasco, but Zworykin's iconoscope fixed that and RCA's interlaced scanning solved flicker by dividing the frame into two intermeshed fields. Meanwhile, Baird had been invited to America by radio station owner Donald Flamm. He was to promote and set up a television service, but the federal regulators rejected Flamm's licence application following an RCA objection to a foreign company entering the US television market. In retaliation, Baird wrote to the Prince of Wales complaining that the BBC was giving 'secret encouragement to alien interests'. The English company Electrical and Musical Industries (EMI), 27% owned by RCA, had perfected the RCA/Zworykin system and was applying for a UK patent. Worse, the BBC engineers were showing considerable interest in the EMI system.

EMI system gains support

Experts who saw the EMI system in operation agreed it was far superior to Baird's. Word of this must have got through to Baird as he started looking at alternative scanners. He developed a film scanner that worked on wet film as it emerged from the developing tank, resulting in a delay of about a minute between camera recording and transmission. He was now aware of Farnsworth's work, which had been demonstrated at the Franklin Institute in Philadelphia. Baird experimented with one of these 'image dissector' electronic cameras, now lagging technically behind the RCA 'charge storage' camera.

The Selsdon Committee

With the rivalry continuing between Baird TV and EMI–Marconi, the BBC and PMG set up a committee under Lord Selsdon to resolve the impasse. In 1935, the Selsdon Committee recommended regular BBC broadcasts as soon as possible, using a minimum 240 line scan and the Baird and EMI systems to broadcast on alternate weeks. The scan line requirement wasn't a problem for EMI–Marconi, whose system was already scanning 405 lines, but Baird's three systems were hard-pressed to scan through 240 lines.

BBC's new TV centre

The BBC converted Alexandra Palace in North London to a television centre with considerable duplication to accommodate the two different systems. A test run at the Radiolympia exhibition in August 1936 had mixed results. Baird's system, operating on the first day with its fixed camera and three types of scanner – Nipkow disc, wet film scanner and Farnsworth tube – suffered breakdowns. EMI's more mobile camera provided trouble-free broadcast the next day. Nonetheless, the service opened three months later with the alternating systems, trumpeted as the world's first 'high-definition' television service. A 405-line system was determined to be 'high definition' so that the German Reichs-Rundfunk-Gesellschaft (RRG) service that was broadcast in 1935 with 180 lines could not steal Britain's thunder. However Britain might define its triumph, the contrast between the EMI–Marconi and Baird systems was obvious from the start. By the end of the month, the Baird workshops burnt down and the following February the BBC dropped the Baird system. John Logie Baird's passion and obsession for fifteen years had come to nothing. He later worked on colour television using cathode ray technology and by 1940 had produced a 600-line colour telecast, but in the war years this went unnoticed. He died in 1946.

The lesson of John Logie Baird

There's a message in the story of John Logie Baird for anyone in the business of television production. Television is a flurry of technological change, fashion and whims of the viewing public. It doesn't stand still for very long. To stay on the front of the wave of change, the television professional must monitor developments as they appear; not necessarily responding to every one – it's an industry full of false dawns and soothsayers – but certainly assessing them and being prepared to pick up on any change that is gaining momentum. Baird, with his single-minded focus on mechanical scanning and its American practitioners, was unable to spot a parallel development that was eventually to prevail and so left himself in a sideshow that television passed by.

First American telecasts

As a footnote, NBC–RCA began making regular test broadcasts from the Empire State Building in 1937, America having lost the race for the first television service. The US service was inaugurated in 1939 at the New York World's Fair, opened by President Roosevelt. The next year, the federal regulator, the Federal Communications Commission (FCC), set up the National Television Systems Committee (NTSC) to determine standards for the service. They decided on a 525 scanning line standard for no reason other than it sat midway between the rival companies, RCA (441 line) and Philco (605 line). In 1941, the Columbia Broadcasting System (CBS) entered the television market and the National Broadcasting Company (NBC) commenced a full commercial service. The commercial approach was to prove critical in the later development of the television industry, but any momentum was lost with the bombing of Pearl Harbor.

1.2   America sets the agenda

TV during World War II

Britain's initial dominance of television would last a mere three years. The BBC closed its television service as soon as war was announced in 1939, cutting off in the middle of a Mickey Mouse cartoon and resuming from the same point in the film when peace was declared in 1945. Domestic sales of television sets were just starting to pick up in the United Kingdom when war broke out. In America, television was wound back after the bombing of Pearl Harbor. Only Germany continued transmission, providing communal television in public rooms. RRG had begun three-day-a-week broadcasts in Berlin in 1935. Because the price of home sets was so high, the German Post Office set up eleven viewing rooms in the capital, which it increased to twenty-eight during the Berlin Olympics. The rooms continued to operate during the war until the Allies bombed the Berlin transmitter in 1943.

Early US regulation

Television in the United States developed along laissez-faire lines as radio had before it. Built and operated by the private sector and supported by advertising, it was regulated to protect the public interest. However, early regulation served mostly to prevent any later shift to higher technical standards. As a result, inferior image resolution and colour quality has characterised American television; but this wouldn't become apparent until much later. RCA engineers had improved Zworykin's tube during the war, developing it for guided missiles and reconnaissance. This image orthicon camera could be used in normal room light and RCA reigned supreme in post-war television.

Origin of US networks

CBS wanted to delay the US frequency-band decision – should it be very high frequency (VHF) or ultra-high frequency (UHF)? – so it could establish a colour television service to offset its entry into the television market after rival network NBC. CBS's pursuit of a UHF decision slowed set sales so much that the FCC became concerned about a stalled industry and ratified the television service on VHF in 1947. However, VHF could only support twelve channels nationally and three or fewer stations in most cities. Licences were intended to be local, but the system soon centred on the networks, with NBC and CBS dominant. The American Broadcasting Company (ABC) and DuMont were smaller participants. The DuMont stations were reorganised in 1955 as Metromedia, a large independent station group that was eventually purchased in 1985 by Rupert Murdoch as the fourth network, Fox. In the intervening thirty years, the three remaining networks consolidated their grip on the television industry to the exclusion of all others.

Early doubts and rapid growth

There was an early belief that commercial television was not viable. Its use would be limited to one or two hours a day since it demanded the viewer's attention, unlike radio which could play in the background. Television's production costs were thought to be prohibitive and would lead to a loss of sponsors. Concern was expressed about the disruption of family life and eyestrain from prolonged viewing. By September 1947, there were 3000 sets in New York bars, where the viewers preferred sports and news, and 44 000 sets in the homes of the city's high-income families, who preferred drama, although the total audience was about the same in each group. By 1950, an explosion of set sales to middle- and low-income families, 60% of them bought on credit, had changed all that.

Colour starts and stops

The early days of television broadcast were a time of settling in the new technology. The FCC put a freeze on new television channel allocations in 1948 until station-to-station interference could be resolved. No new channels were allocated for four years. Although Vladimir Zworykin had taken out a patent for colour television in 1925, NBC and CBS weren't able to demonstrate rival colour systems until 1946. In 1951, colour transmission began in the United States, but the several million existing black-and-white receivers could not pick up the colour programs, even in black-and-white, and colour sets went blank during black-and-white transmission. Colour transmission was stopped the year it started and didn't begin again until 1953. In 1956 France developed its own SECAM (Sequential Couleur à Memoire, or Sequential Colour with Memory) colour system.

Network power grows

After the war, network public relations campaigns headed off antitrust and regulatory reform and attempted to persuade all and sundry of their sense of public responsibility. Advertisers and networks had a common goal to reach as many people as possible, they argued. That had to be in the public interest.

With rising prosperity, ideological conservatism and the scarcity of VHF licences, the 1950s shaped a business model for network television in America that remained unchallenged until recently. Advertisers, who had been paying for complete programs, now moved to joint sponsorship. Programs were licensed now by the networks, with advertisers still retaining informal censorship control. Because the market for independent program producers was so small, networks were able to demand a share of ownership and syndication rights. A network licence fee would be less than the program's full production cost and the production company would have to recoup its deficit in domestic and foreign syndication, but that was generally achievable.

Early days of TV drama

Network television had to meet an early economic challenge from Hollywood as well as philosophical doubters and public policy threats. Post-war suburbanisation and the baby boom in America promoted a rise in variety and situation comedy (sitcom). Drama anthology series in the early 1950s had started the careers of many writers, directors and actors – Paddy Chayevsky, Gore Vidal, Sidney Lumet, Arthur Penn and John Frankenheimer, to name just a few of the first two groups – but dramas gave way to quiz shows and episode series (mostly Westerns), and these talented people moved on to movies and the stage. Low-brow programming was a concern with its potential for poor taste, sacrilege and immorality; but the networks headed this off in 1951 with a Television Code.

Networks keep threats at bay

With the success of shows such as *I Love Lucy* and *Dragnet*, filmed programs were preferred to live drama because of the syndication revenue they generated from re-runs at home and abroad. The major Hollywood studios began telefilm production while trying to buy into television station ownership. Doubts about the ability of advertising to support network television had underpinned a proposal for pay television, its viability supported by market surveys and test runs. The networks campaigned vigorously against it, arguing at cross-purposes that the public was not interested in pay television and that it would destroy network broadcasting and the US economy. Frank Stanton of CBS railed against attempts to 'hijack the American public into paying for the privilege of looking at its own television sets'. In the end, Hollywood's moves at television ownership were thwarted by the FCC, with the US Department of Justice already targeting their attempts to control movie distribution and cinema ownership. A change of tack in the late 1950s saw multimillion dollar deals make Hollywood backlog movies available to the networks, thus removing the most attractive aspect of pay television. If the networks showed movies, who needed pay television? It wasn't considered again until the late 1970s.

The start of a world market

The US networks were never slow to cloak themselves in patriotism to advance their interests. They advocated the export of the American broadcasting system to counter the threat of the Soviet Union. Britain, France and the USSR were the only other nations with a regular television service by 1950. America began exporting to Brazil, Mexico and Cuba, even though there were few sets in these countries.

As services commenced around the world in the late 1950s, the US networks moved into international program distribution. They were in a powerful position from their ability to extract lucrative syndication rights over programs licensed from independent producers. CBS ceased telefilm production in favour of licensing and syndication, its 1961 annual report referring to 'eliminating the need for highly speculative investment in television pilot films and series'. Let someone else take that risk! By 1960, television was poised to grow dramatically and the US networks were set to flood the market with program content. As *Business Week* commented, 'the bigger TV gets, the more it resembles the American product'.

The beginnings of public TV in America

Public interest concerns were being expressed about unbridled advertising and educators were worried that the educational potential of the medium was being ignored. Instead, content was limited to advertiser information and entertainment. Ford Foundation-funded lobbying led to the establishment of educational channels on the UHF band; but they lacked facilities and funds, being dependent on donations, and suffered poor management with little vision. Few domestic sets had a UHF tuner anyway. The result was a public television system with low funding and political interference in its content.

Political advertising

The first political advertisements in the United States appeared in 1952 when the Democrats bought a half-hour slot for Adlai Stevenson, only to be bombarded with hate mail for interfering with the broadcast of *I Love Lucy*. Eisenhower and his team settled for twenty-second commercial spots and won the election. But the mood was changing in both the nation and network television.

Current affairs TV

The Nixon–Kennedy 'Great Debates' in the 1960 presidential campaign were perceived to have helped Kennedy win, establishing national politics on the television agenda. News images of southern action against civil rights' demonstrators shifted public opinion on that issue and programs featuring African Americans began to appear. By 1977, *Roots* would draw the largest audience ever for an entertainment program. Television portrayal of the Vietnam War helped end the US involvement there, not from any editorial position it took, but from daily news showing the inescapable reality of the war. Protesters against the war adopted the slogan 'The whole world is watching', fully aware of a new power in the living rooms of the nation and the world. Nixon became paranoid about the networks and in 1973 blocked funding to the Public Broadcasting Service (PBS), which had been operating as a network for only three years. A hotbed of liberalism, it was changed to a central distribution body.

Network power shifts

The 1960s ratings race had been dominated by CBS, which specialised in sitcoms and had more star names than NBC, whose focus was on action and adventure. The ABC was perennially third, without notable stars, but with more daring programming (*The Untouchables*, *Bus Stop* and *Peyton Place*) and a following among the young (*Leave it to Beaver* and *The Flintstones*). The networks had been using their market strength to pressure stations, independent producers and program distributors into deals more favourable to the networks: increased air time, equity in shows and network-favouring re-run schedules.

ABC as the new leader

In 1970, new FCC regulations curbed network power and restructured the television market, thus restricting prime time access, ownership of cable systems or programs, and domestic syndication for the networks. The ABC was the main beneficiary of these changes and by 1976 was the frontrunning network, with an advertising mania for young demographics and the star system having lost its power. This might have seemed at the time as a mere leadership change in the network oligopoly and it was; but by the next decade, as the television market became a global phenomenon, the once-mighty American networks began to look increasingly parochial.

1.3   The ideal of public television

Public TV

Public television is not necessarily state television (although it can be), but its existence is certainly guaranteed only by the state. It is broadcasting built on principles of universal service, diversity of programming, and providing for the needs of minority audiences and the cultural and educational enrichment of an informed electorate. It is a lofty ideal, but one that has been difficult to live up to.

The BBC

The paramount public service broadcaster is the BBC, the cornerstone of British television. Widely admired, it has continued since the start of broadcasting, emphasising serious and worthy programming that would elevate the intellectual and aesthetic tastes of its audience. Established in 1927 by a Royal Charter, it was given a wide range of powers and autonomy, although the government reserved to itself seldom-used powers to prohibit material. The broadcaster was to be funded by licence fees on homes with television and radio sets. Its founding director-general, John (later Lord) Reith, proclaimed the purpose of the BBC was the education and moral improvement of the public.

Arrival of ITV

After the triumph of 1936 and the interruption of the war, television was developed unenthusiastically by the BBC until the arrival of Britain's first commercial channel in 1955. Independent Television (ITV) was a group of commercial companies franchised by the Independent Television Authority, a public body much like the BBC's Board of Governors. The new channel exposed BBC Television's high-brow dullness and, as ITV's network expanded, the BBC lost viewers at an alarming rate. Its audience share had fallen to 28% by 1957. But the liveliness of commercial programs provoked a transformation of the BBC into an organisation more reflective of living British culture. The arrival of *That Was the Week That Was* in 1962 shook the British establishment, breaking television and social taboos. Both public and commercial networks did well in the prosperous 1960s, but by the 1970s inflation was working against the BBC, by then with two channels and the cost burden of the introduction of colour and a new transmission system. BBC2 was launched in 1964 on UHF using the 625-line Phase Alternating Line (PAL) system that had been developed in Germany. The two systems – the original 405-line EMI–Marconi standard and the new PAL 625-line – coexisted on BBC1 until the old standard was finally closed in 1985.

Export of the British model

The British public television model spread across Europe and the British Empire in a range of variations, all committed to broadcasting for the public good and funded by licence fees, taxes or some other non-commercial source. Some departed dramatically from this ideal and became the mouthpieces of state power, sometimes being used to support totalitarian political systems. The United States didn't follow the British example, however, and instead set up a public broadcasting service as an alternative to the commercially financed and market-driven system that prevailed there.

Educational TV in America

In 1951, Iowa State College launched WOI, the first television station owned by an educational institution, although it operated commercially. Two years later, the FCC reserved 242 UHF channels for non-commercial educational television after the freeze on new channel allocation. Frieda Hennock, a criminal lawyer from Brooklyn, had become the first woman appointed to the FCC and had championed the educational channel set-aside during the FCC freeze. She found an ally in Walter William Kemmerer, president of the University of Houston. Kemmerer thought tele-courses might solve the problem of the flood of soldiers entering colleges after the war. In 1953, the university signed on the first non-commercial, educational television station, KUHT (now Houston PBS). Others followed in rapid succession, but there was no federal cash support until the mid 1960s and even then it was patchy. Many of the stations struggled. The second station, KTHE in Los Angeles, closed after nine months when its benefactor withdrew support after an argument with the licensee, the University of Southern California.

Public broadcasting in the United States

The *Public Broadcasting Act* of 1967 set up funding through the Corporation for Public Broadcasting (CPB), for public service rather than educational programming, and set up PBS to operate as a network. Tensions between the affiliated stations, between PBS and the CPB, and between PBS and the White House left public television in the United States starved of funds. In 1972, a frustrated President Nixon vetoed a law authorising two-year CPB funding. The business culture of the undernourished PBS changed as a result and funds were increasingly raised through public appeals.

Achievements of US public TV

Despite the continuing difficulties, American public television has produced some effective television, particularly for minority audiences, in the children's (*Sesame Street*) and news (*MacNeil-Lehrer Report*) genres, and with its purchase of quality British programs. Co-productions between US public stations and European producers became a unifier of American and European television cultures, something unimaginable with commercial television.

Threat of the market forces model

By the 1980s, the underlying principles of public television were being called into question in many countries. Public service television was accused by conservative critics of being closed, elitist and inbred. With movement towards a global economy, it was argued that the free market was making educational and cultural programs viable as commercial commodities. Their protection within public broadcasting was no longer deemed necessary. Deregulation as a prerequisite to dissolving international trade barriers was being applied to the communications industry as well as to many others. The shifting climate increasingly favoured an American market forces model over the longstanding public trustee model that had been the backbone of public broadcasting. In any case, the cost of production and distribution of programs was increasing at a time of reduced public spending.

Loss of direction

With a more market-driven perception of audience, European public broadcasters found themselves unable to offer an alternative to profit-driven programming. In 1983 in an article in *Screen*, Nicholas Garnham referred to 'a crisis in imagination – an inability to conceive of an alternative to broadcasting controlled by profit-seeking private capital other than as centralised, bureaucratic, inefficient, arrogantly insensitive to the people's needs, politically subservient to the holders of state power'.

Fresh force of Channel 4

In Britain, Channel 4 was set up in 1982 as a commercial company owned by the regulatory authority, the Independent Broadcasting Authority (IBA), and financed by advertising revenue and a levy on the commercial companies of ITV. In the wake of a collapse of British cinema, Channel 4 commissioned a new generation of television producers and filmmakers in a curious mix of post-counterculture liberalism and Thatcher-era entrepreneurialism. For the BBC, the Thatcher government considered privatisation and the introduction of advertising, but settled for pressuring it to challenge union power and making demands to bring in new efficiencies.

BBC and the UK government

In the last few decades, the BBC has gone through a succession of political rows with governments of either persuasion. Back in 1985, the Home Secretary, Leon Brittan, had asked the BBC governors to stop the broadcast of an edition of the current affairs program, *Real Lives*, about extremists in Northern Ireland. The Board viewed the program before it went to air and demanded changes. Then in 2003, a report on *Today* suggested the Blair government had 'sexed up' evidence of weapons of mass destruction to justify the war in Iraq. This time the Board rejected the Prime Minister's demands for a retraction, but following the suicide of the source of the BBC's report, the Hutton Inquiry exonerated the government and was critical of the BBC, triggering the resignations of its chairman and director-general.

BBC under attack

By the 1990s, political and public carping about the privileged position of public broadcasters was endemic. Reports exposed bureaucratic bungling, cost over-runs and the misuse of funds. Amid demands for improved accountability and the partial dismantling or reorganisation of public broadcasters, and with the pressure of multi-channel competition, the BBC began reducing its staff and outsourcing many of its activities. The *Broadcasting Act 1990* mandated that no less than 25% of BBC programs had to be commissioned from independent producers.

New alliances for public TV

Even though an intellectual counterattack was mounted, pointing to the loss of minority voices and the illusion of unlimited choice in 500-channel cable systems – content analysis revealed program duplication rather than diversity – the tide continued to run against public television. Public broadcasters built new alliances with book publishers, computer software firms and commercial production houses. Surreptitious commercial money was used to underwrite program production and the question was moved from whether public broadcasting would survive to how much it differed from commercial broadcasting anyway.

1.4   The coming of cable and satellite

Origins of cable TV

Cable television began in the United States as a means of transmitting network programs to areas of poor reception. Cable operators proceeded to offer more channels to subscribers, but FCC regulation limited their operation in the big city markets. What money they made was from broadcasting to outlying suburbs. Offsetting that was cable television's growing reputation for high prices and poor quality. The much-touted capacity for interactivity on the channels was constantly deferred.

Cable builds

In 1972, the FCC allowed cable television to enter the top broadcast markets in the cities and pay television began in earnest after Hollywood's failed attempt in the 1950s. Within ten years, homes subscribing to cable television had grown from 6.5 million to twenty-seven million and by 1992 had increased further to fifty-eight million. With the loosening of FCC's restrictions on cable television, Home Box Office (HBO) was launched by Time Inc., and was initially unprofitable. After the success of the satellite transmission of the Ali–Frazier heavyweight titles fight from Manila, HBO started distributing its programs by satellite instead of microwave, and built a market as the price of satellite-receiving dishes fell. Ted Turner obtained a transmission licence in 1976 for the Turner Broadcasting Service (TBS) station, distributed through the same satellite as HBO, and in 1980 launched the twenty-four hour news channel, Cable News Network (CNN).

US pay channels

Thematic subscriber channels have proliferated in pay television, many drawing initially from existing archives, but as they diversified they commissioned programs to fit into the channel brand. Some of the more notable pay channels are listed below.

- Discovery, a documentary channel founded in 1988 and drawing mainly on the BBC archive, is now the world's leading commissioner of documentaries. Its spin-off channels include The Learning Channel and a 1998 joint venture with BBC (Animal Planet, People & Arts, BBC America).
- Arts & Entertainment (A&E), part-owned by NBC, first used existing archives, but now commissions programs as well. It has spun off The History Channel and The Biography Channel.
- BBC has a joint venture with Flextech PLC for factual channels under the UKTV brand.
- Canal+, a French channel, has invested in a group of documentary channels called Multithematiques, along with TCI, Havas and others.
- CNN has added a range of sub-niche versions to its original all-news network.
- Cartoon Network, created by Ted Turner and now owned by Time Warner, initially depended on the MGM library, but now commissions its own animation, especially from the European studios.

Building a business structure

The struggle to get a business footing for pay television generated a range of financing and merchandising structures. No longer did movies simply go to television three years after cinema release. Now they went through a succession of releases – airline, video/DVD rental and sell-through, pay-per-view (PPV) and subscription television – to maximise their return before reaching the networks at the end of the line. Licensing and merchandising products associated with television programs were often so profitable that a program might be marketed under value because television exposure would bring a higher return from ancillary rights. Sport became the main driver of subscription television, with a bidding competition that has created the high price now asked for live sports events.

The European experience

European broadcasters tried cable with Sky Channel first in 1982 and The Entertainment Network (TEN) two years later. TEN became Mirrorvision, then Premiere and closed in 1989. Sky and SuperChannel struggled. Sky launched as a satellite television channel later in 1982, but by 1988 had lost £39 million. All found young viewers, although not enough to satisfy advertisers. However, a corner was turned in 1988 when a Luxembourg consortium launched the *Astra 1A* satellite with a mix of English and German programs delivered to roof-top dishes. The next year, Rupert Murdoch's News International launched four Sky channels and, a year later, British Satellite Broadcasting (BSB) began after technical delays and high spending. In the battle for UK viewers, Sky lost £95 million in its first year alongside its £121 million start-up cost. BSB's losses were even higher and at the end of 1990 the two competitors merged as BSkyB. The new broadcasting entity didn't look back.

The threat to free-to-air networks

As the number of US cable channels grew (by 1999 there were more than 200 niche channels in America) they ate into the audiences of the three major networks. UK cable penetration was much lower, but BSkyB's satellite service had forty channels and European free-to-air (FTA) networks were losing audience as multichannel television built its audience. European subscribers grew in the 1990s so that by 1997 cable and satellite television accounted for 12% of all viewing in the United Kingdom and subscriber television accounted for 60% of German viewing.

1.5 Decline of the US networks

Management woes of CBS and NBC

The 1970s had been a decade of management problems for the two former dominant American networks. CBS had a succession of bad chief executive officers with no television experience and NBC wooed Fred Silverman from the ABC with disastrous results. Silverman had been instrumental in the ABC's climb to the top, but was unable to repeat that success. Japanese imports were already killing off television set sales of NBC's subsidiary, RCA. Grant Tinker was appointed chief executive officer of NBC in 1981 and in five years it was back on top through a judicious choice of executives and programs.

Network ownership changes

Cable television produced the first real challenge to the networks with HBO, followed by Rupert Murdoch in 1985 with Fox. CNN became the fourth news force, especially after its coverage of the 1991 Gulf War. While Murdoch was launching Fox, all the original networks were undergoing takeovers: ABC (including its cable networks ESPN, A&E and Lifeline) by Capital Cities for half its valued price; NBC by General Electric, which then shut down RCA and NBC Radio; and struggling CBS by corporate raider, Laurence Tisch. All cut payrolls and reduced perks, but to no avail in the face of competition from cable and Fox, video rentals and emerging satellite services to homes.

Cable erodes network audience share

In 1993, the FCC allowed the networks to produce and own programs again. Two years later, CBS was sold to Westinghouse. Another year on, Disney bought the ABC. Warner Brothers and Paramount bought stations to create small networks for digital television, but with a fragmenting market and the convergence of television and computers, the days of the all-powerful American networks had passed. The three major networks, which held 93% of the prime time audience in 1977, found their share reduced to 49% by 1996, eroded by the increasing number of cable channels and by new non-cable channels, such as those with Fox, United Paramount or Warner Brothers, and the Spanish-language broadcasters, Telemundo and Univision.

World dominance of US television

The world television audience had grown from eighty million in 1970 to 500 million in 1988, by which time the United States was spending one-third of the world's total program expenditure with less than 5% of the global audience. The extended period of profitable stability for networks from the 1950s to the 1990s was the result of the marginalisation of public television, an absence of foreign programming in the United States and the high proportion of the American gross national product spent on advertising. In 1983, the United States imported only 2% of its programs and this one-way trade provided a conspicuous international profile for American television. Although the US dominance of world export markets was faltering by the early 1990s, media exports were still high and helping drive demand for mass consumer goods, such as Ninja Turtles, Coke and Big Macs.

The US industry globalised

The political and economic crisis of the 1990s resulted in a reconfiguration of institutions and audience in the three-network oligopoly in America and public television in Europe. Television became more global with delivery by cable and satellite, consolidation of the telecommunications and computer industries, a trend towards deregulation and the appearance of new transnational entrepreneurs. Foreign-based multinationals, especially Japanese companies, were making significant purchases of US media producers. By the early 1990s, four of the eight major movie studios and four of the five major record labels were in foreign hands.

The new global market

The US domestic box office was giving way to the international market. Typically, a Hollywood film had earned 80% of its revenue at the US box office, but by 1990 it had fallen to only 30%. Studio management had to focus on home video and foreign box office demands for their three essentials of star, action and special effects. *Fortune* magazine referred to a 'one-world, pop-tech civilization' and Bill Roedy, chief executive officer of MTV Europe, observed: 'An 18-year-old in Denmark has more in common with an 18-year-old in France than either has with elders in their own country'. With the new fickle multichannel viewer, long-held constructs of audience by both commercial and public television in the United States and elsewhere were now undermined. Even America was complaining that the cost of the demands of the new global market was a diminishing of the American television culture. In fact, it was out with the old technology and in with the new. The digital revolution had started and it *was* revolutionary, not necessarily bringing in a new era but it did bring a new uncertainty.

Sources and further reading

General reading

Castleman, Harry & Podrazik, Walter J 1982, *Watching TV: Four Decades of American Television*, McGraw-Hill, New York.
Smith, Anthony (ed.) 1998, *Television, An International History*, 2nd edn, Oxford University Press, Oxford.
Wheen, Frances 1985, *Television*, Century Publishing, London.

Specific reading

Baird, John Logie 1988, *Sermons Soap and Television*, Royal Television Society, London.
Boddy, William 2004, *New Media and Popular Imagination: Launching Radio, Television, and Digital Media in the United States*, Oxford University Press, Oxford.
Exwood, Maurice 1976, *John Logie Baird: 50 Years of Television*, IERE, London.
Forrester, Chris 2000, *The Business of Digital Television*, Focal Press, Oxford.

Magazine, newspaper and journal articles

Garnham, Nicholas 1983, 'Public service versus the market', *Screen*, vol. 23(2) (Jul.–Aug.), p. 147.
Huey, John 1990, 'America's hottest export: pop culture', *Fortune*, 31 Dec., p. 50.

Some internet references

'A history of public broadcasting', available online at <www.current.org>, viewed 15
   December 2006.
'A timeline of television history', available online at <www.civilisation.ca>, viewed 15
   December 2006.
Avery, Robert K., 'Public service broadcasting', The Museum of Broadcast Communica-
   tions, available online at <www.museum.tv/archives>, viewed 15 December 2006.
Chronomedia, available online at <www.terramedia.co.uk/Chronomedia>, viewed 15
   December 2006.

Chapter 2

The digital revolution

Digital television had been looming for a decade or two, as computer technology spread throughout our everyday lives, but when it did come, it seemed to come upon us in a rush and we weren't quite ready for it. When digital transmission commenced in Australia at midnight on New Year's Eve 2000, digital television sets were still not available in the stores.

Much of television production had already digitised operations that were previously electronic or even mechanical. Post-production had become a significantly digital process, first in the construction of visual effects and then in the editing process. Digital signals could be manipulated by computers, allowing elaborate modifications. Effects, which were previously brought about by a limited number of formula moves or the finicky operation of an aerial image film camera, could now be done with a few keyboard strokes and with a wide range of possibilities. Non-linear editing was computer-based and imitated the manual craft of film editing, but without the quality loss in each copy generation of analogue videotape. However, for all this progress, it was only a means of operational assistance. It wasn't intrinsic to the system. Software might put shots in the chosen order, but the digital image still had to be converted back to analogue for transmission.

Like many of television's developments, digital technology emerged from military research. Claude Shannon, a research mathematician at AT&T's Bell Laboratories during World War II, had developed encrypted communications signals by separating 'signal' from 'noise'. They appeared to the casual observer to be random and with their capacity for error-correction were particularly effective for military use. After the war, signals coded in this way could be delivered intact to the recipient, unaffected by transmission conditions. Shannon's concept of a basic unit of information (a 'bit'), coded in the binary simplicity of a sequence of 'zeroes' and 'ones', enabled strings of bits to be constructed to convey messages.

The operational basis was established for an expanding range of apparatus under the generic description of computers.

Although digital technology was increasingly supporting television production operations, transmission and reception remained steadfastly analogue with its continuously varying signal. The technology for digital transmission of television was already available. It was a particular application of the technology in use generally in computers. By the mid 1980s, for all its feasibility in theory, digital television seemed unachievable because of its incompatibility with existing broadcasting. A change to digital transmission would require wholesale equipment replacement, both at the broadcaster end and for the consumer. There needed to be an economic reason to force the television industry and the viewing public over the hurdle of re-fit cost even though digital television had clear advantages over analogue. At the same time, planning for the allocation of the radiofrequency spectrum was looming as a growing headache for governments with increasing demands for spectrum use by other new digital technologies. Spectrum demand provided that economic reason.

2.1   Freeing up spectrum for auction

Commercial potential of free spectrum

Most developed countries had already allocated nearly all of or their entire analogue broadcast spectrum by the end of the 1980s. However, the greater efficiency of digital transmission allowed broadcast use with much less spectrum, freeing up spectrum for non-broadcast uses, such as mobile telephones. The return from sale of spare capacity to these users was too lucrative to ignore. The potential windfall to governments from the auction of radiofrequency spectrum provided the incentive to introduce digital television whatever transitional difficulties that might entail.

Stakeholders in digital TV

Digital television meant different things to different players. It meant high definition to the electronics industry, multichannelling to broadcasters and cable and satellite operators, and interactivity to the computer, telephone and retail industries. The approach of digital television threatened traditional relationships among program producers, station owners, networks, and satellite and cable operators. In the uncertainty, it attracted new and powerful economic players and altered existing programming and international program flows across a globalised media landscape.

United States chooses HDTV

In the United States, the electronics industry and broadcasters lobbied Congress to allocate spectrum for high-definition television (HDTV) rather than for the non-television applications for which the FCC already had US$20 billion committed through auctions it had been conducting since 1994. The

Telecommunications Act 1996 decreed a second channel should be allocated without charge to existing broadcasters for simulcast digital services. The only fee would be for revenue from spare capacity. As the technologies are different and generally incompatible, it isn't practical to turn on digital and simultaneously switch off analogue. The two must be run simultaneously for some time so that an acceptable proportion of the public can purchase digital sets, whatever that proportion might be deemed to be. Digital broadcast commenced in 1998 and US broadcasters would have to give back their old analogue spectrum by 31 December 2006, as long as at least 85% of households in a given market could receive digital transmission.

A time of market uncertainty

Digital television arrived when network audiences were fragmented and network share was declining. Napster, an internet file-sharing service as a peer-to-peer operation, haunted the content industry, which was gearing up for legal challenges in response. The year 2001 became pivotal. The 'dot-com bubble' burst – the result of overbidding and overbuilding – and the following year saw the bankruptcy of ITV Digital and Kirsch, a major global content marketer. Advertising markets cooled worldwide, there was a drop in personal computer (PC) sales, and cable and internet subscribers declined. In September, the terrorist attack on New York's World Trade Center put its transmitters out of action.

Slow uptake of digital TV in United States

The Telecommunications Act had provided the Clinton administration with a projected revenue source from later auction of spectrum returned. However, with its accent on HDTV, digital television uptake in the United States was not as strong as expected. Within months of its introduction, broadcasters were worrying about television set costs, lack of viewer interest and conversion expenses. Former chair of FCC, Reed Hundt, commented: 'HDTV turned out to be more a lobbying idea than a business strategy'. Congress has replaced the switch-off deadline with a 'hard deadline' of 17 February 2009, at which time analogue signals will go dark regardless of how many people can receive digital transmission. The 85% threshhold is not expected to be reached by that time.

The European experience

Other countries have fared better with the transition to digital than the United States. In 2003, Berlin–Brandenberg in Germany became the first region to switch off analogue terrestrial television. Since then, several more regions have switched off analogue with the aim for a national switchover to be completed in Germany by 2010. The Netherlands became the first country to go completely digital on 11 December 2006. Britain favoured multiple channels or multichannelling in preference to HDTV and the take-up of digital has been faster than in the United States, despite periods of unstable channel ownership. In 1997, six digital terrestrial television (DTT) multiplex licences were issued: one to Digital 3 & 4 (a joint venture between ITV and Channel 4); one to SDN (a company owned by Welsh channel S4C and others, bought out by ITV in 2005); three to British Digital Broadcasting (later ONdigital and still later ITV Digital), owned by ITV (Carlton Communications and Granada) and operated as pay television; and one to BBC. The digital satellite service, Sky Digital, was launched in October 1998. The next month it commenced a DTT service and in 1999 began digital cable television. In 2001, BSkyB (as the platform had become) switched off its analogue satellite transmission to become the first television platform in the world to operate purely digital transmission.

Break-up of ITV Digital

ITV Digital went into administration in 2002 and its three surrendered licences were offered for tender. One was licensed to the BBC and the other two to Crown Castle International. These two parties then combined forces with BSkyB as Freeview, a free-to-air DTT platform of thirty channels launched in October 2002. The trend continued towards advertiser funding rather than subscriber funding in UK broadcasting. In 2003, the BBC moved its digital satellite services from encrypted (through the Sky card) to FTA and a year later BSkyB launched an FTA service for a one-off connection cost. ITV1 (previously SDN), Channel 4 and Five still have encrypted digital satellite transmission.

Final stage of the switch-over in UK

While analogue services continue in Britain, 27% of households will not be able to receive all digital services because DTT at the necessary level of power would cause interference on analogue transmission. By mid 2006, more than 60% of households were accessing digital television by at least one platform. A switch-off schedule for UK analogue has been announced, starting in 2008 and expected to be completed nationally by 2012.

2.2   Benefits of digital broadcasting

Delivery modes

Digital television can be delivered as a stand-alone channel, or as a multichannel packaged by a single company with market versioning. The FTA broadcasters digitise their existing network and simulcast on satellite, cable or DTT. Digital satellite television can be either direct-to-home (DTH) by satellite dish and receiver, or distributed via cable head-ends to subscribers' homes. Satellite television is now posing a competitive threat to cable with the falling cost of satellite receivers and the wide transmission range within satellite footprints. There is, however, a risk with the high cost of satellite failure and cable is a better option for interactivity. Nonetheless, multichannelling is now principally by satellite DTH, with cable and microwave on a Multichannel Multipoint Distribution Service (MMDS) as an alternative means of delivery.

Set-top boxes

The economic impact of the transition to digital transmission has been eased for the consumer by the set-top box, a digital–analogue converter that receives the digital signal from a domestic aerial, and converts and delivers it to an analogue set with none of the shortcomings of analogue transmission (because its transmission has been in the digital mode). Set-top boxes may be attached to analogue receivers with widescreen capacity. Although they have a history of problems with audio synchronisation, the cost of the set-top box and analogue receiver is far lower at present than the cost of a digital receiver, so that it will remain an attractive option until the predicted fall in the cost of digital sets as the retail market grows. When that happens, the set-top box will have served its purpose and slip quietly into oblivion.

Bandwidth efficiency

Digital television is a more efficient means of broadcasting than analogue. In the digital mode, images and sounds can be transmitted as compressed data so that more services are delivered in less space. A digital multiplex of channels occupying the same bandwidth as an analogue channel (6–8 MHz) can contain at least four digital channels, generally six and possibly more with higher compression. Efficiency of bandwidth use allows more improvements to be incorporated into the broadcast signal without requiring an unacceptable amount of additional spectrum. HDTV, multichannelling, high quality sound, widescreen picture and enhanced services all become practical possibilities with digital compression.

Video compression

Video on digital television is compressed using a standard called MPEG, which has been adopted in Europe and most of the world apart from the United States and Japan. MPEG-1 is the video compression commonly used on PCs, but it is not a broadcast standard. MPEG-2 was set as the standard for full-motion video compression in 1995. Inside each frame, an MPEG-2 encoder records just enough detail to make it look like nothing is missing. The encoder compares adjacent frames and only records the sections of the picture that have moved or changed. In other words, the signal is sent without redundant information. Sport is difficult to compress because it is constantly moving. Movies are much easier, not least because they are shot at twenty-four frames per second, whereas television transmits at fifty frames per second.

Audio advantages

The human ear is much more sensitive to subtle changes in sound, making audio less able to be compressed, but digital sound offers advances in quality instead. Digital audio recordings on CD, with their wider frequency range and finer sampling, took over the commercial music industry while television sound remained with low-range analogue. Digital television sound using the Dolby Digital/AC-3 audio encoding system matches the sound quality available in most movie theatres since the early 1990s and on DVDs. It can include up to five channels of sound, front and back, and a subwoofer bass that can be 'felt'.

The self-restoring signal

The digital signal suffers no loss of quality during transmission or copying because of its inherent capacity for self-restoration. The signal is coded as 'zeroes' and 'ones', so a degraded signal can always be restored to its original code as long as it can reliably distinguish between 'zero' and 'one'. The digital signal is not affected by transmission conditions until it gets degraded to the point where the binary distinction is unclear – then it crashes. In contrast, once analogue transmission deteriorates, it stays degraded whether it's using frequency, amplitude or any other variable as the analogue. The analogue signal will gradually deteriorate as transmission conditions worsen. On the other hand, drop-outs in transmission are much more conspicuous in digital than in analogue.

Undegraded copying

The same principle applies to copying. In analogue, each successive recorded generation produces a slightly lower quality copy. The self-restoration of the digital signal ensures that there is no generational quality loss in successive generations. The quality of the recording might decrease, but the code embedded in that recording remains unchanged and plays out with the same code and, therefore, the same quality that was played in.

2.3   High-definition television

Definition of HDTV

HDTV presents cinema-quality images and CD-quality sound on television. It has a higher resolution than analogue or standard-definition digital television (SDTV) because it has more pixels per line, and it has more lines of resolution (up to 1080). Because of the technical advantages of the digital code, image and sound are received at the same quality as that transmitted; but HDTV is not a fixed standard. Remember that the 405-line service operated by the BBC in 1936 was described as 'high definition'. High definition is now defined as the system providing cinema-quality pictures (or the nearest to it currently available) and this standard is raised as cinema technology is improved. The standard of HDTV gets raised also as its own technology is improved. In other words, HDTV is the best television system currently available and when a better system is introduced, that becomes the new HDTV.

The push for HDTV

US broadcasters had proposed the introduction of HDTV back in the 1980s to prevent non-broadcasters, such as mobile phones and two-way radio, from getting hold of available spectrum. The Japanese public broadcaster, NHK, had already introduced the analogue HDTV systems, Hi Vision and MUSE, to justify increasing television licence fees in Japan. The Dutch company, Philips, and the French company, Thomson (formed by the purchase of RCA and GE consumer electronics businesses from General Electric), successfully opposed Japanese HDTV as a world standard. In looking for an American option, they proposed digital HDTV.

European and US standards

By 1990, General Instruments had produced a digital HDTV system called Digicipher, but it was unable to persuade the FCC of its ultimate merit. Meanwhile, Europe's Digital Video Broadcasting (DVB) Project had expanded to a global consortium and was determining technical standards for digital terrestrial, cable and satellite television. DVB's focus was on multichannelling rather than HDTV. It has been suggested that UK viewers were so used to ghosting and fuzzy reception that when they got digital television, many thought they were already seeing HDTV. The American Grand Alliance retained its emphasis on HDTV because multichannel cable television was already available in the United States. It developed its own technical standards through the FCC's Advanced Television Standards Committee (ATSC) to replace the analogue standards of the NTSC. The broadcasting approach used in Europe and Australia is Coded Orthogonal Frequency Division Multiplex (COFDM), which divides the data stream into parallel bit streams. The United States adopted the less expensive Vestigial Sideband Broadcasting (VSB), with claimed lower power and extended station coverage, but it has developed problems and is generally regarded as inferior to the DVB standard.

Future prospects

HDTV continues to be the government's policy priority in the United States and Australia, although in both countries its broadcaster support is softening and it is struggling to gain ascendancy. HDTV is in danger of being relegated to an option, perhaps at the luxury end of what digital television has to offer. Nonetheless, it does present a superior form of image and sound, the equal of DVD, and may find a place in the television panoply as the digital era settles in. It has already provided an incentive for widescreen presentation across the whole range of digital television.

2.4   Widescreen picture

Widescreen aspect ratio

Conventionally, television is presented on a screen with a ratio of width to height (called aspect ratio) of 4:3. HDTV is presented in widescreen with the ratio 16:9 so as to more closely imitate the cinema experience created by widescreen formats such as Cinemascope and Vistavision. Thomson had developed an analogue widescreen television, called Cinemascreen, in 1993, but the necessary equipment changes to accommodate it meant that it could not get a foothold in the market. With digital television, radical equipment changes were unavoidable so it was an opportune time to introduce widescreen in the package.

Pillar-boxing

When television is fully switched to digital, all screens will be 16:9, whether they are HDTV or SDTV. However, during the interim period of simultaneous broadcast on analogue and digital, the 4:3 or 16:9 option creates considerable confusion. Programs shot and finished on the older 4:3 format are broadcast 4:3 on analogue, but are smaller than the 16:9 frame. They are accommodated on widescreen by 'pillar-boxing' with a black strip either side. The 4:3 picture could fill the widescreen frame by increasing the size of the picture to the widescreen width and cropping top and bottom, but that carries the risk of losing bottom-of-frame text, such as ident supers.

Presentation options on widescreen

Increasingly, as television prepares for the digital era, programs are being shot and finished on a 16:9 format. This can be presented unchanged on widescreen transmission, but the picture is wider than the older 4:3 screen. Widescreen programs in analogue transmission can be presented as either 'letterbox', with a black mask above and below, or as 'centre cut-out', with the sides of the widescreen picture cropped to fit the squarer format. Where the intention is to broadcast as centre cut-out, the program is shot '4:3 safe', using markings in the camera viewfinder as a guide. All essential information in the picture is kept within that part of the frame that will remain after the sides have been cropped. Many channels present a compromise between these alternatives with a 14:9 letterbox format, which reduces the black masking above and below and lowers the risk of losing important information in the picture by cropping less of the frame's sides.

Aspect ratio confusion

The confusion often arises from the belief that letterbox is a 16:9 format. It is not. It is a 4:3 format used to present program material sourced on a 16:9 format. On the other hand, pillar-box is not a 4:3 format but a 16:9 format used to present program material sourced on a 4:3 format, such as pre-digital archive. Figure 2.1 shows how picture sources are accommodated on incompatible aspect ratios.

2.5 Multichannelling

Growth in Europe

Although not the prime emphasis in cable-television-rich America, multichannelling through digital television created much more interest in Europe, where cable hadn't made as great an impact. While American commitment to HDTV faltered, multichannelling never wavered in the United Kingdom and Europe.

Figure 2.1: Presentation of 4:3 and 16:9 aspect ratios on incompatible screens.

As in the United States, European FTA networks lost audience as multichannel television built. Although TEN had evolved into Premiere and closed by 1989, Sky became BSkyB, stepped up its forty analogue channels to 140 in going digital in 1998, and turned around its performance. European subscriber growth in the 1990s was reflected in a growth in UK cable and satellite transmission, with 12% of all viewing in 1997 increasing to 40% of homes with multichannelling by 2000.

Recycling, repurposing and repackaging

Multichannelling is voracious in its programming needs, with increased pressure for low-budget production and greater recycling of programs. Multiple scheduling of programs is the norm in the multichannel environment. Existing programs are repurposed as inexpensive repackaged re-runs for digital channels, raising the concern that generic documentaries, versioned with cheap digital post-production, will replace nationally produced documentaries on specific social and political issues. One side of the cultural–economic coin is a loss of expression of national identity; the other is the possibility of increased revenue from the expanded market for documentary, always a hard genre to work profitably. Others, mostly American, welcomed a single global popular culture, overwhelmingly American in content and origin. American cultural hegemony could be maintained, it was thought, although much of the recent documentary growth in the United States has been overseen by expatriate English, and the advent of lightweight flexible production equipment has generated an international documentary style that owes no more to America than it does to any other country. Its accent is generational (with mostly younger practitioners), not national.

Market failure and success in the United Kingdom

While it's reasonable to assume viewers will welcome a greater choice of programs, there must be a point where the choices become overwhelming or just illusory. As already noted, the dramatically increased number of channels has produced program duplication as much as diversity. Stephen Grabiner, erstwhile chief executive officer of the United Kingdom's ONdigital, remarked acidly: 'There is a market for people who want 200 television channels. They live in dark attics and don't come out very often. ONdigital's market is middle England, people who want more choice in their viewing'. Grabiner resigned in 1999 and sued parent company, ITV. ONdigital, with technical, marketing and management problems, rebranded itself as ITV Digital and went into administration in 2002 with £1.2 million in losses. Meanwhile, BSkyB, once regarded by middle England as cheap, poor quality and for football fans only, powered on, its Australian–American owners out to change the viewing habits of Britain.

ONdigital's problems

ONdigital's corporate woes are a useful insight into the difficulties of growing a business at a time of technological and market fluidity. ONdigital's set-top boxes came late into the market and 30% of households in the United Kingdom could not get its signal, which was prone to fuzziness anyway. The UK government refused to allow it to increase its transmission power. ONdigital had a huge churn rate (proportion of subscribers who elect not to renew their subscription) of 25–30%, its service was widely pirated and, in 1999, it got caught up in a bidding war when BSkyB gave away set-top boxes to subscribers. Finally, ONdigital held on to low-performing in-house specialty channels, such as the Carlton Food Channel, and overbid for second tier football rights. The company collapsed even though the United Kingdom had the world's highest penetration of digital television, reaching 44% of homes with television by 2003. Freeview, the FTA digital service that acquired ITV's licence, was allowed a 300% increase in transmission power, and with only twenty-three channels posed no threat to BSkyB.

Electronic Program Guide

The growth of multichannel television and the intricacy of its programming stimulated the development of its hand-servant, the Electronic Program Guide (EPG). A digital data stream provides extra information, which allows presentation of program options and grouping by category, and then at deeper levels provides program synopsis, cast details and other information about a program. As media commentator William Boddy has wryly noted, BSkyB's 140 channels require an EPG more like an internet search engine than *TV Times*. Second-generation EPGs can select channels and switch on a VCR. They are becoming much more than a program guide. The EPG is now a shop window for the broadcaster, the promotional vehicle for highlighted programs, and is expected to develop further as an entry point for on-demand services.

2.6   Enhanced services

Range of enhanced services available

The technology of digital television makes possible a range of add-ons to the broadcast program, so-called enhanced services. These can be expensive multi-streaming or data and graphics as overlays on the video program. They may be voluntary, in the form of additional information on request, or involuntary, in the form of market-specific advertising or product placement digitally inserted into the picture. However, it's a matter of opinion how much some of this constitutes enhancement.

Examples of enhanced services

Already digital broadcast of sport is showing benefits of program enhancement where viewers can select overlays with match statistics, player information, replays and alternative camera coverage. Since 2001, the BBC's Wimbledon tennis coverage has offered in its digital service multiple feeds from five courts with SMS chat, live score updates, match highlights and interviews via a mosaic menu. *Wimbledon 2003* had four million viewers, but with six streams it was expensive to produce. *Walking with Cavemen* offered additional layers of facts and *Top of the Pops* provided the song lyrics for karaoke. The potential for expansion to other television genres includes, say the opportunists of marketing, the possibility of immediate ordering of products displayed in a program. The viewer will be able to interact with a commercial in real time or switch to a dedicated stream. It's debatable how much this type of marketing will appeal to the viewing public. Telemarketing hasn't managed so far to move significantly from the midnight-to-dawn schedule. The appeal of these programs may be limited to those addictive personalities, the 'shopaholics'.

Virtual advertising

Where use of the enhancement is involuntary, the key issue is: when does the enhancement become too intrusive and viewers turn off? When TiVo began marketing its personal video recorder (PVR) in the 1990s, a shiver ran through the broadcasting industry. In allowing the viewer to skip advertisements it appeared to undermine the basis of commercial television. Advertiser and broadcaster strategies to combat the threat included product placement, on-screen banners and program length commercials. The development of enhanced services allowed a different tack by digitally inserting advertising into programs, placing the message directly in the frame of action and at moments of peak audience engagement. Princeton Video Images' Live Video Insertion System (L-VIS) provided this technology to the San Francisco Giants in 1995 because the baseball team didn't control signage revenue at Candlestick Park. Virtual advertising found a particular place in European soccer where many games are shown in countries other than the one in which the game is played. Different commercials can be inserted in the game for each country in which the game is broadcast.

Industry ambivalence

Reaction from the advertising industry has been ambivalent, with concerns about advertising clutter and viewer backlash. In 1999 CBS began inserting its logo in New York scenes on the daily news show, *The Early Show*. In its New Year's Eve broadcast, it used L-VIS to digitally replace actual Budweiser and NBC billboards with the CBS logo. Press and public reaction was negative and host, Dan Rather, described it as 'a mistake'. CBS executives defended it publicly, although later expressing reservations, but Princeton Video Images was unapologetic, welcoming the increased visibility. However, there's nothing especially new about the commercial practice of virtual advertising. For some time we have seen signage on walls, scoreboards and player uniforms, product placement in movies and digital manipulation of image, such as in *Zelig* and *Forrest Gump*. In any case, the threat from the PVR has not materialised. Sales have been modest, ReplayTV stopped making stand-alone PVRs in 2000, installing them in set-top boxes instead, and TiVo laid off 25% of its staff the next year, selling hard disc storage to advertisers instead. Digitally enhanced services remain a Pandora's box.

2.7   Interactivity

Defining interactive TV

Interactive television is an umbrella term covering all ways that the technology enables engagement with content on television. It can be defined so broadly that it serves no practical purpose, amounting to any engagement with television, such as switching channels. SMS voting independent of the television, as in *Australian Idol*, is pre-digital interactivity at its most basic. The classic conception of interactive television involved a series of plot options in the story, each of which has to be provided as content at some cost. As plot options accumulate, the cost of this approach to interactivity balloons and becomes economically unsustainable. One method interactive television producers have used to contain the cost is to continually bring the options back to the same point in the story, but if the viewer detects this in the interactive pathway, the program loses much of its appeal.

Internet interactivity

Interactivity has long been a major facet of computers. The operator navigates through corridors around a series of obstacles in the game format, or through levels of information in fixed layers. Internet interactivity works by two-way communication through cable between site and user. The early 1990s saw a male fascination with control of simulated interaction that promised to remake or destroy conventional television. Virtual reality pioneer, Jaron Lanier, said that the best thing about virtual reality was that it would kill television. But there were sceptics as well. Sallie Tisdale noted in 1991 in *Esquire*: 'There is something terribly familiar about the flying pillars and smashed television sets, something smacking of comic books and Saturday-morning cartoons . . . Here is technology with massive power stuck in the tiny paradigm of the white American male.'

Difficulties with interactive TV

Television has found it difficult to establish a viable interactive format to match the computer, with several failed launches going back to Time–Warner's Qube system in 1977. Interactive television selects between a small number of transmission streams, but has no back-channel in DTT and digital satellite (Dsat). Return data has to be sent by telephone for these delivery platforms. The process is two-way only with digital cable (Dcable) and here it has enabled viewers to play along with contestants on *Who Wants to be a Millionaire?* and for viewer participants to be scored. The *Big Brother* digital transmission in the United Kingdom has a multistream feed from the house during broadcast, as well as a menu for voting, a quiz, betting on house events and a Pac-Man style game on a pay-per-play basis.

Differences between TV and internet

Television has tried to duplicate the interactivity of the internet with very limited success because it is a technology that is delivered, whereas the internet is technology that is accessed. Television comes to us, but we go to the internet. There are also fundamental differences in the way we use the two media. Television is built on narratives created by someone else and enjoyed passively by the viewer. In the internet's game format, there is no narrative beyond the outcome of preset challenges, rather like a sports event. If interactivity is the capacity to select from a menu of items available to be presented on a screen, television can do that in imitation of the internet. If it's an interaction where the dynamic is determined by user input, the technology is not yet in place for television to match that internet capacity.

2.8   Convergence

Convergence that never happened

There has been discussion about the convergence of television and the computer for some time – the coalescence of computing, telecommunications and media, and information into the one combined entity. In 1990 George Gilder predicted that digital technologies would replace the television set, the 'dumbest box of all', through networks of PC telecomputers, but computers never seemed to seriously threaten to usurp the role of television and, as we have seen, television hasn't always been able to imitate the internet. The two remain functionally distinct even though they share much technologically to achieve their separate functional roles.

Different modes of use

Viewers, especially younger viewers, will surf channels and use the internet or watch television while surfing the internet, but people generally watch television and use computers for different reasons. Internet use is interactive and task-oriented, whereas television viewing is passive, with the medium a convenience for leisure. Are viewers inherently passive or, given the opportunity, hunters for a viewing experience? The proponents of convergence insist the latter and have done so for some time with undampened enthusiasm, but there has been minimal change. William Boddy points out that 'the long tradition of overheated pronouncements about technological change (has) insistently conjured up a reformed and empowered spectator to supplant the disparaged couch potato'. Yet, we still look up the TV guide to see what's on.

WebTV

Microsoft attempted to combine the PC and television set with cable television's set-top box as a platform for interactive television. It acquired WebTV in 1997 to combine internet access and television viewing, but subscriptions stalled for a range of reasons. There were network outages, a high churn rate of programs, a charge of deceptive advertising, and Sony withdrew an interactive television game show. With the internal friction this generated, WebTV was absorbed into Ultimate TV in 2001, with a digital video recorder (DVR) integrated into the set-top box, but within a few months it was trying unsuccessfully to offload this to

News Corporation. However, WebTV's woes seem to relate more to management and content than technology (reminiscent of ONdigital's failure), so it might be that this is an idea whose time is yet to come.

Peercasting

Mark Pesce of the Australian Film Television and Radio School (AFTRS) has put forward an interesting proposition of convergence that may come to pass (or may not). The technology already exists to swap files of television programs between computers. Pesce's view is that consumers will soon make their own programs and swap them without having to go through a broadcaster, a process he calls peercasting. It has its precedent in music file-sharing through Napster and others. Apart from its frustration of the major record companies, file-sharing enabled little-known musicians to get their work out in the public arena, something that was difficult without a record contract. But while interesting music can be made as a cottage industry, it's not so clear whether that is the case with television content. The public might bemoan the quality of television, but is it ready for a diet of domestically made programs instead? And if it is, how does the new multiskilled solo operator recover the costs of production? A business model might emerge, but like most prognostications, we won't know if it is accurate until we get to the future. By then the failed predictions are long forgotten. Often major developments emerge out of dark corners where no-one saw them coming. The engineers at Nokia decided late in the development of the mobile phone to experiment with sending text as an add-on for mobile phone users. They didn't anticipate the impact SMS would have when offered to consumers. The future will come and things will change, but how much the soothsayers of today have powers of divining the future is debatable.

Multiplatform delivery

If the digital communications media have not yet converged into a single technology, they are certainly finding content alliances mutually beneficial. Increasingly, television producers look to the possibilities of multiplatform delivery as a means of extending the market of their program concept. There is nothing profoundly new in this approach. Program-makers have long looked at merchandising spin-off in the form of video or DVD release, a book or even cuddly toys as a means of extending the financial return associated with television production. Now producers are looking additionally at cross-platform options for their program: the possibility of on-demand broadband, an immersive interactive site or mobile phone video delivery. The incorporation of cross-platform delivery into a project is examined in Chapter 10.

Sources and further reading

General reading

Boddy, William 2004, *New Media and Popular Imagination: Launching Radio, Television, and Digital Media in the United States*, Oxford University Press, Oxford.

Forrester, Chris 2000, *The Business of Digital Television*, Focal Press, Oxford.
Hart, Jeffrey A 2004, *Technology, Television, and Competition: The Politics of Digital TV*, Cambridge University Press, New York.
Sinclair, John (ed.) 2004, *Contemporary World Television*, British Film Institute, London.

Specific reading

Cunningham, Ben 2003, *Interacting With Your Television: Key Lessons From The UK*, AFTRS, Sydney (CD-ROM).
Department of Communications, Information Technology and the Arts 2006, *Unlocking the Potential: Digital Content Industry Action Agenda*, DCITA, Canberra, available online at <http://www.dcita.gov.au/arts_culture/policy_and_legislation/digital_content_industry_action_agenda>, viewed 15 December 2006.
Gilder, George 1990, *Life After Television: The Coming Transformation of Media and American Life*, Whittle Direct Books, Knoxville, TN.
Given, Jock 2003, *Turning off the Television: Broadcasting's Uncertain Future*, UNSW Press, Sydney.

Magazine, newspaper and journal articles

Tisdale, Sallie 1991, 'It's been real', *Esquire*, April, p. 147.

Chapter 3

The industry in Australia

Nearly every Australian home has a television set: 67% of homes have two or more sets and 28% have three or more. At the prime time of viewing (7–9 pm) 60% of homes are tuned in with the result that commercial television broadcasters are able to capture a substantial (although not a major) share of the nation's advertising revenue. As in the United States, television broadcasters have enjoyed considerable stability until recent years, with profits ranging from reliable to considerable. A key to this has been a structuring of the industry as a dual system of public and commercial broadcasters. Now, new technology is driving new delivery platforms, with consequent fragmentation of the mass audience. Broadcasters have to worry about a trend to narrowcasting for niche audiences as they try to ensure that they can prosper from the transition to digital television. Pay television and broadband on internet are posing challenges to the dominance of FTA television. Video content on mobile phones and other podcasting threaten to add to this in the very near future, along with mobile television, broadcasting directly to mobile phones. It's in younger viewers that the drift from television is felt most keenly, with the competing attraction of interactive computer-based entertainment. The Australian average daily television usage by viewers under 24 has fallen 20%.

Although there is a claim of an Australian as an early developer of television transmission – Henry Sutton is said to have designed a 'telephane system' in the 1880s to transmit pictures of the Melbourne Cup from Flemington to Ballarat – Australia, by and large, has held back to see what others were doing, to see what worked and what didn't in the early days of television. This characteristic of Australian business as well as its television industry is both a strength and a weakness. It's a strength because Australia was able to launch a television system far superior to that of either the United Kingdom or the United States, who were saddled with systems that resulted from their early involvement with the medium.

However, it's also a weakness because Australian business is stereotypically risk averse and, in the case of television, has probably missed out on opportunities where less faint hearts might have taken a chance. Nonetheless, Australian television has, by and large, been productive for participants in the industry and diverse for its audiences.

3.1   Consolidation of a dual system

Alternative models for Australian TV

The post-war Chifley government planned Australian television as a public monopoly, following the British model. The Menzies government that followed was not persuaded of this approach and in 1953 set up a Royal Commission into television. The government accepted the Royal Commission's recommendation of a dual system with a national service funded by licence fees and a commercial service funded by advertising. The government had been arguing for this prior to the Commission, so its acceptance is hardly surprising. Australian television was to be a mix of the American commercial system and the British public system, but Australia rejected both the EMI–Marconi 405-line standard and the NTSC 525-line system in favour of the 625-line system developed in Germany after the war. The government also accepted the Commission's recommendation against the immediate introduction of colour (available in the United States at the time, but with teething problems and high consumer cost; see Chapter 1) and broadcasting on the UHF band. Colour was not introduced in Australia until 1975 and UHF not until 1980.

Beginnings of TV

With two commercial stations and one Australian Broadcasting Commission (ABC) planned for each of Sydney and Melbourne, progress was to be cautious to ensure reasonable standards, but the Melbourne Olympic Games were approaching and the new medium was expected to bring them to the wider Australian public. Television commenced in Sydney on 16 September 1956 with regular test transmissions from Surry Hills. TCN-9 had rented a church hall as a studio for the first few months because its Willoughby studios were not ready. Official transmission from TCN-9 commenced in October, with transmission starting the following month from HSV-7 and from the ABC stations in Sydney and Melbourne. ATN-7 began in Sydney in December and Melbourne's GTV-9 began in January. Commercial services and the ABC extended to Brisbane, Adelaide, Perth and Hobart, and then to regional areas over the next few years.

Growth of the dual system

The dual system continued to grow incrementally for forty years, without troubling its basic assumptions. It was expanding without any significant threat to the underlying stability of the structure. In 1964–65 a third commercial channel (0/10) began in Sydney and Melbourne, to be followed in Brisbane, Adelaide and eventually in 1988 in Perth. Transport group, Ansett, secured the Melbourne and Brisbane licences, and Amalgamated Wireless Australasia (AWA) the Sydney licence. Following the federal government's aggregation policy, regional commercial services were increased from one to three in the larger regional markets of the four eastern states. With the ABC seemingly transfixed by a British program style, a second public broadcaster with a charter of multicultural programming was introduced into the mix. The Special Broadcasting Service (SBS) began in 1980 in Sydney and Melbourne, four years later in Brisbane, Adelaide and Perth, and then was introduced progressively into regional and rural areas. Since 1992, SBS has been able to run advertisements, although only between programs (until late 2006 when the network began showing them within programs as well) and limited to five minutes per hour.

Community TV

In 1993, a non-commercial licence was issued to community-based groups in Sydney and Melbourne for non-profit community and educational programming on a renewable three-year trial. In 1997 the Australian Broadcasting Authority (ABA) recommended that the last FTA analogue channel (the 'sixth channel') be reserved permanently for community access television and in 2004 permanent community television licences were allocated for Channel 31 in Sydney, Melbourne, Brisbane and Perth.

What is perhaps the most remarkable of the community television channels is not metropolitan. Imparja has been servicing central Australia since 1988 as an Aboriginal-owned mainstream regional commercial station. At the same time, it broadcasts a second channel, Channel 31, of Indigenous programming, news and community information to outlying communities in the Broadcasting for Remote Aboriginal Communities Scheme (BRACS). Run out of PY Media in Alice Springs, it is the successor to pirate stations that operated in the 1980s at Yuendumu in the Tanimi desert and Pukatja (fomerly Ernabella) in South Australia. The station transmits ten hours a day by satellite to northern and central Australia, and much of the content originates from government-funded video units in the communities themselves.

Arrival of subscription (pay) TV

SBS and community television attracted only small audiences and the ABC was constantly at loggerheads over funding and editorial bias with its changing masters in Canberra of either political colour. Australian commercial television continued to be a very profitable business, notwithstanding ownership hiccups in the late 1980s. The belated arrival of subscription television in 1995, after thirteen years of public inquiries and political delays, managed to cause consternation in the commercial sector despite pay television's slow progress in establishing itself. However, by 2005 it was turning its massive early losses into profit. The introduction of the pay sector into the television mix has driven a wedge into the well-established and comfortable dual system. There is now the shadow of an unknown future hanging over the industry, exacerbated by uncertainties in the transition from analogue to digital, and the role of new distribution technologies emerging on the horizon.

3.2   The commercial free-to-air sector

Network origins

It had been intended that stations would be licensed to serve local areas, but from the outset GTV-9 affiliated with TCN-9 and HSV-7 with ATN-7. The first commercial television licences were dominated by newspaper proprietors – Australian Consolidated Press (ACP) with the Nine channels, and John Fairfax and the Herald and Weekly Times with the Seven channels. Under them, de facto networks developed, the Seven Network forming a looser association as a partnership without a common owner. Network affiliates share production, acquisition and distribution of programs, but without cable facilities to transmit television signals between capital cities until 1964, there was no technical integration of the networks. Television markets developed in isolation, with different local programs and regional commercials. They became more unified with the launch of Aussat satellites in 1985–86.

Network ownership

The networks have mostly remained the same since the mid 1960s even though their ownership has changed. Television licences have been heavily regulated in Australia and, until 1986, a licensee was restricted to two televison stations nationally and only one in any discrete market. When the regulations were changed so that licensees were instead not allowed newspaper and television interests in the same market or to reach more than 60% of the Australian population, the three networks changed hands. In 1987, Bond Corporation (Alan Bond) bought the Nine Network, Qintex (Christopher Skase) bought Seven, and Northern Star (controlled by Westfield's Frank Lowy) bought Ten at highly inflated prices. All had lost control by 1990. Lowy returned to shopping centres, Bond went to gaol, and Skase went into exile in Majorca. Now the networks are back in the hands of people whose principal business interest has always been the media, although their interests diversify into related fields from time to time. The Nine Network amalgamated with ACP in 1994 to form Publishing and Broadcasting Ltd (PBL), owned by Kerry Packer. PBL, now under James Packer, controls Nine and major magazines, along with Melbourne's Crown Casino, OneTel (until its collapse), internet provider ecorp, and Ticketek. Kerry Stokes is executive chairman of the Seven Network, which was in a joint venture with the Australian Football League (AFL; now in the courts) and is part of the Docklands consortium in Melbourne. TNQ TV Ltd is the largest shareholder in The Ten Group, but most (57%) of the economic interest is held by Canadian company CanWest Global Communications, which acquired a stake in Ten in 1992 when the network was in receivership.

Network licensing

In 1992 the *Broadcasting Services Act* changed content and ownership rules again, as well as establishing the ABA to oversee them. Licensees are required to broadcast programs of wide appeal ('intended to appeal to the general public'), which are to be received on 'commonly available equipment'. Broadcasters must be licensed by the ABA (restructured in 2005 as the Australian Communications and Media Authority [ACMA]) and only three services are allowed in any one area. No new licences are to be issued before 2010 as part of the digital transition process. The public interest has declined as a licensing policy issue. The focus has moved instead to new technology, managerialism and liberal economics.

Network ownership restrictions

Current ownership of metropolitan and regional FTA commercial television stations in Australia is detailed in Table 3.1. There have been constraints on who can own media in any market and the extent of ownership by different types of owners, but under the *Broadcasting Services Amendment (Media Ownership) Act 2006* the restrictions will be lifted in 2007. Previously, media ownership was restricted to one in any market and that owner could not control commercial television and a radio station or daily newspaper in the same area. These cross-media rules prevented Murdoch's News Ltd acquiring a television network and Packer's PBL acquiring Fairfax. A foreign person or company could not hold more than 15% equity in a company controlling a commercial television licence. Compliance forced CanWest to restructure its interests in the Ten Network in 1997 and scale its shareholding back to 14.5%. Commonly owned television stations could not reach more than 75% of the Australian population. The Seven Network had reached 72%. Under the new laws, in place of cross- and foreign-media ownership restrictions will be a diversity of tests whereby a company can own a newspaper, television network and two radio stations in the same market, as long as there are five independent 'voices' in cities and four in the regions. The changed media ownership rules have triggered a flurry of acquisition activity. In anticipation of the new rules, the Seven Network took a strategic stake in West Australian Newspapers and agreed in 2006 to sell a 50% interest in Seven Media Group to American private equity firm, Kohlberg Kravis Roberts & Co (KKR).

Advertising revenue

The business of commercial television is the sale of advertising time. The purpose of programs, therefore, is to bring audiences to advertisements. Advertisers buy time directly from the broadcasters or, more often, through advertising agencies (who may handle all the company's advertising) or media buyers who bargain on behalf of their clients for bulk deals with broadcasters. With earnings of $3.3 billion, television accounts for 36% of Australian media expenditure on advertising, second only to newspapers (Table 3.2). Television is particularly effective in attracting national advertisers, accounting for 53% of all national advertising. Generally, the network market leader attracts even more advertising, although Table 3.3 shows that this is not always the case. In 2004, Nine had 38.0% of the audience and 39.2% of advertising revenue, and Seven and Ten both had a higher audience share than advertising revenue share. However, Nine's share of audience in 1993 was higher than its share of advertising.

Table 3.1: Ownership of affiliated commercial television stations in Australia.

Network affiliation	Seven	Nine	Ten
Metropolitan markets	*Seven Network* **5 stations** (Sydney, Melbourne, Brisbane, Adelaide, Perth)	*Nine Network (PBL)* **3 stations** (Sydney, Melbourne, Brisbane) *Southern Cross* **1 station** (Adelaide) *Sunraysia TV* **1 station** (Perth)	*The Ten Group* **5 stations** (Sydney, Melbourne, Brisbane, Adelaide, Perth)
Aggregated regional markets	*Prime TV* **3 markets** (Northern NSW, Southern NSW, Vic.) *Seven Network* **1 market** (Qld) *Southern Cross* **1 market** (Tas.)	*WIN TV* **4 markets** (Southern NSW, Vic., Qld, Tas.) *NBN* **1 market** (Northern NSW)	*Southern Cross* **5 markets** (Northern NSW, Southern NSW, Vic., Qld, Tas.)

Table 3.2: Share of Australian advertising revenue (2004).

Media	%	Media total	%
Free-to-air TV	34.8	TV total	36.1
Pay TV	1.4		
Newspapers	40.2	Print media total	50.1
Magazines	9.9		
Radio	9.3		
Outdoor display	3.6		
Cinema	0.8		

Table 3.3: Relative audience and advertising share in commercial television (1993, 2004).

	TV station		
Year	Nine	Seven	Ten
1993			
Audience share (%)	41.2	34.5	24.4
Advertising share (%)	37.3	36.1	26.6
2004			
Audience share (%)	38.0	31.7	30.3
Advertising share (%)	39.2	31.0	29.8

Advertising regulation

Television advertising is regulated by the *Trade Practices Act 1974* against misleading and deceptive conduct. The Broadcasting Services Act restricts time used for advertising, requires advertisements to be produced in Australia or New Zealand, and limits sexual and violent content in them, especially in C-time (only programs classified as suitable for viewing by children). The Act bans tobacco advertisements, restricts medical advertisements and bans political advertisements in the three days prior to an election.

Content regulation

The ABA (and ACMA since 2005) is responsible for ensuring programs on commercial television 'reflect community standards'. Australian content requirements were introduced in 1961 and revised in 2003. The test of 'Australian content' is whether the program is under Australian (or New Zealand under the Closer Economic Relations trade agreement since a 1998 High Court decision) creative control. The regulations also provide for a transmission quota and minimum sub-quotas. The transmission quota requires a minimum of 55% Australian programming (including repeat programs) between 6 am and midnight, averaged over the year (see Tables 3.4 and 3.5). In 2004 all commercial networks met this content quota, Seven with 57% Australian programs, Nine with 63% and Ten with 56%. Minimum sub-quotas apply to drama, documentary and children's drama. With drama the requirement is 250 points of first-run Australian drama per year and 830 points over three years. Points are calculated by multiplying a 'format factor' by program duration, a formula that provides an incentive for more expensive drama. Content regulations also require twenty hours of first-run Australian documentaries per year and twenty-five hours of first-run children's drama. In 2004 Seven screened thirty-four hours of documentaries in Sydney and forty-two hours in Melbourne. For C-classified programs (including children's drama), 260 hours are required per year, with half of them being Australian programs, along with 130 hours of Australian preschool programs. Eighty per cent of advertising time must be occupied by Australian-produced advertisements. Regional commercial television is required to broadcast 90 points of local content per week and 720 points over six weeks. Two points are allocated per minute of local news and one point for other material.

3.3   The two public broadcasters

The ABC

Australia is unique with its two public broadcasters, one with a mandate to reflect multicultural Australia. For half the history of television in this country, the sole public network was the ABC, based on the BBC model, with particular importance placed on locally produced drama, and sport until the 1980s when money and commercial television lured much of it away. Its 'golden age' was from the mid 1960s to the mid 1970s, pioneering current affairs programs (*Four Corners*, *This Day Tonight*), documentaries (*Chequerboard*, *A Big Country*) and drama (*Bellbird*,

Table 3.4: Proportion of Australian content on commercial networks, 1998.

Program	Seven				Nine				Ten			
	Local	Imported	Share of total	Australian content	Local	Imported	Share of total	Australian content	Local	Imported	Share of total	Australian content
Drama	10.3	26.5	36.8	28	4.5	27.7	32.2	14	6.9	11.3	18.2	38
Light Entertainment	11.2	13.7	24.9	45	13.2	2.9	16.1	82	17.9	24.8	42.7	42
News & Current Affairs	16.1	2.2	18.3	88	23.7	1.0	24.7	96	11.1	0.0	11.1	100
Sport	15.3	0.2	15.5	99	13.9	1.9	15.8	88	12.0	1.6	13.6	88
Infotainment	1.6	0.1	1.7	93	4.7	0.3	5.0	94	4.6	0.4	5.0	93
Documentary	0.5	1.8	2.3	44	0.7	1.0	1.7	44	0.4	0.1	0.5	71
Other	0.4	0.0	0.4	80	3.6	0.7	4.5	80	3.3	5.8	9.1	36
Total	55.4	44.5			64.3	35.7			56.2	44.0		

Table 3.5: Proportion of Australian content on public broadcasters, 2003–04.

Program	ABC				SBS			
	Local	Imported	Share of total	Australian content	Local	Imported	Share of total	Australian content
Drama & Comedy	2.0	11.1	13.1	15	0.4	3.5	3.9	10
Entertainment	11.9	0.5	12.4	96	0.1	0.4	0.5	20
News & Current Affairs	13.4	0.0	13.4	100	6.0	35.5	41.5	14
Sport	2.6	0.0	2.6	100	6.9	6.8	13.7	50
Factual	4.4	1.7	6.1	72	0.9	0.3	1.2	75
Documentary	1.5	5.3	6.8	22	2.7	11.0	13.7	20
Children & Education	6.6	18.5	25.1	26	2.1	0.0	2.1	100
Movies	0.1	12.3	12.4	1	0.1	16.8	16.9	1
Other	7.0	1.4	8.4	83	5.5	1.0	6.5	85
Total	49.5	50.8			24.7	75.3		

Certain Women). It had charter obligations with educational programs and those for young people, rural programs and regional obligations, with state-based news and current affairs (until cost-cutting forced its gradual centralisation).

ABC pressures and responses

The ABC has lived under budgetary pressure since the late 1970s. The federal appropriation of $200 million in 1976 had been reduced to $150 million by 1981, but the ABC has found it difficult to rein in costs. Management drifted without a clear vision of how to adjust to the changing television environment until the appointment of David Hill as managing director in 1986. Hill injected a new purpose into the organisation with the strength of his personality, reflected in more purposeful programming, and consideration of new delivery technologies and multichannelling. An inquiry into covert sponsoring of program production and ill-fated forays into pay television and an international television service took some of the gloss off the progress of this period, but it did generate a more commercial, quality drama output through accessing 10BA tax offsets (see Chapter 8), Film Finance Corporation Australia (FFC) funding and international co-production.

Funding cuts

The new federal coalition government in 1996 cut funding by $55 million and set up the Mansfield inquiry, which recommended outsourcing production to the independent sector. The ABC began a well-regarded internet service and an under-funded digital television service, but the level of Australian production had fallen and repeats increased. The network was able to maintain audience levels, with British drama proving to be its best performers. The ABC had become the captive of its success with UK programs, but there were occasional high points with local production, such as the drama series *SeaChange* (1999) and the comedy *Kath and Kim* (2002).

Evolution of SBS

The early days of SBS were a time of technical difficulties, policy confusion and reversals, and tensions between ethnic groups. Proposals to merge the ABC and SBS materialised in a 1986 announcement by the Labor government of a plan to amalgamate them. The public protested vehemently and it was rejected by the Senate. Instead, a national multicultural strategy was followed by SBS being established as a corporation by its own Act (1991) and allowed to accept sponsorship and sell on-air advertising time. The network's programming direction changed to predominantly English-language programs but retained the requirement to reflect cultural diversity, both in Australia and globally. As a matter of policy, any non-English speech was to be subtitled, not overvoiced in English.

Current position of SBS

SBS began to see itself, and be seen, as the network that could take risks with innovative programs (*South Park*, *Pizza*, *John Safran's Music Jamboree*), complementing the ABC's shift to middle-of-the-road quality programming. Its prime interest moved to the second and third migrant generation, away from more folkloric programming preferred by their migrant parents and grandparents. The original output of programs from migrant homelands and well-meaning expositions of Australian multiculturalism was always going to find a limited audience. While people might be interested in seeing a program in their own language and reflecting their own culture, they are not, by and large, interested in someone else's culture or language, even if subtitled. The new direction allowed a growth in audience and gave SBS a clearer role in mainstream television. Its audience was always more urban cosmopolitan than working class migrant and became increasingly so with its AB demographic (the upper two of the five socioeconomic levels from A to E). The network's advertising was constructed to match.

Movement of creative personnel between networks

A feature of the Australian television industry has been the movement of personnel between the commercial and public sectors. Many people, well-established in commercial television, spent their formative professional years in the ABC, which for some decades was regarded as the de facto trainer of the industry, with its established training department and in the absence of much well-regarded training elsewhere. In the era of budget restraint, the ABC has wound back much of its training effort, reviving it from time to time, but without the reliability it once had. Similarly, SBS has been a first port of call for many television workers before moving on to the ABC. Because they are separate organisations there has been an occasional rivalry between the two public broadcasters, but to date it hasn't broken out into serious competition. For much of the time they have recognised their separate roles in the television spectrum and have accommodated each other accordingly, the ABC wedged somewhere between safe, predictable Anglo-centrism and the guardian of choice and quality, and SBS straddling a boutique channel for urban cosmopolitans and the voice of multicultural Australia.

3.4   Changing patterns of programming

The popularisation of Australian programs

Imported American programs played an important role in developing the local television production industry, initially dominating the commercial channels with crime shows (*Dragnet*, *The Untouchables*) and westerns (*Gunsmoke*, *Bonanza*). The ABC preferred British programs. Low-cost imported programs subsidised the production of local programs, especially variety and light entertainment. *In Melbourne Tonight* and *The Bobby Limb Show* rated well in prime time. A 1960 government requirement that all commercials be locally produced signalled the approach of what Albert Moran has dubbed 'import substitution' – the displacement of imported program dominance by popular locally produced programs. From the late 1960s, an increasing and diverse range of Australian programs appeared as a consequence of their ratings success and content regulation by the Australian Broadcasting Control Board (later the Australian Broadcasting Tribunal). Australian programs frequently appeared in the year's top ten most popular shows from the early 1970s. The 1974 Top 10, for example, included *Number 96*, *The Box*, *Homicide*, *Division 4* and *The Great Temptation*.

The Australian vernacular

The surprise success in 1964 of the Crawford Productions' police series, *Homicide*, was followed in the next few years by *Division 4*, *Matlock Police* and ABC's *Contrabandits*. *Homicide* was a watershed local program by an independent local packager, introducing integrated studio and location (film) shooting, and setting a climate for the later rebirth of the Australian feature film. Domestic drama made its mark initially with American-style series in Australian settings and with an Australian vernacular. Consciously made for export, *Skippy* featured Australian scenery and icons. A more distinctive national style emerged, first in ABC's *Bellbird* (1967) and *Certain Women* (1973), and then in the commercial serials, *Number 96* (1972), *The Box* (1974) and *The Sullivans* (1976). Less in action-drama mode and more with an almost documentary-styled ordinariness, these were sometimes rough-edged, unabashedly Australian, and serials rather than series. Their descendents are the successful and ongoing soaps such as *Neighbours* and *Home and Away*.

Drama peak and decline

In 1978, *Against the Wind* started a mini-series boom, piggybacking on the 1981 tax concessions to boost feature film production. Drama peaked in the 1980s and 1990s with such mini-series as *A Town Like Alice*, *Bodyline*, *The Dismissal* and *Vietnam*, and the long-running series *Water Rats*, *All Saints*, *Blue Heelers* and, more recently, *McLeod's Daughters*. From the early 1980s, there have been increasing sales of Australian programs in the international market, with particular success for its soaps in the United Kingdom, but the current decade has seen a serious decline in local drama by commercial television as audiences have failed to respond to what has been offered and investors have become cautious. The ABC's drama output has declined even more dramatically as it struggles with budgetary restraints, although by 2006 it had made the beginnings of a comeback.

The Tonight show format

Early Australian content was provided by variety shows, with their emphasis on music, performance and dance, and quiz shows, many of them versioned American shows. Some, such as *Consider Your Verdict*, *Pick A Box* and *Wheel of Fortune*, had come from radio, whereas Reg Grundy successfully packaged *Concentration* and *Tic-Tac-Dough* for TCN-9. As local programs became more acceptable to the Australian viewing public, the earlier variety style with its ageing audience was superseded by the Tonight show format with broad, vaudeville-like comedy, guest chat and sometimes music, but not in the big production numbers of the old shows. Graham Kennedy made his mark as the 'King of Television' with the anything-goes *In Melbourne Tonight*. Don Lane had some success with a Sydney version of the format. Bert Newton, one of Australia's most enduring television personalities, was common to both shows. Mike Walsh drew a strong following with the format fashioned for daytime audiences and designed to appeal to home-based women.

Australian TV comedy

Comedy is a strong performer on television and Australia has strived to find a distinctively Australian style of comedy to match the success of comedy from America (from *I Love Lucy* to *Seinfeld* and *Sex and the City* and the unflagging *The Simpsons*) and Britain (*Till Death Do Us Part* through to *Monty Python's Flying Circus* and *Fawlty Towers* to *Absolutely Fabulous* and *The Office*). Situation comedy (sitcom) has had patchy success with the occasional popular shows from *My Name's McGooley, What's Yours?* through to *Kingswood Country*, *Mother and Son* and *Frontline* to *Kath and Kim* and *Pizza*. Sketch comedy has been more consistently successful with *The Mavis Bramston Show* and *The Norman Gunston Show*, and the more formula *Comedy Inc.* and *Fast Forward*. A recurring theme seems to be suburban life and middle-class pretension, but the Australian comedy brand is yet to be fully defined.

News, sport and current affairs

The 1980s saw the growth of world-class sports programs in Australia as technical developments enhanced live outside broadcast (OB) production, particularly of cricket, Australian Rules football, Rugby League and tennis. Its peak was coverage of the 2000 Olympic Games in Sydney, with 10.4 million people (72% of households) watching the opening ceremony. News and current affairs is now the cornerstone of the networks' schedules, but there was no current affairs until 1961, when the ABC modelled *Four Corners* on BBC's *Panorama*. Bob Raymond left the ABC in 1963 to make *Project 63* for TCN-9. Current affairs boomed in Australian television in the 1970s, but there has been a shift since to a more tabloid style (Nine's *A Current Affair* and Seven's *Today Tonight*), with a lowering focus on the harder journalism of *Four Corners* and early years of Nine's *60 Minutes*. News bulletins have been with television from the start, at first quite parochial, but after the success of SBS's *World News*, much more international in its content. The news output increased in the 1990s with the addition of late-night news bulletins.

Factual programming

Documentary has never been able to command much more than token interest from commercial television, mostly no more than to comply with content regulation requirements, so this genre has been left largely to the two public broadcasters. Even the ABC gave it little attention until the late 1960s, with the popular series, *Chequerboard* and *A Big Country*. In the following decade, the ABC developed magazine programs successfully (*Torque*, *Holiday*, *Quantum*) as it tried to maintain its output while costs were increasing faster than the federal government's funding. Commercial television followed suit with *Burke's Backyard* and has expanded this genre as 'infotainment' or 'lifestyle programs' (*Better Homes and Gardens*, *Getaway*), but the dramatic new player in the schedules is the reality program.

Programs for children and teens

Once they grew out of *Play School*, *Here's Humphrey* and the other shows tailored to young children, Australia's youth didn't have much specifically for them except pop music shows (*Six O'clock Rock*, *Bandstand*, *Countdown*). Music video compilations became the cheap alternative, but their earlier artfulness has largely given way to repetition and cliché. For young viewers, the ABC would run versions of what adults thought they ought to be watching, and occasionally get it right with innovative series like *Home*, *Sweet and Sour* and *Dancing Daze*. Reality shows, particularly the sensations *Big Brother* and *Australian Idol*, may have helped stem the flow of young viewers away from television. With some exceptions (*The Block*, *My Restaurant Rules*) they are mostly overseas formats 'licensed' and versioned in Australia.

Network programming preferences

Nine has been the industry market leader since the mid 1980s with 64% of its programs being Australian, although its dominance may be coming to an end. It operates on a high-cost/high-revenue business model in contrast to Ten's lower-cost/lower-revenue model. The networks have each found success in different program genres and have tended to build on these successes even if the preferences change over time with new successes in other genres and waning audience interest in previously successful ones. Thirty-six per cent of Ten's programs are imported drama and entertainment (compared with under 40% for Seven and under 31% for Nine) and 61% of the network's schedule is drama and entertainment, including Australian programs. Twenty-five per cent of Nine's programs are news and current affairs (18% for Seven and 11% for Ten), 16% are sport (15% for Seven) and 5% is local infotainment. Table 3.6 shows how commercial television allocates its expenditure and transmission time to the different program genres.

3.5   The third player: pay television

Beginnings of pay TV

The *Broadcasting Services Act 1992* was designed to diversify broadcasting in Australia, in particular with the introduction of pay television and the partial

Table 3.6: Commercial television comparative program expenditure (2003–04) and hours broadcast (2003).

Program expenditure	%	Hours broadcast	%
Drama		*All sources*	
Imported	23	News & Current Affairs	25
Australian	12	Children's	12
Total drama	35	Movies/Mini-series	11
Imported non-drama	10	Drama/Serials/Series	11
Australian non-drama		Light Entertainment	11
News & Current Affairs	12	Sport	11
Sport	20	Infotainment	6
Documentary	<1	Documentaries/Cultural	5
Light Entertainment	21	Comedy	4
Children's (non-drama)	<1	Others	3
Others	1		
Total Australian non-drama	55		

deregulation of the communications industry. The two telecommunications giants, Telstra and Optus, entered pay television in order to gain market ascendancy in the industry. Each installed its own cable infrastructure with the aim of leveraging Australian telephone and online business. By 2005, pay television's 1.7 million subscribers in Australia constituted 22% penetration, although that doesn't compare favourably with the United States (88%), United Kingdom (50%) or New Zealand (45%).

Financial losses and licensee departures

The initial delivery platform for Australian pay television was satellite, providing a revenue stream for Aussat, the national satellite that had been sold to Optus. Allocation of the services through public auction was delayed by speculative bidding. As in the United Kingdom, the sector suffered huge early losses – $2 billion in the first three years – from high infrastructure and program costs, slow take-up and high churn rates. By 1998, with Australis in receivership and Northgate and East Coast TV having already ceased operation, the original six licensees had declined to the three current operators, Foxtel, Optus Vision and Austar.

Foxtel and Optus

Foxtel, owned by Telstra (50%), News Corporation (25%) and PBL (25%), now controls the bulk of programming through ownership and distribution agreements. It commenced on cable in 1995 with twenty channels. Foxtel Digital was launched in 2004 and includes near-video-on-demand (NVOD), enhanced programming and some interactive services. In 2003, the Australian Competition and Consumer Commission (ACCC) approved 'channel sharing' between Foxtel and Optus, allowing each subscriber to get extra channels and enabling Telstra to bundle Foxtel TV with telephone and internet services, something Optus had already been doing with Optus TV for some time. Optus had operated its pay television service at a loss for some years, so part of the deal was Foxtel's agreement to take on $600 million of Optus's liabilities, including those that had accrued from Hollywood studio movie supply. Optus had been bought by SingTel (Singapore Telecommunications) from the UK's Cable & Wireless, which had itself bought out the Bell South (US) interest. Optus resells Foxtel channels along with its own three channels, MTVAustralia, Odyssey and Ovation, its production being outsourced to the digital media company, Omnilab, on a high-speed cable network.

Austar

Austar, 51% owned by US company Liberty Global and 30% by Denver-based United Global Com, provides satellite services to 515 000 rural and regional subscribers in eastern Australia, Hobart and Darwin. It was the first of the pay television operators to show net profit because of the greater need for this service in regional and rural Australia. Austar bundles video, mobile phone and internet services as well as carrying a wide variety of programming from all providers. Austar Digital was launched in 2004. The pay television sector has set itself the challenge of developing digital interactive services.

Ownership of channel providers

By 2003, over seventy channels were available from the three pay television operators. Foxtel Digital had over 100 channels. Ownership of channel providers ranges from pay television operators and FTA commercial broadcasters to joint ventures between local operators, Hollywood studios and foreign producers. XYZ, a joint venture between Austar and Foxtel, owns or distributes Nickelodeon, Discovery, Channel [V], musicMAX, Arena, The Lifestyle Channel and The Weather Channel. The Movie Network, owned by MGM, Disney and Warner Brothers with Village Roadshow as a partner, operates three movie channels. A rundown of the owners of each channel can be found on the Foxtel website at <www.foxtel.com.au>.

Different marketing models of pay and FTA TV

As already noted, subscription television was introduced after years of debate and in the face of vocal opposition from the commercial sector. The two operate on different marketing models. FTA television earns its money while the advertisements are running and spends it during the breaks for running programs. It needs as many viewers to tune in as often as possible. Pay television, on the other hand, earns most of its money when people pay their subscriptions. In theory, it doesn't need viewers tuned in at all. The theory isn't yet turning profit, however. Pay television earned $1348 million revenue in 2002/03, for an operating loss of

$452 million. By contrast, commercial FTA television earned $2934 million for an operating profit margin of 15% in the same financial year, both figures increasing in the following years.

Advertising on pay TV

Pay television was prohibited from taking advertising until 1997. Its advertising revenue, though small compared with commercial television, has been steadily growing since, which no doubt hasn't escaped the notice of its commercial rivals. Pay television's advertising revenue for 2004 was $123 million which, although small (1.4% share of the television market) compared with commercial television's $3.3 billion, was a 32% increase on 2003 and followed a 39% increase the year before.

Regulation and drama quota

Although the impact of pay television on FTA has generally been low, it has been felt in some areas, noticeably movies and sport. ACMA's 'anti-siphoning' list prevents FTA television from being excluded from major sporting events. The 2006 legislation dealt with FTA abuses of anti-siphoning by introducing a 'use-it-or-lose-it' clause. FTA networks still have the first right to bid for major sports events, but the business interests of pay and FTA television are merging anyway as we have seen with shared ownership and other strategic partnerships. The regulator is moving cautiously to encourage the growth of local content in a still not-highly-cashed sector. Licensees and providers of the seventeen drama channels are required to spend 10% of their programming budget on new Australian drama: $18 million was spent in 2002/03, $10 million short of the requirement for that year. By 2004/05, the spend had fallen to $16 million, although principally from the drop in children's drama. Nonetheless, the success of Foxtel's *Love My Way* may be an indicator that the hands-off approach by the regulator may eventually reap benefits. Amidst calls for a documentary quota, the ABA reviewed pay television's local content across the board, but has yet to report its findings to the public.

The growing subscriber base

Pay television has been slowly increasing subscriber numbers and household penetration, while aggregate FTA viewing is falling. Fifty-two per cent of the viewing in subscriber households was of pay television, but spread over so many channels that the top-rating pay television channel has only a 3.9% share, the epitome of niche broadcasting (or narrowcasting, if you prefer). It is worth noting, however, that 18–39 year olds with pay television spent a total of 21% more time viewing television than those without pay television.

3.6   The transition to digital television

Digital TV comes to Australia

In 1998, the federal government released a framework for the introduction of digital television in Australia from January 2001 in metropolitan markets, then progressively in regional markets. Like the American networks, the Australian commercial channels had lobbied for HDTV, arguing that the networks would be carrying the costs of conversion and that they would use no more spectrum after analogue hand-back than before digital. Pay television and the internet industry claimed the proposal for HDTV distracted attention from their real interest in multichannelling and subscription and data services. Their actual real interest was probably to block a fourth commercial player, with Rupert Murdoch reported to be interested in buying into Australian television. Commercial television proposed no new commercial licences during the transition and it argued that this should run over fifteen years. The upshot was no new networks or stations in markets already with three licensees, but only until 2010. The Ten Network began a third commercial digital-only service in Hobart in 2003, then progressively across Tasmania. Ten's digital-only licence for Mildura commenced in late 2005. The proposed timetable for analogue switch-off is currently that it will begin in 2010 and be completed by 2012 or soon after.

HDTV versus multichannelling

The ABA endorsed the emphasis on HDTV and the 1988 legislation gave existing broadcasters access to a second 7 MHz frequency on VHF/UHF for digital transmission, simulcasting until 2008 (reviewed in 2005 and extended to begin in 2010) when analogue spectrum would be handed back. The allocation could not be used for multichannelling or subscription television, although the ABC and SBS could multichannel 'non-commercial' and 'Charter' material under detailed guidelines. Spare digital capacity in the allocation could be used for enhanced services and datacasting (for a fee if as a commercial operation). Any spectrum remaining after allocation would be auctioned for datacasting, for which FTA broadcasters could not bid. Of seven registered bidders for the 2001 auction, four had withdrawn within six months. The auction was cancelled and the spectrum was used instead for wireless internet trials.

Triplecasting

Further legislation in 2000 mandated triplecast. Instead of high-quality 1080i (interlace-scanned) HDTV, it could be lower quality 720p (progressively scanned) allowing simulcast of SDTV. There were concerns about the continuing slow take-up of HDTV in the United States and the high price of high-definition set-top boxes. As the only country choosing the European digital video broadcasting–terrestrial (DVB-T) standard and requiring HDTV, cheaper receivers and set-top boxes from either Europe or America couldn't be marketed in Australia. The new legislation required twenty hours per week of HDTV-originated programming within two years of the start of digital television, except for the ABC and SBS, who were permitted to use up-converted SDTV as the United States was not a main program source for them.

Specialised digital channels

In June 2005, 11% of homes (820 000 households) had set-top boxes or digital sets, but by then DTT services were available to 1.07 million pay television subscribers. The ABC had started two specialised digital channels, Fly TV and ABC Kids, in 2003 but ceased broadcasting when the federal government refused separate funding for their continued operation. It has since started a digital-only channel, ABC-2, transmitting twenty hours per day. SBS began the digital World News Channel in 2003, operating eighteen hours per day. In 2004, the ABC began trialling datacasting with digital 44.

3.7 Regulatory and infrastructure changes

DCITA review of electronic media

This chapter has outlined the principal market in which an Australian producer is operating. After years of stability and growth it has been through a period of rapid structural change, which is just starting to stabilise, although the commercial and regulatory dynamic within that structure is still far from clear. In 2004 the Australian Government's Department of Communications, Information Technology and the Arts (DCITA) instigated a review of:
• possible additional programming by FTA broadcasters (including multichannelling) and modification of programming limitations
• the moratorium on new commercial licences
• the allocation of spectrum for digital television
• under-serviced television markets
• an Indigenous broadcasting service.
Communications Minister, Helen Coonan, has said she doesn't want new services to be a replica of what's already there. The federal government will auction off further digital spectrum for mobile television services using digital video broadcasting–hand-held (DVB-H) technology, currently under trial by The Bridge Networks, and to favour licences for providers of new educational and children's programs.

The issue of deregulation

Many commentators believe the Australian media is over-regulated. The wide expectation of Coalition government deregulation of the media industries proved accurate, with legislation enacted in 2006 allowing foreign and cross-media ownership of commercial television licences. This has prompted fears of a return to the destabilising media ownership changes that characterised the late 1980s and, as noted above, has already seen activity along those lines. The new *Broadcasting Legislation Amendment (Digital Television) Act 2006* also allows multichannelling on FTA networks (each allowed an HDTV multichannel from 2007 and an SDTV multichannel from 2009) and eases restrictions on ABC and SBS multichannels, but there will be no fourth FTA network until at least 2010. There will, however, be a third public broadcaster. The DCITA is drawing up the procedures and infrastructure necessary to operate an Indigenous television network, National Indigenous Television Ltd (NITV). It is expected to commence transmission in 2007. There will also be two new digital licences, usable for mobile television or 'in-home' services, and FTA networks will be allowed to bid for these within their guidelines. The cycle of profound change in the Australian television industry is not yet at its conclusion.

Sources and further reading

General reading

Clark, David & Samuelson, Steve 2006, *50 Years: Celebrating a Half-Century of Australian Television*, Random House, Sydney.
McKee, Alan 2001, *Australian Television: A Genealogy of Great Moments*, Oxford University Press, Melbourne.
Turner, Graeme & Cunningham, Stuart (eds) 2000, *Australian TV Book*, Allen & Unwin, Sydney.

Specific reading

Given, Jock 2003, *Turning off the Television: Broadcasting's Uncertain Future*, UNSW Press, Sydney.
Mercado, Andrew 2004, *Super Aussie Soaps*, Pluto Press Australia, Sydney.
Westfield, Mark 2000, *The Gatekeepers: The Global Media Battle to Control Australia's Pay TV*, Pluto Press Australia/Comerford & Miller, Sydney.

Magazine, newspaper and journal articles

(Anon) 2005, 'Pay television in Australia', Get the Picture, Australian Film Commission, available online at <http://www.afc.gov.au/GTP/wptvanalysis.html>, viewed 15 December 2006.
Encore, a monthly film and television industry magazine covering business and technical developments, published by Reed Business Information Pty Ltd, Sydney, available online at <www.encoremagazine.com.au>, viewed 15 December 2006.
Media Day, a daily bulletin of current developments in the media and entertainment industry with particular emphasis on television, published by PB Media, Sydney.
Moran, Albert 1997, 'Australia' in 'The Encyclopedia of Television', The Museum of Broadcast Communications, available online at <www.museum.tv/archives>, viewed 15 December 2006.

Some internet references

Austar United Communications Ltd, <austarunited.com.au>, viewed 15 December 2006.
Cox, Peter 2006, 'Australian TV: what we watched and what we didn't', Powerhouse Museum, Sydney, available online at <http://www.powerhousemuseum.com/pdf/publications/on_the_box-what_we_watched.pdf>, viewed 15 December 2006.

Foxtel Digital, <www.foxtel.com.au>, viewed 15 December 2006.

Peters, Bob 2005, 'Free-to-air television: industry structure and historical development', in Get the Picture, Australian Film Commission, available online at <http://www.afc.gov.au/GTP/wftvishistory.html>, viewed 15 December 2006.

Peters, Bob 2005, 'Free-to-air television: trends and issues', in Get the Picture, Australian Film Commission, available online at <http://www.afc.gov.au/GTP/wftvanalysis.html>, viewed 15 December 2006.

Chapter 4

Television genres

Television content, as with cinema, can be broken into a number of different genres – groupings of like programs or films – although the purpose and groupings are largely different for each medium. Film genres are the product of screen culture study. They describe differences of content in terms of style and subject matter, but there isn't necessarily a difference in the mode of production. The machinery to produce a comedy film is essentially the same as that for a film noir work, although the films themselves are recognisably different.

Television genres are more practical and group programs by production mode. The content may be different as a result of different production machinery, but not necessarily. Clearly there are differences between drama and current affairs in content as well as approach to production, but the content can be much the same, for example, in documentary and magazine-format programs. Nonetheless, the approach to production will determine style and content to a considerable degree. Generally, different subjects are best served by particular production modes and are usually dealt with in a particular genre.

The genres outlined in this chapter are those conventionally used in television at the present time. There is no hard and exclusive definition of any genre. They overlap. Genre is a convenient means of describing a production by stereotype. It has practical value in alerting someone to whom a project is being pitched to what type of program will be produced and in what production regimen, but it can discourage experiment with format. It is the product of the innate conservatism of television: safety first, low risk and don't frighten the horses. Often the most exciting advances in television come from breaking the genre mould. Ten years ago, the term 'reality television' would have been assumed to describe the existing documentary genre. Now it is a clearly understood, if not always admired, genre that has radically changed the face of television schedules.

What follows is an overview of the principal genres of television and the production resources and approaches generally required for them. Genres are more properly the province of screen culture studies and a whole book (or several of them) could be written on this topic alone. That is not the purpose of this book, but an overview of genres can give the producer an understanding of the range of production modes available to make different types of programs and the resources that might be necessary to do that. There's no one way to make a television program. Each is a variant drawing from the available range of resources and approaches. If producers know what genre they are working in, then they have a general sense of what production regimen might be needed to set it up – and so will any party they want to interest in contributing to the production. But it doesn't necessarily need to be done that way. It's up to the production team – and the project's backers.

4.1 Drama

The drama production pathway

Drama is the high-end fiction genre and, in many people's eyes, the pinnacle of television production. It is also a high-budget genre, demanding for its producers in its logistics, its resourcing and its sheer management. Conventionally, the production pattern involves developing a script, casting actors, designing and building a set and/or selecting locations for shooting, designing and making costumes, making or buying props, and working out a detailed and busy schedule, all in the pre-production phase before shooting commences. At the shooting (production) phase, the actors perform different sections of the script in scheduled order (generally not in script order) over several weeks. Stunts, action props (vehicles), animals, dollies and cranes (as moving camera platforms), and lighting are often part of the production phase as well. In post-production, music, digital vision effects (DVE) and animation may be added to the program as it is being edited, first for picture, and then sound.

Drama formats

Dramas may be one-offs, often at telemovie length of about ninety minutes, or series or serials. Series have common characters, settings and context. Sometimes story elements will thread through more than one episode, but episodes are mostly stand-alone with a main story and various sub-plots contained to the episode. Serials build on continuity of story, often with a 'cliffhanger' ending to an episode to entice viewers to watch the program the following week. Series will run for a season, conventionally thirteen, twenty-six or forty-eight episodes. Serials are usually either long-form formats as 'soaps' (a shortening of soap opera, as the early radio serials were called after their washing powder sponsors) or short-form formats as mini-series, usually three to six episodes and often adaptations of books. The attraction of series and serials is that they allow some of the costs of production to be spread over the series (amortisation), so reducing the cost per episode. A series can build an audience over several weeks instead of relying on a massive and costly publicity effort to pull in an audience for a once-only screening.

Docudrama

There is not much deviation from the pattern of large-crew, carefully scripted, contrived and controlled production found in television drama. 'Guerilla' drama, shot with small crews on low budgets and relying on freshness of ideas and style to offset its rough edge, is little used in television drama, even when it is a genre pursued by feature films. The main departure from the familiar artificiality of television drama is docudrama, in which documentary style is contrived in a fully scripted program that may be fiction or may be based on fact. Originating in English series of the 1970s, such as *Talking to a Stranger* and Ken Loach's *Days of Hope* – with a nod to the pseudo cinéma-vérité of *Hill Street Blues*, the style is intended to invest in the program a gritty realism. It generally does this, although the similarity in appearance to a small-crew documentary production is deceiving. Pools of light in the 'available lighting' style take as much effort to light as a fully lit conventional drama. The raw darting sentences in imitation of naturally spoken speech is as carefully written as the most intricately crafted dialogue. Probably because of its origins and its serious intent, the docudrama style is more often adopted by the ABC than the commercial stations. The mini-series *Scales of Justice* and the later series *Phoenix* and *Wildside* all told fictional stories in the docudrama mode (although *Scales of Justice* drew heavily on rumoured fact), whereas *Blue Murder* and *Joh's Jury* were docudrama presentations of researched fact.

Improvised, fast-turnaround drama

There has been a reluctance to take the logical next step and actually do what the production is purporting to be: a drama made with small crews and improvised dialogue and lighting. However, that mode was adopted by Hal and Di McElroy in making *Going Home* for SBS. This was a nightly drama about a regular group of commuters on an evening interurban train, talking about the actual news of the day and the fictional drama of their lives. Each episode was structured, incorporating overnight news, in the early morning and then recorded via two hand-held cameras directly into a non-linear edit system. The cast improvised dialogue for the scripted structure. The episode was edited that afternoon and broadcast that evening. With a little care, the news under discussion was the same news that had been on the real bulletins an hour or so earlier. But *Going Home* was the exception. By and large, Australian television drama sticks with the tried and tested, sometimes with pleasing results, sometimes disappointingly predictable.

4.2 Comedy

Sitcom

Comedy comes in two principal formats: situation comedy or sitcom, and sketch comedy. Sitcom is made in a production regimen very like that of drama. It is, in essence, drama that aspires to be funny, but there are subtle differences of emphasis. Sitcom generally places greater store in performance and timing, and less in direction and visual aesthetics. The editor is probably more crucial to its success than the photographer. The comedy derives from familiar characters' responses to life's events in a common environment, such as the family home or a workplace. It may revolve around neurotically self-absorbed thirty-somethings in downtown New York, or mother and daughter in Australia's aspirational outer suburbia, or a countercultural mother and geeky daughter in the residue of swinging London.

Sitcom's origins

Sitcom transferred to early American television from radio sitcoms of the 1930s and 1940s, themselves derived from the humour and continuity of comic strips. Radio shows such as *Amos 'N' Andy*, *Li'l Abner* and *Blondie* had a continuing cast in a different situation each week. Because television sitcom is strongly character- and dialogue-driven, the budget-favouring studio was preferred over location for production. Initially it was broadcast live from a New York studio and syndicated by kinescope, but the landmark comedy, *I Love Lucy*, changed that. Lucille Ball and Desi Arnaz were the show's producers as well as its stars. They wanted to stay in California and could do that by recording the show on film. Unlike a movie, they filmed in sequence and before a live audience, called 'three-camera technique'. With this approach, *I Love Lucy* was recorded as high-quality picture, establishing the ability to re-run shows, and setting the pattern for sitcom production.

National styles of sitcom

US sitcoms are typically long series runs of twenty or more episodes from teams of writers. British sitcoms are more often short series of perhaps only six episodes, with one or two writers. They tend to rely more on quirky characters than on plots, and on caricatures of stereotypes. *Till Death Us Do Part*, *Fawlty Towers* and *The Royle Family* come to mind. Australian sitcom takes the middle ground, with usually about ten episodes and often pursuing in its comedy some distinct aspect of the Australian character, as in *Kingswood Country*, *Kath and Kim* and *Pizza*. These days sitcom is often called 'narrative comedy'. Much of television production has moved out of the studio, so sitcoms too (to the extent that they are made at all in Australia) have become more location-driven. The cost difference between studio and location is less significant and there is a search for realism in imitation of drama, although it's not clear why comedy would want to be realistic. One landmark comedy has moved the genre from the television studio to the animation studio. *The Simpsons*, with its parody of middle American lifestyle and popular media, is now one of the significant cultural events of the television era.

Sketch comedy's relentless demands

Sketch comedy is a demanding genre despite its deceptive simplicity of structure. It is a succession of largely unrelated short segments, sometimes one-gag pieces, either butted together one after the other or interspersed with a presentation device, such as a presenter or presenters, graphics and animation or a combination of these. For the writers particularly, the need to keep churning out fresh material is relentless. In sitcom, if the characters have been well-defined and the plot line thought through, the episode tends to write itself. It is in the unforgiving nature of sketch comedy that as soon as one sketch – maybe no more than a minute – is finished, the writer must take up a blank page and start again. To alleviate this, sketch comedy often features a format and characters that reappear frequently in sketches throughout a series. Mark Mitchell's Con the Fruiterer in *Fast Forward* is an example of this. As well as taking some pressure off the writers, such characters can become much-loved by viewers.

Studio presentation of sketch comedy

Sketch comedy may be produced in the studio, although the practical limitation imposed by space on the number of possible sets in a studio puts a significant restriction on what can be done. The cost of set construction and the desire for realism are additional factors. It is more usual for most of the sketches to be pre-produced and dropped into the studio recording of the program, along with a small number of studio-based sketches, perhaps in front of a live audience. Pre-recorded segments are generally shot with a small field crew, often no more than a documentary crew, with minimal art department support. Sketch comedy aims to be low-budget and have a fast turnaround because that's the industry expectation. This enables some instances of this genre to be topical, and programs satirising news and current affairs formats (and other film and television) are common. This can be seen in programs such as *The Chaser, Non-Stop News Network (CNNN), Dead Ringers, Fast Forward* and *Life Support*.

The mavericks: guerilla comedy and mockumentary

A sub-genre that has performed well in Australia is guerilla comedy, pioneered by Garry McDonald in Norman Gunston, continued by several others in this country and reinvented (presumably) in the United Kingdom by Ali G. In this format, the comedy comes from seeing real people unsettled as they handle the apparently gormless interviewer who is, in reality, a character created by a comedian. Another variant is the mockumentary, in which comedy characters are given an edge by appearing to be real people filmed in documentary style. Mockumentary was pioneered by cinema's *This is Spinal Tap*, and followed with some success in UK television, *People Like Us* being a memorable example.

4.3   Documentary

Reconstructed real life

Documentary is the genre that purports to show actuality, although commonly it reconstructs actuality. This is often for reasons of practicality. The way to film a person walking down a street, even if research shows they walk there daily, is not to set up a camera and wait till they come by. The person is directed to walk by at a particular time, after the production has first set up the shot and rolled camera. It's not dishonest, just practical. The onus is on the director to produce a faithful reconstruction of the person's activity, or of anything else that is being recorded as actuality. Most documentary scenes are shot where the people on-camera know they are being filmed and will alter their behaviour accordingly, sometimes subtly by playing up their mannerisms, sometimes unsubtly and performing for the camera, whether that is showing off ('mugging') or subconscious. Perhaps the only genuine documentary footage is that captured on surveillance camera, but an unchanging high-angle wide shot is not likely to interest an audience for long.

Diminishing crew size

The traditional documentary crew was made up of three people: cameraman (infrequently a woman), camera assistant and sound recordist. A director was in charge and sometimes an interviewer or presenter made a fifth person. There could be a production assistant for general support as well. Documentary production moved from recording on film to recording on videotape, as the ability of tape to handle contrasting light conditions improved and the equipment became increasingly lightweight. A camera assistant was no longer needed to load film magazines. The production assistant was already becoming regarded as an unnecessary cost in the field and directors were often doing their own interviewing or conversely interviewers or presenters were taking on direction. These days, the entire crew is often two people with sound recorded with a microphone clamped on the camera, or with a microphone held by the director or with radio microphones concealed (not always as well hidden as they could or should be) on the people talking.

The video-journalism mode

Increasingly, the image recorded on lightweight digital video (DV) cameras are considered acceptable for broadcast, despite their domestic origins. A documentary may be recorded by a single cameraman–director in the video-journalist mode. This production approach has the advantage of considerably lower cost, especially in overseas shooting, and great manoeuvrability and responsiveness to changed circumstances. The almost unnoticed single person with a small camera has a greatly reduced artefactual impact on people on location which compares favourably with the traditional three-person crew with larger professional-looking equipment. As already noted, once people realise there is a working crew around, their behaviour changes in response to that realisation.

Post-production changes

Technological change has had a significant impact on post-production. Documentaries are seldom shot on film these days, but whatever the recording medium, it is likely to be digitised and edited on a computer-controlled non-linear edit system such as Avid or Apple's Final Cut Pro. In these systems, the digitised image is managed as edit decision data and the screen displays the image that these decisions will eventually convert to recorded output. Non-linear editing allows greater ease of digital effects and enhancement, so that documentaries are tending away from pure narrative form towards a more interpretive and personal mode.

Documentary on commercial TV

The documentary genre has been developed in Australia (and elsewhere) mostly by the public broadcasters. Commercial television is wary of the genre because of this association and perhaps because regulatory quotas create a perception of documentary as something that is 'good' for the audience, but not necessarily enjoyable. Nonetheless, there is longstanding audience support for travelogue and nature, and some observational documentary series (*RPA, Border Security*) have recently done well on commercial television.

4.4   Current affairs

Production characteristics

The current affairs genre has much in common with documentary, mostly recording actuality footage but with the additional requirement of currency of its stories. The mode of production is much the same as for documentary with a small mobile crew. Many of the changes in actuality shooting with new digital technology were pioneered in current affairs programs, with its need for mobility and immediacy. Presentation is fairly standardised and usually includes an on-camera journalist who has evolved in some programs to the single-crew video-journalist. Conventionally, current affairs adheres to requirements of actuality, but reconstruction (properly identified) is often used to good effect. Programs may be in long-form format (fifteen to sixty minute segments), more closely resembling documentary, or in magazine format.

Journalism

In many ways, this is a sub-genre of documentary, although its practitioners would dispute this. They regard themselves as journalists, but the issue is semantic (or elitist). It's hard to see why practitioners in either genre shouldn't legitimately call themselves journalists, both being reporters of factual material.

4.5   News

Getting the story quickly to air

News is another variant of the actuality mode of production, covering stories of daily currency. These are shot and compiled into a regular news bulletin for that day, the line-up of the bulletin changing as the day progresses and stories arise or evolve and take on new priorities. The craft is in finding the stories in the first place and in getting them done as quickly as possible without sacrificing their essence or understanding in the haste. Where the news is major and ongoing, or unfolding at the time the bulletin is broadcast, stories will be broadcast live or, alternatively, live updates will be tagged on to the main part of the item produced during the day.

Types of news stories

Items will be a mix of those made by the station during the day, those made by the station's overseas-based journalists that day (and sent by satellite) and overseas agency stories, taken off satellite daily and sometimes revoiced locally. Live updates of major breaking stories overseas (or even locally) are possible by satellite and some stories are of such magnitude that they are now able to be viewed live or in the immediate aftermath. These include such events as New York's World Trade Center attack in 2001, the 2003 invasion of Iraq and the more offbeat police chase of OJ Simpson on a Los Angeles freeway.

The growth of network news programming

Main network bulletins are run in the early evening, between 5 pm (Ten) and 7 pm (ABC). The last decade has seen an extension of news presentation to updates between programs in prime time, a second late evening bulletin and additional news presentation in the morning and midday. Each morning, SBS replays off satellite various national news bulletins in their originating language, under the banner of *World News*.

4.6   Sport

Rich and poor in a big business

Sport is big business on television. Licence fees for major sports with a large following are huge, with players in those sports commanding high salaries. In contrast, a minor sport will struggle to find a television outlet, often necessary to promote and expand the sport, and it may need to find a sponsor to be able to get a leg into television at all.

Advertising slots and delayed broadcast

The mainstay sport program is live (or nearly live) multi-camera coverage of sports events. With the high cost of production (event rights and production resources), FTA channels must maximise their advertising returns. Cricket and tennis provide natural advertising breaks between each over and at change of ends, but the various football codes don't accommodate advertisers so easily. The only natural breaks are when goals or tries are scored, but in low-scoring games this can be problematic. The solution can be delayed broadcast of the game, the delay increasing with each advertising break. The start can even be delayed so long as the telecast begins before the game ends so that the audience can't know the outcome of the game from some other source before broadcast begins. With major games like finals and test matches, networks are reluctant to risk viewer anger and will offset limited advertising breaks during the game with extensive advertising during the hoopla before and after.

'High-tech' coverage

Sports coverage is now a highly specialised art, both in the presentation of the game and the coordination of its resources. Major games might have twenty or more cameras, grouped with downstream mixers whose output is selected by a program mixer for transmission. Most of the cameras might be in fixed positions, but some will be roving. Technology now allows a range of enhancements of the live game coverage. Replays of key incidents of the game – a try or a disallowed try, a wicket, a shot at goal, a great rally – make use the of 'slo-mo' (slow motion) capacity and the ability to see the incident again on different cameras from those used in the live coverage of the incident. The technology allows a range of preformatted analytical pieces.

Major international events

The pinnacle of sports programming is the major international events such as the Olympic Games and the World Cup. Covered by a local host broadcaster and with broadcasting rights managed as a major global marketing exercise, the coverage uses a multiplicity of cameras in downstream units, drawing on all the enhancements current technology can offer. A broadcasting nerve centre houses crews from broadcasters who have licensed various rights, choosing from all of the output lines available and packaging them to send by satellite to their home channels for live transmission.

Sport in magazine format

At the other end of the pecking order, networks schedule sport in magazine format (see next section) either devoted to a particular sport or as a review of what's happening across the spectrum of sport. A more loyal following seems to be able to be built for the unabashedly low-brow, studio-based, variety-format shows, such as *The Footy Show*, as a mix of blokey sports chat, comedy and frequent dressing up.

4.7 Infotainment, lifestyle and magazine programs

An assembly of factual segments

Programs built up from factual segments were known initially as magazine programs, but now are more usually called lifestyle programs or infotainment in view of the content and production style. This is a growth area in factual television – the production cost is moderate, style for the most part is undemanding and content is widely accessible for the viewer. They are designed to deal with factual information in bite-sized, entertaining segments. The newest buzz term is 'factual entertainment'. Typically, a program will be made up of several segments, seldom over five minutes long, often with a 'personality' reporter and often linked by a marquee presenter either in the studio or on some thematically relevant location. The subject area is wide and has been used successfully for food and cooking, travel, gardening, home renovation, and so on – the list is long.

Production crew

This is a small-crew production. The reporter often directs, with a one- or two-person field crew. If there isn't a dedicated sound recordist, audio will be recorded through either a camera-mounted or a reporter-held microphone, or alternating between the two. Segments will often be short enough to be edited online on a non-linear system. In the basic format, the program may have an introduction and 'closer' by its presenter(s), with presented links and/or short animated breakers bridging the segments.

Growth of magazine programs

Magazine production began in Australia with the ABC as a means of its documentary department spreading its budget further when it only paid direct costs (studio use was a negligible cost to the department). The genre has developed in an increasingly populist style as a staple in commercial FTA and pay television, starting with *Burke's Backyard*, a program reportedly taken to Nine after it was knocked back by the ABC. The development of lightweight cameras and flexible post-production systems has ensured that the attraction of the genre remains, as has the continuing popularity of many of its programs.

4.8   Variety and entertainment

Decline of variety television

Light entertainment was the prime live content of Australian television for many years. Now it is the only genre that still makes extensive use of a television studio in the remaining subsets of the genre – Tonight shows, game shows and talent quests. Everything else goes out on location or builds the program in post-production.

The Tonight show format

The lavish song and dance spectacular has become a thing of the past. Costs have risen and tastes have changed. This format has evolved into the Tonight show, revolving around a high-profile presenter and including celebrity interviews, music items with a guest or resident band, some comedy segments (live on the show or prerecorded in the field), game or novelty segments and anything else the producers can dream up to ensure a varied mix. The technology allows much more interaction now with the studio audience and, via live feeds, with the general public. Graham Kennedy was the king of Tonight-style television in his time, with Don Lane and Dave Allen also successful practitioners of the format. Recent Tonight shows derive from Kennedy's very Australian knockabout approach and the formula spontaneity of America's *Saturday Night Live*. The current front performers in this format are Ten's *Rove Live* with the likeable Rove McManus and ABC's more thoughtful *Enough Rope* with Andrew Denton.

Game shows

Game shows are the stayers of television. Even when there isn't a place for them in prime time, they are good schedule fillers for daytime television. They seldom stray outside the studio, where they are shot live with multi-camera coverage. Often a week's programs are shot back to back in a day, particularly if they are 'stripped' (i.e. scheduled at the same time on each weekday). Game shows are highly professional in their production efficiency, low-brow in their aims and entertaining if the formula is right. Quiz shows were the mainstay of the game show format for the first decades of television, despite the early American payola scandals, but by the 1990s they seemed to have run out of momentum. Even the big performer of the 1980s, *Sale of the Century*, was taken off by 2001, although it's since been revived and renamed as *Temptation*. However, the success of *The Weakest Link* and *Who Wants to be a Millionaire?* has shown the television-viewing public was just waiting for a fresh approach to the well-worn formula.

The rebirth of the talent quest

The talent quest was a format that had some of the characteristics of both musical variety and game shows. It also went into decline during the 1990s as a costly and old-fashioned format, but has recently seen a spectacular revival as one of the options in the new reality program genre. Refashioned talent quests have provided two of the more successful programs in the new genre: *Australian Idol* and *Dancing with the Stars*.

4.9   Reality programs

Origins of docusoap

Reality television is the genre success story of twenty-first century television so far, although how long it will last is uncertain. This genre is essentially a game show taken out on location, with coverage influenced by longitudinal documentaries in the fly-on-the-wall (or cinéma-vérité) style. Its antecedents began with PBS's *An American Family* (1973), filmed over seven months at the home of the Loud family going through a marriage break-up. BBC's *The Family* (1974) followed the working class Wilkins family in England and in 1992 the formula was reworked in Australia by its producer, Paul Watson. The BBC/ABC series, *Sylvania Waters*, followed the nouveau riche Baker–Donaher family in the eponymous Sydney suburb. More recent examples of this format are *The Osbournes* and *Newlyweds*. They involve a single crew (for the most part) shooting a lot of material over a long period, the footage later being structured along the lines of soap opera, and hence the sub-genre category of docusoap.

The original reality TV program

In reality television, a location game show is shot in much the same style, documenting an artificial community or contrived social dynamic. The original of this form of the genre (and docusoap is a form of documentary, anyway) was the 1997 Swedish format, *Expedition Robinson*, licensed by Mark Burnett to create *Survivor* in 2000. Participants are put in exotic locations or abnormal situations and their consequent behaviour and interactions are observed by the cameras.

Big Brother

The most successful franchise of the genre, *Big Brother*, was created by the Dutch company, Endemol. With a production style influenced by CBS's *Candid Camera*, dating from 1948, the *Big Brother* format works by containing the participants in a house and observing them through a complex layout of hidden cameras. This introduces a keyhole tone to the program, but has the advantages of being able to take live feeds from the house for regular television and internet showing, and the program can be presented in real time, allowing viewer participation in voting contestants out of the house.

Reality TV in Australia

Other successful formats in Australia have been *Australian Idol* and *Dancing with the Stars*, both licensed formats derived from the talent quest format going back to CBS's *Star Search* (1983), and the home-grown *The Block* and *My Restaurant Rules*. There are a number of variants within the genre, such as the makeover format – be it of backyard (*Backyard Blitz*, *Ground Force*) or personal style (*Queer Eye for the Straight Guy*) – and the challenge format (*The Apprentice*). Another variant of the latter is the dating show format, such as *The Bachelor*, where the selected participant chooses from a group of suitors who are eliminated one by one, a formula derived from American ABC's *The Dating Game* (1965). *Candid Camera*, *The Dating Game*, *Star Search* and *An American Family* have all been reborn in reality television, illustrating a dictum of television: the new is only ever semi-new. Successful formats will return in new forms, perhaps forever in the continuing story of television.

The formula

The reality television formula is one of ongoing filming of participants in an enclosed environment, competing for a prize. The outcome may be decided by viewers eliminating participants by 'disapproval voting' (*Big Brother*, *Australian Idol*), by contestants voting each other off (*Survivor*, *The Biggest Loser*) or by the game controller making the decision (*The Apprentice*, *The Bachelor*). The format of the show is designed by producers who control the outcome to a considerable degree, so they aren't really reality shows at all. The suspicion has been that participants are chosen as heroes or villains with an expected impact on people in the show, but leading reality producer, Peter Abbott, says it's not necessary to be that deliberate in casting these programs (see Chapter 15).

How contrived is the show?

No major evidence has surfaced that programs are rigged beyond the influence of casting participants, although there have been a couple of minor ripples from disgruntled participants. Generally, contracts prevent participants commenting on production and for the most part programs are probably allowed to take their course with only minor contrivance of content. Experienced producers would recognise some of the voiced-over comments as prompted, if not scripted. For a program like *The Amazing Race*, the cost of capturing all the key moments as they happen and ensuring their quality coverage would be so prohibitively high that it is unlikely that they have been serendipitously caught on camera. Do they recreate the moments after they happen or do they take the easier option and simply script them? If the latter, how far does the scripting go? Of course, it's entertainment even if the audience takes it seriously, but then that justification has been used before.

Living history documentary

The term reality television is used for two quite distinct groups of programs: fly-on-the-wall documentary (docusoap) and location-based game shows, although the former is just a variant of the documentary genre. The difference is whether it is actuality or contrivance that is being documented. A format that straddles the two is 'living history', where contemporary people are filmed living under the conditions of a past age. The format began with the UK's *1900 House* and has been versioned in Australia in SBS's *The Colony* and ABC's *Outback House*. Participants are chosen in part for their expected interactions and put in an enclosed, con-trived environment so the program could observe their behaviour. But there are no winners and no prizes and the program supposedly gives insights into life in past times in a dynamic and dramatic format. This is what television is about. It could be argued that this is no more than re-creation, a more commonplace aspect of documentary than most viewers are aware of. However, it does contrast with reality television, where participation is for a money prize and fame. Reality television can make instant celebrities out of ordinary people, although there's not much evidence of lasting celebrity.

4.10   Music

The decline of music performance

Popular music has historically been presented on television as regular studio-based programs (*Six O'clock Rock* through to *Bandstand* to *Countdown*) with strong support from young audiences, and recorded live performance (*Rock Arena*), including genres such as country and western. By the 1990s, live music had given way to compilation programs of music videos on FTA television. With the music industry demanding increasing payment for the use of video clips (initially they were seen as advertisements and handed out free of charge by record companies), these programs have become infrequent on FTA as well. It might be argued anyway that music video has become cliché-ridden, pretentious or just incomprehensible. In any case, what popular music is now on television is mostly to be found on pay television, with Channel [V] the principal outlet. FTA television currently provides more programming of quiz shows about music than shows featuring music.

Classical music

Classical music hasn't fared much better. The ABC has considerably wound back its presentation of music performance. What coverage of this area of music remains is largely purchased from overseas (principally Europe) and scheduled within arts programs.

4.11   Children's programs

Activity programs

While straddling a number of approaches and operating within several of the adult genres, two types of children's program stand out: the activity program and children's drama. The former, aimed primarily at preschoolers, is generally studio-based and made up of educational activities (addressing numerical, alphabetical and motor skills) for the young viewers to imitate. Production is deliberately unsophisticated, but will draw on expert advice about what children of that age are capable of understanding and how best to engage them. Educational television that is entertaining at the same time was revolutionised in the 1970s by *Sesame Street*, produced by the Children's Television Workshop for the National Educational Television (now PBS) networks. It has tended to be the benchmark for preschool programming since. ABC's *Play School* is the longstanding local exemplar of this form, with *Hi Five* both popular and well-regarded in more recent years.

Children's drama

In resourcing terms, children's drama is little different from adult drama. It is shot in much the same way, so the main difference is in content and storyline. It is mostly aimed at preteens and is designed to comply with what appeals to that age group (or sometimes to what well-intended adults think *ought* to appeal to that age group). As a result, children's drama tends to be adventure-related, often drawing on fantasy, and sometimes these days is mildly scatological.

4.12   Animation

Cel animation

Traditionally, animation has been a slow, labour-intensive process of artists creating a succession of cartoon frames combined into a film (cel animation), or physical models positioned and filmed, then moved slightly and filmed again (stop motion). In cel animation, artwork is painted on clear plastic sheets, called cels (they were originally made of celluloid), one for each frame of filming. This can be shortcut with animation loops for sequence repeats such as walking, and by painting only the elements that move (e.g. hands gesturing, a talking mouth) in successive frames and aligning those cels on top of a common background using registration pegs. This method is near extinction. Recently, Disney closed its animation studio in Australia.

Computer animation

The first stage of phasing out cel animation was the computerisation of colouring and animated motion, although still working in two dimensions. These days, animation is done with three-dimensional (3D) imaging software, such as Autodesk Maya, developed by Alias Systems Corporation and now owned by Autodesk, which was released in 1998. Computer animation involves modelling, motion generation, addition of surfaces, and then rendering to produce a succession of frames with some aspect of the image varied. Animation is not drawn or painted, but animators choreograph movements and facial expressions with the software in each scene. Maya can simulate particle and fluid effects (e.g. smoke, fire, water droplets), human limb movement, cloth movement, fur and hair, and objects colliding and deforming under pressure. 'Shaders' allow variations in colour and texture to shape objects and reflect different lighting conditions.

Three-dimensional animation

3D programs move through three dimensions with a complexity not possible in the moving parallel planes – foreground moved faster than background – of traditional and two-dimensional (2D) animation. Initially, massive camera movement was used to show it off, but the novelty wore off and it was settled for movement required by the story rather than a gratuitous display of technical wizardry. The production of Disney's *Bambi* went well over time as animators tried to make antlers moving on a turning head look realistic, but now the rotation of antlers by computer is relatively simple and with life-like motion (as can be seen in sequences in *Brother Bear* and *Fantasia 2000*). Ironically, 3D animation is now often designed to look 2D to keep the traditional 'drawn' look that is still favoured by the market, and seen in the carriage in *Cinderella* and the Japanese animated feature *Howl's Moving Castle* with its black outer edges defining objects. The 2D look can be programmed more easily, reducing production costs and adding to its attraction. The American animation company Pixar is able to devote significant funds to technical research and development (R&D) and has an output of three seconds per week. On the other hand, television animation with its limited funding has very little capacity for R&D and generally uses tried and tested animation effects. It works to an output of about thirty seconds per week.

Flash

A low-cost alternative to Maya is Flash, a 2D, vector-based animation program used by website developers and garage animators. It is familiar in its use on the internet for animated novelty cards. *South Park* has the appearance of Flash although it is actually made with Maya with the 2D look as a design choice and for efficiency of programming. However, *South Park* commenced life as a pilot made by stop motion with paper cut-outs.

Stop motion and claymation

Stop motion continues as a boutique animation option with clay animation (or claymation) where clay (or similarly pliable material such as Plasticine) is shaped and animated, frame by frame, in a small set construction. It is labour intensive but with an instant result. It also has the advantage of realistic lighting, unlike 3D animation, where lighting looks unauthentic. Recent examples are *Wallace and Gromit* and Adam Elliot's Oscar-winning *Harvey Krumpet*.

Animation–gaming rivalry

Movies often have 3D shoots for games and DVD as part of their back-end exploitation. There is, in fact, a technical rivalry between animation and gaming, similar to that between film and videotape in the 1970s, where technical advances in one spur further advances in the other, the craft leapfrogging from incremental improvements in the two rival areas. The two may converge in the future, but for the moment the two cultures remain at arm's length, one interested in narrative and story, the other in challenges along a linear pathway. Convergence remains a prediction yet to be fulfilled here as elsewhere (see Chapter 2).

Sources and further reading

General reading

Bonner, Frances 2003, *Ordinary Television*, Sage Publications, Thousand Oaks, CA.

Specific reading

Bignell, Jonathan 2005, *Big Brother: Reality TV in the Twenty-First Century*, Palgrave Macmillan, Basingstoke, Hampshire.
Murphy, Kerrie 2006, *TV Land: Australia's Obsession with Reality Television*, Wiley, Brisbane.
Murray, Susan & Ouellette, Laurie (eds) 2004, *Reality TV: Remaking Television Culture*, New York University Press, New York.
Patmore, Chris 2003, *The Complete Animation Course*, Thames & Hudson, London.
Turner, Graeme 2005, *Ending the Affair: The Decline of Television Current Affairs in Australia*, UNSW Press, Sydney.

Part B

Massage parlour: development and funding of a project

Chapter 5

The concept

Part A looked at the television industry, where it has come from, where it is going (to the extent that anyone knows or thinks they know), the styles of production it interests itself in and the particulars of the Australian industry. The producer has not featured greatly up to this point, but now is the time to introduce that person because the story of the business of television production is the story of the producer.

The television producer shepherds the program from concept to delivery and often on further to marketing and distribution. As implied, the first stage to examine in this process is the concept – where it might come from and what form it might take. But before that, there is the question of what exactly a producer is. The title sounds precise enough, especially if expressed with no hint of uncertainty, but it can be used with a lack of clarity about what it entails and how crucial an effectively functioning producer is to the ongoing wellbeing of a production project. What sort of people does this role require, what sorts of skills and knowledge should they have, and what are their principal functions and responsibilities in a production project?

5.1 The role of the producer

The label of producer

'Producer' is a self-designated role. It requires no specific training, background or knowledge and, as a result, there are often abuses of the title. People will call themselves producer with little idea of what responsibilities they have taken on. Some star production personnel – actors or directors, perhaps – will demand the title for friends or lovers. Others will demand it in return for access to key program material or funding. A producer can be anyone who calls themself producer. Whether they can produce or not is another matter.

Pivotal role of a producer

Does this mean that the role of producer is a role of no real substance in the production of a television program? If it did, that would reduce this book to an analysis of an indulgence, but the reality is the opposite. The producer is the cement that holds the production together through its long and often complex pathway. The producer brings an accumulation of experience, insight and instinct that is central, indeed crucial, to the production process. Without a competent producer, a production will always struggle to stay afloat.

Differing role in cinema and television

Understanding the producer's role is further confused by the nuances of differing functions in cinema and television. In cinema, the producer develops the idea and then obtains and manages financing for the project. The director has creative control. In series television, the producer oversees every aspect of the production, guiding it creatively from concept to delivery, obtaining finance and managing expenditure on the production's resources. The television producer is the key decision maker for the length of the production pathway. Cinema and television producers differ also in the delay before they can get market indicators for their product. A cinema project will have a long development period before its first market testing in the form of finance and distributor interest, which will not take place until the project has got to full script. Television projects, on the other hand, can often get indications of broadcaster interest at treatment stage (see Chapter 6) even if the commitment doesn't come until later. The broadcaster *is* the market for a television project and it is speculating that there is an audience for the program. Investors will often only come in when there is broadcaster commitment. For a cinema project, the financiers are the market and they too are speculating about audience.

A dual role

A television producer is two people rolled into one. He or she (the role can be filled effectively by either male or female and is perhaps hermaphroditic anyway as it combines skills that are stereotypically regarded as male with skills regarded as more female) will be someone skilled in the management of money, resources and logistics. In other words, the producer is a 'bean counter', but will also be a person who can 'mother' a creative team through the stages of development of the project from concept to eventual realisation as a completed and (with luck and good management) satisfying program. At one extreme is the line producer, the person who tabulates, books and supervises all the resources necessary to carry out all the steps of production. Their objective is the mantra of 'on time and on budget'. At the other end is the so-called creative producer, who isn't so concerned about the specific resources that are required or when (there are others to do that) but instead is the empathiser and encourager of the creative team to draw on its inner resources and produce a work of imagination and significance. However, a fully rounded producer is both of these people at once – a modern renaissance person, a marriage of left brain and right brain, a person who can count beans and guide and support the creative team.

Types of producers

There is a hierarchy of producers at varying levels of responsibility for a production or a slate of productions. These variants are outlined below.

- Executive producer – the most senior level, often overseeing a number of projects, but generally not involved in the day-to-day operation of production. This producer is in charge of all creative and technical personnel, makes sure the production is on budget and meeting its editorial brief, and is responsible to broadcasters and/or investors for the proper contracted use of their funds.
- Supervising/series producer – oversees a series or a number of related productions, often with an emphasis on the day-to-day management of resources and the budget, sometimes with less oversight of editorial and creative aspects.
- Producer – oversees the production at the day-to-day level for editorial/creative and resource/budget aspects, indeed, all aspects of physical production.
- Line producer – oversees resource/budget aspects of a highly resourced production; in other words, a producer with more focused responsibility.
- Associate producer – works for the producer in one area of their responsibilities, such as overseeing research or post-production or magazine segments.

Developing projects through to completion

Producers are generators of projects and will often work on the development of several different projects simultaneously. They are the leader of the team that will build and carry the production machinery through a complex succession of integrated events from which will emerge a completed television program. They are rather like a commanding officer in a military operation, constantly assessing the state-of-play of the project and making judgements on how to respond to subtle (and sometimes not so subtle) deviations from anticipated outcomes of events along the production's pathway. The producer may or may not be the originator of the program concept. However, somewhere in the genesis of a program, if not at the very outset then in its embryonic stages, a producer will come in and put together the first elements of a production team and start to build the machinery of program development which will evolve into program production.

Structuring the development

If the concept is created by the producer, they may well carry out the first stages of turning that into a proposal by themselves, at the same time giving consideration to who might work on the production and perhaps having preliminary discussions with those people. With a concept originating from someone who isn't a producer, that person will take some of these first steps until linking up with a producer, who will then start to structure the development and give direction and leadership to the building of the program. But whether the concept is the brainchild of the producer or another person, it is always the germinal moment of the production process.

5.2   Sources of the concept

The bottomless well of program ideas

Where does the concept for a television program come from? The answer is: anywhere and anyone. The potential sources of program ideas are, to all practical purposes, limitless. A concept may be in some pre-existing form, such as a novel or a magazine or newspaper article, or it may simply pop up in someone's head, although usually something has to trigger that. It may be a casual remark from a person with no involvement in television or it may come for a professional looking for a producer to work with them on their idea or script. It is important to keep eyes and ears tuned to the possibilities and maintain an open mind. It can sometimes be hard to recognise the potential in a program concept, not least of all because we don't always know what works on television. We know what has worked in the past, but that doesn't always tell us what will work in the future. It's not always clear what *made* it work in the past. Audiences are both predictable and unpredictable.

Independent and commissioned development

Concepts can be created independently of the marketplace with a view to developing them to a stage where they can attract funding for their further development or production. In the early stages this will be an individual or a small team running on enthusiasm for the concept and its potential as a television program. They will continue until the means of production of the developed program are secured (known as 'greenlighting' the project) or they get to the point that all possible avenues of production backing have been exhausted. Alternatively, programs may be commissioned from a pre-existing concept provided by a body with the funds for development or, better still, production. This might be a broadcaster, a production house or any other party, such as a sponsor or a facilities house, with the necessary finance and interest in a particular program being made, either as investment or promotion of some other business interest. A common example is a broadcaster buying a pre-existing format, already successful in an overseas market, and commissioning a local version of the formatted program. Where the project is commissioned, the range of sources of its concept is the same as those outlined above. A commissioning body is a producer in that sense.

Brainstorming and clustering

When a subject has been decided but ideas are needed on how to visualise it, two methods that are sometimes used are brainstorming and clustering. They are related in their approach, the latter being more organised, the former being less restrictive. In brainstorming, the people in the team throw ideas off the top of their heads, each following on the last with a spontaneous or subconscious connection, no matter how tenuous or obscure. The session is recorded and later played back to see if anything strikes a chord that can be developed further as a new angle on the subject. Clustering is a solo variation where ideas are written down instead of called out. Again, it starts with a key word or phrase and runs lines of related phrases in clusters.

Sources and reconceiving

Like the sources of concepts, the ways of arriving at them are limitless. Program concepts can come from anywhere. Some very successful programs have surprising or quite incidental origins. *Fawlty Towers* was the result of John Cleese and Connie Booth staying at a hotel run by a man as ill-suited to that job as Basil Fawlty. On the other hand, *Chequerboard*, a seminal ABC program of the early 1970s, was modelled on a UK program of the time, *Man Alive*. Sometimes a great idea comes as a bolt of lightning. You wonder why it took so many years of your life to come to you when its potential is so self-evident. Sometimes it is elusive and has to be teased out of the nether regions of your brain. Something that at first seems of limited interest or practicality can, on rethinking, be an original and refreshing approach to an exciting story. Some successful programs do not originate as the program that is eventually made, but evolve during the development process. The UK comedy *Absolutely Fabulous* was conceived as a satire of the magazine publishing world with a reversed mother–daughter relationship as a subplot. This was the concept that was piloted (with Dawn French playing the daughter, not Julia Sawalha), but after evaluating the pilot the relationship became central, publishing moved to the background and the daughter was recast.

5.3 Is it a good idea and who else thinks so?

Testing the idea

Is your concept a good idea? If it originated with you, you will be persuaded it is good for that reason, but you might be the only person who falls in love with it. If the idea has come from someone else, a producer is at least able to be more objective in assessing it, but either way the aim should be to build up a consensus, a straw poll of what the viewing public might think. It is useful to sound it out on a range of people, not limited to people in the industry. A television audience draws from the whole community and the straw poll should attempt to reflect a cross-section of the viewing public. The idea should not be presented too enthusiastically, and a producer will sometimes need to read between the lines of people's comments. There is a general reluctance to be critical of something that a person seems passionate about. Friends and relatives are particularly susceptible here. The completed straw poll will be the first assessment of the project. It's not foolproof, but it's a start.

Similar concept with another producer

If it is a good idea, some other producer might also think so. A producer needs to be alert to the possibility that there might be another production overlapping dangerously with their own project's concept. This is not such a problem with fiction, but is a particular concern with factual programs. A network is unlikely to want to acquire two programs on substantially the same topic. Antennae should be kept up. When dealing with people involved in the subject of a project, the alert producer will ask whether they are aware of any others pursuing a program on the same subject. It's also worth sounding out a commissioning person in the network(s) in mind for the program to find out if there is any existing commitment to a program on that subject.

5.4　It's a concept, but is it a program?

Log line

A concept may sound good and it may feel good, but if it isn't able to be developed into a viable program it will be of little practical value in the long run. The concept may come in nearly as wide a range of forms as its range of sources. It may be no more than a thought floating around in someone's mind or it may be a long and detailed exposition in a published work. In whatever form it comes, it needs to be converted into a short written statement that captures the essence of the idea. This is the log line, the central conceptual statement that underpins the proposed program. It is a one-sentence summary of the meaning and theme of the program. This is the practical starting point of the program and, until the concept – floating thought or published work – is consolidated into a log line, there is no means of assessing and developing it as television. If it is a thought it has to be converted into a less ephemeral form that others can consider; if it is a published work it has to be digested to something capable of being turned into the shorter time span of television.

Fundamental differences between script and prose work

A log line is drawn out of a published work in order that the program can be developed from this statement rather than from reworking the source prose as script. Stories need different treatments in different media. Published prose works as an interaction between the written word and the reader's imagination with no real restrictions on the world described beyond the author's inventiveness or perhaps the reader's capacity to understand it. Television scripts, whether for drama or documentary, must be tailored to what images can be captured by the technology, mostly the camera, within the restrictions of available finance to access that technology and those images. Their narratives are constructed with that reality in mind. A prose work is not.

Log line as consolidation of the idea

An idea floating around in someone's mind might be pondered over for a while, but must eventually be written down and subjected to intense scrutiny. This might demonstrate that it's still a half-formed idea and needs further work to mould and shape it. As series producer of the revival of ABC's *A Big Country*, episode producers were asked to capture the essence of their proposed program in a sentence that explained what it was about. This didn't mean it would be about a rodeo, for example. What the sentence needed to do was clarify what it was about a rodeo that the program would explore. Writing the concept down forces an examination of its essence in concrete form.

One-paragraph summary

The log line is the essence of a single paragraph that is written as a brief summary of the proposed program. Until an idea can be captured in a sentence and a paragraph, its originator is still trying to work out what that idea is. The paragraph should be an expansion of the sentence and the sentence should be the core component of the paragraph. It doesn't really matter which of the two comes first, but the one should generate the other. Both will later have key roles in a proposal document if the concept survives the rigours of evaluation. Someone reading a proposal should get an immediate grasp of its selling point if the proposal is to serve its purpose.

Criteria for program feasibility

The concept needs to meet certain key criteria if there is to be a commitment to the considerable effort and investment, both emotional and financial, of development. The criteria aren't necessarily examined in any particular order, but are pondered together to arrive at a view of how feasible the project is. An important consideration is the type of program format that best serves the idea. What is the natural vehicle for its production? Is the subject matter factual or fictional? Is it better dealt with in long-form documentary or magazine format, drama series or as a one-off? Is it presenter-led or can the subject drive the program? The questions can be endless, but in practice the subject raises many of its questions and answers at the same time. Knowledge of available genres helps, but anything that enhances the story could be considered, with the proviso that it is harder to sell a non-established genre in a notoriously risk-averse industry. The producer must weigh up the newness of the program format against investor and broadcaster fear of failure with the unknown.

Visualisation of the concept

The essential practical question about a concept is can it be produced? While thinking about what form the concept's program might take, a producer will want to know how that will be possible. At its simplest, television is a visual medium and if the concept doesn't provide something at which to point a camera, it's hard to see how a television program can be made out of it. An imaginative but nebulous concept might be stimulating to talk about over a bottle of wine, but may not lend itself to visual presentation. With no visuals, there is no television program. Where it *is* possible to visualise the subject, it must be able to generate pictures that will excite viewer interest. Are the pictures so produced likely to be attractive, unusual, or dynamic, or likely to have any of the other qualities that will engage the viewer with its content? Formats, where they have already been produced in other territories, give some insight into this issue. They are low risk because they demonstrably *can* be produced.

5.5   A market for the program

Who is the audience?

As the concept is developed into a program proposal there needs to be an understanding of who will want to watch the program and therefore who will want to broadcast it. Who is the principal audience and what is the best market to reach that audience? Many proposals assert their program will reach a broad audience of all ages. While this would be good if it were true, it might indicate the program's developers are uncertain just who might watch it. Most programs are skewed towards either female or male viewers, or towards younger or older audiences. Some viewers look for programs that are informative, whereas some look to be diverted or entertained. Few programs have strong appeal to all demographic and interest groups. An appreciation of which audience is more likely to be drawn to a particular program means the program can be constructed to ensure and maximise that appeal.

Fashioning the program to its audience

If a program has inherent appeal to female viewers, building on relationship interest should increase that appeal more than adding action sequences. Older audiences prefer a conventional narrative approach to a program. Younger audiences, reared on commercials, music video and computer games, are more receptive to the use of visual effects and more syncopated editing. The use of demographic-oriented styles won't, however, attract a younger or older audience to a program that is not inherently of interest to it. The use of such style should be to build the program's natural audience, not pull in viewers that are marginally interested at best. A documentary about a political issue is not likely to hold younger viewers just because of extensive use of effects and fast-paced editing.

Designing the program to the broadcaster

Connected to this is the issue of which broadcaster is most likely to be interested in the program. It is developed to appeal to that broadcaster's style and apparent needs. If the prime broadcaster is Australian, the profile of network scheduling will reveal where each channel's emphases lie. A close examination of the network's schedule in a TV guide is a good starting point for understanding a broadcaster's program interests. Any reports about network preferences in both general media and industry journals, and comments by people in a position to have some insight into network preferences, all add to the understanding of what each network is looking for in the way of programs and – equally as important – what it is not looking for. The program should be developed to appeal to the target network, once that has been determined. There is no point in trying to appeal to all networks, although variations to the program may be considered later for pitching secondarily to other networks.

Broadcaster preference for TV series

Producers should bear in mind that, in general, broadcasters are more receptive to television series proposals than one-off programs. A series has the capacity to build an audience, even if it is a short series. A one-off program has to draw immediately whatever potential audience it might have. There's no opportunity for word of mouth to deliver follow-up audience. As well, a series enables the broadcaster's publicity and promotion dollar to be spent more cost-effectively. Publicity investment is highest prior to the first episode as it is principally awareness-raising. Subsequent episode promotion carries a smaller cost as follow-up, building on review and word of mouth from earlier episodes. Because of its nature, publicity for a one-off program must be of higher cost and awareness-raising. Spending the preponderance of the publicity dollar on awareness-raising for one hour of television is less cost-effective than spending on, say, ten hours of television. Press preview will pick up more readily on a series for much the same reason: it is covering several hours of television rather than one hour, so there is a greater impact on its readership. In the chapters that follow, the discussion will often cover one-off rather than series production for simplicity of description. Nonetheless, the reader should not lose sight of the broadcaster preference.

Appealing to overseas broadcasters

Some programs are inherently of interest to Australian audiences only. There is little point in trying to 'internationalise' such programs to secure an overseas sale. All that might do is prejudice the Australian sale by losing its clearer local focus. Programs about Australian social issues are not likely to be of interest to broadcasters outside Australia. Other programs might be of global appeal and developed for an overseas network as the principal broadcaster, although this is generally the harder way of approaching the market. Information about the preferences of overseas broadcasters can often be found in trade magazines or on the broadcasters' websites. Overseas networks often want to see evidence of local broadcaster commitment before they will commit to a project. This issue is examined in more detail in Chapter 8.

Ancillary markets

Some early consideration can be given to the potential for merchandising spin-off and cross-platform delivery of the concept content. The former is more traditional and includes the possibility of a book or music release to capitalise on market interest in the program, or manufacture of any non-media consumer goods that can be promoted on the back of the program, be they Ninja Turtles, Bananas in Pyjamas or Fat Pizza T-shirts. Cross-platform delivery is the result of diversification into new media, the possibilities of websites, content distribution through mobile phones and iPod, or the more established video sell-through on DVD (see Chapter 11). This is only preliminary thinking at this stage of the production cycle.

The main objective is developing the core product – a television program – but, nonetheless, thought is given to what other market opportunities might roll off a successful program. Planning as it proceeds should ensure that the components necessary for follow-on marketing are being considered and developed at the same time as the core product.

5.6   Optioning an existing work

Rights in an existing work

Sometimes the source of a program idea is an existing work, most commonly a novel or short story. The right to base a program on such a work has to be obtained from the copyright owner (usually the author), and with a well-known work this can be expensive. The producer is unlikely to have the finance to obtain rights in a book until the production is fully funded, when it would become a budgeted item. Indeed, rights aren't needed before that stage, but the producer would not want to spend time and money developing a program adapted from a book only to find some other party has licensed its own adaptation. The solution is to option the work.

The option agreement

In the optioning of a work, the copyright owner doesn't license the producer to adapt their work, but contracts not to license it to anyone while the option is in force. For a fee, an option agreement will give the party taking out the option an exclusive and irrevocable right and option for a specified period to purchase nominated rights (generally very wide-ranging) in an existing work. The agreement will usually allow the producer to extend the option for a further period with the payment of a second fee. The option agreement will also state the principal conditions and rights if the option is taken up. It should include an agreement that both parties will pursue a legal remedy if a third party infringes on the work's copyright. If the option is exercised, the parties would then enter into a more formal long-form agreement consistent with the conditions and rights in the option agreement. If the option has not been exercised by the time it expires, all rights in the work return to the original owner, who can deal with them in any way that they choose.

The option fee

An option fee is considerably lower than a licence fee. It doesn't give anything in return other than an agreement not to license another party and this gives the licensee breathing space to try and get their project up without the fear of losing the right to use the source property. A one-year option in a fiction work might typically cost between $1500 and $2500, and more if the work has a high market value or its author (or their agent) believes it has. It would be unwise for a producer to option a work without a belief that they know where to find development money for it. The producer may talk to potential scriptwriters while considering optioning a work to sound out their interest in the project. It goes without saying that the producer should not contract any of these writers until the work has been formally optioned.

Author as scriptwriter

The producer might get the author of the work to do the first draft script. This could be a strategy to reduce the cost of licensing the work or it might be to value-add to the work. In this situation the contract should provide for the producer to bring other writers into the scripting process, including, without penalty, the possibility of not proceeding to later drafts with the author. Where the work's author is also a scriptwriter, the option agreement and writer's agreement should be separate contracts, so the writer's agreement can be incorporated into a Chain of Title (see Chapter 6) without ambiguity, and any copyright issues that might arise from the scriptwriting can be clarified.

Rights to a person's life story

Another type of option agreement is in the right to a person's life story or part of it. The option payment in these circumstances is usually not high because a person doesn't have copyright in their unrecorded life story (although nor do they have an obligation to share it), but the agreement will include a much larger payment if the option is exercised. The agreement is that the person will not share their life story with another party or otherwise deal with it while the option is in force, and if it is exercised the person will cooperate with the producer (or writer) in developing storylines and scripts from their life story and assist in getting consents from other people with whom their story connects.

Optioning non-fiction works

Only works whose use would involve breach of its copyright need to be optioned, and these are principally works of fiction. Non-fiction, such as history, true stories or biography, don't generally need to be optioned unless there is some original aspect in the treatment of this factual material and that aspect is to be incorporated into the proposed television program. Alternatively, there might be some strategic reason for arriving at an agreement with the author, such as the program's promotion riding on association with the recognition factor of a successful book. Sometimes a biographer or historian will appear in the program anyway and may be paid a fee to do so. This is not a licence fee, but an appearance fee. It is contract law, not copyright law.

5.7   The stages of production that follow

The producer's role

At the beginning of this chapter, the role of the producer as the source of television program ideas was outlined. It is also the producer's role and responsibility to guide the production through all the stages that follow in taking a concept through to a finished program. An overview of these stages is provided below (Fig. 5.1)

Development

If the concept has survived scrutiny of its suitability as a potential program, it is taken through the first production stage of development. This builds the concept as a blueprint for the program, usually called the treatment, describing its principal editorial line if it's a factual program or its dramatic arc if it's fiction. The treatment is incorporated into a proposal document, which is used to raise finance for the program's production. The development stage may also involve the writing of scripts (drama or comedy) or shooting scripts (documentary), preliminary or extensive research, or the production of a pilot, a sample sequence or episode of the proposed program, or some similar audition video. The proposal document will also be the basis of a program 'bible' if it is a series. Here, aspects of the production, such as characters, writing and production style, are defined to ensure consistency over a series with different writers, directors and editors for the different episodes.

Pre-production

When the production is financed, pre-production can commence. This is the stage where a shooting schedule is planned, drafted and confirmed step by step, and where resources are determined in detail and booked. It is also the stage of finetuning the blueprint for the program as a result of further research and in the light of the practical realities of shooting that emerge.

Production

Next comes the production stage, in which the principal content of the program is recorded on videotape or film (or, in the digital era, on any other new recording medium) or transmitted live. It is here that pre-production's detailed planning and finetuning is put to the test. The proof of the 'pudding' of pre-production is in the 'eating' of production. The naming of this as 'the production stage' can be confusing given that the whole process is also termed 'production'. This is sometimes clarified by referring to this stage as 'the shoot'. Ambiguity (and vernacular simplicity) is anathema to legal documents, so this stage is generally referred to as 'principal photography' in contracts and the like.

Post-production

The final stage of the traditional production cycle is post-production, where the material (vision and sound) gathered during the production stage and from other sources is fashioned into the television program through the process of editing. Image and sound are, to some degree, dealt with separately, but they have to match, complement and supplement each other so that they can be effectively married at the final stage. The outcome of post-production is a broadcastable program. With a live broadcast, there is no post-production and the production

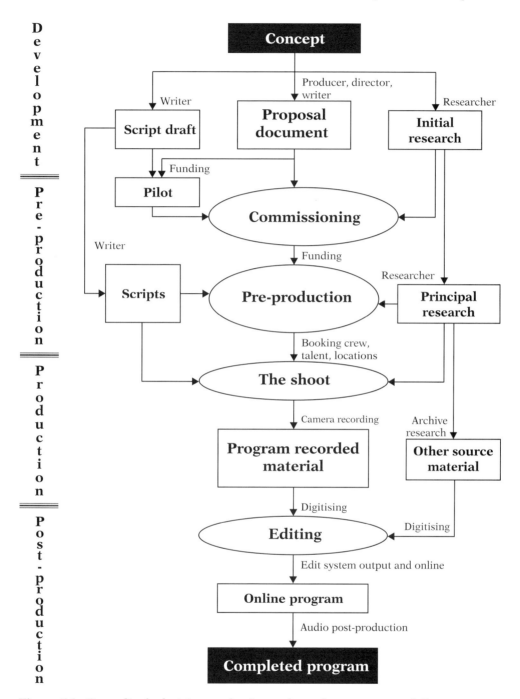

Figure 5.1: Generalised television production pathway from concept to delivery.

stage is broadcast, putting an even greater requirement on pre-production to get its planning right.

The production cycle

Pre-production . . . production . . . post-production. What it lacks in imagination, it makes up in simplicity. It might otherwise be characterised as: planning . . . shooting . . . editing. Figure 5.1 is a schematic layout of the elements that typically make up the production cycle.

Beyond delivery of the program

These days the production cycle doesn't necessarily end with delivery of the program for broadcast. Production funding is much tighter than it once was and often involves exploitation in ancillary markets or of ancillary products to recover the costs of production. Further back-end marketing will be pursued to generate financial returns to the production's investors. This may involve versioning the program for different markets or reusing content to present the program's themes in other modes of delivery. Some of these options are dealt with in Chapter 11.

Sources and further reading

Magazine, newspaper and journal articles

Messenger, Naomi 2003, 'You talkin' 'bout me? Basing stories on people's lives', *ART+law*, June, available online at <http://www.artslaw.com.au/ArtLaw/Archive/03YoutalkinboutmeBasingstoriesonpeopleslives.asp>, viewed 15 December 2006.

Chapter 6

Development of the project

Development is the most intensively creative stage of the production cycle. It is creative in the sense that it starts with very little, just a germ of a program – the concept – and builds from that, giving it definition, fleshing it out so that it is a realisable entity, which is capable, with the necessary resources, of being fashioned into a television program. Other stages have their creative aspects, both in production and post-production, but these are creative enhancements, finetuning of the program, rather than the creation of a program blueprint in the form of a script or shooting script, or detailed treatment from the trickle of an idea.

This aspect of the creative realisation of a program is often overlooked because of the more obvious creative input of directing and editing, but it is a mistake to think that development is just the accessing of resources and people to commence the creative production of a program. The development process is the interchange of ideas and testing of alternative treatments to determine how best to make the program so that it will successfully engage and entertain or inform its audience.

The output of the development stage will be, at minimum, a proposal document designed to sell the envisaged program to investors and/or broadcasters. The proposal's purpose will be to take the enterprise to the point of 'greenlighting', industry jargon for when funding is sufficient for the project to proceed into production. It will contain, inter alia, a treatment, a production plan, and other relevant elements that will help give potential funding sources a solid idea of what the program should look like and what return its financiers can expect from it, either as revenue (for investors) or audience response (for broadcasters). Other products of the development stage are likely to be a fully detailed production budget estimate and a sample video or a pilot sequence or episode of the program. The principal steps of the development pathway of a program are shown in Figure 6.1.

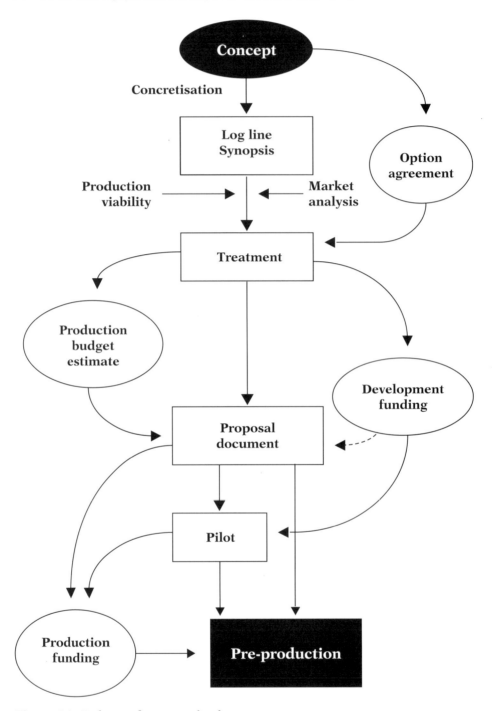

Figure 6.1: Pathway of program development.

6.1 The development team

Make-up of the development team

Usually a small team will carry the creative development of a program concept through to a fully fleshed-out treatment that is capable of attracting the necessary funding to go into production. It should also provide the bedrock of pre-production. The three key roles in development are producer, director and writer. They are not always three different people, but the roles will be carried out in one form or another by members of the development team.

A blueprint for production

Director and writer are the two creative functions that build the log line and the summary paragraph (see Chapter 5) into a detailed and visualisable narrative. This describes a program of a particular length, or a series of a specified number of episodes of particular length. The program can be intended as a one-off and be self-contained, or it can be part of a generic schedule slot, or an episode-based series or serial. The writer is responsible for the instructions on how the program will be constructed; the director is responsible for the visual realisation of these instructions. Together, they will describe the narrative of the program or the series of visual events that will comprise it; they will determine the style in which the program will be presented and specific stylistic elements that will be devised, in both its shooting and its post-production (unless it will be broadcast live); they will indicate the people, circumstances and characters that will feature in its production, any pre-existing material (e.g. archive) that will be incorporated and any animation or computer-generated imagery (CGI) that will be commissioned. They will produce a treatment and a script or shooting script that will be the blueprint for production.

The producer's role

The producer manages and guides the development team through this creative process, acting as a sounding board for the ideas they are generating, testing their proposals against the practicalities of production that will later be faced, and encouraging them to work further on aspects of the emerging program that have not yet gelled, not yet fully formed. They may sometimes act as the devil's advocate to allow the team to test its embryonic ideas of characterisation, concept links or whatever. A producer has to take charge of the development process from the outset. Where no-one is formally designated in that role at the early stages, someone will be performing the function anyway until there is a person designated as producer or, more often, a producer is brought into the team. The producer will supervise the production of the proposal document and may write a substantial part of it as well, putting down the ideas as they are generated by director and/or writer as well as their own contributions to this organic process.

Drafting the budget

The producer will also oversee the drafting of a budget from the time when development has reached a stage that meaningful preliminary figures for the cost of production elements can be committed to paper. The budget will often be in two parts: a development budget (see section 6.5) and a production budget (which will incorporate the development budget). The compiling of the production budget is the subject of Chapter 18. Depending on their skill with this level of production accounting and the complexity of the production, the producer may draw up the budget or perhaps just the development budget. More usually, a production manager will join the production team at some stage within the development phase and begin to estimate the cost of the production and make preliminary plans for and inquiries about intended production resources. The larger the production, the more imperative it is that this is carried out by a specialist production manager.

Researchers and consultants

If it is a factual program that is in development, the team is likely to include people who will gather information or people who will advise on evaluating and ordering this information. A researcher may be hired, initially to find background information on the subject and then to find people, events and other visualisable material that might be filmed for the program (see Chapter 7). Depending on the subject, there may be an archive researcher to source historical or other pre-existing footage, both from commercial archives and from informal sources such as home videos. The development team of a factual program might also include a specialist consultant whose expertise is not in program-making, but in the subject matter of the proposed program. This person will provide the production with informed analysis of the research material, providing an expert perspective on it and insights into relationships within it, and identifying its key elements. The consultant is also likely to be able to point the team towards people and organisations who might assist in production, either in providing access to relevant material or in revealing a telling aspect of the story for inclusion in the program.

Other contributors

Other people who might participate in the development team include an associate producer (sometimes the source of the program's concept or assisting in producer functions) or someone from a production craft (e.g. designer, director of photography, editor) to provide preliminary advice on what is feasible in their craft area and how it might enhance the developing ideas of the production.

6.2   Contract with the development team

The deal memo

A producer, in driving the development process, is advised to formalise relationships and responsibilities in the production team before development or production funding is in place. While team members should think their contribution is critical, it is counterproductive if they have an exaggerated idea of their ownership of the process. A deal memo is a means of clarifying any potential misunderstandings along these lines. The group that is working on the creative development of intellectual property will document what each person is expected to contribute to the process, what his or her rights will be in the product of this development, and what fee will be due in each case, whether deferred or paid on completion. The deal memo is a short version of a contract that outlines the roles and rights as agreed between the parties making up the development team. Once there is an agreement on the rights and responsibilities in working together, a deal memo of perhaps a page can be drawn up. A lawyer could do this, but it could also be drawn up by the producer or by the development team collectively. Once a producer has drawn up one deal memo, they have a starting document for any future agreements of this kind that might be needed.

Key elements

The key elements of a deal memo include:
- the parties to the agreement
- roles and responsibilities of each person and their anticipated credit in the eventual program
- expected duration of work on the development stage
- fee for this work and terms of payment, particularly if it is to be deferred
- copyright ownership that results if work is carried out on the project as agreed
- a process of dispute resolution should it become necessary.

Another document, later in the production process, is also called a deal memo and it has a similar purpose, but it is not the same document as the one described above. The deal memo in the production process is a preliminary document to contracting production crew and is described in Chapter 14.

6.3   Chain of Title

Disputes about ownership of the project

The ownership of the concept and the stages of development that follow it can become complicated if a number of people work on different stages of a program's development, especially if they come and go, making a contribution to just one part of the process. It can be disheartening (and sometimes fatal to the project) to get to the point of financing the production and find that there are disputes about who actually owns the project. A source of production funding is unlikely to sign off on the commitment until this issue is resolved. The document that does this is called Chain of Title (or, more correctly, a record of chain of title) and is often specified for delivery in the production funding contracts outlined in Chapter 8.

Participants in title

'Chain of title' is a legal term originating in real property law which describes the succession of title ownership from the present owner back to the original owner.

In media usage, chain of title (or copyright 'chain of title' as it is sometimes more pedantically called) lists all the people who have contributed to the development of the program from concept to treatment or script, and who hold some intellectual property ownership in it as a result. Where some other work was the source of the concept, this would include the author of that work. It would list any other party with underlying rights in the work (copyright material from another source that has been incorporated into the work), but only if that underlying material has been incorporated into the concept or the treatment developed from it. Chain of title includes all contributors to any of the drafts of the script for the program, and any development of the program by another producer prior to the current producer, or any input into the program's development by a director, even if that director is no longer working on the project. The proviso is that the contribution of the previous writer, producer or director must still be part of the program proposal. A person who participated in a stage of development but whose conceptual contribution has not been incorporated into the current treatment does not have any rights in the treatment.

What is not part of the chain of title

Facts are not subject to copyright, so concepts based on history, true stories or real people cannot be owned unless the treatment of these facts is original in some way. A researcher who provided factual information that supports the concept's treatment does not have any copyright in the treatment. Although these people are not part of the chain of title, it may be advisable to list them with a note explaining why they have no intellectual property rights in the proposed program. This will make the issue easier to deal with if they claim rights in the program when it is made.

Inclusions of the document

The Chain of Title document usually includes:
- a written summary of the project's development history and the personnel involved
- all related documentation, including transfers of rights agreements, writers' agreements, option/purchase agreements, publisher's releases and all other agreements to show that the producer holds the rights to the concept and any underlying creative material, and has the right to produce, distribute and exploit the project
- co-production and/or joint venture agreements, if applicable.

Covering possible claims

It is questionable whether it's necessary to hold rights to the concept itself as ideas are not capable of copyright. A log line does not have copyright except in its precise wording. The idea it embodies has no copyright. Nonetheless, most financing parties would want ownership of the concept clarified anyway. They are wary of a project that has a disgruntled concept source threatening litigation, and there can be issues of confidentiality even if the copyright issue doesn't stand up. Financing parties may want chain of title certified by a lawyer.

6.4 Fee deferral

Budgeting for deferred fees

Depending on the nature of the project and who is involved, it may be possible to take it through the development phase without funding. This is not because development has no cost, but because participants in the team may be prepared to defer their fees until the production is funded. It could be an agreed sum for the development phase of the project, or it might be a time-based fee. If the latter, a running record is kept of fees that would have been paid for actual time spent in development if the payment hadn't been deferred. The accumulated and anticipated total costs of all deferrals are included in the production budget as part of its development cost. They are calculated at a rate that should be acceptable to the eventual investors, either the industry rate for that work or a defensible market rate for that person.

Arrangements for paying deferrals

The agreements that are documented in a deal memo should include agreements about fee deferrals, the rate that will be the basis of the fee (if it isn't an agreed one-off fee), what will trigger its payment and any payment priorities that will apply to it. Payment will generally be deferred until the project is sufficiently funded to go into production, based on a specific production budget that includes all deferrals incurred in development, as well as out-of-pocket expenses paid by members of the development team. In hard-nosed economic terms, only the remaining expenditure is necessary to go into production and complete the program. If funding is sufficient for this but less than the total budget, the production could further defer current deferrals and expense recoveries. It would require agreement of the people owed for the project to defer payment until revenue from sales. Any excess of funding over remaining production expenditure could be disbursed at the funding stage according to pre-agreed priorities, with only the balance held over to be recovered from sales revenue. Usually, expense recovery will have first priority because it is a cash input into development from people's own pockets, followed by fee deferrals that are due to an input of time. Reimbursement of deferrals where there is incomplete finance to cover all deferrals will generally be made in proportion to total deferral at that time.

Writers' contracted deferrals

What development is possible when it is funded just by fee deferrals? For a start, it must involve people who are sufficiently motivated by and committed to the project to be prepared to defer payment and take the risk that there may never be a payment if the program developed is unable to attract production funding. They will be people who can afford to work unpaid, at least for the time being, either because they have other paid work while working part-time on the project or because they are living off savings until a paying project materialises. A writer who has been involved with the project from the outset (and may be the originator of its concept) might be prepared to take the pilot episode script through several draft stages with payment deferred. Rather than a deal memo, the writer is contracted using the Standard Writer's Contract that is annexed to the relevant Agreement between the Screen Producers Association of Australia (SPAA) and the Australian Writers Guild (AWG). This contract should stipulate that the fees are deferred, the terms of that deferral and the conditions for eventual payment of the fees.

Where deferral may not be possible

Where the hire of a specialist is necessary to provide some component of the development, this will be an expense that requires development funding. It may not be reasonable to expect an outsider to join the team and make a full-time professional contribution to a project's development (e.g. as a researcher) on deferred payment. Some people might be prepared to make occasional unpaid contributions to become attached to a project in which they see good potential, but it is unlikely that a project can be taken unfunded through development if a key component involves a cost that is not feasible to defer. Production of a pilot episode involves a whole range of expenses where negotiation of deferral is not realistic. An unfunded (or even underfunded) development stage is unlikely to be able to produce a pilot episode that could sell the program without being fatally compromised by its limitations. With the advent of the DV camera, however, pilot sequences are now possible in some instances without specific funding. Sample scenes and audition videos can be shot on DV camera (borrowed, if necessary), with intention and resources made quite clear. This is particularly useful with factual programs where the shooting style will approximate that of documentary shooting and the broadcaster may want to feel assured that the proposed talent will be convincing on screen.

Development without funding

If development funding has not been secured, it is still possible with a mix of goodwill, new technology and strategic compromise to take a project through development so that it is in a position to pursue production funding. The principal product of the development process is a proposal document whose purpose is to attract production funding. Anyone with access to a PC and some skill in operating Microsoft Word has the core requirements to produce a proposal document. With these operational skills, the main resource needed for the process detailed in section 6.7 is time, not funds. Whether the necessary editorial and marketing skills are there is another matter.

6.5   The development budget

Estimating costs of development

A development budget is much more speculative than a production budget (which is covered in detail in Chapter 18) because it is a cost of resources, including time, expended on a project that is not yet developed and therefore unknown to a considerable degree. Nonetheless, an accurate estimate of the expected time and resources should be made. Any party investing in project development will want an itemised breakdown of its cost. All development expenses, whether they are expected to be paid out of development funds or held over as deferrals, should be included. This will ensure that investors of funds don't get a disproportionate idea of their contribution to the cost of development.

Budgeting deferrals and out-of-pocket payments

As noted above, the time of all people working on development should be properly costed and recorded. Deferrals should be treated as a genuine investment in the project alongside other investor funding. All out-of-pocket payments by members of the development team on legitimate development expenses should also be incorporated into the development budget pending reimbursement. Often development funds from government agencies cannot be used for retrospective payments, only future costs. Deferred development costs can, however, be recovered from production funding or revenue so it is important they be on record from the outset.

Development budget format

The Australian Film Commission (AFC) has a useful format for a development budget in its development funding application form. There are columns for AFC Investment, Applicant Contribution, and Other Funding. The AFC Investment, as already noted, cannot be used to fund retrospectively. It should be allocated to anticipated cash costs in development (e.g. materials, travel expenses) and payment of some of the fees that will be generated by the development team, with the balance being deferred. The Applicant Contribution is particularly relevant where the applicant is a production company with a reasonable level of resources at its disposal. A funding body would generally expect such a company to invest some of its financial reserves into the development of its own project. Where the applicant is an individual or individuals with limited personal resources, the funding body may not expect them to commit personal funds to the development, even if the applicant(s) have formed a small private company. Some or the entire fee owing for their contribution to development would be deferred and should be recorded as such under Other Funding, along with third party contributions to the project's development.

Transferring development costs to the production budget

As development proceeds, items in the development budget are converted to actual costs, whether they are paid from development funding, are deferred, or are reimbursable expenses. These costs should be incorporated into the production budget (including any interest or premium to be paid to development funders) so that the producer will be in a position to return the development funders' investment and interest, reimburse legitimate development expenses and settle deferred payments from within that budget.

6.6   Development funding

Reluctance to fund development

The sources of development funding have much in common with the sources of production funding (see Chapter 8), although there are fewer of them and there is generally a greater reluctance to fund development than production. Government agencies are an exception to this since their brief is often to assist development. The reluctance of some investors isn't without good reason. Whereas production funding produces a program that can go into the marketplace and perhaps recoup its investment, development funding only produces a proposal (or pilot) whose purpose is to attract further investment from which a marketable product can be produced. There are no direct earnings from the product of development. Its investment is a generation removed from recoupment and, therefore, carries a higher level of risk. The next round of funding may not eventuate.

Recoupment from the production

A production budget will include all unpaid development costs, including amounts due to investors in development. Developers will recoup their investment (plus interest) when the production is greenlit, but they may be investors in the production as well. In that case, they are recovering their own money. That's not necessarily a problem as parties invest in development in order to generate a proposal that will attract the higher amount required for funding a production, which will in turn produce the program that will generate returns to all investors (or not, as the case may eventually be).

Australian Film Commission

The government funding agencies are the main source of development funding. The principal body is the federal AFC, which supports development through a General Development Investment (GDI) and specific strands in drama, documentary and animation (Table 6.1). Detailed information is available on the AFC's website, <www.afc.gov.au>. Generally, the AFC recoups its investment plus a 10% premium from the project when it commences production. The project should be budgeted for that recoupment. The GDI, which is for more experienced teams, is recouped plus 10% from the applicant's next one to four productions, whether they were in the application slate or not.

State agency development support

The state agencies also provide a range of development funding opportunities (Table 6.2). The NSW Film and Television Office (FTO) assists television series, telemovies, documentaries (one-off or series) and animations (one-off, pilot or series) reach the stage where they can attract production finance. It funds general script development, final stage assistance, travel assistance and shooting of development or research footage. Film Victoria will provide seed funding for script development, invest larger amounts in projects with established producers and

Table 6.1: AFC development program (as at 2005).

General Development Investment (GDI)

Description	Assists infrastructure and development slates of experienced practitioners.
Funding	Up to $70 000.
Use of funds	Drama or documentary projects for writer; consultant and key creative fees; option payments; market attendance; legal fees; running costs.
Eligibility	Producer with at least 2 recent credits on substantial projects (or writer or director of substantial project) with commercial or critical success.
Recoupment	GDI plus 10% premium from applicant's next 1–4 productions, whether in the application slate or not.

Short Feature or Short TV Drama Series Development (Strand A2)

Description	Supports development of short features (44–55 min), animation projects of up to 25 min, or short TV drama series ($4 \times \frac{1}{2}$ hour, $6 \times \frac{1}{2}$ hour or 3×1 hour).
Funding	Up to $10 000.
Use of funds	Next draft of script (professional development of writer is key to strand).
Eligibility	Writer with short or feature film or TV drama credit. For TV series, producer attached and broadcaster interest preferred.

Documentary Early Development (Strand J)

Description	Assists early development of one-off documentary or series.
Funding	Up to $5000.
Use of funds	Proposal document; trailer or selected rushes assembly to raise production finance.
Eligibility	Team member must have screen credit as producer or director and demonstrated ability to source finance from pitching materials.

Documentary Development (Strand K)

Description	Supports development of outstanding documentary projects.
Funding	Up to $15 000 (one-off documentary) or $25 000 (documentary series).
Use of funds	Detailed treatment; proposal document, trailer or selected rushes assembly to raise production finance; approved shooting.
Eligibility	Team member must have screen credit as producer or director.

Shooting Time-Critical Material (Strand L)

Description	Supports shooting at short notice of time-critical documentary (one-off or series) material integral to success of project, to attract finance.
Funding	Up to $15 000.
Use of funds	Costs of shooting; specified material; and making trailer or selected rushes assembly.
Eligibility	Only experienced writer/directors or writer/producers or teams. One must have released screen credit as director or producer.

Animation Development (Strand S)

Description	Assists animation filmmakers develop pitching materials for short animation (up to 15 min) projects or series.
Funding	Up to $5000 for one-off animations ($7000 if producer attached); up to $7000 for animation series ($10 000 if producer attached).
Use of funds	Development of pitching materials.
Eligibility	May apply as individuals (writer) or teams; one of team must have produced animation credit. Further funding possible with written expression of interest from broadcaster.

Table 6.2: Contact details for state funding agencies.

NSW Film and Television Office
Website: www.fto.nsw.gov.au
Phone: +61 2 9264 6400
Street address: Level 13, 227 Elizabeth St Sydney NSW 2000
Postal address: GPO Box 1744 Sydney NSW 2001

Film Victoria
Website: www.film.vic.gov.au
Phone: +61 3 9660 3200
Street address: Level 7, 189 Flinders Lane Melbourne Vic. 3000
Postal address: GPO Box 4361 Melbourne Vic 3001

Pacific Film and Television Commission
Website: www.pftc.com.au
Phone: +61 7 3224 4114
Street address: Level 15, 111 George St Brisbane Qld 4000
Postal address: PO Box 15094 City East Qld 4002

South Australian Film Corporation
Website: www.safilm.com.au
Phone: +61 8 8347 0385
Street address: 3 Butler Drive, Hendon Common Hendon SA 5014

ScreenWest
Website: www.screenwest.com.au
Phone: +61 8 9224 7340
Street address: Level 7, Law Chambers, 573 Hay St Perth WA 6000
Postal address: PO Box 8349 Perth Business Centre WA 6849

Screen Tasmania
Website: www.screen.tas.gov.au
Phone: +61 3 6233 6995
Street address: Suite 27, Level 1, Salamanca Square Hobart Tas 7000

Northern Territory Film Office
Website: www.filmoffice.nt.gov.au
Phone: +61 8 8951 1162
Alice Springs Cultural Precinct
Larapinta Drive Alice Springs, NT 0870 PO Box 3521
Alice Springs, NT 0871

broadcaster or distributor attached, and support documentary development with broadcaster or distributor interest. Its Commercial Script Development Scheme invests in experienced Victorian producers to develop over two years a slate of high quality, commercially viable projects with market flexibility. Queensland's Pacific Film and Television Commission (PFTC) will fund the development of mini-series, telemovies, drama and animation series with broadcaster investment, or documentary development with broadcaster interest. The South Australian Film Corporation (SAFC) funds television drama and documentary, requiring producer attachment except in very early stages. Western Australia's ScreenWest gives priority to long-form television drama (animated and live) and documentary series, preferring sustained development of selected projects rather than spreading funding thinly over a large number of projects. Except in early script drafts, an experienced producer should be attached and there should be 'firm market interest'. Screen Tasmania assists development of scripts (with producer attached or demonstrated market interest required beyond second draft), and successive stages of drama and documentary development so that the project can attract production finance. Funds can be applied to a project or a slate of projects. The Northern Territory Film Office (NTFO) supports development of screenplays for series, miniseries or telemovies, of documentaries (broadcaster interest an advantage for both categories), and of interactive digital media (one member of the team must already have a digital media credit).

General conditions of state agency funding

Government agency funding is almost exclusively for drama (including animation) and documentary projects. Although drama nominally includes sitcom, there is little evidence of this in practice. Only FTO and Film Victoria make specific reference to sitcom. The agencies generally require applicants to be producers, based in the state or working with writers from the state. An exception is early scriptwriting funding, where writers can often apply. The majority of the production spend should be in the state also, but regardless of where the rights' owner lives, funding is not for purchase of rights or options. When the project goes into production, the agency is to be repaid its investment along with a 10% premium (20% for PFTC) by the first day of principal photography. Some bodies require an ongoing percentage of net profits from the finished program. ScreenWest requires an additional 100% penalty premium when a project intended for production in Western Australia is filmed elsewhere.

Network support of development

Outside the government agencies, broadcasters will sometimes invest in project development. In practice this is usually only for major productions – television dramas, high-end documentary series or major reality programs. The program would need to be one of high importance to the network, otherwise networks prefer to wait and see what comes out of the development pipeline without their assistance. They are more likely to invest in the production of a pilot program (see section 6.10) where the prior development is substantially completed. This is a 'safety-first' approach to series production as much as an investment in development, since a smaller investment is put at risk before committing to the greater investment of production of a whole series.

Production house and distributor investment

Sometimes one of the larger production houses or distributors, such as Southern Star, Beyond Productions or Granada, will invest in development of a program, particularly if there is evident broadcaster interest, but they will also be likely to want to take substantial equity in the program in return for their investment risk. More rarely, private interests might be persuaded to invest in development, but if they are reluctant to invest in production (and they are) they are going to be even more reluctant to invest in development. Unless they are doing it because of a personal connection to someone in the development team, the few private investors that might be interested would limit themselves to projects whose principals have a substantial track record. Private investors aren't in the business of assessment of the creative merits of a proposal. Their interest is in its business merits.

Interest group support

The remaining group who will occasionally provide project development funding is parties with a commercial or administrative interest in the subject matter of a program. This is more likely to be for factual rather than fiction programs because that is where their subject interest will lie. It can be a commercial interest, not necessarily a specific product (which could create later problems in pitching to ABC or SBS) but an area of interest in which it has commercial dealings that would benefit from exposure of the general subject. A pharmaceutical company, for instance, might be prepared to invest in a documentary that creates public awareness of a branch of medicine in which it markets a particular product, even if the program doesn't refer specifically to that product. By the same token, a government department or non-government organisation (NGO) may see some benefit in assisting the development of a program promoting awareness of its area of administrative responsibility.

6.7   The proposal document

Purpose of the proposal document

The proposal document is the watershed of a project's development. It is the means of attracting funding from either broadcasters (as pre-sale of the program) or investors or both. Because it plays this crucial role, it is a document that must sell the program, and at the same time describe it in sufficient detail that broadcasters and investors will get a clear idea in their mind's eye of what they are buying or investing in. Broadcasters particularly want to know how the program will look so they can form a view of who its audience is and whether it would have a place in their schedules. Investors may like to have some idea of the proposed program, but their particular interest is the return they can realistically expect for their investment, and whether the producers are able to manage the project competently enough to ensure this.

Layout and design

A proposal document is not unlike an investment prospectus and will have many characteristics in common. Layout can be an important aspect. An appealing design creates a positive expectation of the program in advance of reading the proposal. A presentable document can be produced on a PC with a number of software applications designed for the purpose – QuarkXPress, Adobe PageMaker, Adobe Photoshop or Adobe InDesign – but even Microsoft Word can produce a quite professional-looking document. Microsoft Word has sufficient functions which, with a little imagination, can make a strong impression. Because the proposal is describing a visual product, the use of pictures is advantageous and, once they are in the computer system, they are easily transported, cut and pasted into position, resized and cropped to taste. Pictures that are representative of the program give a clearer impression of what the program will look like. To the extent that they are available, they should be used liberally in the proposal document. Ultimately, though, it is the content that will sell the proposed program.

No pro forma but common features

There is no pro forma for a proposal document and no one way of doing it. Different programs have different features and emphases, and are therefore presented in different ways to convey their main strengths. Nonetheless, common to these documents are features that have passed the scrutiny of commissioning executives and investors in the past, and have been found to provide the necessary information.

Part 1. Selling the program

As already noted, one of the prime functions of the proposal document is to sell the program. Its main attractions are highlighted in the first page or two of the document. The principle operating here is: sell the program, then explain it. Typically, there will be a cover page with the title of the proposed program, a picture that evokes the program, a practical description of the product (e.g. a ten-part comedy series of half-hour episodes), the program's log line (see Chapter 5) and the production entity's name. The log line will be like a short description in a TV guide and has a similar function. It captures the essence of the program in one sentence. That essence needs to be expressed so that people will want to see the program, whether they are viewers or a broadcasting executive.

Whereas the front page relies for its impact on presentation, and the interaction of image and limited copy, the next page is focused on text. It functions as an executive summary (although never labelled as such), but with the added purpose of subtly selling the product by providing reasons to want to read more about it. It can be as short as a paragraph and should not run over a page. The copy on this page contains the main thrust of the storyline (built up from the log line), the principal characters in the program (whether factual or fiction) and some key salient points about them, an indicator (not necessarily much more than a sentence) of the style in which the program will be made and a reference to its genre (this will underline the production style and indicate the resource regimen for its production; see Chapter 4). It may refer to some of the principal creative personnel in the production and will probably reiterate the format and production entity. Someone reading these first pages should be ready for an elaboration of the program, now persuaded that it is worthy of their attention. Already the selling points of the program and where its main interest lies should be clear in their mind.

Part 2. Content of the program

The next part of the document gives an outline of the proposed program itself. Components of this include:
- a synopsis or storyline
- treatment, including discourse on style and tone of the program and its dramatic highlights (in factual as well as fictional programs)
- short descriptions of the main characters or participants
- a production schedule, even if it is in summary form and laid out as time required for each stage rather than actual dates
- a rundown of sources of material for the program if it is multisourced
- possibly a list of anticipated main sequences (if a one-off factual program).

If the program is a series, the proposal will have an episode breakdown, outlining the central storyline, theme or subject of each episode and how it develops in the context of the series as a whole.

One school of thought holds that the proposal should include a director's statement, discussing the main creative aspects of the program. This is an approach borrowed from feature film proposals, and derived from the theory of director as 'auteur'. This theory seems to have less relevance in television, which is commonly more producer-driven and made more as a production line (without the pejorative connotations of that term). Television production is framed by deadlines and budget restraints, with various creative inputs from the whole production crew, in Australia if not elsewhere. The director's statement, thus, can be seen to be somewhat indulgent. It can be an invitation to intellectualise the production at the expense of simplicity of vision. That apart, perhaps it has no real disadvantage in practice, so it can become a personal choice. Some government agencies specifically require a director's statement in their funding applications. In those instances there certainly should be one, even if it just reflects the greater importance they place on feature films. The content of a director's statement would otherwise be contained in the discussion about treatment.

The material in this part of the document should be written in a straightforward narrative or descriptive style with a few turns of phrase to make it lively reading. It should avoid the flourishes of what could be called 'aspirational rhetoric', which makes great claims to excitement on behalf of the program, but doesn't actually explain how that will be achieved. All commissioning editors are familiar with certain phrases that they see time and time again in proposals – expressions such as 'fast-paced', 'cutting edge' and 'open a bold new horizon in television'. These are clichés and don't convey any meaningful impression of how the program will look, so serve no useful purpose.

Part 3. Marketing the program

The next few pages of the proposal document cover the planned marketing and distribution of the program, and relevant information to support it. Issues addressed include the intended audience and the types of broadcasters most likely to reach that audience, potential back-end exploitation of the program, the costs of making it, and the predicted returns from marketing it. Components of this section of the proposal will include:

- notes about the intended audience
- possibly a suggested timeslot for the program in the recipient broadcaster's schedule layout
- a report on any key cast or crew confirmed
- a copyright statement
- a marketing and distribution plan
- a list of any broadcasters or investors already attached, including in-kind contributors, and terms of investment or rights reserved (where they aren't confidential)
- a budget estimate for the production (and a separate budget for a pilot episode if that is proposed)
- revenue projections from sale of the program.

The audience analysis should avoid insistence that the program will appeal to all viewers (see Chapter 5). It is there to provide insight into where the program's strongest following is expected to be found. A suggested timeslot isn't strictly necessary as a broadcaster doesn't actually want to be instructed where to schedule a program it has bought, but it does give some indication of the style of production that is in mind. A program made for late-evening viewing will have different characteristics from one aimed at a prime-time audience.

Care needs to be exercised in the marketing plan to bear in mind the business interests of the party that will be reading the document. There is not much point in having a marketing plan that targets the public broadcasters in a document submitted to a commercial network. The marketing plan will probably need to be versioned for different broadcasters to whom it is submitted, especially when they are operating in the same market. The program should have been developed with a particular broadcaster in mind, but that doesn't preclude offering it to others (perhaps with some reversioning). There is no knowing what particular programming needs (often short-term) have surfaced within a broadcaster at any one time. Sometimes the timing of a proposal's arrival can be serendipitous.

The AFC budget format is widely used in the industry and can be found on its website at <www.afc.gov.au>. It's a good idea to use the familiar format. Opinions differ on whether to use the detailed budget or the budget summary in a proposal document; however, the summary is generally preferable. In truth, it is hard to evaluate items in a budget for a production when you don't have intimate and detailed knowledge of it – the position of anyone to whom the proposal is submitted. Although they might be able to spot outrageous padding, generally the broadcaster or investor is relying on advice from the producer about the viability of the budget. In any case, the project's budget at this stage is often fairly tentative (see section 6.9). Revealing the itemised budget at this stage of its development might open the gate to ill-founded inferences about budget detail, the sort of signal noise a producer doesn't want disturbing the thoughtful evaluation of a project. In addition to the budget, the document might include cash-flow requirements for each stage of production, although this might be better left as a later deal point if negotiation proceeds.

Revenue projections are highly important to investors – that is the supposed reason for their involvement, so they will need to believe the projections are informed and reliable. Notes about the sources of sale figures can give some authority to them and assurance to the investor who wants to weigh up risk and potential return. Investors also like to get regular reports on the financial well-being of the production. A proposed schedule of budget reports helps investor perception of the production.

Part 4. Production personnel

Finally, the proposal document will list key personnel in the production, including short biographies and possibly photographs. If the program is a drama or comedy, it should list the main actors, with photographs and short biographies listing past roles. If it is a factual program with presenter or reporter, or with a narrator already decided, a separate page should be used for their biography. If the narrator is not yet decided, notes discussing the options for choice of narrator may be appropriate.

The behind-camera production team will also be listed, including short biographies. Usually photographs are not used unless there is a particular reason to do so, such as to emphasise the youth of the team or its cultural diversity, if these are selling points. As with the actors, the biographies are generally about half a page, and never more than a page. They should be written to highlight people's past experience that is of relevance to the proposed project, rather than being a standard all-purpose biography. All contact details for the production entity are often put at the end of the production team list, and this is usually the last section of the document.

Inclusions

Under some circumstances there may be additional items that accompany the proposal document. With a drama or sitcom, there may be a sample script of one of the episodes, separately bound. With a documentary, there may be a shooting script, although generally this is unnecessary and, in any case, research may not be completed at the time of submission of the proposal, in which case a shooting script is not available. Another type of inclusion is background information on the subject area of the program, or on the production company proposing it. Care needs to be exercised not to provide more reading matter than a commissioning executive or investor is interested in seeing.

Finally, a sample video might be provided. This could be for audition of the program's principal participants, or it might be a live performance if the program is built from that, or it might be a promotional video if some material has already been shot for the program (or shot for the promotion), or it might be an indicative video from some other program that features the same people that the proposed program will feature. The value of a sampler video cannot be overestimated if it is feasible to make one. When the purpose is to persuade people of the merits of a visual product, a video can contribute to this in ways that a written document can never do, no matter how skilled the writing might be. The sampler video might even be a sample (pilot) episode, but more commonly the proposal is to raise finance for a pilot in order to secure funding to go into production of a series.

Broadcaster and investor versions

There are two principal groups to which a proposal document is addressed. Broadcasters want to be persuaded that the program, when made, will be an asset on their schedule line-up. Investors want to be persuaded that the program will return their investment, and then a substantial profit on top of that. The document should be prepared in at least two versions to target the different needs of these groups, although both versions will derive from a common source document.

Broadcasters are interested in the production schedule and consequent delivery date (so they can plan for their transmission schedule), the style of the program, the on-screen merits of people who will appear in the program, and its audience profile. In other words, all the things that will make it a distinctive and successful program on air and, if it's a commercial broadcaster, what attraction it might have for advertisers. They will not be greatly interested in speculated revenue earnings from the program unless they are going to invest in it in addition to committing to a licence fee.

Conversely, for the investors revenue projections are the main point of the exercise. They want to know what revenue returns the program might realistically expect to draw and the authority for figures quoted. They want to feel comfortable that the producers are able to manage an effective business, so the program's earning potential is maximised. They want to know the track records of the key production personnel. They are not interested in reading scripts. They have no expectation that they would be able to make a practical assessment of them, but they do want to feel the producers have that ability. They are interested in the treatment only to the extent they can infer from its description that it has the potential for market success.

The core proposal document is versioned to address these separate prime concerns. In either case, layout is important (and not significantly different) because of the positive initial impression it can make. Content is varied to cater to the different emphasis required.

6.8   Choice of format

Matching format to market

A technical decision that should be made, at least tentatively, is the format that the program will be shot on. This will be a proposed format that cannot be confirmed until a broadcaster has committed to the program. The broadcaster will have delivery requirements and the format for shooting will need to be compatible with that. The different formats have different budgetary implications. Shooting on DV camera is generally of low cost, whereas shooting on film is generally expensive. There should be some idea of the market the program is aimed at, and the delivery format preferred by that market. A draft budget is based on a shooting format that would produce that delivery format. There is no point reducing production costs by shooting on a Mini DV if the targeted broadcaster will not accept programs shot on that recording stock. By the same token, the extra expense of film is of questionable value for a broadcaster who would see no particular additional value in a program recorded on film.

Stock and aspect ratio

With the advent of DV cameras and the current transition to digital television, the options of recording stock have consolidated. Analogue videotape is close to extinct and film is used only for some high-end or specialist productions. The other format issue is aspect ratio (4:3 or 16:9), which was discussed in Chapter 2, and how to deal with simulcast transmission and mixed sources. The technical options and issues of choice for broadcasters are covered in more detail in Chapter 14.

6.9   Estimate of the production budget

Process of estimation

It is not possible in the development stage of a project to produce a budget for the production that can be guaranteed in every detail. There are too many aspects of the production that are not yet known. Nonetheless, a producer who is pitching for production funding needs to know what amount to seek and at what point sufficient funds have been secured to be confident that the project can proceed to production and deliver a completed program to investors. If the production is relatively complex, a reliable production budget may require funding and a production manager is hired. Otherwise, producers with a rudimentary knowledge of budgeting could produce a first draft budget themselves. Notated clearly, this can give at least a preliminary idea of what the program's cost might be. It should be cautious enough to ensure production funding won't get underway with insufficient funds, yet not so cautious that it creates a possibility of not getting off the ground for want of unneeded dollars. The process and considerations are essentially the same as those for the working budget for the production (called the final budget), which is the product of several revisions of the initial production budget anyway. With the draft budget there is far more educated guesswork. Chapter 18 looks in detail at the process of budgeting, whether it is for a draft or final budget, or for any of the revisions in between.

Early budget assumptions

The budget prepared in the development phase is hypothetical. It is built on preliminary costing estimates, general industry costs, assumptions about certain aspects of the production, intuition and experience. Sometimes crew and locations are known, but more often they are not – or not with any certainty. Where they are not known, the budget uses a figure that aggregates the usual fees for each planned member of the crew. If, when the production is funded, a desired crew member cannot be hired for the budgeted amount, either the increase in fee is offset by a reduction elsewhere in the budget or the production must shop around for another person to fill that role at the budgeted fee. Similarly with cast. Many actors will play characters at award rates and they can be budgeted at those rates, although for an estimated length of engagement. Some actors will be able to command personal margins at their market value and the budget should anticipate where this is likely to happen and how high the production should be prepared (or can afford) to go. Where an actor will work only for a higher rate than budgeted, that is either accommodated by offsets or the actor has priced themself out of the production's market.

Travel cost estimates

A similar approach is taken with locations. If they are remote with a general idea of where they might be but not known specifically, then indicative locations can be costed. Costs (e.g. travel expenses, per diems, costs at the location) won't vary greatly from one location to the other in the same general area, so any location chosen will give a reasonable estimate of location costs, particularly when erring on the side of caution. If the program is to be shot in central or northern Queensland and may be Rockhampton, Townsville or Cairns, the budget estimate should be based on the cost of shooting in Cairns with its higher travel cost. If the actual location turns out to be nearer and slightly cheaper, the saving is available as an offset for the production costs that go over. Where the location is local and doesn't involve travel costs, locations of a similar type will generally entail similar costs, so an estimate for any would serve the purpose, again with cautious conservatism.

6.10   Pilots

Reasons for pilot episode

A pilot is a trial episode of a series (often, but not necessarily, the planned first episode) to evaluate the proposed program before committing to the cost of making the series. The first question the pilot is designed to answer is: does it work as a program? If the answer to that question is 'yes', the second question is: what finetuning of the production would still be useful to make it that much better a program? If the production can afford it, a pilot should be made without the expectation that it will be broadcast, even if the series goes into production. If the pilot prompts some major changes (e.g. recasting), then that episode, or parts of it, will need to be remade for the series.

Components of a pilot

A pilot is generally made with the same resources and under the same conditions as the series will be made. Although an approximation of the program might cut costs significantly, television executives cannot necessarily factor this into their assessment (even when they say they can) and the risk of a negative response as a result makes it a false saving. It is more likely that they will respond to what they see, as a television audience does. There are a few exceptions to this rule of thumb. Series titles can be expensive but the cost is amortised over the series. As they tend not to influence the decision about the program greatly – you wouldn't proceed with a program just because it has great titles – a rough approximation of the titles can be used without too much risk. It is usually obvious that they are temporary, they are at the front of the program and they are clearly separated from the rest of the program. Temporary music, off commercial disc or some other free source, may be used in the pilot to indicate the type of music that will be commissioned. It will probably be used as part of the brief to the composer. As the pilot is a private communication, it is not 'published' and use of music here doesn't breach copyright. If the music were to be used in the program, of course, it would then have to be licensed for that purpose.

Performers

Generally, the same performers as intended for the program are cast in the pilot. Use of other performers is no way to ensure that the program will be assessed on its true merits. This also enables a judgement to be made about casting for the program. It's not unusual for casting changes to be made as a result of the pilot (see Chapter 5 regarding the pilot of *Absolutely Fabulous*).

Who sees the pilot

The principal audience for a pilot is the network executives who will decide whether to fund the series. They are not necessarily representative of the program's target audience, but that may not be a point they are interested to ponder. It is, however, useful for a producer to screen the pilot to the program's intended audience to feel greater confidence in arguing for commissioning of the series, and to pick up things that need adjusting before moving on to series production. When SBS made a pilot for the proposed sitcom, *Pizza*, the network was apprehensive about how far it could push the bounds despite its success with *South Park*. Are the instincts of middle-aged television executives a reliable guide anyway to teen taste? The pilot was shown informally to two children in their late pre-teens, who were so enthused that one child immediately rang a friend and told her to come over and watch this new show. It indicated that *Pizza* could be the success it became with its target audience.

Other pilot material

If funds are not available for a full pilot episode, an option is a pilot sequence. A sequence is selected to show the main stylistic components of the program. Again, it is made under much the same conditions as the program and will show the style of production, the quality of performance (whether actors, or people featured in a factual program) and the skills of the production team. Sometimes the pilot material will be put together to demonstrate the on-screen presence of people in documentaries. This might be more appropriately called an audition or sample video and can be shot on DV camera or Mini DV as long as the camera operator has the necessary skills to provide vision at a professional standard.

Sources and further reading

Magazine, newspaper and journal articles

Davis, Alison 2002, 'Deferred payments', *ART+law*, July, available online at <http://www.artslaw.com.au/ArtLaw/Archive/02DeferredPayments.asp>, viewed 15 December 2006.

Some internet references

ABC, 'Submitting a proposal', available online at <www.abc.net.au/corp/pubs/documents/abctv_doing_business_broch.pdf>, viewed 15 December 2006.

Australian Film Commission, available online at <www.afc.gov.au>, viewed 15 December 2006.

How to submit a proposal to SBS Independent (SBSi), available online at <http://www.sbs.com.au/sbsi_new/about.html?type=0>, viewed 15 December 2006.

Chapter 7

Approaches to genre development

Chapter 6 outlined the main components in a general process of program development. It didn't go into variations of this process for different genres, but in practice each genre has distinctive characteristics within the general approach to development. In the same way that the basic proposal document has different emphases for broadcasters and investors, the generic approach to program development is varied to meet the particular needs of the program.

Within the variations of approach that are commonly used, there are typical conventions for each television genre. Television drama and sitcom development, for instance, revolve around defining the characters and their circumstances, and then developing scripts. On the other hand, documentary development is about research. As an actuality genre, it has its characters and their circumstances already defined, along with a lot of peripheral and irrelevant material. Here the task is to unearth this information through research and sift through it to find underlying themes that can ground the program. Game shows and reality television are about the rules of the game and the complexity of the production machinery. Sketch comedy is about assembling teams of writers and performers and devising a production schedule that can sustain the necessary relentless output of sketches. And so on.

7.1 Drama characters and setting

The log line

Like all television programs, a drama series (or a telemovie or sitcom) starts from a log line, a one-sentence description that captures the essence of the program. It may be: 'The community is a safe harbour when society outside is disintegrating and anarchy is on the rise.' Or: 'An aspiring upwardly mobile mum and her self-centred daughter somehow find a partnership in pursuing their own needs.' Or: 'What a thirty-something girl has to do to have fun in New York, a city full of unmarried men with a fear of commitment.' Working from the log line, the first stage is defining the main characters and their relationships with one another, and the circumstances in which the story (or stories) takes place – the setting.

Good characters

Good characters are primarily a matter of inspiration, not a checklist of characteristics, but certain qualities seem to be common to characters that work. In the hands of a skilled actor, the well-defined and well-written character connects the story to the viewer. This character need not necessarily be realistic unless the program is in that style, but it should be credible. If the style is exaggerated or caricature, the characters can be as well but they still need to be believable within the circumstances of that story. The job of the producer is to recognise good characters (and sometimes they're only potentially good characters, with some way yet to go) and good stories in their embryonic form. For a start, they must be believable in their role in the story.

Dimensions

Compelling characters will have dimensionality. They will not be too predictable or too hackneyed, but they will have characteristics that give them those little rough edges and signs of individuality that mark them out from two-dimensioned personalities. Well-drawn characters show emotional range. There should be more to them than just the actions necessary to achieve their goal in the story. However, there can be a point where dimensionality has been taken too far. Characters should be interesting and unusual enough to take them away from stereotyping, but care needs to be taken to avoid being so off-beat that viewers don't quite know what to make of them. They can be quirky so long as the audience doesn't sense them as contrived – that is, quirky for the sake of being quirky. Traits should sit comfortably with the character, not swamp it. Done well, this layered dimensionality allows heroes to have flaws – so long as they have enough admirable points to sustain them as heroes – and allows villains to have saving graces.

Characters defined in their setting

In the early stages of development of a drama project, the main characters and their circumstances are defined in considerable detail to provide back-story to the scripts, not all of which will be revealed in the opening episode. This will help avoid inconsistencies of character, behaviour or background creeping in across the episodes. In long-form drama, there will be a common setting in which different stories unfold week by week. Sometimes the story will be contained within a single episode, sometimes a storyline will reappear over several episodes, but the setting will remain the same with the same people occupying it: a suburban street in *Neighbours*, a forensic workplace in *CSI*, a local council in *Grass Roots*. In a mini-series, as in a telemovie, there is usually a beginning (the catalyst) that sets up the unfolding drama progressing to a resolution, the classic three-act structure. In either form, characters and their circumstances must be defined early in the development process. There may be changes made to these definitions as the program develops and scripts are written, but the changes will be applied consistently when they are worked into the character biography.

7.2   The drama treatment

Overemphasis on dialogue

Too frequently, Australian writers move straight on to writing the script once characters and setting are decided, rather than outlining the plot through scene breakdown (see section 7.3). This is not a practice recommended by experienced writers. It can consolidate character traits and setting details in a way that constrains the drama of later episodes. It tends to produce scripts that rely too much on dialogue rather than action. It doesn't allow time for the development of stylistic elements, or mood and tone. It could be argued that overemphasis on dialogue is a general problem in Australian drama. Once characters and setting are drafted, the stage is set to consider the intended treatment of this material in the program, not to turn it immediately into scripted material. Treatment describes the style and tone that the production will adopt in telling the story. Like character and setting, it is in draft form only at this stage and may evolve. All aspects of the emerging program are subject to revision as development progresses. Changes in one aspect, such as character, can have a flow-on to some or all the other aspects.

Decisions about director

First, there is consideration of genre or sub-genre. Is the program to be an action drama, a comedy drama, a docudrama, or a sitcom? This decision will influence the choice of director(s) for the program because they would be expected to have a track record in that type of production. As the ultimate determiner of style and tone will be the program's director, there ought to be a director involved with development by this stage, making a contribution to drafting the treatment. In a long-form series, where there is likely to be more than one director, it is the person earmarked as senior director who will follow the development process through. A series needs unity of style notwithstanding that its episodes might have different directors. A style blueprint is established for all episode directors to work from and work within.

Impact of style and tone

Style and tone are the means of determining the impact that is wanted for the program on its audience. The same impact can be achieved with quite different stylistic approaches, and conversely the same style can be used to create quite different impacts. Tight action-oriented production has been the hallmark of American crime drama through to *CSI: Crime Scene Investigation* and *Law and Order*. Contrast this with the use of musical set pieces as ironic counterpoint to the essentially grim drama of *Pennies from Heaven, Changi* and *Blackpool*. The uncompromised realism in the documentary style of *Frontline* and *The Office* makes their humour even more discomforting. Realism is used to add to the sinister nature of *Blue Murder* and *The Sopranos* or to increase the pathos of *The Leaving of Liverpool*. Melodrama combined with humorous social observation in *Hard Times* and *Our Mutual Friend* highlight a different approach to the Dickensian reality of Victorian England. On the other hand, there is unabashed nostalgia in the art direction of period pieces set within living memory, such as *The Sullivans, True Believers, Bodyline* and *The Shark Net*. Other escapist drama, such as *SeaChange* and *Hamish MacBeth*, will bring in off-beat characters, the humour of human foibles and romance (or at least romantic tension). Stylistic elements can create a point of view, as in the emphasis on suburban consumer crassness in the locations, personal references and malapropisms of *Kath and Kim*, and in the sardonic narration used in *Sex and the City* and *Arrested Development*. All these illustrate the way choices about style and tone will influence the way a drama is presented and the different ways the finished program can be expected to engage its audience. These are decisions that should be made early in the project's development so that they can be integrated into the program's scripting from the outset. The scripts can draw in elements of the intended style as they are being built, rather than these being imposed on the script by the director at a later stage.

7.3 Turning story into screenplay

Step 1: Story outline

At the same time as the development team is pondering issues of style, the writer commences the scriptwriting process, but this is still not a draft of the screenplay starting at page 1. The first step of the writing process is the story outline, only one if it's a telemovie, or one for each episode if it's a series of limited length. For a long series, story outlines are written for sufficient episodes to demonstrate the series viability over many episodes, possibly ten to fifteen.

The story outline, one or two pages long, is a prose precis of the sequence of events that will make up the screenplay, and it is written like a short story. Its focus is on the significant events of the story in the sequence order intended for the script and written in simple English without literary flourishes. The layout should be in short paragraphs, each a separate scene or sequence of events that advances the action of the story and the characters, with little or no dialogue. The story outline is sometimes called the treatment, although this leaves no term to cover matters of style. Whatever it is called, it describes how the events of the story relate to one another, how one sequence will flow into the next, which characters are involved in which scenes, how they will influence events in the story, and how events will influence them. The story outline allows the development team to look critically at the broad structure of the script to see if it has balance and momentum, whether it has the elements of a three-act structure (e.g. catalyst, turning points, resolution) and, most importantly, whether there are any holes in the logic of the story's events. Logic lapses are much more easily spotted in the bare bones of an outline than in a fully fleshed-out screenplay.

Step 2: Scene breakdown

In the development phase, usually only one episode of a series is chosen to take through to a screenplay. This will serve to demonstrate the quality of the writing to a potential broadcaster (as noted previously, investors feel less competent to judge scriptwriting and are more interested in the business plan) and would be the episode earmarked for piloting. The other episode outlines will provide an insight into the series, along with notes about characters, setting and treatment. A telemovie will continue on the path to finished script. In either case, it is probable that the production would seek development funding before embarking on the next stages, unless the development team and particularly the writer is prepared to continue the process on deferred fees (see Chapter 6).

The next step in the scripting process, whether funded or with fee deferral, is the scene breakdown. Here, the story outline is broken down to one-line scene headings, showing where and when that scene happens, and describing briefly the main action of the scene. Each scene that emerges logically from the story outline is listed in the same order as the outline. Figure 7.1 shows an example of story outline and scene breakdown.

A scene is that part of the story that happens continuously in the one place. Generally, a room is a place in this sense, not a building. Different rooms in the same building in the story are treated as different places in the scene breakdown, even if it is anticipated that they will be shot in the same building because the scenes will be shot separately, nonetheless. In any case, rooms that are adjacent in the story may not be adjacent in the building in which the scenes are shot, or a room that serves the story's purpose better may be found in another building. They will, however, be shot in such a way that editing can make them appear adjacent in the finished program. An exception could be when the action is thought likely to flow without break from one room to the next. In this case, the adjacent rooms should be treated as a single place and the action in the two rooms regarded as a single scene.

Step 3: Story review

At this stage of the script's development, the story is reviewed to see if it has the structural elements that classically engage an audience. Early in the story there must be a catalyst, some event to trigger the story, and involving or about to involve the main characters. The main characters are introduced – or reintroduced if it is a series. They are incorporated in the central action of the story or through a subplot, which will merge with the main plot. Where the only purpose of scenes is to provide background information to characters, the pace of the program slows. Such scenes have an inherently backward perspective, the reverse of where the program's momentum is trying to propel it. The audience doesn't need to know all the biographical detail about a character, only what can be revealed through

EPISODE 5: BUZZ'S BIRTHDAY BASH

Story outline

Susan writes the date up on her class blackboard, then realises it's the day before the birth date of her long lost son and breaks down.

Jimmy is arranging the RSL auditorium for Buzz's birthday bash as Brian and Terry set up for karaoke.

The girls, Sally, Sandra and Kylie, have just finished a netball game, talk excitedly at cross purposes about their social plans, and decide to go and watch the boys finish their football match. It's a tough match, with Stan on the sideline having an injury dressed. Coach pooh-poohs his injury and sends him back on. In his fury Stan scores the winning try as the girls arrive. As they leave the field through cheering spectators, Wayne, Shane and Buzz discuss their plans for Buzz's party that night.

The boys continue discussing their plans as they get ready for their big night out. They smoke bongs, rib each other, rummage through dirty clothes and skol beers. At the same time, the girls are getting ready too, squealing and playing with hair. While Mrs Kane does Sandra's hair, the girls quiz her about the Adult Study Group, then Sandra confides she's going to make a move on Wayne. Sally and Kylie advise her to wait until Wayne is drunk.

Shane gives Buzz a homemade birthday card and Wayne says they're going to pick up some dope as a birthday present for Buzz.

Scene breakdown

1. INT. CLASSROOM, DAY. **Susan realises it's her lost son's birthday tomorrow.**
    (SUSAN)
2. INT. RSL AUDITORIUM, DAY. **The RSL is preparing for Buzz's birthday bash.**
    (JIMMY, BRIAN, TERRY)
3. EXT. NETBALL COURT, DAY. **The girls are excited at the end of their netball game.** (SALLY, SANDRA, KYLIE)
4. EXT. FOOTBALL GROUND, DAY. **The injured Stan scores the winning try and the boys plan their night.** (WAYNE, BUZZ, SHANE, STAN, COACH)
5. INT. BUZZ'S HOME, DAY. **The boys get ready for their big night out.**
    (WAYNE, BUZZ, SHANE)
6. INT. SALLY'S BEDROOM, NIGHT. **The girls get ready and Sandra confides her passion for Wayne.** (SALLY, SANDRA, KYLIE, MRS KANE)
7. INT. BUZZ'S HOME, DAY. **Buzz gets a birthday card and a promise of a present.**
    (WAYNE, BUZZ, SHANE)

Figure 7.1: Sample television drama story outline and scene breakdown.

action and response to get a general sense of the character and to generate interest in them. As the story unfolds, a viewer accumulates more understanding of the characters and learns their back-story from their actions, but this will not then be at the expense of program momentum.

The spine or dramatic arc of the story will thread through the program, giving it its dramatic direction. The characters play out the unfolding story through the episodes of a mini-series or in each episode of a long-form series. In a mini-series, the catalyst is in episode one and the resolution in the final episode, the intervening episodes passing through a number of dramatic turning points (often at the end of an episode) that sustain the momentum of the series. In a long-form series, each episode has the three-act structure. The series is too long to sustain such a large number of turning points as continuing momentum.

Key structural elements in the main body of the story are the turning points, turning the action in new directions. They take the audience into a new arena with a different focus for action, all the time carrying viewers towards the resolution. Turning points are often a moment of decision about a main character, raising the stakes for that character. They are a particular and important instance of actions that drive the story forward, called action points. These are dramatic points that cause a reaction and they work best when expressed visually rather than through dialogue, such as a character reacting to a miscalculation about another character. In addition to turning points, an action point may be: a barrier, occurring where a character tries something that doesn't work and is forced into a new decision about action or direction; a complication, not paying off immediately but with a reaction that comes later; or a reversal, turning the direction of the story around, reversing actions or a character's emotions.

Conflict is another key ingredient in any drama. American script consultant, Linda Seger, suggests five basic types of dramatic conflict in cinema:

1. *Inner conflict*, where characters are unsure of themselves or their actions. This works better dramatically if projected on a person or object rather than being done in voice-over or in confidence with another character. The Australian movie *Muriel's Wedding* is an example.
2. *Relational conflict* from mutually exclusive goals of the protagonist and antagonist. *High Noon* is a classic example and *LA Confidential* more recently.
3. *Societal conflict* between a person and a group or from a person against a larger system. *Strictly Ballroom* and *One Flew Over the Cuckoo's Nest* are examples.
4. *Situational conflict*, where characters confront life-and-death situations. They are often relational at the same time from the tension and are difficult to sustain otherwise. *Titanic* and *Alien* are examples.
5. *Cosmic conflict* between a character and a supernatural force, which is usually projected into another character. *The Exorcist* and *Groundhog Day* are examples.

In practice, it's possible to think of a number of films or television dramas where the nature of the conflict doesn't really fit any of these five categories, but nonetheless conflict is a central component to drama and Seger's classification gives us insight into the ways it can be used.

This section is an overview of the writer's craft that is brought to bear in fashioning a script. The producer, of course, won't be writing the script (except as a producer–scriptwriter), but they need to be aware of the classic elements of good script crafting if they are going to be able to provide practical guidance to the writing process. The producer must ensure that these elements are there or, if they are not, be satisfied that the script has been able by some other means to overcome the diminished product that would ordinarily result.

Step 4: Expanded scene breakdown

The next stage of the writing process varies from writer to writer. Either they move on to writing the first draft of the actual script (in which case, each scene in the script breakdown will more likely be two to five lines of description) or they write an expanded scene breakdown preparatory to writing the script. The expanded scene breakdown takes each scene heading and expands it in prose, building into its description all the detail of actions, atmosphere, thoughts and emotions of the characters, paraphrase of dialogue, any aspect of location, or any props that will feature in the scene – in short, anything that is part of the action and emotion of the scene. The writer works through the entire script, scene by scene, arriving at a description of how the entire program should appear to its audience.

Proponents of the expanded scene breakdown say it enables the writer to keep focused on the dramatic elements of each scene and not get distracted by witty but peripheral dialogue or activities that don't advance the drama. Because it is still one step away from the screenplay, there is not so much disinclination to change things. It is not yet at the stage where Pygmalion can fall in love with his creation.

If there is an overemphasis on dialogue over action in Australian drama, which appears to be the case, the expanded scene breakdown can help redress the balance. Dialogue is easier to write than dramatically relevant action and, if it is witty, is more instantaneously satisfying. But dialogue often fails to engage the emotions as effectively as action that illuminates character, and underscores motivation and dramatic direction. As a result, Australian drama can sometimes be very 'talky' and, because dialogue rather than action is propelling it, it can meander without a clear sense of dramatic purpose. Characters might become well-defined by what they say (although their definition can be enhanced by their decisions and indecisions and their ways of dealing with events), but what they say doesn't imprint the direction of the story as strongly as what they do.

It should be noted that action does not necessarily require car chases or running down corridors, which are common elements of so-called 'action drama'. It is anything that is done (or not done) that progresses the narrative, sets up dramatic highlights, or illuminates the characters and the emotions driving them. It may be acting on impulse or doing nothing in the face of a threat. Inaction can be as revealing of character as active response and gives us a stronger and more dramatically satisfying insight into people's inner world than cleverly written dialogue articulating that world.

7.4 Critical assessment of script drafts

Assessing the script

The expanded scene breakdown or the first draft of the screenplay are opportunities for the development team to look critically at the detailing of the story, to form a consensus of what's not yet working and, just as importantly, what seems to be working particularly well. It should always be a constructive process where the mechanism of things that have worked can be applied to other parts of the script in pursuit of a similar outcome, and the things that don't work are fine-tuned or replaced to see if that produces a more satisfactory result. It is the job of the producer to ensure that the people involved in this process, and especially the writer, are viewing it as a constructive process. Depending on the story, there are a large number of things that can be potentially reviewed at this stage. The following text highlights a few of the aspects that are commonly assessed. It's not an exhaustive list, but should give a good sense of what issues can be pursued. Over time, producers build a repertoire of issues that experience and instinct tell them are the important ones to examine in developing drama programs.

Opening scene

It is good to start the program with a strong image that provides a visual reference to place, mood, texture and theme. Dialogue as an opener is usually unable to generate the same power and is harder to understand. A moody scene of a lone horserider creates a much stronger entry to the story than dialogue about solitude. This should lead into the catalyst that triggers the story. Is there a catalytic event? Does it satisfactorily set up the central dramatic spine of the story? Have the main characters been introduced sufficiently for the audience's needs at this stage? Conversely, is there character information superfluous to this stage of the plot's development?

Momentum

The script must maintain its momentum. It can be lost with unrelated scenes, by characters talking without doing, or by the story unfolding too quickly or too slowly. Lack of momentum isn't always solved by increasing pace. This may only serve to make it more difficult for the audience to follow the story. The problem with the script's momentum might be that the story is too predictable, or that it lacks other dimensions, or that the characters are too stereotyped. Things that are foreshadowed should pay off; things that pay off should be foreshadowed. Have these connections been satisfactorily made? Have the devices chosen to foreshadow events and pay off what's come before avoided the crime of being glaringly predictable?

Subplots

The story is made up of a main plot, carried from catalyst to resolution by the unfolding drama, and a few subplots, sufficient to add interest and variety, but not so many as to confuse the audience. Subplots feed into the main plot, providing texture and dimension to the story. As a rule of thumb, plot carries the action, subplot carries the theme. Subplots reveal extra dimensions about characters, about their goals, dreams and desires. Like the plot, they have turning points. Are the subplots unstructured and rambling? Do they lack a connection to the plot or are they played out before the plot has got substantially underway?

Character and action

The theme is best expressed through character and action, rather than dialogue, and can be expanded with telling images. Characters should have something at stake in the story, be it survival, love, self-respect or a need to understand

something. Do the characters have emotional range, not just the actions necessary to achieve their goal? A script should avoid explaining motivation through
dialogue instead of action, or showing it through flashback set too far in the past.
The script should look to expand or extend emotional moments. A strong emotional response is generally more dramatic than a weak response (even if the weak
response is more likely in actuality). A script is a dramatic interpretation of the
world, not a dispassionate recorder of it in the manner of a security camera.

Successive drafts of the script

The above are typical of the questions to be asked and issues to be raised with each
succcssive draft of a screenplay until there are no more questions and no more
issues. After each review, script notes are provided for the writer (who is on the
review team) to take the screenplay to the next draft. The review process should not
be faint-hearted about anything that could be improved. There is nothing wrong
with a script going through ten drafts or more, and it is not unusual to do so.
Indeed, some scripts do not work properly because a producer was not prepared
to bite the bullet and ask for another draft. As a result, an underdeveloped script
goes into production. By the same token, there's no point in requiring changes
just for the sake of it. If the script is working at the third draft, it should be left
as it is. Whether arrived at remarkably early in the drafting process or only after
an agonising number of redrafts, a finished script is a very satisfying thing. As
Linda Seger puts it, 'Great scripts are clean, clear and easy to follow . . . and each
character has a reason to be in the story'.

7.5   When things aren't working

When a script doesn't work

We have just looked at the process that produces a script of which everyone
involved is proud, but what happens when there are differing points of view in the
team about how well the script is working and whether further drafts are necessary? Specifically, what do producers do when they think the script needs further
work and the writer is reluctant or refusing to do another draft? Experience says
there is generally only one bite of the cherry with any one broadcaster or investor,
so a script that falls short will probably not have a second chance as an improved
version. That opportunity is lost. The script represents the producer's reputation,
which can create producer anxiety about whether it is ready to submit. Scripts
can always be taken a little bit further coming into production, but by then they
are over the commissioning/funding hurdle. What we are interested in here is
what producers can do when they believe the script is not yet at the standard that
will get it over that hurdle.

The replacement writer

What sounds like the most logical solution is not necessarily the best. A writer's
contract may allow for another writer to be brought in to take over if there is a

stalemate, but the wide experience of replacement writers is that they will write a new script, not a revised version of the existing script. However difficult the relationship with the writer has become, a substantial part of the script is from within that writer and a new writer cannot build from that, they can only retell the story in a way that comes from within them. A writer might be hired to write draft 5 of an existing script but the result will almost certainly be draft 1 of their interpretation of the story. That may not be a bad thing if the script needs substantial work, but if it is finetuning that is needed, that would be a backward step.

Independent assessment

If the difference revolves around subtle issues of style or interpretation, a better approach might be to bring in a third opinion. A good script editor might shake out the problem where the idea originated with the writer. If the issue is more deep-seated than that, the solution could be an independent assessment by someone the writer respects and who has a perspective of the market in which the script is intended to operate. Producers must be open to examining their own position, to put their ego to one side and to think about what is needed and what can be done to achieve that. They should ask the writer to do the same and then swap notes. If the writer is not budging because they lack confidence in the producer's judgement, then that is a good reason to bring in a third person to resolve the issue.

Identify the issues

Where the stand-off is between writer and director, the producer should get both to identify what the real issues are in their minds and proceed into discussion from there. Sometimes the director might say to the producer: 'I'm the director, you have to support me!' Late in development that position might be reasonable, especially if the producer is inclined towards the director's point of view. If the producer has doubts, then maybe the project would benefit from a different director. The object is always to get to a completed script that all, and particularly the producer who has to sell it, think has reached a level from which a great program can be made.

7.6   Documentary development

Finding an underlying narrative

Like drama, a documentary project follows the general pattern of program development, but it has its own distinctive features. As a genre that interprets actuality, it has to know what that actuality is, and that is uncovered by research. From the information gleaned, producer and director (often the same person) will determine a central theme to underpin the proposed program. A narrative is constructed to tell the story that unfolds from an arresting starting point of the central theme, not dissimilar to the way a drama unfolds from a catalyst event. The narrative may be unfolding events in an observational or historical documentary or an unfolding argument in an essay-style documentary. Bob Connelly and Robin Anderson's *Rats in the Ranks* is an observational documentary about the machinations of Leichhardt Council, Grahame Shirley's *The Road to Tokyo* is a historical documentary about the closing stages of the Pacific War, and Michael Moore's *Fahrenheit 9/11* is a documentary essay about the political misuse of the New York attack by the Bush administration.

Components of documentary proposal

The documentary proposal will have a front page that captures the main selling points of the intended program, a summary of the storyline over a few pages, some notes on treatment, style and ranges of source material that will be used, notes about the presenter if there is to be one and possibly about any on-camera people who will feature prominently, notes about the target audience and the production team, and a budget summary. In other words, the features of a generic proposal document. Unlike drama, where the material is usually purpose-shot for the program, documentary will often draw on a number of sources, such as archive and amateur footage, still photographs, animation and graphics. There are also various ways that this material might be treated in post-production: colouring, composite framing, reframing and slow motion, to name a few. These approaches raise technical issues in dealing with them and they should be indicated in the proposal document so that the commissioning broadcaster is confident the technical challenges have been addressed.

The evolving story

The engine that drives documentary development is research. The story that the documentary tells can be an evolving organism that grows and changes as elements of research come to hand. The development of Trevor Graham's *Lonely Boy Richard* (2003) gives a good insight into this process. The proposal was for an observational film examining why so many young Indigenous males end up in jail. Although they expected it to be alcohol-related and knew the program would need strong characters to sustain it, the production team didn't know who the characters would be at the time of proposing the program. The production spent six months in Arnhem Land looking for the right talent. It was only late in the piece that they came across Richard, who was in court, and focused the program on him.

Hiring a researcher

Substantial research requires development funding to hire a program researcher. In the absence of this funding, the director might do sufficient preliminary research to enable a reasonably detailed proposal document to be assembled. Production budgeting would then include the hire of a specialist researcher to carry out more detailed and production-specific research so that a shooting script can be prepared prior to the shoot. The next section covers the full process of program research, whether funded in development or pre-production.

7.7   Program research

Shooting script

Research is the cornerstone of factual programs and, particularly, documentary. It is the source of the information on which the shooting script will be built and which will be the basis of the ultimate program. The shooting script is an outline of the anticipated documentary prior to its shooting. It allows a degree of flexibility in its realisation to accommodate the practical reality that documentary shoots are never exactly as they were planned. Other genres may use research to background a script, but for documentary it is its lifeblood. It's the means of having something at which to point the camera. Without that, there is no documentary to shoot.

Practical information

Research is more than just a list of the things that can be recorded on camera. It includes detail of how to contact people for access to things to be filmed, whether those things are people, places or events. It includes practical information about light conditions, potential noise interference, travel and accommodation options, the best times to shoot certain scenes and the availability of key people for them, the people to deal with, and notice of people who are difficult to deal with. It includes assessment of the potential of people and events to make interesting scenes. It includes footage already in existence that might be worth acquiring for the program, how to go about obtaining it, and the likely cost. And it includes traditional academic research as background information. A research report is a practical document with all the information necessary to plan and carry out a documentary shoot – and nothing more. As important as what is in the report is that information which is left out about the subject where it is not relevant to the angle the program is pursuing. There is nothing more frustrating for a documentary director than to have to sift through a mountain of superfluous research material. A professional researcher will judge what should go into the report and what is unnecessary for it.

Background research

A research project goes through four principal stages. First comes background research to the subject or to the story idea if that has been the starting point of the project. This is similar to academic research and doesn't have the requirement at this stage of being able to be captured on camera. As this information is assembled, the development team should be looking for those parts of the background research that might translate into visual and sequence treatment. The skill here is to be able to spot a good story angle. There is no instruction that can be given on how to spot a good story. It's a combination of instinct and experience under the general description of journalistic skills. If you have the skill, you will know the story is good when you see it.

The remaining stages

With a story angle determined, the researcher draws up the second stage of the process, a detailed plan for the research project: what to pursue, what to explore further. This plan may be revised as the research progresses and new information suggests further leads to follow up. The third stage is the bulk of the research project, detailed below, and the final stage is writing up the research report. The length of the report should be proportional to the length of the program or segment researched. A report for a five-minute magazine segment would be expected to run for a few pages only, generally no more than four or five. A report for a documentary program would be significantly longer, maybe ten or twenty pages, or perhaps more.

Types of research material

The material a researcher will produce for a factual program falls into four general categories:

1. *Information*. You can't point a camera at this, so it is background information and possible narration material. The researcher should sift through the material available to prioritise it, and not simply include everything known to humanity on the subject. Information should be sourced through people as well as libraries and the internet, and its accuracy should be verified, bearing in mind that there can be shades of accuracy.
2. *Existing vision*. This includes still photographs and artwork as well as motion pictures, and covers material sourced from professional archives and that tucked away in people's garages. Where relevant, the research notes should include such detail as source organisation or person, item file number, format, licence fee and any restrictions on its use.
3. *Actuality sequences*. This details what is usually the bulk of the material that will be in the finished program. The report will indicate when and where sequences relevant to the program will happen, or when they can be set up. It will include practical considerations, such as conditions for shooting, and impediments to shooting, such as noise, other people's requirements at the location, or electricity sources. The director needs to know the nature of the event to be shot: can the action be directed or must it be followed? The researcher should brief those involved so that they know what to expect. It is unwise to assume people outside the industry understand production needs.
4. *Talent*. This is the industry term for non-professional people (as regards television production) who are used for interview or to carry out some activity on camera. Research should cover what they have to say and/or what they might do, suggesting suitable and relevant locations for shooting them (if it's not self-evident) and suggesting any visual support that might be suitable to overlay an interview. The researcher should find out what the talent thinks about the subject under research, and not boast about the things the researcher already knows. The report should also comment on their likely presentation on camera and how articulate they are. In the age of easily operated Mini DV cameras, it

can be useful for some footage of key talent to be recorded so that the director can make this judgement for themself. Talent who is intended to perform for the program might require a fee and might have a publishing contract covering this material. This should be clarified.

Practices of research experience

There are a number of rules of thumb that contribute to successful research. All possible sources of information should be tapped. Libraries and the internet are obvious sources, but the telephone is one of the most useful research tools. Researchers should make use of any contacts they already have and follow up any leads that crop up, finding out who can tell them what they need to know. Researchers are usually the first contact for the production and will affect people's attitude to it. They should be courteous, develop their trust and try to let them feel they can escape if they need to (particularly when dealing with sensitive subject matter). Directors need to be aware that people may change their views on a subject when they later mull over their conversation with the researcher. Sometimes the research meeting will be the first time they have looked at their subject from the angle of the story. Researchers should be sceptical and keep their 'nonsense antenna' operating. They should keep an open mind and be prepared to change initial assumptions. Most importantly, researchers should bear in mind that if they don't understand something, the viewers of the program probably won't either. The solution is to get information paraphrased and simplified. An unfathomable program is not something that will engage viewers.

7.8   Development of reality programs

Comparison with docusoap

By way of comparison and contrast, we now look at the development process for the newest of the major genres, the reality program – not the observational documentary format sometimes given that description, but the genre with competing participants in an enclosed environment (see Chapter 4). Far from differing radically from either drama or documentary, it has features in common with both. In many ways, it is a docusoap in a contrived setting. Like docusoaps, a reality series is planned as a narrative structure with a dramatic arc and action points, much as a drama series would be conceived. It brings together a range of archetypal characters that could be expected to react with each other in sometimes predictable, sometimes unpredictable, but hopefully dramatic, ways. This is the classic 'ship of fools' scenario that is often employed in drama, but here the scenario isn't translated into a script. It is more like a documentary shooting script where there are expectations of response to the introduction of various elements into the story, but no certainty. Whatever the outcome is in actuality, it will be recorded as it happens and incorporated into the story, as in the classic process of documentary production. A reality program must have a degree of responsiveness built into its production machinery to capture both the expected and the unexpected.

Packaging the concept

The starting point for this type of program, as in any other production, is the idea. The producer's first task is to flesh out that idea – with the people who brought it to them, or with associates, or by themself – to determine what is in the concept that can be turned into the narrative structure of a drama series. Consideration is given to how to package the concept. What length of series best accommodates it? What might be the action points that can be inserted into the narrative to propel it along? Because the setting is enclosed, the production can choose what to insert in order to disrupt the settled narrative. It could send in an outsider to join the participants, or it could put a demand on them via a master of ceremonies, or it could use the disembodied voice of *Big Brother*. Development investigates the scale of production and technical support needed to mount the project. The producer estimates how much audience interest there might be in each potential component of the developing scenario and how much screen time each can sustain.

Resources for production

The development of a reality program, once the narrative structure has been determined, is primarily a working out of the types of technical facility necessary to cover all aspects of the scenario and the level of resourcing to do this with reliability. Integrating these can be a complex and fraught business, but setting up production machinery for a long series with levels of uncertainty cannot allow compromises to creep in or detail that hasn't been fully thought through. Initial decisions are based on the accumulated experience of the producer and technical advisors to the project.

Planning technical facilities

Reality television is driven heavily by production management. Development focuses more on planning and detailing staff, and technical facilities rather than on experimentation. It is important to get the right technical people – and particularly a good technical director – to ensure appropriate coverage. This is a process of concretising the visual concept. The right production machinery must be specified and coordinated to achieve this. The producer may have to fight for funding for resources that are identified as necessary. It's not a format where cutting corners can be absorbed into the production process. Over a long series with uncontrollable and unpredictable material, this could eventually come back to bite the production. Peter Abbott, a specialist reality television producer, says, 'It's like being a trapeze artist, so you need to be sure all the rings and bars will be there when you jump'. Redundancy (or better still, 'headroom') is built into the technical back-up, so the production has the capacity to pick up the unexpected without sacrificing the expected.

Generation of costs

This is not generally a low-cost program to make, although packaging enables amortisation of the high cost. For a start, there is often a fairly high capital cost in setting up a location that is the setting for the program. *My Restaurant Rules* involved substantial leasing and refurbishment costs, much of which were not recoverable. On the other hand, *The Block* involved a cost of purchasing the building, but the program's success drove up its market value so much that it was sold at the end for a considerable profit. *Big Brother* had a costly set build and technical facilities for concealed coverage. The production itself is often costly, with multiple crews and high staffing levels, but the more spin-off programs (such as *Big Brother Up Late*) that can be devised, usually at relatively small marginal cost, the more the high production cost is spread over higher output. A key point in negotiations with networks is how well they can accommodate the various components of the package in their schedule to allow amortisation of this high cost. Channel 10 was the favoured network for *Big Brother* because it was able to schedule the extensive package that attached to the program and gain the full benefit of its success.

Technical rehearsals

The cost of production is sufficiently high that a pilot episode is seldom made. In any case, the success of a reality program depends ultimately on the unscripted performance of its participants. No pilot can test this. You can't check the drama, but you can refine the coverage. Instead of a pilot, there are technical rehearsals over the week prior to going on-air, checking the detail of coverage with dummy performers, making sure that wherever some interesting action will happen there is a camera placed that will be able to pick it up. The drama won't reveal itself as successful or otherwise until the program is broadcast, but development of the most intricate detail allows movement of action points to tweak the dramatic arc. It makes more salvageable a program that's not yet working on-air.

7.9   Other genres

Every program is different with common features

The development of all programs follows the general pattern outlined in Chapter 6, but no two projects follow exactly the same set of steps. There is no prescribed pathway for program development, no steps laid down that, when assiduously followed, will provide certainty of a successful program. The same caveat applies to the development of program genres. This chapter has outlined the process that will generally be followed in drama, documentary and reality programs, but it is not prescriptive. These are guidelines to be varied according to the particularities of the anticipated program. A documentary that will rely on recreated scenes will differ in the detail of its development from an observational documentary, even though both will also have much in common with each other and with other documentaries. A reality program about home renovation will not be developed in an identical fashion to one about survival in an exotic location.

The needs of the program

There is no useful purpose to be served in this book by describing general approaches to development of all the other genres. Like the three genres described, they would derive from the general pattern given in Chapter 6. Also like the genres described, they would be guidelines only, to be departed from to the extent that the particular program requires. That is the role of the producer: to determine what is the process that will work best for the needs of the program being developed, by introducing variations into the established broad pattern, and by guiding the development team down that pathway.

Blueprint for a program

The objective is always the same: to come up with a blueprint for a program that will engage and excite its audience, and at the same time produce a proposal document that can persuade potential financers – broadcasters, investors, distributors – that it will do that. Accompanying that requirement is the need to know how much finance must be pursued. While the blueprint of the program is being developed so is a detailed budget for the cost of its production. The producer then knows the level of funding they must pursue, armed with the proposal document, in order to turn the blueprint into a program.

Sources and further reading

Specific reading

Bignell, Jonathan 2005, *Big Brother: Reality TV in the Twenty-First Century*, Palgrave Macmillan, Basingstoke, Hampshire.
Creeber, Glen 2004, *Serial Television: Big Drama on the Small Screen*, British Film Institute, London.
DiMaggio, Madeline 1990, *How to Write for Television*, Prentice Hall, New York.
Drouyn, Coral 1994, *Big Screen, Small Screen*, Allen & Unwin, Sydney.
Johnson-Woods, Toni 2002, *Big Brother*, University of Queensland Press, Brisbane.
Kelson, Gerald 1990, *Writing for Television*, 2nd edn, A&C Black, London.
Seger, Linda 1987, *Making a Good Script Great*, Dodd, Mead & Co, New York.

Some internet references

Keane, Christopher 'Hollywood's best kept secret: the expanded scene breakdown', available online at <http://www.writersstore.com/article.php?articles_id=525>, viewed 15 December 2006.

Chapter 8

The pursuit of funding

A critical stage in the production pathway is the pursuit of funds so that the project can go into production. The rest of the development team may finetune content and creative elements at this stage, but for the producer this is the 'make or break' time. Without sufficient funding, it's hard to see how the project can proceed further. Occasionally, producers will commence production with the project only partially funded in the belief, like Mr Micawber, that something will turn up. This is not recommended and often it is not possible anyway. Smart investors will tie their money contractually so that production cannot commence until it is sufficiently funded to go to completion. This is still no insurance against overspending or under-budgeting.

Funding for production comes from two main sources:
1. pre-sale of the program, most commonly to a broadcaster, in advance of it being made, or via a distributor advance or guarantee
2. investment contracted in return for equity in the project and a share of its revenue from sales.

From time to time, depending on the nature of the program, a third group may come into the picture, namely, parties with an interest in the subject matter of the program. Sponsorship may be a particular kind of investment, although its objective is not a monetary return but promotion of a commercial or policy interest of the sponsor through the program's content. Sponsorship wouldn't ordinarily impart a right to equity in the project.

A pre-sale is not actually a sale of the program at all. It is a licence to broadcast the program, not a sale of the program itself. The program remains the property of its copyright holders. A pre-sale usually takes the form of a licence agreement with a broadcaster, be it commercial or public, FTA or subscription (pay) television, domestic or overseas, for a specified fee. Earnings on this agreement are known from the outset. Pre-sale can also be a distribution guarantee, where only the guarantee is known at the outset and further revenue from distribution will depend on the success of the program in the marketplace. A pre-sale licence doesn't give the broadcaster any right to equity in the project because it has already gained value in return for its money from the right to broadcast the program, unlike investors who must wait for its performance in the marketplace.

Sources of investment funding fall into three main groups:

1. government funding agencies (either state or federal), where there are policy and cultural factors in the choice of projects to back, as well as a nominal expectation of financial return
2. private investors, who are looking initially for tax breaks from the investment and then earnings from sale of the program
3. companies, including broadcasters, who have some strategic interest in the program and its distribution and exploitation.

The principal sources of funding for TV production in Australia are the Australian FTA broadcasters, as both pre-sale licence fee and investment. Table 8.1 gives an indication of where the funding has come from for the two main genres of drama and documentary in recent years. Other genres, notably lifestyle, will generally have an even greater proportion of broadcaster investment (in many cases, 100%) since they are unable to qualify for government agency funding.

8.1 Australian free-to-air broadcasters

FTA networks as key financers

In the vast majority of cases, the cornerstone of an Australian production's financing strategy will inevitably be an Australian FTA broadcaster. Without this, both overseas broadcasters and investors are likely to be quite wary of the project.

Table 8.1: Sources of funding of Australian independent documentary production (2000–2003) and television drama production (2000–2005).

Funding source		Documentary (%)	Drama (%)
Government, including public broadcasters		56	25
Private investors, including Film Licensed Investment Companies and 10B/10BA tax deduction schemes		4	6
Commercial broadcasters and pay TV	7		
Distributors	<1		
Production companies	6		
Other local finance	11		
Australian film/TV industry		24	53
Foreign finance		16	17
		100	100

The FFC (see section 8.5) requires commitment from a domestic broadcaster, and foreign broadcasters generally only consider Australian projects with a local pre-sale. Programs that are likely to appeal only to Australian audiences would not attract an overseas broadcaster and are unlikely to interest investors. It would be difficult to see where their return on investment would come from. These projects would seek 100% funding from a domestic broadcaster as a mix of pre-sale and investment. A producer's first funding approach, therefore, will generally be to Australian FTA networks. The producer will be familiar with network priorities for scheduling, and often with people in a network's commissioning machinery. They are the best understood of the funding sources. It's imperative to decide where the principal interest in the program lies, and who is most likely to be in the market for it.

Network preferences

The first consideration is deciding which Australian network is the prime target for a program. Each has its preferred genres and styles of programs, generally related to the profile of its viewers. Network Ten, for instance, has built its success on targeting younger audiences and it is more likely to be interested in entertainment programs that appeal to this demographic than many others. SBS, on the other hand, has built its reputation on its preparedness to take risks with its programming, so it would be more likely to be interested in an innovative program with untested features than the other networks. In identifying the network most likely to be interested in the proposed program, the producer tries to ensure the proposal is fashioned as much as possible to the attributes generally favoured by that network. There is not much point in presenting to SBS an interestingly risky program that will offend some community within Australia or whose budget is way beyond the means of SBS, or to present to Ten a youth-oriented program that is worthy to the point of dullness or that relies on a personality already contracted to another network.

Network scheduling

Some network preferences are widely known, some are not clear, and all are prone to unannounced or gradual change. The priorities of a particular network can often be inferred by examining the make-up of its schedule in the TV guides. The type of audience may change across different times of the day, and may even change over different days of the week. Some channels, for instance, may build up a comedy night on one day of the week. The art of scheduling is discussed in more detail in Chapter 24 and provides the framework in which networks commission programs. Television networks are innately conservative and they tend to schedule the same things this year in the same pattern as they scheduled them last year – as long as they consider that they've been working. Having said that, if they are offered a program they think will knock their competitors out of a timeslot, they will do anything that is necessary to make that happen. Unfortunately, they often prefer to see someone else take the risk first.

The delusion of universal appeal

Many program-makers make the mistake of persuading themselves that their program is of such universal appeal that it will attract all viewers of all ages and interests. Few programs do this. In truth, probably none do. Most programs described by their proposers as appealing to all ages are usually so bland they don't have any particular appeal to any demographic group at all. They aren't bad, just unremarkable, and there's enough of that on television already.

Pitching to a second network

Although the proposal is initially conceived to meet the scheduling needs of an identified principal network, this doesn't preclude pitching to a second or even a third network. If necessary, the proposal document could be re-versioned to increase its appeal to other networks. Sometimes a program that isn't in the mainstream of a network's thinking comes along at just the right time to offer a solution for the network programmer – a solution to a problem a producer would not necessarily know about. Timing, coincidence, personal preference, alliances and serendipity all play a part in the inexact science out of which one program proposal gets picked over others on offer. But if a program is to be versioned for another network, it should not be obvious that it has been done. Commissioning executives don't like to think that other networks have been approached first, even though they know that is always a possibility. Reworking a proposal will generally require more than simply throwing in another component. For instance, adding some ethnic component to a proposal to try to appeal to SBS after the proposal has been passed over by another network (or all of them) will not necessarily guarantee acceptance.

Network options of pre-sale or acquisition

Networks will generally pay more for a pre-sale than for acquisition of the finished program, even though they can see what they are buying with acquisition and cannot with a pre-sale. A pre-sale is based on what the program aspires to be. However, the broadcaster can have editorial input into the making of a program that has been pre-sold to it, and can mould it to network needs. How much the network exercises that right varies from network to network, and from network representative to network representative.

Another reason to go down the path of the higher priced pre-sale is to ensure that the production is financed, and at less cost to the broadcaster than if it were to fully fund the production. This is particularly the case for ABC and SBS, with policy pressure to schedule documentaries. It requires the producer to find other parties to complete financing, but an Australian FTA commitment often makes that more likely anyway. Waiting to acquire a program when it is completed may be cheaper, but it is a false saving if the greater likelihood is that the program will never be made due to lack of funding. This is especially possible with Australian documentaries, which may have limited marketplace potential to attract equity investors.

Pre-sale of drama programs

Pre-sale licensing tends to follow distinct patterns in each genre. With television drama, the Australian broadcaster may provide up to 90% of the budget, although some of this might be assigned as investment, and some as licence fee. The balance would be made up as distributor finance (see section 8.4), where the distributor would hope to recover its guarantee, and then profit, from sales of the program in other territories. Increasingly, the Australian broadcaster might, with the producer, seek overseas broadcaster pre-sale to reduce its own funding, although these additional broadcasters also reduce the territories available to the distributor to market the program and hence make the deal less attractive to a distributor. Other broadcasters might produce the drama series in-house and contract a distributor to market the program overseas or market it themselves.

Pre-sale of documentaries

Documentaries are mostly broadcast by ABC and SBS. Until 2006, the two public broadcasters each had an accord with the federal FFC, under which the FFC provided investment funding of a specified number of documentary projects annually where the broadcaster had committed to a pre-sale of the program for a specified licence fee. Although these accords no longer operate as such, the FFC will invest in documentary projects under similar conditions of co-funding with any domestic broadcaster, as outlined in section 8.5. ABC and SBS will generally pay about $90 000 per program hour for a documentary pre-sale licence. Commercial networks don't invest in documentary to a great extent because they feel it has limited audience interest. They mostly buy just the number of programs to fulfil their regulatory obligations (see Chapter 3). Commercial television is likely to pay market rates for non-prime time (about $30 000 for the program hour in 2006) and schedule accordingly. From time to time, this attitude changes and commercial FTA broadcasters will actually pursue certain types of documentary and schedule them in prime time. This is currently the case with docusoap.

Pre-sale of other genres

A pre-sale of other genres doesn't have much potential for shared funding with government agencies because the agencies are interested in only a few genres, and often the programs are too locally oriented to interest overseas broadcasters. A program made exclusively for the Australian market may require a pre-sale of 100% of its budget, but there can be sponsorship and ancillary marketing opportunities in the content of sport, lifestyle and reality programs, for example, so that the broadcaster's cost might be offset by a sponsor's contribution. In some sport programs, usually live broadcasts of sporting events, the administering body of the sport is so much in need of a higher profile for its sport that it will fully fund the program's budget, an obvious financial attraction to a broadcaster.

8.2   Australian pay television

Commissioning by pay TV

Pay television can sometimes be a useful second source of Australian licensee financing of a project. Pay television channels will complement their scheduling of purchased overseas product and acquired re-runs of FTA-broadcast shows with locally commissioned programs. Some have no expected life beyond the network, which might be the sole funding source in mostly low-budget programs. Where it has the potential to 'travel', the channel will try to recover some of its costs from overseas pay networks, especially in New Zealand. Foxtel has a platform-funding approach to investment. It pools its funds for production and allocates thcm on behalf of its owned and operated channels, which have to pitch for the funding. Foxtel will invest in what it sees as the wider benefit of the platform, preferably in a program that can be scheduled over time across several of its channels. Independent channel providers commission their own program material and have to be approached individually. As a general rule, the pay networks prefer to produce programs in-house or commission with well-established producers.

Documentary projects

Documentary producers find very little investment in their projects from pay channels. Foxtel's Crime and Investigation Channel (CIC) has, however, commissioned Australian producers to revisit major Australian crimes for international syndication. Documentary producers may be better placed by approaching the US or UK head office of channels, such as Discovery, National Geographic or The History Channel, for a pay television pre-sale. While a producer could approach these through the Australian subsidiary, there's generally no particular advantage in doing so.

Drama projects

In drama, pay television has to consider the 10% quota, noted in Chapter 3. Foxtel has invested across its drama channels, the Movie channels, Turner Classic Movies, Hallmark and The Cartoon Network (animated drama is counted towards the 10% obligation), but the largest investor has been Showtime, often in projects in partnership with FTA networks. *Love My Way* is a successful drama whose second series was produced by Foxtel and Austar. Foxtel had initially funded it for Fox8, gathering funds from sources that needed it for the drama quota. Showtime is funding the third series, ensuring this well-regarded program will continue, but it may reduce the opportunities for other drama projects to secure Showtime investment. Production difficulties with Kennedy–Miller's *Mango River*, partnered by Austar and Showtime, might make pay television channels generally cautious about local drama. On the other hand, the producers of *Love My Way* started production in late 2006 on a new eight-part drama, *Dangerous*, to run on Fox8.

8.3   Overseas broadcasters

Attraction of Australian broadcaster attachment

If a project has the potential to find an audience outside Australia, a pre-sale to an overseas broadcaster becomes a possibility. This is more likely if there is already an Australian broadcaster attached. Overseas interests feel more confident when the project is backed locally, not least of all because the backer would be familiar with the producer's and director's track record. Generally, the potential for an overseas broadcaster pre-sale is higher with documentary than drama projects, although not all broadcasters are interested in documentary.

Market research

The first stage is to research the market for the most appropriate pre-sale partner. This might involve an internet search, talking to the FFC, or approaching a distributor (see next section) for guidance and advice. Only some FTA broadcasters have an interest in documentaries, and these are mostly public broadcasters. However, commercial broadcasters might look at event documentaries or docusoap. Cable television broadcasters tend to specialise in genres that are detailed on the network's website, if it isn't already obvious from their name. Indicative prices currently paid by broadcasters in a number of territories around the world are published in trade magazines from time to time. *Variety* magazine publishes a global programming price guide, World Screen has a program price index and C21 Media has its Programme Prices Map.

Order of approach to networks

The producer should first approach FTA networks in major territories – the United Kingdom, United States, France and Germany – followed by second-tier territories such as Canada, Holland and Scandinavia. The next to approach is the cable networks. US networks often have preferred suppliers, but they will sometimes back a project from outside those sources if they believe it could work for them. The reason for approaching FTA networks first is that cable networks may take only international pay television rights, making it difficult to sell FTA rights as a second run.

Drama

Only a key broadcaster is likely to be interested in Australian drama. The location of the drama would need to have some connection to the broadcaster's country. Without this, it is more likely to wait to view the finished program as a possible acquisition. However, with an overseas connection the pursuit of a co-producer in that country can be worthwhile. The co-producer is more likely to succeed in approaching its domestic broadcaster than a producer from outside the territory. In any case, it's hard for an Australian producer to secure an overseas broadcaster without an existing relationship. An alternative approach is to work through a sales agent.

8.4   Distribution advance or guarantee

Minority financer

A sales agent or international distributor could be a minority financer of a project, with a distribution advance or guarantee, where the majority financers are already attached. Beyond International and the Southern Star Group are the two prime distributors of television product in Australia. Others, such as Becker, Verve and the two public broadcasters, have particular program interests, and some distributors of features and feature documentaries will distribute to television as well. A distributor often provides the balance of funding where a project is just short of its target. The objective is to secure the program ahead of its commercial rivals and, by completing the financing, ensuring a program with good sales potential will actually be made. The other investors are more likely to be broadcasters than government funding agencies (see next two sections) because of the different priorities that the agencies and distributors place on choosing projects.

Distributor preferences

The terms 'agent' and 'distributor' are used fairly interchangeably in the industry. Generally, an international distributor will only be interested in an Australian project if it has confidence in the creative team and the project has potential for overseas sales. If that is the case, the producer may even talk at the development stage to an overseas distributor, especially if there is an Australian broadcaster attached. This would provide a good guide to the international market, at least, and may lead to something more tangible. It is the distributor's business to know the international market and determine the key buyers for a program. Distributor preference is for series rather than one-off programs because networks have a greater interest in series and there is a bigger return for each sale. Although one-off programs can be difficult to sell, a distributor might take on one if it believes it has sufficient sales potential – an event documentary, a big-budget program, or a notable telemovie. It would also look at a program that could be included in an existing series strand that it already has in the marketplace. On the other hand, distributors are unlikely to commit money to a project by someone with no track record, or where there is not an existing relationship. They are not in the business of taking risks.

A cautious relationship

In the first instance with any producer, a distributor would probably take on a program only after completion. If that goes well, it might consider an advance or guarantee for the producer's next project. An exception is possible where the producer or director has already made programs within a broadcaster or production house.

Advances and guarantees

Distributor financing of a project will be as either an advance or a guarantee. With an advance, the distributor contracts to pay the agreed amount before or on delivery of the program. Some distributors regard the financing as an advance if it is paid after delivery but too soon for any reasonable expectation of revenue to cover the advance. A guarantee is a contract to pay an agreed amount at an agreed date after delivery, usually one that should allow sufficient time for sales to cover the guaranteed amount. If they haven't done so, the balance of the guarantee is paid to the producer by the distributor. It won't make further payments until sales have recouped the contracted amount, whether guaranteed or advanced. A distributor will require a completion guarantor on a project where an advance is to be paid before delivery (see section 8.12).

Amount advanced by the distributor

The conventional distribution arrangement is a commission of 30%. A distributor will be looking for a wide grant of rights, preferably all rights in all media, including the internet, mobile receivers and ancillary rights. It is in the producer's interest as well to sell the program and attached rights as widely as possible. Some will work on the theory that distributors have differing areas of speciality, and that distribution rights should be spread across the specialists. The amount of the advance or guarantee is a negotiated figure, with the distributor wanting to err on the side of caution so that it doesn't contract to an amount it can't be reasonably confident of recouping from sales. If the producer is pursuing a higher amount, a distributor may agree to that with a tightening of the terms of the agreement in its favour: a longer contracted period, higher commission, no termination clause, or a right of approval over some creative components. The distributor might also, in these circumstances, look at some equity in the project, so it could get additional return from its back-end exploitation.

International connections

Early distributor attachment to a project might be instrumental in brokering an additional pre-sale, using its existing international connections with major FTA or cable channels in the United Kingdom or United States. Here the distributor will contract the broadcaster as part of fulfilling its distribution agreement with the producer. Where there are producer obligations demanded by the broadcaster, it may be more appropriate for broadcaster and producer to contract directly rather than setting up a mirror agreement between distributor and producer to pick up the obligations.

8.5   Film Finance Corporation

Genres supported

While the state funding agencies principally support the development of television programs (see Chapter 6), investment in their production is left mostly to the federal funding agency, Film Finance Corporation Australia Ltd. The FFC's objective is growth of private sector investment in film and television production, although this hasn't yet happened to the extent hoped. The agency limits its investment to drama mini-series and telemovies, children's mini-series drama, and documentaries as the genres it regards as culturally important in reflecting Australia to both itself and overseas. Popular genres, arguably of greater interest to private investors, are left to fend for themselves. Although sitcom is nominally included in its targeted genres, there hasn't been much FFC support for it in practice. Sketch comedy is excluded. More than half of FFC's funding is directed towards feature films, with 35% for television drama and 12% for documentaries.

Criteria for projects

The FFC funds primarily through equity investment, but it will also consider acquiring and dealing in rights, loans, underwriting agreements and joint ventures. It assesses projects on the basis of:
* the level and appropriateness of broadcaster and distributor commitment (called marketplace attachment) and their commercial terms
* the amount of FFC investment requested and its prospect of recoupment
* the track record of the production's principals
* the level of Australian participation.
The project must have a provisional certificate under Division 10BA of the *Income Tax Assessment Act 1936* (Cth) (see section 8.8). This means that its key creative personnel must be freelance – they cannot be on broadcaster staff – nor will FFC finance a drama developed by a broadcaster and subcontracted to the producer.

The application process

Only Australian producers and production companies that are Australian owned, controlled and registered can apply for FFC funding. Applications can be lodged at any time (except for special funds noted below), but producers should discuss their projects with the FFC first. If the FFC board decides to invest, the producer will receive a letter setting out the terms and conditions of investment, and the documentation (including Chain of Title) required by the FFC before cashflow can begin. A Production and Investment Agreement (PIA), drawn up by FFC's lawyers, is signed by both parties. There is a fee to apply, ranging from $50 to $300, and administration and legal fees for projects that have been funded, starting at $2910 for budgets up to $500 000.

Investment terms and conditions

The terms and conditions of FFC investment are fairly standardised. The agency requires a completion guarantee on each project, on terms it approves, and the usual production insurances. It must approve any sales agent or distributor for the program, and prefers collection society, merchandising, music publishing and ancillary rights to be excluded from a distribution agreement. The FFC encourages productions to hold sequel, remake, series, spin-off and ancillary rights, and expects to share revenue from exploiting these rights. It will not invest in a television project unless the producer has the right to exploit a subsequent series, including a reasonable opportunity to secure a third party for this if the initial broadcaster is not interested.

Equitable returns to the producer

The FFC also sees its role as securing an equitable return for a producer's investment in project development. For equity investments (i.e. money invested other than to secure use of the program), FFC encourages 50% of the profit to go to investors and 50% to the producer, although it recognises that this will be subject to negotiation with other investors. Producers' overheads must be funded in the budget.

Adult TV drama

The FFC will invest in mini-series totalling up to eight hours, single telemovies or a package of two or three, and animated mini-series up to thirteen episodes of at least half an hour. Generally it will not invest more than $4 million in any one project, or more than 40% of the production budget, with preference given to projects seeking 35% of the budget or less. FFC assessment of projects looks at market potential, prospects for recoupment, subordination of FFC investment, and track record of the creative team. It also has a brief to put together a diverse, culturally relevant slate. A television drama must have an Australian FTA or pay television pre-sale, with no more than four runs over seven years. The licence fee must not secure equity in the project, and a domestic FTA licence must not include pay television, satellite or New Zealand rights. A mini-series pre-sale must be at least 30% of its budget, or $400 000 per program hour, and a telemovie pre-sale at least 35% of its budget, or $400 000 per program hour. A sales agent must be attached to the project for rest of the world (ROW) sales.

Children's drama

The FFC will invest in children's mini-series up to thirteen hours in total length, animated series of up to twenty-six episodes (each no less than a quarter of an hour), or telemovies. It will not invest more than 43% of a mini-series' budget (and gives preference to projects seeking no more than 38%), or more than $4.5 million for a twenty-six-part series, or $2.25 million for a thirteen-part series. A mini-series must have a domestic broadcaster pre-sale of at least $95 000 per half hour (with no pay television or satellite rights included in an FTA licence fee), a pre-sale in a major overseas territory, and attachment of a sales agent for ROW sales. The foreign pre-sale requirement is a response to Australia's reputation and success as a supplier of children's programs to the world market, but the agency recognises that there may be programs of merit without international appeal. To encourage distinctly Australian programs that may not have international appeal, up to $1.5 million is reserved in the Distinctly Australian Children's Drama Fund for two lower-budgeted children's projects, with no international pre-sale requirement. These must have a domestic FTA pre-sale of at least $90 000 per program half hour and a budget of no more than $225 000 per program half hour. Applications have a closing date.

Documentaries

The FFC will support one-off documentaries or series with an Australian FTA pre-sale, but not reality television, infotainment, current affairs or sports programs. Documentaries are dealt with in three strands:

1. a 'domestic door', requiring local television pre-sale only
2. an 'international door', requiring local television pre-sale and an international pre-sale or guarantee
3. a Special Documentary Fund for innovative projects, with no marketplace attachment requirement.

The domestic door requires the broadcaster to put up a cash pre-sale of 40% of the production budget, with the FFC investment capped at $200 000 for one-off projects and $600 000 for a series. International marketplace attachment is not required, but producers must develop marketing strategies for international sales at rough-cut stage. The international door is divided into two equally funded levels. Level 1 requires a domestic pre-sale of at least $110 000 per program hour, an international sales agent, and an international pre-sale or agent advance of at least 10% of the budget, with the FFC investing up to 50% of the budget. Level 2 requires an appropriate domestic pre-sale, a pre-sale to one major or three minor international territories, and an advance from an international sales agent, with the FFC investing up to 40% of the budget. The Special Documentary Fund offers $150 000 each for up to five projects. It calls for applications by a fixed date each year, and preference is given to experienced program-makers.

8.6   Other government agency funding

Focus on development

Because their funds are limited, the federal Australian Film Commission (AFC) and the state agencies concentrate on the development of projects rather than their ultimate production. Nonetheless, these agencies reserve some funds to support a few productions each year. While they are limited in their funding and their genres, and parochial in their support, they can serve a useful function of funding a gap that still exists to complete financing of a project. As production financers, the state agencies see themselves for the most part as minority investors with this practical function of gap funding.

Australian Film Commission

The AFC will invest in short features (up to one hour with a budget of no more than $500 000), short television drama series, and documentaries. Drama support is regarded as a development opportunity for directors with some experience. The agency will invest up to $400 000 in a short feature and up to $100 000 per program hour of a drama series. It will fund documentary production or post-production to complete a program or series, with up to $85 000 for a one-off program and $100 000 for a series. The AFC won't co-fund with the FFC or Film Australia, but will with other agencies, broadcasters and investors. It won't release funds until the full budget is raised.

NSW Film and Television Office

NSW's Film and Television Office (FTO) will invest up to 10% of the program budget in a television drama, comedy or animation that has confirmed broadcaster commitment. It will also invest up to $80 000 in a one-hour documentary with a 'reasonable level of television pre-sale', or more at a lower hourly rate for a low-budget documentary series, and will fund post-production where there is a broadcaster pre-sale offer or some funding indication from another source, such as the AFC. The FTO calls for applications as expressions of interest four times a year. These are documents of about four pages which include applicant, creative team and cast details, a synopsis of the project, and a proposed financing plan.

Film Victoria

Film Victoria invests in productions by Victorians of drama series, telemovies, sitcoms, documentaries and children's drama as strategic minority funding of projects. Investment is usually limited to 10% of the total budget, with Australian FTA attachment necessary before the production can apply for funding. Like all the state agencies, Film Victoria requires proportional and simultaneous (pro rata and *pari passu*) recoupment of its investment along with other investors, without a producer corridor, unless a co-investor is prepared to allow this from its share of receipts. A producer corridor allows some revenue (usually about 20%) to flow to the producer while the investors are still recouping their investment. Film Victoria also expects to share revenue from ancillary rights. It may invest in post-production, but not to fund deferred costs, and generally won't accept deferred fees in the production itself. The agency charges an administration fee of about 2% of its investment.

Pacific Film and Television Commission

Queensland's Pacific Film and Television Commission (PFTC) will invest up to $350 000 in drama projects, or 10% of the Queensland spend, whichever is less. The producer, director or writer must be Queensland-based, filming must be in Queensland, and 70% of the below-the-line budget must be spent in Queensland. Projects other than serial drama must have Division 10BA certification, and they must have a completion guarantee before production starts. The PFTC's Revolving Film Finance Fund will cashflow a television production by lending up to $4 million or 10% of the production budget against approved security, and with a completion guarantor in place. Acceptable security is a distribution guarantee, pre-sale or financial instrument, without unacceptable risk. The PFTC will also fund documentaries that have a Queensland-based producer and post-production occurring in the state. At the time of applying, projects must have a broadcaster pre-sale, a distribution guarantee, and the majority of their financing in place. The agency will match the pre-sale up to $65 000 per program hour or 30% of the Queensland spend, whichever is less.

South Australian Film Corporation

The South Australian Film Corporation (SAFC) will invest up to $200 000 or 10% of the production budget, whichever is less, in a drama series, telemovie or documentary. The production must have an economic benefit for South Australia, and preferably be produced in the state, with a South Australian cast, crew and facilities. The SAFC will be a minority investor only, but will consider projects with FFC or AFC funding. From time to time, the agency invests under a specified accord with an enduser such as ABC or SBS. The SAFC also has a $3 million revolving loan fund to cashflow productions with a secured pre-sale, and distribution guarantees or advances. As well, it provides in-kind post-production investment of sound facilities to documentaries with creative merit and market potential, but which have exhausted other production support options.

ScreenWest

ScreenWest assists television production in Western Australia to achieve full financing by complementing other funding sources as a minority investor, generally investing no more than 10% of the total budget. It may also make a loan secured by pre-sale or distribution commitments, corporate guarantees, letters of credit, personal guarantees, or some other acceptable security. A loan is recouped along with a 10% premium prior to equity investor recoupment, but ScreenWest has no share of profits. For loans or investments, the project must have a completion guarantor.

Screen Tasmania

Screen Tasmania funds the production of television series, telemovies and documentaries as a loan, or equity investment as a minority investor, to enable Tasmanian productions to reach full funding in conjunction with other financing. It will invest up to $250 000 in television projects with a significant marketplace attachment, such as domestic television pre-sale, or an advance from an international sales agent of at least 25% of the production budget.

Film Australia

A government company of a different kind is Film Australia, which invests in documentary projects that qualify for its National Interest Program. It funds development under the supervision of one of its executive producers and, if it decides not to move into production, will allow buy-back by the producer with a 10% premium on the development budget. If the project proceeds to production, Film Australia will act as executive producer, investors' representative and completion guarantor. It adds a 20% charge to production budgets to cover production, promotion and administrative overheads, and will include producer expenses in the budget. The company has an output deal for documentaries with ABC and SBS, which can help to secure a pre-sale to the network. Where a producer brings a developed project to Film Australia, the producer will be entitled to 20% of return on investment to Film Australia (after sales commission, marketing costs and third party investor entitlements). Where producers bring investments or international (but not domestic) pre-sales to a project, they are entitled to an equivalent proportion of gross returns or a one-off 15% commission on the pre-sale. Film Australia requires 100% copyright where it fully finances a program or a negotiated share where there are other investors.

8.7 Private investment

The elusive private investor

The El Dorado of production funding is private investment – and it's just as elusive. But once a private investor is on board, it's reasonable to expect them to be interested in future projects, if the first one has a positive outcome and they continue to be in a position to invest. It is a process of building a relationship. Unfortunately, there is no identifiable body, no institution or directory dealing in people interested in investing in film or television production. So, where does a producer look for private investors? It's largely a matter of contacts and sometimes intuition. A good source of the former is family and friends, but that's dependent on having family and friends with sufficient disposable income or a financial need to invest. Sometimes intuition will lead to people or organisations with an interest in the subject matter of a program, but it can just as often be inspired guesswork or no more than luck.

The investment sector

A more structured approach might be through professional financial advisors or lawyers working in the merchant banking sector. This may involve making an offer to the public through a prospectus, a costly and well-regulated way of reaching investors. The requirements and cost of this may not be justified by the returns and, in any case, should not be attempted without appropriate professional advice. It's a high-risk approach with very low likelihood of return for someone with little experience, or insight, into the investment sector. The prime concern of investors is return on their investment, which takes place in two stages. Investors will look first for a tax break. Division 10BA of the Income Tax Assessment Act allows a 100% tax deduction on a certified Australian television or film production (see next section). The balance of the return on investment is revenue from marketing the completed program, as broadcaster acquisition, sales in the video or education market, or from associated merchandising and other ancillary activities, called back-end return.

The history of Division 10BA investment

In 1981, Division 10BA was introduced with the purpose of encouraging investors with a genuine interest in seeing the Australian film and television industry grow. It offered such generous tax concessions (150% tax deduction on investment and 50% deduction on earnings) that many investors had no interest beyond the tax breaks, unconcerned if the film (they were mostly feature films) was never released. Films of limited commercial and artistic merit were made and languished on the shelf, with no real likelihood of release, and Division 10BA developed a notoriety that has dogged it ever since. The deduction on investment was reduced to 125% and subsequently to 100%. Now that there is no windfall tax saving, opportunist investors are not interested, but production investment has had to cope with the lingering reputation. It is going through a slow rebuilding process.

The investment environment

Those who have trawled through the venture capital market for production investment funds know not to expect to find philanthropists in the private investment industry. Investors want to feel assured that their investment gets every chance of return, and that the risk is minimised. They want to see evidence that the production's controllers understand their business and know how to manage it, that they can provide detailed and credible revenue projections, that they are able to put appropriate controls in place and monitor the production process, and that they are able to track expenditure and provide reliable financial reports. They are not interested in reading scripts or getting excited about styles or technical innovation, simply because they do not regard themselves as equipped to evaluate those. They don't know what makes a good script. They are more interested in being confident that the people running the production have that skill. Investors, it would seem, are not interested in investing in something because it's creative or innovative. Their interest is whether it is a good business proposition. If it is, then whether it is art or dross is neither here nor there to them.

A frisson of glamour

The view of the financial sector as a cultural wasteland may be over-cynical or it may be the unglossed reality. Others are prepared to take a more wryly positive approach. Their view is that investors may be attracted to production investment over more conventional investment sectors because it gives them something more exciting to talk about at dinner parties. Actors and the process of production have much more conversational appeal than pine plantations or sewage disposal, even if their investment carries a higher degree of uncertainty. Investors would still want that risk minimised, the argument goes, and would want to feel assured it was prudently managed. They would be unlikely to acknowledge glamour as a factor, however, and it would be unwise to sell it as one. The social spin-off may only be secondary, but a producer should ensure anyway that investors get something personal out of the experience, if only because no-one likes to be taken for granted. Investors should not be ignored once they have parted with their money and it is good policy and good business practice to let them know how the production is progressing, organically as well as financially. An invitation on to the set allows them to feel a part of the process. If they're not interested, that's fine, and if they are, it adds to the possibility of further investment.

Investor order of returns

Whatever their passing romantic notions might be, investors are in the business ultimately to get the best financial return that can be negotiated, using whatever leverage is available to them. There is a view among private investors that they should not be sharing initial returns with government funding agencies on a *pari passu* basis. Rather, the agencies are seen as types of 'socialist' bodies with a cultural as much as a financial agenda. The investors' position is that they should recover their investment up front and only after that should other contributors – the government funders and intellectual property rights holders – share in the proceeds. This is an extension of the government agency view that investors, including themselves, should recoup their investment, principally if not completely, before the producer has a share of revenue.

Portfolio investment

A financing structure that might have more appeal to investors is an offer of a portfolio of production projects, rather than inviting investment in the productions individually. A suite of projects might be developed within a company, or as a partnership or joint venture, allowing investors to hedge their risk. They would bank on some productions doing sufficiently well to offset the ones that don't perform as well. In an industry where there's so much uncertainty about what projects will succeed, although there is good money to be made when they do, this opens up the opportunity to get it right in a package rather than relying on a single serendipitous choice. But whatever the financing structure they invest in, investors are looking to maximise their return in marketing and distribution of the program and its ancillary products, the second of the two stages of return on investment and the subject of Chapter 11.

8.8   Division 10BA and 10B tax deduction schemes

Deductions under the schemes

Division 10BA of the Income Tax Assessment Act provides a 100% tax deduction for an investment acquiring a copyright interest in a new Australian television program. The investment must be in production of the program, not financing, packaging or marketing, and the deductions are available only to Australian residents. Division 10B of the Act, which is available to resident and non-resident taxpayers, allows a 100% tax deduction to initial investors in units of industrial property (including television programs) over two financial years, starting when the program is first used to derive income. Division 10BA deductions can be more beneficial to investors, so their eligibility is far more stringent than that under Division 10B. This is the tax deduction scheme of prime interest to television producers.

Deductions against marginal tax rates

As it currently operates, tax deductions under Division 10BA are claimed in the year that the investment is made. Investors with sufficient assessable income benefit at the highest tax bracket, being otherwise required to pay 45% of the investment amount as tax. Similarly, a company investor would benefit from the 30% of the investment that would otherwise have to be paid as company tax. Any returns to the investor from sales of the program are taxable, but where a schedule of coming tax cuts is announced, as was the case with the 2005 budget, Division 10BA would enable investors to time-shift their tax burden.

Certification by DCITA

To qualify for a Division 10BA tax deduction, the project must be certified by the federal Department of Communications, Information Technology and the Arts (DCITA). Information sheets and application forms can be accessed via the DCITA website (see sources below). The form requires a budget, script or synopsis and a list of intended cast and crew. Tax cuts under Division 10BA are not available for development investment funding, or for a portfolio of projects, only for individual projects.

Criteria for certification

To be certified, the project must be an 'eligible film' and an 'Australian film'. Eligible films are feature films, telemovies, documentaries and mini-series, either serial or anthology, and no more than thirteen hours in total, except children's drama, which may be twenty-six hours in total. Specifically excluded are commercials, panel and quiz shows, variety, training films and public event programs. To qualify as an Australian film, the project must be wholly or substantially made in Australia with significant Australian content, or be an official co-production. Content is determined by creative control, subject matter, locations, residence of cast and key creative personnel, copyright ownership, and sources of finance. Projects with significant non-Australian content may be refused certification under Division 10BA, but not under Division 10B. Certification is also required for FFC funding, which can be acquired along with Division 10BA investment in the same project.

Authorisation of deductions by ATO

The producer applies first to DCITA for a provisional certificate, which must be issued before investment funds are spent. To secure the investor's deduction, a final certificate must be sought within six months of completing the program, and this should include a final budget, script and video of the program, and a statutory declaration. Finally, the program must be completed and in the marketplace within twenty-four months of the end of the financial year in which the investment was spent on production. Tax deductions are authorised by the Australian Taxation Office (ATO), not DCITA. However, the ATO accepts DCITA certification as prima facie evidence that it is eligible.

The 'at risk' requirement

The investment must be at risk, determined by the factors that are likely to reduce the loss to the investor if the program derives no income. A pre-sale, as a licence fee or distribution guarantee, is generally not considered to reduce the investor's risk because if the program is not delivered, the producer usually loses the fee. Non-tax-deductible investors, such as the FFC or the state agencies, cannot provide funds for investors to claim a Division 10BA deduction, but an investor can receive a loan to leverage up the deduction. The ATO will look closely at this transaction to see whether the loan is genuine, and whether the investor remains at risk of repayment of the loan, and at arm's length. If the investment is not at risk, it may still qualify for a deduction over two years under Division 10B.

Division 10B certification

Certification under Division 10B of the Act is more flexible. Programs must be wholly or substantially made in Australia and may be feature films, documentaries, mini-series, television series, short dramas, multimedia, promotional, variety, educational, training and large format projects. There must be significant Australian content, although there can be significant non-Australian content as well. There is no requirement that the investment be at risk, but under Part IVA of the Act, the main purpose cannot be to secure a tax benefit rather than to invest in a production with significant Australian content, however that might be determined. Films that qualify under Division 10B are not eligible for FFC funding.

Balance of financing for a project

Within a month of the end of the financial year in which the investment is spent, a declaration must be lodged with the ATO that there is a production contract with agreement on a budget. This document will specify investment funds received and money spent on production. Where a Division 10BA investment only partly covers the budgeted cost of producing the program, the producer must secure the balance of the budget before the end of the financial year in which production commences. If the other investors agree, the producer can underwrite a budget shortfall, or get a third party to underwrite it, with deferrals or a guarantee. There is nothing to prevent a producer raising further funds during production to enhance production values, although raising finance incrementally during production is not recommended. There is no longer a deduction on earnings, not even foreign earnings. The federal government will review the operation and effectiveness of Divisions 10B and 10BA to stimulate greater private investment in Australian films and television programs.

8.9   Film-Licensed Investment Companies

The FLIC scheme

A government-supported private investment scheme is available, at least in principle, for investment in television production. In practice, it is the product of lobbying by the feature film industry and its main focus is on investment in feature films, but an interest in investment in television projects with good profit potential would make sense. The Film-Licensed Investment Company (FLIC) scheme was introduced in 1998 with a 100% tax concession. An upper limit of investor revenue on which tax concessions will be allowed is set for each year of the licence period. Investors receive deductions for buying shares in a FLIC, which in turn is invested in qualifying Australian film and television projects. This differs from the Division 10BA and 10B schemes, which only gain tax concessions for investing in specific projects.

The licensees

The two original licensees, Capital Content Ltd and Macquarie Film Corporation Ltd, could raise up to $20 million capital over two financial years to June 2000, but found attracting finance difficult. In a new tender in 2005, only one FLIC, Mullis Capital Film Licensed Investment Company Ltd, was licensed. It was able to raise up to $10 million in 2005/06 and and again in 2006/07. It became The FLIC Company after the Mullis Capital Group withdrew from the company in 2006. Project eligibility for applying the concessional funds is determined by DCITA and includes adult and children's short-form drama, documentaries, short films, children's long-form drama and short-form animations. Projects in which the FFC has invested are not eligible.

8.10 Corporate investment

The types of company investment

Companies that might be interested in investing in a production fall into two principal groups: those with an interest in the program's subject matter and promoting public awareness of it, and those with an interest in participating in some part of the production process. The latter are generally production companies and may be broadcasters as well. Co-productions have their advantages and difficulties, as will be discussed later in this section. As noted in section 8.1, it is not uncommon for broadcasters to invest in production in addition to a pre-sale licence as part of its 100% funding of a production that would not attract funding from other sources. There might be a third group, namely companies with an interest in investing for equity in earnings from the production, but the risk here is generally high and the tax breaks are not as attractive as for private investment.

Commercial interest investment

The companies that could be interested in the subject matter of a program are as varied as the range of subject matter that a program might be about. It might be the actual subject of the program, as may be the case with documentaries, or an interest in the context or theme of the program, which is more commonly the case with drama. It might be a local company if the program has a regional setting, or a tourism promotional body if that location has potential to attract tourism. It might be an industry peak body if the program is likely to create public awareness of some commercial activity of the industry. Such investors will want to ensure that awareness will be beneficial to the industry. They are hardly likely to want to invest in an exposé story, even an exposé of a commercial rival. Such strategies have considerable risk of backfiring.

Public sector interest

Sometimes the corporation will be a government body if the subject matter or some other aspect of the program falls within its sphere of administrative responsibility. Some might have a track record of past funding of productions relevant to them. Over the years, CSIRO has funded a number of science-related documentaries. These things come in policy waves, and past willingness to contribute funds to production is no guarantee that an organisation will continue to do so. Other government instrumentalities are more likely to contribute resources for which the production would otherwise expect to pay. The Australian War Memorial, for instance, is more likely to assist with a waiver of archive costs than direct funding of a production. For the most part, this type of company investment is a form of sponsorship to promote a commercial or administrative interest. There is no need for these investors to receive equity in the project in return for their investment. Their return is the public awareness that flows from the program.

Production sector interest

The other source of corporate interest in a project is from a production company or production-related company that has an interest in sharing in the production for some equity in it, rather than for fee for service. An Australian production house is more likely to be a competitor, but a facilities house that supplies a specialised production service that is vital to the project may be persuaded to come in on it as an equity partner. An overseas production company is unlikely to be in direct competition and can have an interest in a co-production partnership where the co-producers have broadcaster clients in their own territories and an interest in sales to any other territories. Hilton Cordell Productions, now evolved into two different companies, has made a number of programs in co-production with overseas partners. Examples are the Irish–English–Australian production, *The Irish Empire*, with Café Productions (UK) and Little Bird (Ireland), and the French–Australian *The Hacktivists*, with Dominant 7. As co-producers, the partners would share editorial responsibility and may version the program for their respective territories.

Official co-productions

Some television projects can become 'official co-productions' with financing arrangements under the provisions of government-to-government treaties. Australia currently has co-production treaties with the United Kingdom, Ireland, Canada, Italy, Israel and Germany. Australia also has memorandums of understanding (MOUs) with France and New Zealand, under which projects may be treated as official co-productions. The treaties and MOUs require an overall balance of creative and financial elements across the co-productions. The AFC administers the International Co-Production Program and determines whether productions are eligible to qualify. Official co-productions benefit from the tax incentives that are available to eligible Australian films (see section 8.8) as well as incentives that are available in the foreign co-producer's territory. This dual access to incentives is a major attraction for entering into these arrangements. There are downsides as well that should be borne in mind when considering co-production. These include: the need to comply with two sets of legislation, and difficulties where the guidelines for the two countries are different; the need to spread elements of the production, including key personnel, over the partners' two territories; taking account of exchange rate movements; and the complexity of recoupment schedules.

8.11   Production funding contracts

Types of contractual agreements

When a party is persuaded of the value of funding a production, whether that's in the form of a licence fee or investment or a combination of these, negotiations follow to determine the terms and conditions for the agreement. The outcome of these discussions, as terms are agreed, will be reflected in a Production and Licence Agreement (PLA), a Production and Investment Agreement (PIA) or a Production Investment and Licence Agreement (PILA), depending on the nature of the funding. The term 'agreement' is commonly used. It is synonymous with 'contract' as generally understood.

When does a contract exist?

It is worth noting at this stage that the written 'contract' is not a contract in strict law, but evidence of a contract. A contract is the agreement on terms in the minds of the negotiating parties, not its expression on paper. The expression on paper is clear evidence of what those agreed terms are – otherwise they have to be inferred from the parties' behaviour. The main implication of this legal pedantry is that the assumption that there is no contract until the parties have signed the document is not correct. If one party has given the other to believe that there is agreement on terms (and the other can persuade a court of this) and the second party acts in reliance on that understanding, a court may well rule that a contractual relationship exists between them and that both parties are obligated under inferred terms of that agreement even though they do not yet have a mutually signed document. This appears to have been the situation between a broadcaster and the producers of one particular program. The broadcaster wanted to discontinue negotiation of the project, but proceeded when the producers threatened legal action after acting on an earlier undertaking that the production would go ahead. Fortunately, the program went on to be a major success for the network.

Negotiation of contracts

To return to the process of arriving at a production agreement, the parties will negotiate, horse-trade perhaps, sometimes exercise some brinkmanship and eventually arrive at a set of terms that are incorporated into a draft (and successive drafts) of the Agreement. Sometimes the terms are as expected, or the producers are too anxious about the outcome to argue the toss too much on the detail, and the negotiation takes place quickly. One party, often the broadcaster, who will have a legal department, drafts the Agreement. Lawyers for both parties then exchange comments on the draft. These will be incorporated into a redraft or rejected until the parties have a document that they are both prepared to sign. Issues under negotiation in a PLA include territories and repeat rights, rights to back-end exploitation of the program, rights to subsequent series, editorial rights and responsibilities, and anything else that either party deems important. Issues in a PIA include formulas for disbursement of program sales revenue, equity issues and producer accountability. The Agreement will also include a schedule of payments that will, in all likelihood, commence on signature of the contract. This schedule will enable cash flow of the production and, with cash flow, pre-production can commence. The description of this part of the production cycle is outlined in Part C.

8.12　Completion guarantee

Role of the completion guarantor

As noted earlier, many investors and particularly government funding agencies require the production they are co-funding to contract a completion guarantor. This serves as a sort of executive producer to ensure that the project will be completed on budget and on time, and will fulfil the technical requirements of delivery to the various interested parties. Completion guarantors in Australia are generally a local arm of an overseas company, with production management and legal expertise. A prospective completion guarantor will look closely at a project to determine its feasibility before committing to it as a guarantor. Having done so, it will monitor production as it progresses in consultation with the producer, and can do so as a disinterested party with no potential conflict of interest. The completion guarantor will continue to monitor progress until delivery of the program is completed in accordance with its distribution agreements.

Supervision and Completion Deeds

The documentation of a completion guarantee includes a Supervision Deed, between the completion guarantor, the production entity and the principal investor or investors, and a Completion Deed, between the completion guarantor and the investors. The Supervision Deed enables the completion guarantor to take control of the production if the producer will be unable to complete the program within the terms of the agreements that funded it or if the production company goes into receivership or ceases to exist. If necessary, the guarantor will provide additional funds to enable completion. This outlay will be recovered from any party that can be shown to have legal liability for it or else from revenue from exploitation of the completed program. In a Completion Deed, the completion guarantor undertakes to the investors, both equity investors and pre-sale licensees, to ensure completion of the program as contracted with them by the producer.

Creative management of the project

The completion guarantor does not have any responsibility to oversee the creative or editorial aspects of the program, only its production management. Within the constraints imposed by the guarantor, creative management remains in the hands of the program's producers, using their personal skills and those acquired by experience. The exercise of these skills is examined in detail in Chapter 9.

Sources and further reading

Specific reading

Film Finance Corporation Australia 2003, 'Doing business with the FFC', FFC Australia, Sydney.

Film Finance Corporation Australia, 'Investment guidelines', 2006/07, available online at <http://www.ffc.gov.au/investment>, viewed 18 December 2006.

Gonski, David 1997, 'Review of Commonwealth Assistance to the Film Industry', available online at <http://www.afc.gov.au/archive/afcnewspdf/156.pdf>, viewed 18 December 2006.

Magazine, newspaper and journal articles

Holding Redlich 2004, 'Film and Television Production in Australia', Holding Redlich, Melbourne.

Some internet references

Australian Film Commission, 'Filming in Australia – Tax & financials', available online at <http://www.afc.gov.au/filminginaustralia/taxfins/fiapage_28.aspx>, viewed 18 December 2006.

Department of Communications, Information Technology and the Arts, 'Film-Licensed Investment Company scheme', available online at <http://www.dcita.gov.au/arts_culture/funding_programs_and_support/film_licensed_investment_company_scheme_flics>, viewed 18 December 2006.

Department of Communications, Information Technology and the Arts, 'Film tax incentives – 10BA information sheet', available online at <http://www.dcita.gov.au/arts_culture/funding_programs_and_support/film_tax_incentives_10ba_and_10b/film_tax_incentives_10ba_information_sheet>, viewed 18 December 2006.

Chapter 9

Management of a creative project

As noted in Chapter 5, a producer of a television program is more than a person to keep tabs on resources and budget. Television production is an exercise in project management and this requires, among other things, people management skills. The people that have to be managed sometimes have idiosyncratic personalities. Massive egos can come into play. The television production pathway may sometimes resemble a manufacturing production line, but these are not process-line workers to be managed in a disciplined regimen of 'carrot and stick', even though the occasional subtle use of both carrot and stick might sometimes be a useful strategy. These are (hopefully) gifted professional people and among the tasks in the producer's leadership of the creative team is encouragement of them and providing the environment that allows them to produce their creative best. A good producer may draw more out of the individuals in the team than those people thought they had to contribute, with a combination of encouragement, cajoling, flattery and insistence at different times.

This chapter looks at the personal qualities that contribute to the making of a good producer and how they are exercised in the leadership and management of a creative team. They are relevant not only to interactions with members of the production team, but also with the people that producers deal with on behalf of the team – broadcasters, investors, potential contributors to the program, to name just a few. It involves a range of judgements about people and editorial strategies for which no right answers are written down anywhere. A producer's ability to manage a delicate balance of the professional and the personal is part of the recipe for success in their external relationships. The other side of the creative management coin is their ability to lead a production team and draw the best out of that team. It's not something that's been widely addressed in tertiary media education in Australia to date, yet ironically it is probably more inherently teachable than the current staple of media courses, craft creativity.

9.1   The qualities of a producer

An unpredictable industry

Certain qualities are central to the make-up of a capable producer. The television industry is not always logical or predictable. Audiences are constantly shifting ground in their tastes. The industry consists of sometimes erratic, sometimes visionary people who are trying to second guess the viewing public. Sometimes their greatest skill is peddling nonsense convincingly. It's hard to find objective and quantitative measures of good television, even in commercial television ruled by ratings. In this mercurial professional environment a producer needs to have determination and tenacity, the ability to keep plugging away. The process of developing projects for someone else's endorsement can be disheartening at times. Producers need to be able to soldier on, but also to know when the time has come to give a project away.

The positive qualities

On the more positive side, producers need to have good creative instincts and to be able to detect where the heart of the story is. They need to be resourceful and be able to think laterally, knowing what the production process is about (and also what they don't know and who can fill the gap until they do know) and what television audiences are about. They need the interpersonal skills to be able to negotiate with people and to resolve conflicts as they arise or threaten to arise. Producers need to be dogged, thick-skinned and persuasive. What could be simpler?

9.2   Choosing the right team

A reason for making a program

A program has to have a reason to be proposed. There might be an identified hole in a network's schedule, an enthusiasm to showcase particular talent, a writer's need to express a point of view, or a concept that is too attractive to be ignored. Any (or all) of these, and more, will provide an engine for a show to develop. The reasons for getting a team on board to pursue a program must be more than just money. The team must understand and want to make the idea. It must have a commitment to it and be able to bring a level of creativity and professionalism to its development and realisation. Producers exercise professional judgement in bringing the right team together to advance a particular idea, the right team for that idea.

Basis of choice of key creative personnel

Chapter 6 discussed the balance of director and writer functions in creating a narrative for the program and defining the style with which the narrative is to be treated. Most often, the writer is on the project before the director and may well be the originator of the concept. Among a producer's considerations in deciding whether to become involved in the project – apart from assessment of the concept's potential as a program – is whether the writer has the scripting skills to do justice to it. This is gauged from the writer's track record. Another crucial consideration, weighed up before inviting anyone to join the team, is how constructively the writer will work with the producer and with other key personnel. It is often more about personal chemistry than personality flaws, and creative judgements that are inherently subjective, but it is important that the team works collaboratively. People will often work with those with whom they have had a previous productive working partnership to reduce the risk of personal or aesthetic incompatibility.

Balance of director and writer

Sooner or later a director joins the development team but the director need not put their stamp on the production at this early stage. The director joins the producer in guiding the writing and providing a sounding board, while formulating thoughts on visual treatment of the script. Sometimes writers can be reluctant to let their baby fall into the grasp of another and may resist changes that appeal to the director. In the early stages, it's more likely that the producer will back the writer to enable the full extent of their input, but at some point the producer has to exercise a judgement about the right time to go with the director and leave the writer in the background. This can be a sensitive transition and must be handled with understanding so that the writer can accept that the script must be taken over by the director and taken into production. A script could be described as 'a working document'. It is the function of the producer to convince the writer of the practicality of that description as a professional necessity. Like so much else of the producer's role, this is a matter of managing interpersonal relationships and egos constructively.

9.3   Production team interaction

Conductor of the production orchestra

The production of television runs on relationships. It's an exercise in teamwork where a number of skilled people contribute their particular expertise towards the cooperative realisation of a program concept. When that works they build it up to something better than any one of them could have imagined or managed on their own. In one sense, it is an orchestra of production professionals, and the conductor of the orchestra is the producer. How the producer encourages each person's contribution to the enterprise and manages the creative interaction between individuals in the production team is crucial to the success of the program.

The guardian of the vision

The producer isn't the sole guardian of the vision. The metaphor of orchestra can be applied in another sense because the director also guides the creative realisation of the program, but in a more concentrated way. If the director is more correctly the conductor of the production orchestra (and it depends how narrowly 'production' is defined), then the producer is the manager of the orchestra company and the guardian of the vision of the enterprise, in this case the project. The director is then the guardian of the vision of the program, the outcome of the project. Sometimes, particularly in documentaries, producer and director are the one person, but for the most part they are separate people. The first relationship, therefore, to consider is the producer's relationship with the director.

Professional relationships

There are no hard and fast rules about how to relate to the people you work with and especially in a creative industry. There are, however, certain conventions that are worth keeping in mind. Generally, people find that they work in subtly different ways with different individuals, ways the two of them have evolved without thinking too consciously about it. Each way presumably relates to their different natures and the chemistry between these natures. If a working relationship with someone is productive, there is little reason to change it – or even ponder why it works. It just does! The best that can be offered on how to work with people is some rules of thumb that generally produce good working relationships.

9.4   The producer–director relationship

Producer and director working to a common end

The producer–director relationship illustrates the essence of professional creative relationships as well as any other relationship. The director is focused on making the best possible program and, in the ideal world, nothing should stand in the way of that. The producer, on the other hand, wants to manage the production so that it can be made *within the resources available to it*. But neither can achieve their objective without the other. They are like escapees from a chain gang still joined by leg irons. The astute producer will recognise that the director, no matter how unrealistic they might sometimes be about practical restraints, is essential to the producer's goal. The smart director will work out that the person who manages the finances and logistics of production is essential to the making of the program. Both objectives can be reached to the extent that there is a willingness to meet in the middle. The word 'compromise' is a reality in television production from which no-one should shy away.

The best possible program within the resources available

A brilliant program that cannot be finished through lack of money is an unhappy result for everyone; but a dull program on time and on budget is still a dull program. The objective that producer and director work towards is the best possible program within the resources available to it. It requires give and take on both sides and an understanding and appreciation of each other's role in working to this common goal. The director must realise that we don't live in a perfect world where all things that could contribute to the production are available to it. Producers need to ensure that directors are aware of practical reality, not by treating them as naughty, irritating children, but by explaining the restraints as they arise and seeking how best to meet the director's needs within those restraints. Any compromises should be in less essential components of the production so that the impact of reality's constraints on the finished program is minimised. The producer must build in the director's mind the confidence that this is the principle being followed and that these decisions will be consultative.

Trust

A major element then in the producer–director relationship is trust. Trust by the producer that the director has the visual, dramatic and/or editorial skills to make a program of considerable merit and appeal. Trust by the director that the producer will work to ensure that every possible resource that is within the production's capacity will be made available so that they can exercise their creative function to the best possible outcome. Like any relationship this is a two-way street, but there is additional responsibility on the producer, as leader of the enterprise, to ensure this mutual trust is generated and maintained.

Troubleshooting as a team

When problems arise centre stage, that is, on the shoot on the day, director and producer (and first assistant director usually) will confer on how best to deal with them. The director's involvement there is unavoidable. In the shooting of the final episode of ABC's *Winner Take All*, an integrated OB/studio drama, two of the OB days were virtually rained out and, since some of the leads were unable to extend beyond the contracted final studio day, extending the shoot wasn't an option. The viable options were discussed and a new schedule was arrived at, with two scenes able to be shot in rain under a verandah awning (appropriate weather for a story about a recent widow finding her expected inheritance had evaporated). One scene was reconceived in a studio set and added to the upcoming studio schedule and an extra OB day was scheduled instead of one of the two studio rehearsal days. With goodwill on all sides and lateral thinking, the revised schedule made the most of what was still available. When problems arise on the periphery, however, or in the planning stage, the optimum is for solutions to be found before the director becomes aware of them.

9.5   The team with a leader

Monitoring production progress

Various logistical upsets and people problems will arise, but they should not distract a director from their prime purpose any more than is absolutely necessary. The best outcome is where these are resolved before they can have a substantial impact on the production as a whole. This is achieved if the producer is perpetually monitoring the progress of production and its preparation, not by personally supervising every detail, but by encouraging each senior member of the production team to monitor their area's preparation and report regularly to the producer. When problems arise, senior staff should have been encouraged to exercise their initiative in dealing with them, but at the same time to consult with the producer and affected production personnel to ensure their solutions won't have detrimental impacts on other areas of the production.

Lateral thinking

Producers must be able to think laterally when dealing with problems or potential problems, but this doesn't mean that they are the person to come up with a solution to each and every problem. A culture of initiative and lateral thinking is encouraged where everyone in the production team feels empowered to, at least, offer suggestions on how to deal with emerging issues. This tends to be the norm in Australian production crews anyway, where there is less standing on the ceremony of hierarchies, so it is not difficult for a producer to make it known that this tradition is to continue in the current production.

Everyone has a part in the project's vision

An important quality in a producer's dealings with members of the production crew is their communication skill, the ability to articulate the project's vision to each member of the team and to emphasise the importance of that person's role in it. Producer John Eastway (*Grass Roots*, *Life Support*) says that everybody in a production, 'from tea lady to lead actor', should have a sense of his or her role in the production machinery and feel that their 'contribution' is a key part of making the program possible. Everyone involved should believe that they are an important cog in the creative machine, even if they are not the flywheel.

Crew sociability

A producer should be a conversationalist, be seen doing the rounds of all areas of the production, making sure that everyone knows where they fit into the production and what is expected of them, encouraging feedback on how things are going, chatting to all and sundry, not just about the detail of production (although that's the prime purpose) but also to maintain an atmosphere of convivial sociability. Keeping in touch and keeping a finger on the production pulse enables problems to be headed off as they arise instead of waiting till they grind production to a halt.

The vital leap

A concept in management theory that might give some insight into the producer's role is the 'vital leap'. When workers are promoted to a supervisory level, they have to engineer a change in mental attitude in themselves and in their former workmates. If they remain 'one of the boys', they can find it hard to exercise the authority sometimes necessary in supervision. If they are forcefully authoritarian, it is hard work maintaining that position. The ideal is to convey the authority (and be perceived to have it) without needing to force it on workers. Much of it can come from confidence in the role and the respect of the workers that can come from that. Supervisor and workers can maintain friendly relations so long as both know where the new boundaries are and respect those boundaries. The producer should have the personality that accompanies the vital leap. The rather democratic nature of Australian television production makes 'quiet authority' a better model than 'boss-man'. There will always be hard decisions that have to be made and the person vested with the responsibility to make them should do so.

9.6 Negotiation skills

Dealing with people outside the production

Relationships within a team revolve around ideas of collaboration and a common goal. Relationships with people outside the production team can have quite different characteristics. Central to them is often a negotiation process and generally it revolves around the pursuit of some resource the production needs and for which the supplier will be looking to get the best deal. That deal is often money, but not always. It might be promotion of a commercial or some other interest. It might be a desire to participate in the production. The negotiation might be to persuade someone to participate in a program. Although the dynamic of the interpersonal relationship has changed in moving outside the production group, a person's nature and personal style doesn't need to (if indeed that was possible), especially with contemporary ideas of the practical process of negotiation.

Mutual gains bargaining

Classic negotiation is the advocacy approach, often called win–lose negotiation, where an advocate for one party to negotiation attempts to obtain the most favourable outcomes possible, generally at the expense of the other party. This began to be superseded in the 1970s with a different approach called principled negotiation or mutual gains bargaining. The product of Roger Fisher and William Ury at the Harvard Law School, it looks at satisfying underlying needs rather than achieving stated positions. From their theoretical studies, a list of practical considerations has evolved as the basis of most successful negotiation in contemporary business.

Insights into self

What are some of the factors that can contribute to positive outcomes in negotiation by producers on behalf of their production? For a start, people negotiating should try to get a good insight into themselves, not only to understand their own nature, but also how other people see them. They should assess their personal feelings about negotiation, and whether they tend to give in too quickly or give away too much. Do they have a need to win at any cost, creating a negative and defensive relationship between the parties, or accept the pyrrhic victory of an outcome that is no longer of any value to them? They should develop the art of external listening when the negotiation discussions are underway. They should try to avoid conducting an internal dialogue with themselves about their next move when the other party is talking because they might miss some non-verbal message, a facial expression or a voice inflection.

Insights into the other party

Negotiators should try to infer the personal attitude of the other party to them from non-verbal signs (or verbal if they are there). Are they comfortable with them or do they seem to find them abrasive or unclear – or slippery even? Often off-hand, jokey remarks can have meaningful comments embedded in them. At the same time, they find out what they can about the people with whom they are negotiating from those who have done so in the past or by reviewing past encounters with them. What is their reputation? They should give some thought to how best to work with the insights they have about themselves and the other parties prior to the negotiation.

Negotiation with alternatives

Before they go into negotiation, they should work out their best alternatives to a negotiated agreement. What are their options? What other choices are there and what are their advantages and disadvantages? They should also anticipate what the other party's alternatives are likely to be, so that then they will be in a position to practise double think and triple think: don't just know what *you* want, anticipate what the other party wants and what they think you want. In other words, be the devil's advocate. They should go into the negotiation knowing what a positive outcome for themselves is. What is their best result and what is their worst result? The area in between is called the settlement range. The important principle to draw from this is: don't drop below your bottom line – know what point is the time to walk away from the deal.

Moving position to promote an outcome

Negotiators might state their position at the outset of the negotiation, but they aim to move beyond positions. They should build trust, honour commitments and respect confidences. By doing these, they avoid manipulation and suspicion masquerading as communication as parties manoeuvre their way around their mutual distrust. If they have avoided this, they are in a position to risk honesty and identify their true interests, leaving their original stated position behind. They can ask questions to reveal the needs and interests of the other party. In a supportive and open climate, answers will be more honest and outcomes more lasting.

Avoiding the other party feeling pressured

Negotiation should give the other party the feeling they have room to move, so they don't react to a sense of being pressured. In a *Four Corners* story about culpable driving causing death, in this case of the best friend of the young driver, the father of the dead boy was rung to ask if an interview with him could be filmed about the feelings of a family in a tragic event like this. Not surprisingly the father was not keen. The response was a suggestion that he should not make up his mind immediately in reaction to an unexpected telephone call but perhaps should talk it over with his wife before coming to a decision. It was put to him that sharing the experience could have a public benefit. He was told that he'd be rung back in a few days and that if they had decided no, he wouldn't be pursued any further on it. When he was rung a few days later, he said he'd talked it over with his wife and felt comfortable doing it. If instead he'd said no, there would have been no point in pressuring him further on it anyway.

Be philosophical and enjoy the negotiation

The above is a quick saunter through some of the guiding principles that are currently thought to underpin successful and meaningful negotiation. Negotiation often seems to come down to an exercise of power. A party to the negotiation might have a commanding position in some hierarchy or hold resources that are wanted, but this external power can fluctuate over time. Today's rooster is tomorrow's feather duster! People should be philosophical about the power relativities of the day and ensure they keep their personal power of self-esteem and self-confidence. These will see them through the process with no scars, whatever the outcome. Withdrawing from a negotiation that no longer offers anything useful is as professional as achieving the best result. It is not a defeat. If the outcome is disappointing, the next best option should be looked at. Most importantly, the business of television production should be enjoyable. No-one should let a hard negotiation take away their enjoyment.

9.7   Knowing how production works

Familiarity with each part of the production process

A successful producer will have an instinct for a good story, the ability to spot a good idea that can work on television. It is an instinct that builds out of experience, working on the innate editorial skill to recognise a fresh and engaging idea – or, more correctly, one that can be turned into fresh and engaging television. Experience teaches what audiences have liked and have not liked in the past, although it doesn't tell how they will respond to something they have not previously been confronted with. An understanding of genre will assist in appreciating how the idea might be realised as television, and a knowledge of the production process will inform whether that idea is indeed producible. Producers must know enough about the production process to know how to get an outcome. They need not necessarily have all the craft operational skills to carry out all aspects of production themselves, but they do need to know what outcomes are likely from each of these specialist personnel. Among other things, if they are going to lead a production team, they have to instil in them the confidence that they know where it is they are taking them and how they are going to get there. Even when the team's advice will be the means of getting there, they need to be aware of the general means of doing that and have an informed view of how feasible it is.

Expectations of the producer

Producers need to know what people both within and outside the production team expect from them so that they can make their decisions and provide their recommendations. Sue Murray is an executive producer of feature films, but her observations about the needs of financiers apply just as validly to television. They need to see you as a straight-shooter, she says, and will draw a view of this from casual conversations. They respect well-prepared and researched information. What doesn't work for them is deliberate misleading, withheld information, sloppy paperwork or a failure to meet deadlines.

A generic process with individual variations

Producing is not just about the application of general management skills. It is a particular craft that is built up from exercising the particular skills of television production. No two productions are the same so there is no single prescribed set of steps to take any given production through to bring it to completion. There is a generic process that has individual variations according to the particular needs of each production. The producer constantly assesses the status of the production and makes professional judgements of what adjustments need to be made to keep it on track. This will not work without the producer having a thorough and detailed knowledge of the production process.

9.8   Networking

Keeping in touch and forming alliances

Interaction with people outside the production team is not just a matter of negotiation for specific outcomes. It can also take the form of networking, keeping in touch with people who might have some future usefulness to production, and maintaining a profile within the industry. In a business where so many judgements must have at least an element of subjectivity – much of television doesn't lend itself to objective analysis in advance of its creation – it is useful to position yourself to benefit from that. There is an element of 'it's not what you know but who you know' that lurks in the television industry. People form alliances of mutual self-help, not necessarily to the extent of supporting a bad idea, but there is always some uncertainty about whether an idea is good. Producers work on creating an environment where they get the benefit of whatever doubt there is from positive personal perceptions of them.

Being seen as part of the industry

To be seen as part of the industry is established, at least in part, by networking, by doing the rounds of industry events and hobnobbing with peers sufficient to maintain cordial relations. It's easier to make a positive decision about someone when you have a positive impression of them as a person as opposed to no real impression at all. Their assessment will still be principally on any proposition's merit and their expectation of your ability to fulfill it (or it should be), but their view of the person behind it can influence that assessment and often tip the scales in its favour. There is an expectation that producers who are well-grounded in the industry have the ability to maintain that level. People always prefer talking to people they know than people they don't know. Some producers have established their business to the point that they seldom have to offer a concept document as the first step to project development, but know in advance from conversations with broadcaster contacts, usually over a meal and several wines, that their interest is in a particular concept. Of course, the relationship with these people has to be developed first before a producer can get to this degree of contact. It's not a development that can be pushed easily beyond its natural speed of progress. Too unsubtle a pursuit of industry contacts can be counterproductive. One does not want to become known as a 'serial networker'. Even the most hardened industry cynic wants sometimes to feel that people are interested in them for their personal qualities rather than just for what benefits will flow from knowing them.

9.9   Building a business

Collaborative relationships

Networking has a second role apart from building potential future sales, and that is to prepare the ground for future collaborative relationships. Producers don't just look for jobs. They create jobs. They should be in the business of building businesses. A flow-on from the need to have several projects in development (and hopefully some in production) is to keep open the possibility of projects involving partnerships with a range of people with differing expertise. If this results in some productions going ahead, there may then be the opportunity to establish the core of a business with a small team as business management and office support, a joint executive producer perhaps and some key creative personnel who work frequently on projects with the group. A good example in the Australian industry is the building of the business Beyond International on the back of the magazine program *Beyond 2000*.

A core of mutual support

Such relationships should not develop into a closed shop, but should include a mix of people with ongoing roles and people with particular expertise who come in on particular projects. Broadcasters and investors both have an interest in the production entity in which they are investing having some business solidity. If it is only one person hiring individuals for each task, they may have reservations. A core group who is part of a working team will give them more confidence in the business skills and the ability to deliver. Another advantage of working collaboratively with fellow industry professionals is that there is a quid pro quo of favours. An editor with whom a producer works frequently is likely to be quite happy to put together a show reel for them during development of a future project.

Producer initiative and enterprise

Unlike in America, where many directors in cinema have production companies, Australian directors mostly do not create businesses. They are 'guns for hire', many moving between feature films and television drama as the work becomes available. This puts the onus on producers to take the initiative in creating businesses rather than being producer 'guns for hire'. Enterprise must start somewhere and producers are the more logical people to do that. The enterprise issue is different in documentary, where many of the senior players will both produce and direct, either simultaneously or on separate occasions. The problem here is that the documentary sector is crowded and this makes it difficult to build a business. A partnership between producer and director is one way of building some project critical mass, although this is often with partners who would otherwise be competitors.

9.10   Ethics

The need to think through ethics in advance

It might surprise some to see a heading of 'ethics' in a book about the business of television production, but producers need to decide what their general positions are on the range of ethical issues that will inevitably arise in the process of developing and making television programs. It is not the intention here to instruct would-be producers in what their specific ethics should be, but it is to alert them to the need to think through where they stand on some of the more likely issues in advance of being confronted with them.

An example of the ethical decision

During pre-production of the controversial ABC documentary about policing in Redfern, *Cop It Sweet*, the producer grappled with a concern that the people they would film in Redfern might think that they were associated with the police because the film crew would appear on the scene behind them and with their obvious agreement. The executive producer assured them that this was what the Redfern residents would think and that if this disturbed them, they should ask themself whether they were able to make the documentary. If the producer went ahead, they would have to accept that reality of people's assumptions and live with this knowledge. The production went ahead and was an eventual critical success.

Ethical decisions outside the guidance of the law

Production is full of such decisions. Some of these decisions are determined by law, making them relatively easy to decide. There is statutory law about copyright and defamation, which determines what you cannot use without permission and what you cannot say. There is common law about confidentiality, which determines what you cannot do with information shared in business confidence. These issues are all covered in Chapter 25. But no law advises on where chequebook journalism, the propensity of current affairs programs to pay people, some of them unscrupulous ratbags, for exclusive access to their sordid story, should draw the line. Anyone who is working in factual programming will, from time to time, be confronted with the question of the right to privacy protecting people from the camera poking into their personal lives. One can take the existential view that these are moral choices that every individual has to make using their own moral framework as a guide. A correct moral framework cannot be imposed on others, but producers should arrive at their own framework to guide them when confronted with the dilemmas of professional ethics in production.

9.11   Risk taking and commercial prudence

The network commissioning executive's view

Producers need to understand the environment in which they are working and where external stakeholders' interests lie. Network executives occupy relatively well-paid positions with a regularity of income for at least the duration of their current contract and further if their contract is renewed. Non-renewal can result from a disastrous program (in network terms) slipping through on their watch. It wouldn't matter if it were an honourable failure, an attempt to push the envelope that didn't pay off. There's no such thing in the network lexicon. It would still be a failure and the executive's name would be permanently attached to it in the network's eyes. It probably makes little difference these days whether the broadcaster is public or commercial. On the other hand, a series of unremarkable programs that pick up an average audience would be seen as fine. Peter Herbert, an independent producer now at AFTRS, has a scenario that encapsulates the network environment: a producer is trying to sell an excitingly fresh program idea to a commissioning executive. The producer thinks they are offering the executive a marvelous program opportunity, but the executive is thinking: 'Will this be the person who costs me my job?'.

Innovation without risk

The business of television production in Australia is a paradox. It is an industry constantly crying out for exciting new ideas and, at the same time, is extraordinarily risk averse. It is reluctant to commit to a project unless someone has already made a fairly similar program that has already been successful. But the excitement of taking risks and pursuing exciting new ideas is often what attracts people into the industry. Push too far into the unknown and you may find you are there by yourself. Hold back from the opportunities and you will not have got out of the industry what it is capable of providing. Perhaps the solution is a balanced slate of projects, some risky, some safe. Perhaps it's a fine judgement of how far the risk-taking can be pushed within the restraints of commercial prudence. An exciting program is not so exciting if no-one wants to fund its production.

Sources and further reading

Specific reading

Shell, G. Richard 2000, *Bargaining for Advantage: Negotiation Strategies for Reasonable People*, Penguin, New York.

Ury, William 1993, *Getting Past No: Negotiating Your Way from Confrontation to Cooperation*, Bantam Books, New York.

Ury, William, Fisher, Roger, Patton, Bruce 1991, *Getting to Yes: Negotiating Agreement Without Giving In*, Penguin, New York.

Chapter 10
Multi-platform projects

For all its desire to be creative, to reflect the society it finds itself in, and to pursue other worthy and intellectually satisfying ends, television production is a business. Its producers look for people and organisations to fund production so that they can earn a fee from their participation in it and, in many cases, share in profits from commercial exploitation of the program produced. The financers of the production invest in it to share in the expected profitable return from marketing the program when it is made, or so that they can broadcast the program to reap advertising revenue (if they are a commercial channel), or to fulfil their obligation to subscribers (if they are a pay channel), or fulfil their statutory obligations (if they are a public broadcaster).

The first phase of generating return on investment is to license the program to as many broadcasters around the world as can be secured (see Chapters 8 and 11), some of whom contract by way of pre-sale to buy the program in advance of it being made, and so contribute to the production's funding. The next stage of marketing is to find other means of delivering the program to audiences apart from broadcast, which might mean cinema release, or videocassette (VHS) and DVD sales. A third marketing outlet, under the general umbrella term of new media, is growing in importance as new options in this broad category continue to emerge. This doesn't put the program itself on the market, but takes the content of the program, both media and subject matter, and refashions it as a different 'program' for delivery on technological platforms other than broadcast television or a diffusion service such as cable. It is in the investors' interests to pursue every avenue of market exploitation of the product in which they have entrusted their funds, no matter how indirect that might be.

There's nothing new in this, or in the concept of multi-platform exploitation of a program's concept, although the description of it as 'multi-platform' is recent, and has grown out of the escalating jargon of digital media. Merchandise

172

associated with a program has been considered for some time, and continues to be. The growth is in the range of emerging technologies and delivery modes generated from the new digital media. Some of these have market futures that are still highly speculative, despite the number of future-gazers who will confidently predict their ascendancy, as already noted in Chapter 2. However, skepticism notwithstanding, there are people and organisations interested in exploring the potential of new delivery modes. And no matter how inaccurate some predictions may turn out to be, one thing is certain. There will always be new technologies that do ascend, whether they were predicted or emerged when no-one was looking.

It is in the interest of producers and their financial backers to examine the potential for a program concept to be adapted to products other than a linear television program. Early attempts at this had been to refashion (or re-version) the television program itself to other products, but media produced for television broadcast isn't always the most suitable for other modes of delivery. Although other modes will use much of the information researched and media recorded for a television program for their own purposes, they will have additional needs for purpose-created material. An interactive website, for instance, might make use of media captured on a 360-degree camera, something for which a television shoot would have no place. It could be included, along with other website-specific requirements, if this platform got investor backing. For this reason, it is prudent to plan for cross-platform products to be part of the development of the project as a whole.

10.1   Established merchandising

Publications

Producers and broadcasters of programs have long looked at the commercial and promotional potential of their programs with an associated book or some other publication. This can be particularly successful with lifestyle series, *Burke's Backyard* and *Gardening Australia* being two well-known examples among many. Documentary research content can often be recycled into a non-fiction book, but drama has much less success in publishing spin-off. Fiction doesn't always translate well from video to prose form, although sometimes in non-fiction a prose version of past events is easier without the challenge of having to find a means of visualising them. Some drama programs are adapted from a pre-existing novel. A successful television drama series can generate a second wave of sales for that book. If a publishing spin-off from a program is envisaged, the decision should be made early in the project's development. Writing and publishing a book can often take longer than producing a television program, and the spin-off is best exploited when it is released at the time that the program is broadcast.

Children's merchandise

More recently, there has been a growth in other merchandising spin-off from television programs. Children's programs have the potential for lucrative market exploitation with associated toys and other merchandise. Ninja Turtles, Power Rangers and Bananas in Pyjamas have all found a place in children's bedrooms and hearts, and produced additional investment returns to program producers. *Teenage Mutant Ninja Turtles* originated as a cult comic book in 1984, published by Mirage Studios as a parody of the long-form comic, *Ronin*. The animated television series followed in 1987, produced by Murakami-Wolf-Swenson, and during its run Playmates Toys produced action figures, vehicles, play sets, and accessories, followed by Nintendo video games in 1989. *Mighty Morphin Power Rangers* was broadcast from 1993, accompanied by the associated marketing of action figures and other branded paraphernalia. *Bananas in Pyjamas* began as a component in ABC's *Play School*, but its popularity triggered a separate show, with merchandising of games, toys and clothing with Bananas in Pyjamas branding.

Accessory merchandising

Adult programming has also supported a range of accessory merchandising. Branded clothing, such as T-shirts, is sometimes used to publicise a program, but it can also be sold successfully given the right program and the right product. Fat Pizza T-shirts and caps sold well through the internet off the back of SBS's *Pizza*, at a time when e-commerce was struggling to work. This was low-priced wear for an enthusiastic audience that turned into a market. The most conspicuous success of accessory marketing can be seen when it is associated with a program with a younger following, such as *The Simpsons* or *South Park*. There's no real limit to what might get program branding and sell well. It's a matter of good market judgement and maybe an element of luck, much the same as any other retail enterprise. It inevitably needs the program to be a broadcasting success. The market is unlikely to respond to products branded with a program it hasn't seen or doesn't like.

Telephone merchandising

Another venture that can successfully and lucratively attach itself to a television program is the marketing of telephone traffic. Many programs will be extended with a rudimentary interactive element (see Chapter 2), where viewers ring in and vote on something, either for a prize (Nine's Classic Catches in its cricket coverage) or to participate in an outcome (voting participants off a reality program such as *Big Brother* or *Australian Idol*). The number of telephone calls can be enormous on a high-audience program, and revenue from telephone call charges are generally shared between production, the broadcaster and a telecommunications company (telco).

10.2   Online platforms

Early website attachment to TV programs

The internet provides an online platform for video and related content. Generally known as interactive websites, they often require broadband connection.

Setting up program content on a website is the most established use of new media platforms, but it has gone down a bumpy path and taken some time to find directions that might prove productive. Websites such as the video-sharing <www.youtube.com> are popular and exciting, but they involve the free exchange of material, not commercial enterprise.

The early approach to website use in conjunction with a television program was to regard it as a publicity vehicle for the program, and a repository for unused research and footage. The former was as a result of most early program websites being located on a broadcaster's website, the latter in the largely mistaken belief that people who enjoy a program will be interested to see the material that wasn't considered good enough to go into the program. The next wave of online development was through people with a vision that interactive broadband was going to turn the media industry upside down. They wanted to get in at the front end. A lot of 'crazy money' was blown in the early stages, but the objectives have narrowed, and a glimmer of a productive future is starting to emerge. Government bodies are still interested in the exploratory development of new media, but the marketers are returning their focus to the bottom line.

Advertiser interest

New electronic platforms are testing the waters to find where the markets are. The question for the entrepreneurs of new media is how to drive viewers to money-making platforms. The greatest commercial interest at the moment seems to be in gaming, gambling and sport. There is an observable drift of advertisers from non-television media, and online advertising is starting to yield returns where there is a match between its users and the advertiser's market. It's a matter of looking for the right sponsor, and infotainment programs seem to be particularly suited to commercial sponsorship. The website for SBS's *Who Do You Think You Are?*, a celebrity genealogy program, will be used by Ancestry.com to sell its genealogy services to user subscribers. Prospero Productions' *Eco House*, a competitive greenness reality program, will look for green image sponsors, such as state utilities, for the interactive website that will accompany the television series. Essential Viewing's *Is Your House Killing You?*, about alternative products, will look for housing industry advertisements and product placement on the associated website.

The UsMob example

The Australian broadband project, UsMob, shows how to manage a multi-platform project to take advantage of the strengths of each platform. Set in the town camps of Alice Springs and telling Aboriginal and youth stories, the project was conceived by director, David Vadiveloo. In addition to a television series for ABC's digital channel, an immersive, interactive site was produced by Adelaide-based Katalyst Web Design. The project targeted 8- to 14-year-old viewers, and the website design process was started by exploring how that age group used online sites. The original home page that was developed showed a 360-degree outback scene with an abandoned car. Entry to the website was by clicking on a car door, duplicating the challenge enjoyed by this age group. Although the website has now been updated, once in it, viewers follow multi-path storylines, activating video and text diaries, and participating in forums and games offering a virtual experience of the town camp and surrounding deserts. Participants can also upload their own video stories to the website. Part of the success of the project, according to David Vadiveloo, was in partnering with a smaller but committed website design group and, as a result, designing the website on its own merits, not as an extension of an associated television series.

Development of the website concept

Although an online project is assembled as fragments that can be visited in any order, unlike the linear structure of a television program, the success of an interactive website is still dependent on having a good story to tell. SBS Manager of Digital New Services, Paul Vincent, says, 'You should ask yourself what's the hook in the program that makes me interested in doing more? That hook should then become the website concept'. It's a mistake to make the website too comprehensive. Rather, the website should cater for a need created by the television series, and make sure that this is done well.

It's important that the decision to pursue an online platform as part of a production project is made at the development phase of the television program. Partnerships in production should be sought at this stage. Funding for the website can then be sought as part of the investment package. This gives time for the website to be developed as a separate entity from the program, not as an add-on, and for material to be shot as content for the website, even if it is not needed for the television program. An example is the previously noted 360-degree camera shot, often used in website design. Media specifically for a website is generally more efficiently gathered at the same time as the same subject matter is shot for the program.

Proof of concept

The usual form for a website proposal is as a sample of the main elements of the website, called a 'proof of concept' (POC), with a written proposal, a main menu linked to a sample page or video, artwork in a portable document format (PDF), video material, and a flow chart of the architecture of the website. The POC is an online equivalent of a television pilot, and should demonstrate the production values of the project, reflecting the core concept and working elements of interactivity. Funding for purely artistic online projects is limited to the AFC, the state agencies and the Australia Council for the Arts and, even then, they encourage partnership with a third party investor, such as a telco interested in R&D or content distribution, or a gallery or community group. Private sector investors will require a business plan to indicate how revenue will be generated. This has been discussed above regarding lifestyle program sites. Internet service providers and telcos might be interested if there is a possibility of generating high hit rates on their websites.

10.3   Mobile (hand-held) platforms

The mobile developments

In recent years there have appeared on the market, or are appearing, hand-held mobile platforms for delivering video content. Adoption of video content by 3G mobile phones has been more cautious than the big online hopes in the middle of the dot-com explosion. Alternatively, media can be downloaded onto a video-enabled iPod, used as a portable PVR, and replayed at will. The new player in mobile platforms is DVB-H (see Chapter 3), which uses a broadcast signal, not telephony, and allows proper interactivity with a back-channel, making it attractive for betting use. Here the receiver picks up the signal, and can double as a mobile phone. The 3G mobile phone must dial in to a portal to get the signal. The Bridge Networks, owned by Broadcast Australia, trialled DVB–H with Telstra in 2005–06, offering fifteen channels to 400 handsets. Preliminary findings reveal content to be important, suggesting screen size is not a great issue, and viewing sessions to be twenty-five minutes long on average.

Video content on mobile phones

It's mostly in the 3G mobile network that mobile content delivery is currently being explored. Although still quite speculative, it's much more driven by marketing and corporate product strategies than its online relatives were at the same stage of development. Overseas, much of the content is tie-ins with popular television shows and sporting highlights. In the United Kingdom there have been picture slide stories from the teen soap, *Hollyoaks*, and 'behind the scenes' shots from *Celebrity Big Brother*, ITN news updates, and 'today in history' clips from their extensive archive. Vodafone has offered twenty-four 60-second 'mobisodes' (mobile-delivered episodes) based on the television series, *24*, but written and shot exclusively for the 3G mobile network. Frank Chindamo makes mini-comedies for mobile platforms in the United States. He has made short, two to five minute comedies for pay television since 1999, and one of his videos was demonstrated on a mobile (cell) phone at an industry conference in 2003. The following year, he had a deal to run a content aggregator channel, Fun Little Movies, on the Sprint Vision wireless phone network. In 2005, he launched *Love Bytes* on the network, a mini-comedy about internet dating made for mobile delivery.

Mobile video in Singapore

Closer to home, Singapore mobile operator, M1, has offered a range of video content since mid-2005 through twenty different channels on its Watch-a-Video service. This has included live streaming of Channel News Asia, celebrity interviews and other entertainment programming, a serial drama (*PS . . . I Luv You*), a thriller made for the 3G mobile network (*POV Murder*), and a drama serial adapted for mobile from the Mandarin television drama, *Love Concierge*. It is too early to judge the success of these products, sourced from television or imitating television product, but there are doubts about whether this is the best approach. If it isn't, television producers will need to think through their strategy carefully if they are to tap successfully into this market as part of a multi-platform project.

Challenges for mobile carriers

In Australia there are over eighteen million mobile phones, 62% of which can access multimedia services. Mobile carriers are under threat from the lower cost of competitors, such as Voice over Internet Protocol (VoIP) telephony. They need to build content value to confront the challenge. Fear of high data charges may discourage Australian consumers from off-portal options, so that the most successful content sellers will be found on carrier portals. A producer is best served working with mobile content aggregators with existing relationships with telco carriers. Pre-existing content often fails to excite on mobile phones. Putting television or website product on the mobile phone doesn't seem to work in the long run, once the novelty has worn off. It appears it should be tailor-made, appropriate to the audience, and not available elsewhere. If the mobile platform is to flourish, carriers must probably find or develop content that can exist on 3G mobile phones in its own right, similar to the approach now pursued for online content.

The accent is on mobility. Output from widespread video cameras showing Bondi surf or traffic at major city intersections, along with goal-mouth action and fall of wickets in sports content, are all indicative of new content experiences that might be well provided by mobile platforms. The prevailing wisdom is that this medium will only work with snack-sized programs, but research is suggesting that this is not necessarily true. As with wireless phone handsets, people will walk around the house with a mobile television and happily watch it for half an hour.

A new grammar of mobile content

The mobile medium, ultimately, is still about storytelling, and about finding what forms of content make sense for audiences on the move. It may be that television grammar will not work on a tiny screen and a new grammar will have to be found. In the meantime, some practitioners, such as Frank Chindamo, have assembled some basic rules for producing mobile content:
- Content needs to be in series form to gain traction with consumers.
- Producers should try to wrap it around a product or service, in order to bring in sponsorship.
- An episode must be able to tell its story in two to three minutes.
- Don't shoot on a mobile phone, but shooting from a mini DV camera or better is fine.
- Don't pan quickly.
- Don't clutter the visuals or the acoustics.
- Use large, screen-friendly fonts and text colours (primary colours show up well on the tiny screen).
- Use a black background where possible.
- The vision needs close-ups and therefore good actors.

- Make scenarios and settings interesting and avoid subtlety.
- Use locations extensively.
- Physical comedy works better than dialogue comedy (and travels better).

10.4 Range of rights

Securing rights for future media use

New digital media is an area of enormous change and unpredictability. The 'next big thing' never materalises, and something instead comes out of left field, dominating the media landscape before we realise it's there. With these potential exploitable media, not yet known to us but just around the corner (maybe), it's important that a producer secures as wide a range of rights in the material that will be incorporated in the project's content for as long as possible. The ideal rights term is: 'in all media, whether now known or yet to be devised, throughout the world in perpetuity'. This allows for the possibility of extending the life and value of the project's intellectual property. It's a question of what to do with website and other material which is associated with a television program that is past its 'use-by' date. If platform content has been designed for the merits of its medium, then it can have a life beyond the television program. Producers should make sure they have the rights to re-contextualise media and materials outside the original product. If that means sharing the spoils with investors, that's not a bad thing. It encourages future investment.

Sifting opportunity from future speak

The prime message about new media, multi- or cross-platform, or multimedia – call it what you will – is that it is developing, and therefore both experimental and speculative. It attracts a number of grand visionaries, who will talk up a storm and move on when the storm doesn't materialise. But at the same time, there are emerging commercial possibilities for the canny producer with a practical nose for marketing opportunities. Some of the delivery platforms are starting to show signs of their potential, whereas in others the lack of real progress gets buried in the buzz of future-speak jargon. It's a matter of picking the right opportunity and developing it in a business-like procedure.

Sources and further reading

General reading

Flew, Terry 2005, *New Media*, 2nd edn, Oxford University Press, Melbourne.
Gillezeau, Marcus 2004, *Hands On*, Currency Press, Sydney.

Specific reading

Lugmayr, Artur, Niiranen, Samuli, Kalli, Seppo 2004, *Digital Interactive TV and Metadata: Future Broadcast Multimedia*, Springer-Verlag, New York.

Magazine, newspaper and journal articles

Kaufman, Debra 2006, 'Are pint-sized films a big business opportunity?', *Film & Video*, available online at <www.studiodaily.com/filmandvideo/currentissue/6287>, viewed 18 December 2006.
Yiacoumi, Roulla 2006, 'Get the picture', *The Age* 19 January.

Some internet references

Ancestry.com, available online at <www.ancestry.com>, viewed 18 December 2006.
Romney, Jason 2006, '21st century mobile content and services', AFTRS Centre for Screen Business, June, available online at <www.aftrs.edu.au>, viewed 18 December 2006.
UsMob, available online at <www.usmob.com.au> or <www.abc.net.au/usmob>, viewed 18 December 2006.
YouTube broadcast yourself, available online at <www.youtube.com>, viewed 18 December 2006.

Chapter 11

Marketing and distribution

Usually a program is offered in the marketplace two times. First, it is offered as a program proposal, for broadcaster pre-sale among other production funding sources, as a means of cashflowing the cost of production. This was the subject of Chapter 8. A broadcaster will commit contractually to rights in the program when it is made in return for securing those rights exclusively for its territory. Most commonly, the commitment comes initially from a local broadcaster, as a result of which the possibility of an overseas broadcaster or investor being prepared to commit to the project increases. If no other funding source is secured, the first broadcaster may consider an equity investment in the production on top of the pre-sale, or it might decide to withdraw from the project. The reason a broadcaster commits to a program that has not yet been made, rather than waiting until it is completed and can be assessed, is primarily to assist the program get funded, and thus ensure it is able to be made. It also enables the broadcaster to have an input into the program, so it best fits its schedule needs. It is hard in Australia to raise the full budget for a television production. Without broadcaster pre-sale, the majority of Australian programs would never be made. As noted in Chapter 8, the program may also be offered to a distributor at this time, to seek a financial commitment for the rights not acquired by the local broadcaster. The attachment of an international distributor is also important for a producer who wishes to approach a federal or state funding body for top-up funding.

The second time a program is offered to the marketplace is as a completed program. Any residual broadcast rights, that are not tied up in pre-sale or by a distributor, are available for purchase at this stage, which is known as acquisition. It would be offered to much the same list of broadcasters that might have been approached for pre-sale, although not usually to the same section of the broadcaster. The program proposal is submitted to the commissioning arm, the finished program to acquisitions. Ironically, broadcasters will pay less for acquisition, when they can see exactly what they are buying, than for pre-sale, where they buy on the aspirations of a proposal document. The ability to have input into the product is increasingly valuable to broadcasters. The pre-sale price must be high enough to ensure that, with investors or other pre-sales, the project will be sufficiently funded to proceed to production. Past experience is an indicator of what level this needs to be. Where it might be an investor, the FFC now dictates the proportion of budget to be covered by pre-sale, and the amount of distributor's attachment it requires. Acquisition, on the other hand, need cost no more than the market value of the program, which is little more than what competing broadcasters, if there are any, are prepared to pay. There is no need to worry about whether the production will find its funding, since the program has already been made.

This chapter is about the second round of marketing a program, by offering the finished program to broadcasters, and other parties interested in securing some of its uncommitted rights.

11.1 Marketing options

The distribution option

There are two options for approaching the television market. One is to work through a distributor or sales agent who has marketplace experience with the type of program that has been made. The other is for producers to market it themselves. The advantage of working through an agent is that they have a good working knowledge of the marketplace, and have established useful sales contacts overseas, many of whom are difficult to meet as a do-it-yourself (DIY) marketer who is not well established. Agents attend the international markets and are in the business of monitoring marketplace trends. Sometimes, they can package programs with others on their books to enhance sales. Association with a distributor with a strong programming catalogue brings with it access to potential buyers that a DIY marketer may not be able to reach. The disadvantage is that there is a distributor commission, usually 30%, which producers will keep if they go the DIY marketing route. There will be marketing costs due to the distributor's expenses in canvassing the market that producers will need to offset, but the DIY marketer will also generate costs, and these cannot be amortised as effectively as with the distributor's larger slate of programs.

Distribution expenses

A distribution agreement will generally allow both commission and marketing expenses to be deducted from gross receipts, the former being a percentage of gross receipts, the latter a calculated amount. The marketing expenses are effectively deducted from the balance after the distribution commission, so there is no real incentive here for a distributor to contain marketing costs. However, with the possibility that sales won't eventuate and costs will come from their pocket, the distributor will usually cap expenses to ensure that they will be able to recover them from the sales they think they might make. It is prudent, nonetheless, for a distribution agreement to cap marketing costs. The producer needs to decide which is likely to be more remunerative: save the distributor commission and contain marketing expenses, with the risk of unfamiliarity with the market, or view commission and potentially greater expenses as a fair price for market knowledge and contacts, and time spent in pursuing them. By and large, the advantages of a distributor's experience and economies of scale far outweigh the disadvantages. The AFC provides a list of distributors and sales agents on its website (see sources below).

Marketing to the viewing public

Producers need to be clear to whom they are marketing their program. The natural assumption is that they are selling it to the viewing public, but this is not really the case. In fact, they are marketing to broadcasters who, if they buy the program, will in turn market it to their potential audience to maximise viewers for their investment in the program. Any attempt by the producer to sell the program to the viewing public is probably largely wasted effort and expense, or at best doing the broadcaster's work. A broadcaster is unlikely to thank a producer for this. Rightly or wrongly, broadcasters believe they know best how to reach their audience, and a producer taking over this function is generally not appreciated. What the broadcaster does want from a producer is the materials to assist in running an effective publicity campaign for the program. These are dealt with in the next section.

Marketing budget

The production budget should include a marketing budget. Even if the program will be sold through an agent, there will be costs to the production in providing materials to support the agent in selling it, as well as publicity materials for a network that has bought it, so that it can promote its broadcast of the program. If producers intend to market the program themselves, they will incur further costs in doing so. An agent would recover much of the marketing expenses from sales. Where marketing expenses are not contained within the production budget, this limits the sources of such funding for the completed program. The AFC might invest in the program's marketing, or the producer could seek additional funding from its investors. It might be to their commercial advantage to provide it, given that their return on investment doesn't come until the program is out in the marketplace, but they won't necessarily be happy to have been put in that position. Otherwise, the producer may have no option but to find a sales agent interested in distributing the program.

11.2   Publicity materials

Publicity kit

Every project requires a publicity kit of some sort to provide for the publicity needs of its broadcasters and also to market it to broadcasters. The kit might include: preview copies of the program on VHS or DVD (increasingly the latter, and remembering that the North American market operates in NTSC); program details such as duration, gauge, genre and major credits; one-line, one-paragraph and one-page synopses; background information about the program and anecdotes about the making of it; any awards or favourable press reviews; biographies of key cast, director, writer and producer; contact details of the producer or the production company; and ten or more still photographs relating to the program and its production. Conventionally, the press kit is printed and bound, but producing multiple copies of a glossy document with an attached video can get expensive. The digital press kit, a CD-R version of the printed kit, can be a viable alternative. All text and stills are already available in digital form, an attraction to a journalist who can then adapt the text instead of writing a story, and transfer the chosen pictures. Any video items can be played instantly from the CD-R, saving a journalist the bother of finding a VHS or DVD player. If the production's funding included a broadcaster pre-sale, many of these items will have been required in the PLA as deliverables, as is discussed in Chapter 23.

Publicity photographs

The key item in a press kit is still photographs. They are an added incentive for newspapers and particularly magazines to run a story related to the program. Indeed, they may be the main incentive for doing the story in some cases. Publications prefer particular styles of photographs. The more posed production stills often work best for drama, and strong observational shots for documentary. 'Happy snaps' that include crew are of no interest to print media because their readers don't want to know about the crew. Hiring a professional photographer is worth spending any marketing budget the production might have. Some publicity photographs may be shot in black and white, but the demand for them is decreasing. Photographs in newspaper TV guides are mostly colour these days, so the demand there will be for colour stills.

Colour transparencies

Colour transparencies (slide film) have been the preferred format for the print media because of the high-quality printed image they produce. They are processed by a professional laboratory and kept on their roll, not mounted on slides. Laboratories can also scan images from the stills at high resolution (usually 600 dpi at A4 size) on a drum scanner, and save them in TIFF or JPEG format. Some magazines will accept scanned images instead of a copy of the transparency, which they would then have to scan. Some prefer to do their own scanning. For magazines or newspapers that require prints of images for preview, these can be provided more cheaply with a colour ink-jet print from a scanned image on CD-R. Increasingly, publicists are using images in high-resolution JPEG format, and marketing people are emailing these to their buyers.

Digital-sourced stills

Digital stills taken on a high-quality digital camera are increasingly becoming the norm for publicity stills and, as noted above, these can be delivered to buyers by email as a high-resolution JPEG file. Most laboratories can provide prints of digital stills transferred to CD-R if a magazine insists on receiving it in that form, but the resolution is not particularly good. It is preferable not to have to go down that path. Video stills can be taken from the program's video by any non-linear editing system (see Chapter 23). This saves a single frame of video and exports it as a TIFF or JPEG file. At 72 dpi, the resolution of video stills is inferior to transparencies, but as long as they are not enlarged too much they can still be useful. Software such as Adobe Photoshop can improve the image quality with contrast, brightness and saturation changes, as well as cover over any blemishes.

11.3 The television marketplace

Direct and indirect approaches to broadcasters

There are some optional avenues for selling completed programs. One is by direct approach to broadcasters. These are, by and large, the same broadcasters that might be approached for pre-sale of the project. Some broadcasters, who, for a variety of reasons would not have been interested in pre-purchase of the proposed program, may well be interested in acquiring it when completed. As well as approaches on their home turf, broadcasters might also be approached at international markets, and even sometimes at film festivals. The approach can be indirect through agents or distributors, who might also be approached at the markets. Some producers, particularly of one-off documentaries, set up a website to attract buyer interest in their program.

Broadcaster priorities

In the first instance, approaches are made to the principal overseas FTA networks. In most cases, a domestic network would already have secured Australian FTA broadcast rights to the program, otherwise it is unlikely that the program would have raised the funding to go into production. The second round of options is the larger cable and satellite channels. Their fees are lower, although they can offset that by buying rights in a wider range of territories than any one FTA network, to cover their wide broadcast footprint. The next level is Australian pay television, and broadcasters in developing countries. These generally offer a fairly low licence fee, but it strengthens the argument with domestic pay television for a hold-back on their broadcast until some time after the domestic FTA screening of the program. A producer intending to approach a broadcaster will need to research its key strands, timeslots and programming preferences on its websites and in trade publications. Agents will generally be familiar with this information.

International television markets

The international television markets are gathering places for a large number of major broadcasters from around the world, although they are also attended by equally large numbers of producers and agents. Competing for attention of the buyers is intense. It is advisable that producers organise meetings with prospective buyers (or investors, if they are pitching a program proposal) in advance of the market, using the official delegate list circulated prior to the event. Cold-pitching to key buyers at bars and in corridors is probably just one more in a constant barrage of pitches and, most likely, doomed to failure.

MIPTV and MIPCOM

Traditionally, the biggest of the television markets has been MIPTV, at Cannes in April. It is an event that is more likely to be productive for experienced producers, and has an encouraging record for factual series, but is probably not so good for selling one-off documentaries. MIPTV has a focus on development deals and pre-sales to international broadcasters, as well as acquisition. MIPDOC, held immediately before MIPTV, allows a specialist focus on documentary and other factual programming. MIPCOM, held in Cannes in October, is similarly high profile with a strong interest historically in Australian product, telemovies, mini-series and general interest documentaries. MIPCOM Junior, held in Cannes prior to MIPCOM, specialises in children's programs. The main difference now between MIPTV and MIPCOM is timing. They are held six months apart to allow buyers and sellers of programs a half-yearly market opportunity. The AFC has stands at both MIPTV and MIPCOM, and will provide a range of assistance and sometimes funding support to Australian producers intending to be at these markets.

Other international TV markets

Two other markets worthy of note are MIFED, which is held in Milan in October, and is a film and television market, although the former predominates, and NATPE, which is held in Las Vegas in January, and is a large television programming market for very commercial product. For a few years, there have been two congresses of specialist factual programming, the World Congress of Science Producers and the World Congress of History Producers. As of 2006, the latter has been absorbed into the former as the World Congress of Science and Factual Producers. Closer to home, there is the Asia Television Forum (ATF), which is held in Singapore in late November. Its purpose is to foster business connections between Asian broadcasters, producers and international distributors, and it has been encouraging Australian participation through Austrade. The ATF is an opportunity for selling future production and co-production, as well as completed television programs, although the latter predominate.

Multimedia markets

There has been a trend in the international markets recently for cross-media platforms. MIFED promotes itself as a television and multimedia market, and the Reed Midem group, which runs MIPTV, MIPCOM and ATF, also has MILIA, which it markets as a digital media market at the same time as MIPTV. This is a strong movement in the production and acquisitions marketplace, although audience enthusiasm is currently lagging behind the industry's hype in the area.

Industry conferences in Australia

Locally, there are a few industry conferences that attract a useful cross-section of overseas delegates. The SPAA Conference is the main industry conference, now to be held at the Gold Coast in November. Perth's Small Screen Big Picture attracts a similar broad range of delegates, and the Australian International Documentary Conference (AIDC), although more focused in scope, is also well-attended by overseas buyers and agents. The AIDC is held in a different venue each year.

Festivals

Screening at festivals can provide some momentum for one-off programs, especially if they pick up an award. The AFC profiles over fifty international festivals on its website (see sources below), although many of these are cinema-relevant only. Producers supply the festival with VHS preview tapes, flyers, production details, and a media kit. Many festivals in Europe are free to enter, but in North America they can be expensive. Sometimes the result may be better at a specialised festival, for wildlife or ethnographic programs, for instance, or for those on women's issues. Among the more productive festivals are the Amsterdam International Documentary Film Festival (IDFA), the Annecy International Animated Film Festival (in France), the Banff World Television Festival (in Canada), and Hot Docs, the Canadian International Documentary Festival (in Toronto).

Website marketing

Some producers claim that a website can be a powerful sales tool for television projects, and that programmers, distributors and buyers will research a project they are considering on the internet. This may reflect a naïve assumption about the thoroughness of network buyers, who may not be surfing the 'net' looking for great programs to buy. However, if producers decide to build a website to market their program, it should contain a home page with the spirit of the program and the production company, images and key artwork, production notes, a trailer and sound grabs, quotes and reviews, its screening history, and contact information. It should be listed on search engines, be easy to navigate, fast to load, and user-friendly. Marcus Gillezeau, in his useful handbook, *Hands On*, claims buyers and the public are suspicious of a project without a website, especially if it is aimed at a mainstream audience. He advises looking at existing projects, and using broadband connection. The website can be at one of three levels: a billboard website (an electronic brochure derived from the publicity kit, easy to set up and requiring little maintenance); an informational website (background or extended information regarding a factual program); or an interactive website (with chat rooms, video segments and other online activities, similar to the UsMob website). It is probably more practical and more commercially astute to conceive the website as a platform in its own right, along the lines described in Chapter 10. If it serves a marketing function as well, so much the better. Websites are still unproven as marketing vehicles. They may be a reasonable alternative to the high cost of multiple glossy hard copy materials and freight, and they may be an option for a documentary producer unable to find an agent willing to take on the hard work of distributing a one-off program.

11.4   Marketing beyond television

Cinema release

Marketing the program beyond television leads to other platforms. These include new digital platforms, where the program or parts of it are streamed, although this doesn't currently yield significant revenue, or the program content could be refashioned to take advantage of the technical attributes of the platform. This was the subject of Chapter 10. A program could also potentially find a revenue return from cinema release if it is a one-off program, either a tele-movie or a documentary. In practice, the deal for cinema release is much more likely to be part of the funding of the production. It usually involves a contractual hold-back on television broadcast until after the cinema run. There is not a high likelihood of a program securing theatre release after its television broadcast.

Non-theatrical sales

Another marketing opportunity that can be lucrative for some programs is non-theatrical sales. Here, the program is bought to play to non-paying audiences, the purchasers being schools, universities, training organisations, libraries, hospitals, non-profit organisations and corporations. These sales often operate through specialist distributors such as Marcom Projects (the biggest of them in Australia), Maxwells and VEA, and many distributors subcontract to them for their non-theatrical marketing. Film Australia and Ronin pursue non-theatrical sales along with their other marketing activities.

Screenrights returns

The return comes to the producer, not just from sales on the non-theatrical market, but as a share of subscriptions paid to the copyright collecting society, Screenrights (see Chapter 25). Schools, libraries and other educational institutions pay an annual registration fee to Screenrights for legitimate copying of videos they hold, and they report usage over the year. Distribution of these fees to copyright holders is based on the reported usage, but the producer must have registered the program with Screenrights. The society will also collect from equivalent organisations overseas, although it is principally an English-language market, and educational use of video in the United States and United Kingdom is more curriculum based. The Australian non-theatrical market is lucrative because it is interested in a broad range of material. Even videos of football matches can sometimes generate a useful return.

Expansion of the non-theatrical market

This is an expanding market. EnhanceTV will copy programs off air and sell them to schools, which will further generate returns through Screenrights to the producer. The UK-based Compact Collection is now operating in Australia, and will chase up collection societies worldwide for a fee, unlike the more passive approach of Screenrights. Whether the increase in returns will be greater than the fee is a question that producers should ask themselves when considering this option. Another development is the offer of digital downloads of programs to subscribers. Concerns have been expressed that this will generate pirated copies, but it is just as easy to pirate a video bought through a retail outlet. If producers want to put their program into the digital download market, they should ensure that the program has the necessary rights.

11.5   The video market

The rise of DVD

Another opportunity to exploit the program is through video, marketed through international cinema distributors such as Buena Vista, or Australian distributors such as Roadshow Entertainment, Magna, Madman and Shock Entertainment. Video rental and sales have long provided additional revenue to the equity holders in some television programs, including series. Children's programs, animation and comedy have been strong in this market, along with some documentary and drama. Until a few years ago, returns have been primarily through VHS videocassette, but DVD has overtaken VHS as the main form of home viewing and, significantly, turned movie viewers into buyers instead of renters. DVD has revived old movies and television shows for contemporary audiences, and tapped different audiences with added features.

DVD's sell-through boom

By 2004, 62% of Australian homes had a DVD player. Two years earlier, DVD sales had passed those of VHS, and by 2005 wholesale sales of DVD disks had risen to $1032 million, whereas VHS sales had declined to $17.6 million. This represents a doubling of total video sales figures in just a few years. The boom is in 'sell-through' (sales as opposed to rental) because of the technical quality of DVD, and its convenience, the special features added in the product, and its earlier move into the retail market. Previously, retail was held back for a twelve-month rental window. The market has widened through music CD outlets and retail chains. The shift from VHS to DVD has seen an increase in sales of television series from 2% of DVD sales to 16%. Non-movie product is now 34% of DVD sales.

Online program rental

There has been a growth of DVD rental through online access in the United States. NetFlix has three million subscribers. In 2003, Australia's Hoyts and HomeScreen

Entertainment announced an internet-based DVD home delivery service, Home-Screen. It was acquired by QuickFlix in 2005. The industry expectation is that video on demand (VOD) will eventually cause DVD's rapid growth to plateau, but there is probably still considerable growth to happen before that position is reached.

11.6   Rights management

Rights in the project and underlying rights

The key to marketing a television project is management of the rights that relate to it, the rights in the project itself and underlying rights in copyright material that has been incorporated into it. The former rights belong in the first instance to the producer or production house that has made the program, but a portion of these is usually traded off in return for investment financing that enables the production to be mounted. All copyright owners of the program have control over how it is exploited in the marketplace, although there is generally a common interest in maximising the revenue from that process. The latter rights are for underlying material, such as script, music and footage from other sources. These are owned by other parties, but the production is licensed to use the material for specified purposes in particular territories. Copyright law is covered in greater depth in Chapter 25.

Extended rights in music

It is the underlying rights that require particular management. In contracting for use of this material for the primary product, namely the television program, the producer will be looking for as extensive a range of rights, without paying an extensive price for rights that may never be needed. When a fee is arrived at for music, for instance, the negotiation moves on to the rights that are covered by this – the range of different media, the range of territories – and as much as can be agreed without increasing the fee is to the advantage of the production. Where the musician is insistent on an additional fee for use of the music in other media or territories, that fee is agreed and stipulated in the contract. The contract, however, will require the fee to be paid only when the producer seeks to exercise these rights for sale to that medium or in that territory.

Rights in the script

The position is similar with rights in a script, which will be subject to a scriptwriting contract. The contract will bind the parties to agreed fees for different rights, should the producer wish to license those rights. Ideally, all potential uses of the program will be covered in this way. It is always easier to negotiate rights in a program when there's no sale pending, and no-one knows whether it will be successful or not. Once it's known to be a runaway success, a smart supplier will realise they are in a very strong negotiating position. If pushed, the producer might consider replacing the music, but the script can't be replaced.

Rights for archive footage

Licensing of archive footage from a commercial supplier is more straightforward. They usually have card rates for all potential uses. The producer should ensure that the licence contract for the immediate use also commits the archive to adhere to its card rates (or less, if it can be negotiated) for all other uses. Some rights, once paid, allow a number of sales of the program to follow at no extra cost. If world television rights have been obtained for a sale to one overseas broadcaster, there are no further rights payments necessary for sale to further foreign broadcasters. The rights for that were secured for the first sale.

Marginal cost of rights

The purpose of rights management is to contain future licensing costs, by negotiating their amount when the environment is most favourable to the rights buyer, namely when the success of the program is unknown, but postponing payment of these fees until they are actually required. What this also means is that agents will be offering the program and any ancillary material to the marketplace, knowing the marginal cost (economist-speak for the additional cost) of providing the product for each use. If servicing the sale will cost more than the price to be paid for it, the sale is of doubtful value.

Sources and further reading

General reading

Gillezeau, Marcus 2004, *Hands On*, Currency Press, Sydney.

Some internet references

Australian Film Commission, 'Australian distributors and broadcasters', available online at <http://afc.gov.au/profile/pubs/marketing.aspx>, viewed 18 December 2006.

Australian Film Commission, 'International festival profiles', available online at <http://afc.gov.au/marketingyourfilm/festivals/default.aspx>, viewed 18 December 2006.

Australian Film Commission, 'International sales contacts for Australian and co-produced television drama completed 2005+', available online at <http://afc.gov.au/profile/pubs/marketing.aspx>, viewed 18 December 2006.

Australian Film Commission, 'Marketing documentaries internationally', available online at <http://afc.gov.au/profile/pubs/marketing.aspx>, viewed 18 December 2006.

Maddox, Garry 2003, 'The video industry in Australia 2003: the DVD revolution', in Get The Picture, Australian Film Commission, available online at <http://www.afc.gov.au/GTP/wvanalysis.html>, viewed 18 December 2006.

UsMob, available online at <www.usmob.com.au> or <www.abc.net.au/usmob>, viewed 18 December 2006.

Part C

**Riding the tiger: management
of the production**

Chapter 12

Commencement of pre-production

Part B dealt with the development of a program from concept and the pursuit of funding for production of that program, an exciting and intensely creative process that can be heartbreaking as well. Without the necessary funding to cover the costs of production, it is unlikely that production will commence and the program will then never be made. The unfortunate statistical reality is that a majority of program concepts that go into the development process do not end up as programs shown on television. They fall by the wayside somewhere along the line, most commonly through insufficient funding.

For those projects that do move into production, the environment of the project changes dramatically. No longer is it a semistructured, freewheeling exchange of ideas run on enthusiasm, hope and a modicum of desperation. The prevailing mood switches to one of structure, and the application of professionalism. There is still room for creativity and new ideas. That never stops until the program is delivered, but these are applied in a long, integrated and managed process, a matrix that is business-like and follows clearly laid-out pathways.

The intensity eases for the producer at this stage. There is a mood of relief at having got the project over the major hurdle that stands between the idea and its realisation, the 'green light' of funds that enables the project to go into production. There will be other hurdles between this point and completion of the program, and times of self-doubt, but none are ever as insuperable or as seemingly final as a developed project with no real prospect of funding for production.

The pressure also changes in another important way for producers at this point. No longer are they the driving force of a small, intense creative group, sometimes pushing into uncharted territory without reliable maps. Now, with the necessary funding, a team is being built with the funding ability to hire support and key creative staff, and the workload is spreading over an increasing number of people. The producer is now overseeing a team of professionals following a pathway that should be familiar and to which they will contribute those extra elements of creative expertise. The detailed work, especially in the early stages of pre-production, is carried principally by the production manager, with creative heads paying close attention to their own craft areas. The producer can afford to sit back and review how it is all going.

As outlined in Chapter 5 and diagrammatically in Figure 5.1, the traditional production cycle is made up of three stages: pre-production, production and post-production. Central to these stages is the filming stage, often called principal photography, recording or, simply, 'the shoot', where the raw material of the program is recorded. Filming is a broadly used term, whether the program is recorded on film, videotape or transmitted live. Pre-production precedes it and is the stage in which the production team is put together and all preparations are made so that production can proceed as smoothly as circumstances allow. The better the planning, the fewer the problems that will come out of left field during the pressure of the shoot. No amount of planning will ensure that no problems emerge, but the more detailed the planning the more these are kept to a manageable level.

As with development, there are variations in the detail of the production process from genre to genre. Some of the more significant characteristics of genre production will be highlighted as each phase of the production cycle is dissected. But television production has a common general approach that straddles all of its genres, so genre-specific aspects will be examined *en passant* as a variant of the general. For the most part, the following chapters will describe the paths of production for drama and documentary series in parallel, using the one description for both when they are substantially the same and describing separately those parts that diverge, such as script breakdown (drama) and shooting script (documentary).

12.1   Key production personnel

Production manager

The first person to join the team at the onset of pre-production is often the production manager. This person may have been involved in earlier discussions with the producer, or they may be picking up a draft production budget prepared by another production manager or by the producer. Either way, they will be brought up to date with decisions already made regarding the production and given copies of existing production documentation, particularly agreements with production investors and distributors (if any), and delivery requirements that attach to these. Where these have been drawn up, the production manager will also be provided with copies of Chain of Title agreements, completion guarantee agreements, and any agreements, letters of intent or deal memos with crew or cast.

Engagement of key production personnel

Among the early tasks of a production manager are setting up the production base and engaging key production personnel. Many key personnel will already be decided by producer and director. Generally, the director will have the principal voice on selection for these roles as they have to form a creative partnership with these people, but there may be budgetary aspects that have to be considered by the producer at the same time. In any case, a smart director in a constructive working relationship with a producer will want to make use of that person as a sounding board for these major decisions. The roles under consideration at this stage for a drama production are typically director of photography (DOP), first assistant director (1st AD), production designer, editor, sound recordist and location manager. With a documentary, there may be no more than DOP and editor, and with a studio production there would be early involvement of a technical producer (TP). By the time pre-production is underway, some of the key production personnel will already have committed themselves (or as good as) at some earlier stage of the development process, some will be under strong consideration and may have been involved in discussions, and a few key roles may not be considered until pre-production has commenced. None should be contracted until budgeted funding is in place, but the main terms of the intended contract might be outlined in a deal memo or a letter of intent.

Production departments

In a large-scale production, such as drama, comedy, live telecast, variety or reality television, the production personnel are grouped in departments, typically camera (which may include location sound), art department, production support and post-production (editing and audio), with key production personnel as heads of departments (HODs). With a smaller, more mobile documentary or magazine production, there will be the field crew (often no more than cameraman and sound recordist, sometimes with an assistant and at other times just one person), post-production crews (editing and audio post-production) and a production assistant (or production coordinator). The post-production personnel may have only a consultative role in documentary pre-production, and may work at a separate facility from the production office. The production coordinator has a wide-ranging production support role, principally to assist producer and production manager but with an expectation by them of a considerable degree of initiative about what is needed to progress the production process, from arranging meetings to checking travel and accommodation availability.

Hiring of HODs

After the producer and director have made their final choices of key production personnel, these are confirmed and negotiated by either the producer or production manager. The available budget is kept in mind in arriving at an agreed figure for their fees. Where many of the terms of engagement are already spelt out in a deal memo, there is limited room to move in negotiation (for either party). Once HODs have been engaged, they will start to give thought to the personnel to hire for their own department and how they will run that department. This is done in consultation with the production manager to ensure that what is desired is within the scope of the production budget. HODs will often choose the same people regularly for their teams (if they are available) as the HOD knows the quality of their work and they, in turn, know how the HOD likes to operate.

12.2   The production base

Finding a production office

Even before the key personnel are brought on board, a production office needs to be found and secured so that the activities of pre-production can commence under the one roof. If the producer has already been working out of office space that can accommodate the production's needs, the next step is to equip it specifically for the production. If the development phase has operated out of a home office or a small business office, this is no longer practical once pre-production is underway. Thought must be given to the most suitable location if a production office is to be set up for the project from scratch (see also Chapter 26). Considerations include closeness to where the bulk of the shooting will take place (if practical), convenience of the main suppliers of production resources, availability of transport and parking to the extent required by the production, and access to the building, especially out of normal working hours.

Equipping the production office

The office needs of each project vary according to the size and nature of the production. It is preferable for all the production's departments to operate under the one roof. This facilitates the exchange and coordination of planning notes between different areas. Drama and comedy, with their discrete departments, have more diverse office requirements than does documentary, where a smaller, more flexible production entity is the norm. Essential equipment, such as telephones, workstations, fax machines, photocopiers and office furniture, is installed before personnel move in substantially to start on the project. This is followed up by organising letterheads and business cards, a meeting room and kitchen facilities. Depending on the size of the production, some of the production support staff might join the team at this early stage also, most notably the production coordinator.

12.3   Script breakdown

Purpose of a script breakdown

In a drama production, the production manager breaks down the script to see what areas will require specialist crew and facilities, where there might be particular budget implications that the producer should be alerted to, and so that a preliminary production schedule can be drawn up. The script breakdown provides familiarity with those areas of the production that are likely to require particular attention as pre-production's planning proceeds.

Choice of studio set or location

The script breakdown will note scenes that might be considered for shooting in a studio, involving set design and construction, with attendant costs. The reasons for building a set might be a low expectation either of finding a suitable location for the scene, or of getting access to the location for the length of time required. A shop or office location would necessitate finding an appropriate vacant building and renting it for the duration of the shoot, which is particularly problematic for a drama series where the location might be required for successive episodes. There can be restrictions on moving camera shots or access within a building for positioning the camera. On the other hand, a set with moveable flats (i.e. sides of the set, usually walls) has considerable flexibility. The ABC series *Patrol Boat* used a set of the interior of the patrol boat, whereas all other scenes (including on the deck of the boat) were shot on location. The marine architect's designs for an actual patrol boat were used as a source by the production designer, but the interiors of these vessels are cramped and pokey. The set design scaled the dimensions of a patrol boat up 10% to give more leeway for camera angles, tracking shots and cast and crew movement. Walls could be moved to enable preferred camera angles on any scene, a consideration a real patrol boat could not offer.

A studio set would need several scenes scheduled in it (if a telemovie) or would have to be a recurring location across a series to warrant the cost of set construction. With the greater mobility of both modern cameras and modern shooting styles, along with the increasing costs in building a set, the use of sets in television drama is declining.

Preliminary thoughts about locations

Another important piece of preliminary information is where locations for shooting might reasonably be expected to be found and what sort of support they will require. Chapter 16 deals with the process of looking for and negotiating locations, but an informed guess is a useful planning tool at the early stage. Would they be expected to be found within easy reach of the production base, or in the outer suburbs, or in another city or even a rural or remote locality? These options impact on the schedule (how much of the day will be spent travelling to and from or between locations?) and budget (what will be the cost of getting crew and cast to the location?). The type of location will indicate whether it might require specialised patrol or support assistance, such as traffic control or police assistance, overnight security, or boat or other location access support.

Specialist crew inferred from the script

Other specialised crew and their equipment will be inferred from the script rather than as a consequence of the location. There may be aerial shots or underwater shots, requiring helicopters, divers or a camera with underwater housing; there might be scenes with animals, requiring hire of the animals and their handlers (called 'wranglers'); there might be car chases, high falls or other action requiring stunt performers; there might be extended dialogue or action scenes inside a travelling vehicle, requiring camera attachments or a trailer-mounted vehicle; or there might be scenes with firearms, requiring armourers, or with explosives, requiring a special effects crew. As well as the production expense of these requirements, they usually take up additional schedule time for set-up, rehearsal and ensuring safety requirements are met.

Night shooting

The script will be split into day and night shooting. Night shoots may impose penalty payments to cast and crew and, with an external location, may require a larger lighting kit. A night shoot followed by a day shoot can impose penalty payments if the award requirement of an 11-hour break between shifts cannot be scheduled. The script breakdown will alert the production to the danger of this. The schedule can look at ways of working around this, by backing the night shoot onto a weekend break or staggering the starts of following days through a couple of day/night shooting days (see Chapter 19 for more detail of these strategies).

Cast analysis

Finally, the cast is analysed to identify the number of speaking roles and their general configuration. This can also highlight lapses in the logic of who is present in the script and who is not, and characters who seem to be in two places at once or who disappear from a location in mid-scene without explanation. It gives an opportunity for an initial assessment of the number of extras required and identifies characters that are likely to be played by actors under the age of 15 years. Each state has regulations requiring notification in advance where children are to perform in a production (it's the age of the performer that matters, not the age of the character) and places regulatory limits on hours worked and other requirements for the wellbeing of children in production (see Chapter 15).

Adjustments to departmental budgets

As well as the production manager breaking down the script, each HOD will go through the same process as it is relevant to their area and work out a preliminary budget for labour and materials. Where the estimate is higher than the budgeted amount, this has to be resolved, after discussion between producer and director, so that either the HODs pare down their activities or some other department has to work within a reduced budget to allow the higher production priority to proceed. It's not a case of equity of access to production funding, but what has been identified as the priority needs of the production. The HOD breakdown also serves as a back-up to the production manager's analysis to ensure something has not been overlooked.

12.4 Refining the production budget

Production department budgets

Each HOD is advised at the outset of the budget for their respective department and how it has been broken down into line items. The budget and its main components may be committed in negotiations with investors, so that there could be limited room for variation. Certainly, the total budget for the production is fixed and set at the total of production funds that have been raised for the project. Budget for individual items can generally be varied, but the departmental bottom line can be increased only at the expense of another department's budget. A documentary project won't have interdepartmental considerations. Instead, the entire budget is under the direct management of the producer without a need for broad consultation. However, the production manager will still prepare financial reports and advise on budgetary action from their detailed familiarity with expenditure progress and the cost of resources.

Adjusting a budget with offsets

An early task for the production manager is refining the budget as specific details of the production consolidate, within what capacity there is for adjustment of the figures. This process will have started with the detail generated by the script breakdown. As pre-production progresses, elements of production will be examined closely – be they transport to location, ancillary camera equipment or support staff – and one factor weighed up will be whether the budget can afford them. If the element is over budget, the HOD decides whether to drop it in favour of an alternative that is within budget, or offset the additional expense by holding a line item under budget with reduced expenditure elsewhere in the department's share of the overall production budget. An over-budget cast member could be offset by casting in a different role a performer who was able to be hired for a fee under the budgeted amount. Similarly, a crucial location with a travel cost that is over budget can be offset by restricting another location so that the amount over (called an 'overage') can be recovered. If acceptance of an over-budget item is being considered, the producer will rely on the production manager's advice of where offsets are realistic.

12.5 Timing the script

Importance attached to program duration

If it hasn't already been done in the development phase, another key task that is carried out at this early stage is timing of the script (or each episode's script for a series) with current drafts. This is of particular importance for television drama because networks are insistent about upper limits of program duration. They want to start programs on advertised half-hour time junctions (even if they ignore their own stringent rule when it suits their strategic purposes). Generally, the commercial television hour is up to fifty-two minutes and the networks do not want programs to restrict their capacity to schedule advertising, which is, after all, how they make their money. Even the ABC is not enthusiastic about one-hour programs that run over fifty-six minutes.

Reasons for script timing

The timing should be done by an experienced continuity person, preferably the person who will work on the production. That person will have an understanding of the pace at which the script translates into program time, and should consult the director to get an insight into their likely interpretation and the timing implications of this. It's not a perfect prediction, and editing allows flexibility in the final timing of a program anyway, but it does alert the production to a program or episode that is inherently overlong. This is better and more economically solved by tightening the script at this stage rather than relying on editing to excise expensive but ultimately unusable production effort (and cost). In any case, a planned but overlong sequence may not be easily tightened, which creates continuity difficulties. A highly skilled editor may eventually find a path around the problem, but it is better to avoid putting the program in that position if the problem can be foreseen.

12.6   Pre-production schedule

Early production schedules

The production manager draws up an overall production schedule for the producer's endorsement. The schedule includes the major dates for commencement of pre-production, principal photography, any CGI or other specialised image generation, vision and sound editing, and delivery dates (consistent with any contractual obligations for delivery). Then, generally in conjunction with the 1st AD and with further input from HODs, a detailed pre-production schedule will be drawn up. This schedule will be handed out to all production staff and crew, and is usually also drawn up on a central whiteboard for convenient reference – the start of widespread use of whiteboards in production planning.

Elements of the pre-production schedule

The pre-production schedule will detail key meetings (and who should be at them) at which various production decisions will be made, and the periods when various personnel will be working on the team. The budget cannot necessarily afford the whole crew to be engaged for the entire pre-production period. Some people wouldn't be usefully employed for some of that time anyway. Some key production personnel might work on pre-production in two stages, the first to participate in important initial production decisions and later to set up for the production stage itself.

The next stages of pre-production

With tabulation of some of the major issues to be addressed before the shoot, and with the pre-production schedule laid out, the wheels have been set in motion for detailed planning of the shoot and confirmation of all the necessary resources (including people) for that shoot to take place and proceed smoothly. The next chapters look at the major areas of preparation for the shoot, all designed to ensure that what is needed will be there on the day and that it can contribute to the production with maximum effectiveness, whether we are talking about a skilled actor or a special effect with explosives. However, we will commence our discussion with setting up an office system to keep track of the information that accumulates as planning of the shoot proceeds.

Chapter 13

Documentation and office systems

No-one thinks that paperwork is exciting, but without it the coordination of the logistics and management of a production – and especially a large and complex production – is just not possible. It is the means of tracking all the elements that must be in place at each step along the production pathway, and of making sure that the production isn't generating unnecessary costs that will result in compromises – which are equally as unnecessary – in the final product. The objective is to make the best program within the resources, not the best program despite the waste of resources.

As noted in Chapter 12, setting up an office starts with the commencement of pre-production, if not before. The production manager is one of the first people hired on the production team, and they will inherit some key documents that have been generated during development (see Chapter 12). They will also be instrumental, in discussion with the producer, in selecting an office and establishing furnishings, fittings, filing cabinets and communications, as described in Chapter 12, unless this is already in place as part of the production company, and suited to the needs of the project.

What follows in this chapter is an overview of the office systems and their supporting documentation that enable the production office to monitor and report on production progress. The objective is for the project to be productively and cost-effectively managed throughout the entire production process, all the way to the delivery of the completed program and beyond.

13.1 Office systems

Sources of paperwork design

The need to order the design and printing of letterhead and business cards was noted in Chapter 12. These should include production office and contact details as well as the ACN, or ABN if the production entity isn't a company (see Chapter 26). Order books for supplies and services are purchased, and a range of forms are copied from existing formats or designed for the production's purposes. These days, production forms are less likely to be photocopied and more likely to be distributed widely as e-forms, which are filled out on computer, distributed by email, and only printed if a hard copy is required or for filing.

AFC/AFTRS pro formas

Form design is often done by versioning other forms that the production manager has used in previous productions. Where this is not possible, the sample forms provided in the AFC/AFTRS handbook, *The Production, Budgeting and Film Management Satchel*, can be used as a starting point. In adapting these to the production's specific needs, it should be borne in mind that they are designed for feature film production and, in some cases, may be out of date. The forms pre-date GST legislation in Australia in the most recent edition, although that might be rectified in future editions. Nonetheless, it should not be difficult to version these forms for television production use. Larger productions may find that they are working with accounting packages that generate some of these forms.

The range of forms that might be needed

The production may need a memo system with a recognisable memo format, or it may settle for using email or intranet communication. There will also be a call for Daily Progress Reports, Extras Salary Vouchers and all the other daily production paperwork that enables a production to run smoothly (see section 13.8). There is a comprehensive list of financially related forms (either on paper or as e-forms) that a production might use: account forms, overtime sheets, cheque requisitions, remittances, petty cash forms, and so on. Whether these are available as multiple copies on paper or on computer will depend on how the office operates and who will be using the forms, but increasingly, television production, like all businesses, prefers to steer away from accumulating paper files. This can, however, prove difficult. The forms might be generated in the computer, but they often have to be printed to be sent to the appropriate people, who will then file them. If this is the case, it may be useful to print the forms on different coloured paper so that they can be quickly recognised.

Filing on shelves and on computer

The office traditionally sets up a filing system to keep all its paperwork in a logical and accessible system. Although many of the items that go into these files can be sent electronically and held in a folder within a computer, productions often operate a duplicate hard-copy filing system at the same time. This might be out of habit or the comfort of familiarity, but there are still some advantages with files in lever-arch folders on shelves. The main one is accessibility. Anyone who needs a particular piece of information, and is familiar with the office's filing system, can find what is needed, even when the production manager or the production coordinator is not in the office. There is a trade-off here between accessibility and confidentiality of information, but the information becomes more readily available than when held on computer. Files that are kept in a securely locked cabinet may not be any safer than those in a secure computer, but if they arrive in paper form, there is little alternative but storage in a physical file.

Range of files

The AFC/AFTRS handbook lists a typical range of files that should be set up in a production office. It's as good a starting list as any other:
- 2nd AD Reports/Continuity Reports
- Art Department/Wardrobe
- Call Sheets
- Camera and sound sheets
- Cast
- Crew
- Financial
- General correspondence
- Insurance
- Legal
- Locations
- Memos
- Post-production
- Progress Reports
- Schedule and revisions
- Script and amendments
- Travel and accommodation

This list of files is appropriate for a drama shoot. The production office would adapt it to the needs of different genres accordingly.

13.2 Financial organisation

Production accountant

Unless the production is small, it is likely to have a production accountant, who is responsible for the payments of wages, accounts, tax, and so on, and for cost reporting. The position might be full-time or part-time, depending on the scale of production. A production accountant will provide support to the producer and the production manager in monitoring the financial position of the project. The three will determine which financial reports are required for their own monitoring and management of the project, and to fulfil contractual reporting obligations to the investors.

Cash-flow schedule

The production manager prepares a schedule of the cash flow of investor funds, and then breaks the budget into cost-reporting periods. These might be weekly for a major production, or fortnightly or monthly for a smaller production, or during post-production when expenditure falls off. An estimate is made of that part of the budget that is expected to be spent in each reporting period, bearing in mind suppliers who require pre-payment or give a discount for pre-payment. It also allows for the time that invoicing typically takes to follow supply, unless the accounting is to be set up on a commitment basis (see Chapter 22), in which case costs are estimated from the time that they are incurred. Development expenses may have to be paid from the first cash flow. The scheduled payments by investors for production funding, and the estimated timing of production expenses will indicate if there might be a timing problem with the cash-flow schedule. Funding must always flow ahead of expenditure, or the production will have to be adjusted to enable it. Alternatively, a change to the funding cash-flow schedule could be negotiated with an investor. Table 13.1 lays out production funding cash flow and production expenditure flow as a means of calculating if the timing of funding is viable.

Production accounts

An early task for the production office is to set up its financial procedures and structure. Production accounts may be on a computer-based general ledger, operated by software customised for film and television production, or it might be on generic software such as MYOB. A manual cashbook is seldom used these days, even for small productions. Whatever system is used, it will be based on double-entry accounting, where every entry is balanced by an entry somewhere else in the accounts. It is useful for producers to have a general understanding of how double-entry accounting works so that they can follow reports from the general ledger and any other financial reports that are generated. The basics of accounting are covered in Chapter 22.

Bank accounts

A bank account or accounts are opened for the production. The bank will usually require a copy of the certificate of incorporation, if the production is a proprietary company (see Chapter 26) or a certificate of registration of business name, if it is a partnership (see Chapter 26). An investment agreement may specify some conditions for this account and signatories. If it doesn't, the production will determine who will be the account signatories. These should include people with appropriate authority, such as the producer or executive producer, but not so restrictively that the system is dependent on someone who is not readily available. The project should have separate bank accounts from those ordinarily operated by the producer or the production company, which is something usually required by financing parties anyway. On a large production, the production entity may be set up as a separate company to limit liability of the production company for any losses of the production.

Table 13.1: Spreadsheet of production funding cash flow and estimated production expenditure flow.

'Wandering with the Ancients'

	Pre-production			Production				Post-production			Budget
	Wk 1/2	Wk 3/4	Wk 5/6	Wk 7/8	Wk 9/10	Wk 11/12	Wk 13/14	Wk 15/16	Wk 17/18	Wk 19/20	
Development	1 200	340									1 540
Producer & director	5 000			15 000		16 000				20 000	56 000
Production unit fees	500	1 500	3 000	6 400	12 000	13 000	1 500	800	500	500	39 700
Cast			200	100	200						500
Locations						100				500	600
Videotape stock		500				100					600
Equipment			500	1 000	2 500	2 500	500		240		7 240
Rentals & storage		500		500		500					1 500
Travel & transport		1 300	3 200	2 100	1 200	500	200				8 500
Accommodation & meals		600	1 200	500	600	250	140				3 290
Insurance	1 500									1 000	2 500
Office expenses	450	100	100	70	50	50	50	50	30		950
Post-production		200	450	600	1 350	1 800	4 100	4 100	4 600	5 400	22 600
Special effects/CGI				15 000		25 000		30 000	70 000	45 000	185 000

											Total
Post-production sound										4 100	4 100
Music									2 000		2 000
Publicity							500				500
Legal & business				1 000		2 000		2 000			5 000
Contingency	2 000	2 000		2 000	2 000	2 000	2 000		2 000		14 000
TOTAL EXPENSES	10 650	5 040	8 650	44 270	19 900	62 300	8 490	36 950	79 130	80 740	356 120
CUMULATIVE EXPENSES	**10 650**	**15 690**	**24 340**	**68 610**	**88 510**	**150 810**	**159 300**	**196 250**	**275 380**	**356 120**	
CASH FLOW	50 000			100 000		100 000			50 000	56 120	
CUMULATIVE	**50 000**	**50 000**	**50 000**	**150 000**	**150 000**	**250 000**	**250 000**	**250 000**	**300 000**	**356 120**	
Excess of funds over expenditure	39 350	34 310	25 660	81 390	61 490	99 190	90 700	53 750	24 620	0	

Production credit cards and delegations

The producer will also determine delegations, that is, upper limits on the authority given (i.e. delegated) to which members of the production team can approve expenditure on behalf of the production. If the producer is to manage the budget, they don't want to give HODs carte blanche to approve all spending in their area, but they also don't want to have to authorise every trivial purchase of, say, a rubber eraser or a pen. The production manager and accountant set up cashing facilities, and procedures for processing invoices. A production credit card is fairly essential for a production manager these days, when many suppliers prefer to take a deposit on hired goods. With a large shoot at a remote location, the production may need to establish a cashing authority there with a local branch of the production's bank. With a smaller production, the production credit card accessing funds from automatic teller machines is more convenient, although delegations need to be clear here too.

Petty cash and orders for supplies

Petty cash floats are set up, and order books issued for those that will require them. In a small production, only the production manager may require a petty cash float, but in a bigger production the HODs may also get one. The production's Petty Cash form will be used to reconcile each float with every item noted and receipted. The production manager will have an order book, and HODs might also on a large production. Each order must be written out with the full details of the supplies, including the amounts and quoted cost, and signed by an authorised person. The order forms are in triplicate, with a copy going to the supplier, one to accounts, and one remaining with the order book as a reference. The orders allow the production manager to note budgetary commitments and the production accountant to validate the invoice when it comes. For this reason, copies of orders should go to accounts daily. The production manager does not want the invoice to be the first notification of a committed cost.

13.3   Regular reporting

Weekly production meetings

Preparation for a production requires communication, and pooling of relevant information as it comes to hand or is decided. Weekly production meetings are a vehicle for this, usually chaired by the producer and attended by the director, HODs, the production manager, 1st AD and anyone else who is involved on an issue that is to be discussed. These meetings enable coordination of the overall planning, and cost-effectiveness. They report on progress in the areas of production and any issues that have arisen, on costs and the state of the production budget, and on any additional requirements that have come into the schedule. Minutes are taken to ensure that people don't rely just on memory or on notes scribbled on a piece of paper. Decisions, and information that comes out of the meetings, are circulated to the relevant crew.

Final production meeting

A large meeting of all crew should be held just prior to commencement of the shoot – the final production meeting. This ensures that all participants have all the information they need, that concerns that any crew member might have are addressed, and that the crew has a definite sense of being part of a functioning team. The 1st AD, as the person who runs the shoot on behalf of the production, goes through all aspects of the shoot to ensure that everyone is properly briefed and to clarify any issues that arise. A sense of being part of a professional and creative machine is important in motivating the crew for the shoot, and in preparing it for working to one common purpose over the following weeks.

13.4   Insurance

The production determines its insurance needs early in the production process, so that necessary insurance arrangements are in place before their cover starts. Some, such as workers compensation, are required by law; some are required by investors and the completion guarantor; some are simply prudent; and some are of questionable value in many productions. A judgement is made for each production of what insurance is desirable and, where it is considered necessary, the extent of coverage required. On a major project, it is customary to seek the advice of an experienced film insurance broker. No production wants to spend money unnecessarily, but ignorance about insurance can put the production at unwarranted risk. A copy of all insurance policies should be given to the completion guarantor, if there is one, and to investors, if contractually required. Often the completion guarantor and investors will require the production to note them as an interested party on any insurance policy.

Types of insurance

Workers compensation insurance
Workers compensation insurance is mandatory under different legislation in each state and territory of Australia, although the requirements of the statutes are similar. The NSW system described below is indicative of all the jurisdictions. The specifics of each can be found on the websites listed in Table 13.2.

Every employer in New South Wales must take out a workers compensation policy with a licensed insurer to cover its employees and any others brought under workers compensation by the legislation. This includes casual workers, trainees and most individual contractors – anyone who is paid wages or a commission, even if they work away from the production's premises, unless they are hired as part of a capitalised business they operate. Thus, it may not include an editor hired with their edit suite or people in an audio post-production suite, but would include an editor who hired a suite on the production's behalf or for whom the production hired a suite. If a worker's own business (usually a proprietary company) or some other company is contracted to supply the worker, that company is responsible for workers compensation. However, the production is required by law to

Table 13.2: Workers compensation authorities in Australia.

State/Territory	Authority	Website	Act
ACT	ACT WorkCover	www.workcover.act.gov.au	*Workers Compensation Act 1951*
NSW	WorkCover NSW	www.workcover.nsw.gov.au	*Workers Compensation Act 1987*
NT	NT WorkSafe	www.worksafe.nt.gov.au	*Work Health Act 2006*
Qld	WorkCover Queensland	www.workcoverqld.com.au	*Workers' Compensation and Rehabilitation Act 2003*
SA	WorkCover Corp of South Australia	www.workcover.com	*Workers Rehabilitation and Compensation Act 1986*
Tas.	WorkCover Tasmania	www.workcover.tas.gov.au	*Workers Rehabilitation & Compensation Amendment Act 2004*
Vic.	WorkSafe Victoria	www.workcover.vic.gov.au	*Accident Compensation (Workcover Insurance) Act 1993*
WA	WorkCover Western Australia	www.workcover.wa.gov.au	*Workers Compensation and Injury Management Act 1981*

ensure that the company has done so. Failure to check may make the production liable for unpaid premiums.

In New South Wales, the employer must keep records of wages paid, keep a Register of Injuries at the workplace, have an approved summary of workers compensation legislation displayed at the workplace, and establish a return-to-work program for rehabilitation of injured workers. The employer must notify the insurer within forty-eight hours if a worker will be absent through injury for seven days or more. Penalties for failure to comply with these requirements are severe, with high fines, and in New South Wales can include prison sentences in serious cases. Workers compensation insurance is discussed further in Chapter 26.

Film producers' indemnity
Film producers' indemnity (FPI) covers costs caused by postponing or abandoning the shoot through death or disability of any of the nominated personnel, generally lead actors or presenters, and sometimes the director. FPI should cover pre-production and go through to the end of the shoot, and the people covered will be required to have medical examinations at the production's expense. This insurance is most relevant to a major drama production, where the marketing of the program has a considerable investment in the marquee names in the cast.

Smaller projects would be more likely to cut their losses and recast quickly, but there can be substantial reshoot costs to insert a new performer into a program.

Negative film risk
Negative film risk covers costs to the production from accidental loss, damage or destruction of film or tape stock (raw, exposed with or without processing, or recorded), recorded soundtracks and tape. This cover can be extended to the cost of reshooting footage lost to faulty stock or camera, or in processing or copying.

Multi-risk insurance
Multi-risk insurance covers the cost of repairing or replacing props, sets or wardrobe, or the full range of production equipment (i.e. camera, lighting, sound or grips) for loss, damage or theft. Action props or fragile articles are unlikely to be covered. Where equipment is owned by the production company it would be covered, but responsibility for insurance needs to be clarified where equipment is hired.

Public liability insurance
Public liability insurance covers the legal liability of the production company for damage to property belonging to others while it is under the production's care, and it indemnifies the production against death or injury to persons other than employees of the company. Employees are already covered under workers compensation insurance. The cover is usually for the entire duration of the production. In Australia, evidence of public liability insurance cover, usually to the extent of $10 million, will often be a condition for production access to property.

Motor vehicle insurance
Motor vehicle insurance is necessary when vehicles are hired or borrowed from a person who has insured it only for private use, or where the vehicle is not otherwise insured. Vehicles hired from a commercial hirer are more likely to be insured by the owner. Marine and aviation insurance may be necessary where the production uses boats or planes in the shoot.

Travel insurance
Travel insurance should be taken out whenever the production will be shooting overseas.

Errors and omissions insurance
Errors and omissions (E&O) insurance indemnifies the production against legal action for defamation, breach of copyright or other intellectual property rights, or breach of contract. In most countries, including Australia, E&O insurance is rarely required for television production, but US broadcasters are usually adamant about it. A requirement is that clearances have been approved by the production company's solicitor and that title clearance is obtained. A title clearance can be provided by the American title search company, Thomson & Thomson.

13.5   Cast and crew contracts

Registrations regarding employees

Several matters relating to the engagement of crew and cast are dealt with in pre-production. The production is legally required to take out workers compensation insurance to cover people who will be on the payroll, generally whether they are employees or individual contractors (see section 13.4), but not if a company is contracted to supply a person's services. The premium is initially based on an estimate of the numbers and duration of people engaged and this figure is eventually adjusted to the actual figures when the production has been completed. The production must also register with the ATO to pay group tax instalments of pay as you go (PAYG) withholding from wage payments (see Chapter 26). An estimate will be made of the peak monthly wages bill for the production to determine if it will exceed the threshold for payroll tax in its state. If it is liable, the production entity will be registered with the appropriate state authority for payroll tax (see Chapter 26).

Deal memo

A crew or cast contract should be issued before a worker commences on the production. A deal memo is filled out to provide the necessary information for drawing up the contract, and for payment of wages cross-referenced to the AD's daily report of starting and finishing times of cast and crew. The deal memo is described in Chapter 14. It will include tax status and superannuation fund details, period of engagement and fee, method of payment and bank account details, any equipment or motor vehicle allowance details and, if contracted as a company, its ACN and workers compensation policy details. An actor's deal memo will also include the rights contracted at the time of performance.

13.6   Script amendments

Sources of script changes

The script for a dramatised production, whether drama or sitcom, will change as development of the characters, their subplots and the dramatic arc takes place. It will also change as practical issues, such as costs and available facilities, determine the reality of the production. Dialogue might be revised, action changed, different props might be required, or scenes might be added, deleted, extended or contracted. Changes can come from discussions between director, script writer and producer about the direction of the story, from the resources confirmed as available to shoot the program, or as a result of rehearsal of the production. Amendments might be either replacement pages or a listing of minor changes. Sometimes the change will be a single word. Scene numbers are not adjusted to the changes. If a scene is deleted, it is noted as such ('Scene 15 deleted'). If a scene is added, it is notated with a letter, such as new Scene 15A to follow original Scene 15 before original Scene 16. If a new page is issued, the changed parts are indicated with an asterisk.

Colour-coding amendments

Replacement script pages are conventionally issued in a different colour for each amendment, to avoid confusion with earlier amendments. The date of issue is noted on the revised page as well. The original script is on white paper, but the standard colour code for subsequent script amendments is:
- first amendment – blue
- second amendment – pink
- third amendment – yellow
- fourth amendment – green.

Amendments after the fourth are an arbitrary colour choice, but the usual practice is to go through the blue–pink–yellow–green cycle again and note it as '2nd blue amendment' and so on, with the date.

Distribution of amendments

Script amendments should be distributed widely, erring if necessary on the side of caution. They should go to director and producer, cast and HODs, but also to any crew member who needs to be up to date with the blueprint of the production for which they are preparing. People working to different versions of the script can be catastrophic for the production. If scenes are added or deleted or changed significantly, the script's timing should be adjusted from that done early in pre-production (see Chapter 12).

13.7   Safety Report

Conditions requiring a Safety Report

Productions have a duty of care under occupational health and safety (OH&S) law to provide a safe working environment for the workers, and for members of the general public on whom its working activities might impact. Where there is hazardous action planned in production, such as stunt work, special effects with explosives or pyrotechnics, firearms use, potentially uncontrollable animals on set, use of boats or vehicles in the action, or any other potentially dangerous activity, on-screen or off, the production commissions a Safety Report. It will be provided by a Safety Consultant, accredited by the Media, Entertainment and Arts Alliance (MEAA). Usually, a large-scale production will get a Safety Report as a matter of course, whether it has identified specific potential hazards or not. The MEAA's position is that all productions should commission a Safety Report, but smaller productions usually don't do so unless there is known to be potentially hazardous activity in the production. If an injury occurs during the shoot, it can be used to argue that adequate measures were taken to protect people's safety, the injury notwithstanding. On the other hand, a Safety Report is an added cost to the production that may seem unnecessary or of limited relevance in a small actuality shoot. The absence of a Safety Report is not of itself evidence that reasonable measures were not taken for a safe workplace, but would place an onus on the production to show how they were taken instead.

Procedure

The current script, schedule and location list are sent to the Safety Consultant, who will confer with the 1st AD regarding the director's intention in shooting the scenes, inspect locations, and have discussions with HODs where relevant. The completed report will specify requirements for the production to ensure that it takes all the necessary steps to prevent accidents or injuries to production staff or the general public. These steps are added to the production schedule if they are not already part of it, but usually the producer, 1st AD, production manager and HODs will have discussed safety requirements in advance of the Safety Report, and anticipated much of its content.

13.8　Daily production paperwork

Principal forms

A number of forms are used during production to report to the production office on the reality of the shoot, as opposed to scheduled activities. This information gets processed into Daily Progress Reports, which are a running diary of the production for its ongoing management. They are also the basis of payments through accounts. Call Sheets, the AD's Report and overtime sheets are all usually the responsibility of the 2nd AD if there is one. There are Continuity Daily Reports, and Stock Reconciliation forms for the camera department. The crew have camera sheets and sound sheets to note each shot recorded.

Call Sheets

A Call Sheet is issued daily, and provides the details of the day's planned shooting activities, specifying what is required and what time it is required. Figure 13.1 shows the layout and components of a typical production Call Sheet. Call times for each unit of the crew are listed. Each location is described by address, contact and road-map reference. Tide (when relevant), sunrise and sunset times are provided. The nearest emergency services and contacts are listed. Each scene that is scheduled to be shot is noted with the cast involved and call times. Information about major props, action vehicles, livestock on set, and make-up and wardrobe facilities is provided, along with special requirements of the camera crew, grips and electrics. There are notes about the location, parking availability, and any particular safety provisions such as traffic control. Scheduled catering times are provided. The Call Sheet is designed for a large production in a drama shoot, but a modified Call Sheet is used in any production, regardless of size. It includes those elements of the expanded Call Sheet format that are still relevant to the smaller production. The production crew should have access to all practical information relating to the day's planned activities.

AD's Report

The AD's Report includes start times and wrap (finish) times for each cast member (except extras who are recorded on a separate extras sheet, usually also filled out

PRODUCTION TITLE

Producers: *Producer's name(s)*   Director: *Director's name*
Production office: *Street address*   Telephone number   Fax number
Postal address: *Postal address office* Mobile contact: *Production Coordinator or Production Secretary*
Editing Suite: *Street address* Editor *telephone number* Assistant Editor *telephone number*

CALL SHEET 6

LOCATION: 1. SCRIPT LOCATION
        All locations @ *street address*
     2. SCRIPT LOCATION
     3. SCRIPT LOCATION
     4. SCRIPT LOCATION

UNIT BASE: *Street address*

ON-SET MOBILES:
2nd Assistant Director: *name, mobile*
Unit Manager: *name, mobile*
PRODUCTION MOBILES:
Production Manager: *name, mobile*
Production Coordinator: *name, mobile*

SHOOT DAY: 6
DAY: *Day*
DATE: *Date*

Unit called @ 0545
M/U & W/R called @ 0645
Pre Grip & Elex. @ 0645
Crew call: 0730
Breakfast on arrival @ 0715-0745
Est. wrap: 1815

Est. screen time: 04:50
Sunrise: 0552
Sunset: 1925

WEATHER: 19-25 °C Λ few showers, chance thunderstorm. NE winds.

Sc. #	Script timing	Set synopsis	Character	Artists	Travel	M/U W/R	On set
47A	D10 0.05	**Int – SCRIPT LOCATION – Morning** *Scene description*	Name	Name	0630	0700	0745
22	D2 0.25	**Int – SCRIPT LOCATION – Day** *Scene description*	Name Name	Name Name	0630	0700	Cld 0830
40	D7 0.50	**Int – SCRIPT LOCATION – Day** *Scene description*	Name Name	Name Name	0830	0915	Cld 1000
54	D11 0.55	**Int – SCRIPT LOCATION – Day** *Scene description*	Name Name	Name Name			Cld Cld
96	D18 0.75	**Int – SCRIPT LOCATION – Day** *Scene description*	Name	Name		Cld	1315
STAND-BY SCENE							
101	D19 0.10	**Int – SCRIPT LOCATION – Day** *Scene description*	Name	Name			
END OF DAY 6							

CAST PICK-UP: 3rd Assistant Director (*mobile*) to P/U *cast member* and *cast member* from their
            accommodation @   0630 and travel to location
            Runner (*mobile*) to P/U *cast member* from home @ 0830 and travel to location
            Runner (*mobile*) to P/U *cast member* from home @ 1300 and travel to location

PARKING: Please park on the streets surrounding *street address*.
            ****DO NOT PARK ON CERTAIN STREET****

PROPS: Sc 22 – CAD computer screen, cake
            Sc 54, 40 – CAD Computer screen
            Sc 47A – Graphic 'card' same as Sc49
            Sc 96 – Flowers
            Sc 101 – Camera @ top of stairs

COSTUMES: Sc 96 – Characters' changes
            Sc 102 – Hawaiian shirt

CAMERA: Sc 22, 40, 47A – Computer screen to be seen
            Sc 96 – Hand-held

ADDITIONAL LABOUR: 1 × *security person* ex *company* called @ 1830-1000 to *street address*
                 Crew member replacement *name* (*mobile*) (Best Boy) called @ 0645

CATERING:
Breakfast for   #   at   0715-0745
Lunch for   #   at   1245-1330
Afternoon tea for   #   at   1600-1615

RUSHES:
EXPOSED NEGATIVE to taken by *runner's name* and then to be **picked up by** *Laboratory* (*contact name, mobile*)
@ *location*.
EDITOR'S PAPERWORK to be **put in 'EDITOR'S' envelope** and dropped to *Editing Suite*.
DATs to be dropped to *Editing Suite*.
CONTINUITY AND MARKED-UP SCRIPT to be faxed to *editor* (Editing Suite Attn. *editor, fax number*) morning
after shoot.
OFFICE PAPERWORK, camera, sound, AD reports and continuity to be **placed in 'TO OFFICE' envelope** provided
and handed to *runner* (*name, mobile*) the morning after wrap.
All office paperwork then to be given to *Production Coordinator* (*name, mobile*) by *runner*.
DAILY DVD RUSHES will be provided **for screening** at the *Production Office*.

TELECINE: (Day 4 rushes) 0600 @ *Telecine location*

ADVANCE SCHEDULE:
SHOOT DAY: **7**   EST. CREW CALL: **1115**
ACTUAL LOCATION: *Street address*
SCRIPT LOCATION: *Script location*
SCENES: 67, 95, 37, 60, 61, 101, 83

Name
1st Assistant Director

Figure 13.1: Layout of a typical Call Sheet for a television drama.

by the 2nd AD) and crew member, and any late arrivals. It will also note when meal breaks began and their duration and, of special importance, any delays or accidents and their cause, equipment failure, or late delivery, even when it didn't actually delay production. Accidents, or anything else with OH&S implications, are also reported on an Incident Report in greater detail, whether they resulted in injury or delay or not. If the production, and particularly the producer who carries a considerable responsibility for the production's duty of care, knows of potential or looming safety problems, there is a greater chance of heading them off before a serious accident does happen.

Continuity Daily Report

The Continuity Daily Report tabulates details of the shooting of scheduled scenes, their estimated timing, and cumulative timing in the shoot to date. It will note scheduled scenes that were not shot or not completed and will have to be rescheduled, and unscheduled scenes that were picked up opportunistically. It will note crew call times, time when set-up of the first scene of the day was ready, and wrap time for the day's shoot, as well as any delays, as a cross-reference with the AD's Report.

Daily Progress Report

The Daily Progress Report is compiled by the production office from reports that came from the shoot the previous day. It will include:
- start and wrap times, meal breaks and first set-up
- scenes shot and scheduled scenes not shot
- cumulative program timing and its variation from the original program timing
- shooting ratio (estimate of the ratio between footage shot and footage that will be in the finished program, calculated as the ratio of duration of footage shot to program timing to date)
- shooting days to date, estimated days to complete the shoot, and whether there is a change in the scheduled total days
- stock usage to date
- cast call and wrap times, and days worked on the production to date by each actor.
    The report will also list additional crew and equipment on the day, including props, action vehicles and livestock, and provide details of any accidents or delays. Because the Daily Progress Report is a major instrument of a producer's ability to keep the shoot under effective management, it will list anything of any sort that they should know about as a management issue, whether it caused a delay in production or not. The preference is to head off the potential for delay before it becomes a practical reality, whether that's from a chronic latecomer or an accident waiting to happen. A sample Daily Progress Report is shown in Figure 13.2.

Variations in different scales of production

Where there is no continuity person or no 2nd AD, their reports are probably unnecessary (even delegated to another person), as would be the case in the

'HEARTS ENTWINED' – DAILY PROGRESS REPORT

PRODUCER:	**Jennifer Sing**		SHOOTING DAY	6
DIRECTOR:	Akhim Tiporasov			
DIRECTOR OF PHOTOGRAPHY:	John Steele		SHOOTING DATE	29/06/06
FIRST ASSISTANT DIRECTOR:	Lindie McConnell			

Unit call:	0545	SHOOT DATE START:	22/06/06
Crew call:	0730	SCHEDULED FINISH DATE:	04/08/06
M/U/Hair called:	0645	REVISED FINISH DATE:	
W/R called:	0645	**SETS/LOCATIONS:**	**1.** ABLE HOUSE – 17 Smith St, Woodville
Turned over:	0820		**2.** BACKYARD SHED – 17 Smith St, Woodville
Lunch from:	1250		**3.** NEIGHBOUR'S HOUSE – 19 Smith St, Woodville
to:	1335		**4.** SHOPPING CENTRE – Woodville Mall
Wrap location:	1830		
SHOOTING HOURS:	**1015**		

TRAVEL TIME:		Scene nos. shot today:		Unscheduled scenes shot today:
TOTAL HOURS		47A, 22, 40, 54pt, 96, 106, 107, 94, 102		94
SLATES:	107–137	Scheduled scenes not shot today: S/B 101		Scenes deleted today:
NO. OF SET-UPS **PREV.:**	106	Cumulative scenes not shot:		Cumulative scenes deleted:
TODAY:	**31**	30, 62, 94, 101		
TOTAL:	137			

SHOOTING DAYS			SCRIPT	Scenes	Est. time	Act. time		RATIOS	
Scheduled:	20		Prev. shot:	31	23.09	24.37		Scheduled ratio:	**16.6:1**
To date:	6		Shot today:	8	4.45	5.02		Daily ratio:	12.1:1
Estimate to			To date:	39	27.54	29.39		Average ratio:	12.2:1
complete:	14		To be shot:	73	58.47	58.47		Daily average:	4.57
Est. total:	20		Total:	**112**	**86.41**	**88.26**		Original timing:	86.41
								Cumulative +/–	+1.45

STOCK	Loaded	Gross	Expos.	Print	N/Gs	Waste		S/End		SOUND		STILLS	
										DAT	Tsfer	Colour	B/W
Previously	12 000	11 220	10 720	8 680	2 040	500		780		7			
Today	2 000	2 290	2 220	1 440	780	70	+	450		2			
Total	14 000	13 510	12 940	10 120	2 820	570	–	740		9	0	0	0
	0	0	0					490					

∞   Please note test stock previously loaded = 2000

								EXTRAS		
Cast	Character	Pick-up	Make-up	Wrap loc.	Return accom.	Meal break	Total hours	No.	Cl d	Wkd
Dwayne Proud	Charles Able	0630	0700	1630	1705	0045	0950			
Larissa Hunn	Connie Baker	0630	0700	1630	1705	0045	0950			
Bill Schmidt	Charlie	0830	0915	1830	1915	0045	0830			
Giuseppe Po	Sergio Delta	1300	1330	1830	1915	0045	0415			

CATERING: BREAKFAST for 20 at 0715–0745
LUNCH for 23 at 1250–1335
AFTERNOON TEA for 22 at 1805–1820

ADDITIONAL PERSONNEL: Replacement Best Boy – David Stock – 0645–1900
1 × Security Person ex Acme Security 1800–0600

ACCIDENTS: Grips Asst, Colin Shakespeare, cut thumb; required 3 stitches. Key Grip has organised replacement for next week (no Grips Asst required Friday), name to be notified later today.

REMARKS: Stand-by Props, Silvester Slack, arrived on location 40 mins late; claimed traffic congestion had held him up.

John Briggs

John Briggs – Production Manager

Date: *30/6/06*

Figure 13.2: Daily Progress Report for a television drama shot on film.

production of most factual programs that don't include substantial reenactment shooting. In these productions, producers are likely to be able to be more intimately involved with the full breadth of the production, and less likely to need a Daily Progress Report to keep their finger on its pulse. They may need to make periodic reports to their superiors on the progress of the production. The form that these should take would be determined by the people involved at an early stage. Whatever the scale of the production, documentation is a necessary part of its management.

This chapter has outlined the main types of documentation in television projects, but any individual project will structure its office support to its particular needs, doing no more than is necessary, but sufficient to ensure its contractual obligations are met, and that the project can be guided efficiently to its end point.

Sources and further reading

General reading

Ritchie, Julia 2002, 'How to manage a film', in Case, D., Gailey, L., Knapman, C., et al., *The Production, Budgeting and Film Management Satchel*, AFC/AFTRS, Sydney.

Chapter 14

Crew, equipment and facilities

In pre-production, several strands of generic activity – assembling crews and identifying facilities needed, casting and location hunting, to name a few – are underway as the production unit prepares for the shoot. Each of these will be examined in detail separately, with no real significance to the order as they operate at much the same time. We will start with the assembly of the various teams that will make up the production crew.

Decisions are made about the positions needed in each crew, the individuals to fill those positions, and the equipment and facilities necessary to carry out the requirements of production. These are matters of constant consultation and refinement, of discussion between director and HOD about the creative demands of the production and how to meet them, with producer and production manager about the capacity of the budget to provide those needs, with the 1st AD about how to plan the logistics of the activities identified for efficient and achievable production scheduling, and between a HOD and key members of their team on how best to organise the components and procedures of their craft area. Because this is the team that is actually recording the program (the main purpose of the production phase), we will deal first with the camera crew, but all components of the production crew are equally as necessary to a successful shoot.

14.1 Choices of format

Format of the program

One of the first practical decisions to be made regarding the camera crew is the format on which the program will be shot. To some degree, the choice of format will determine the make-up of the camera crew. The subject of format has already been discussed in Chapters 2 and 6. It will have been considered and possibly decided by the beginning of pre-production. It may be mandated or implicit in funding agreements with broadcasters and, in any case, it is likely that a format would have been indicated in the program proposal. At whatever point along the development and pre-production pathways these decisions take place, they involve a routine set of options.

Film or videotape

The first decision is whether to record the image on film or videotape and, if the latter, on analogue or digital tape. Increasingly in television, the choice is narrowing to the single option of digital tape. The transition to digital has progressed sufficiently that there is little advantage in shooting now on analogue tape. For some time, even before the advent of digital tape, videotape had been replacing film as the preferred medium of recording for television. Videotape has greater technical compatibility with an electronic broadcast system. Technical improvements in videotape have closed the gap between it and film (especially 16 mm film, the conventional format in television's earlier days). Also, videotape costs less than film to purchase and doesn't involve processing and printing expenses on top of that. These advantages increase with digital tape, which has the capacity for duplication without quality loss and is more technically compatible with the digital post-production systems that are widely used now in the industry (see Chapter 23).

Circumstances in which film is used

Film is still retained for some high-end production, principally of drama and commercials. It has a visual quality and resolution in its larger formats that digital tape doesn't quite match, although HDTV comes close to it. The former standard, 16 mm film, is near to an extinct species. A television production planning to shoot on film will probably use 35 mm stock; 70 mm film would achieve the objective of high quality even more, but the higher cost generally precludes it. Indeed, television transmission may well reduce 70 mm film to the same quality as 35 mm film on broadcast. Since a program sourced on 35 mm film would be replayed off videotape for transmission, how much of the superior quality of film will be retained for broadcast? In fact, use of film for television drama is generally limited to programs where an overseas broadcaster has specified it or the production company believes that this will increase the likelihood of overseas broadcaster sales, or there is some expectation of cinema release.

Aspect ratio

Another option to consider is aspect ratio, an issue that has cropped up with the advent of digital television and the possibility of transmission as a widescreen picture. The alternatives for recording are the standard ratio of 4:3 and the widescreen ratio of 16:9, with options for transmission presentation of the picture, as outlined in Chapter 2 and illustrated in Figure 2.1. If a broadcaster pre-sale agreement specifies a delivery format, then the program should be shot in a format that enables this. However, the producer may want to keep open the possibility of further sales of the program on completion and would want to provide the program to that market in any of the formats it might require. Australian FTA networks generally now require delivery in widescreen format, although the bulk of their viewers still receive on standard (4:3) sets. The practical approach is to shoot 4:3 safe on 16:9 to maximise flexibility. In this approach, the camera records 16:9 but the cameraman is instructed to keep the essential picture within a 4:3 frame marked in the viewfinder. A program recorded in this fashion can be broadcast acceptably in either format. The reverse process of converting 4:3 material to widescreen is also possible through an aspect ratio converter (ARC), by cropping the top and bottom of the picture. This will lose some resolution quality as well as some of the picture, so it is possible, but not preferred.

Digital video cameras

Most productions decide to shoot on digital videotape (DV) these days, so the question is which DV format to use. The choices from least sophisticated to most are:

- Domestic DV camera – versatile and affordable with handling mobility, less technically sophisticated, but very user-friendly. It is used particularly in documentary, current affairs and other factual shoots.
- Professional DV camera – a more robust camera providing higher quality pictures and sound. This is a development by Panasonic (DVCPro) and Sony (DVCam) from the domestic version.
- Digital Betacam – a high-quality camera for drama and high-end documentary, colloquially called 'digibeta'. With 800 lines to the image, it has better definition than other DV formats (625 lines) and better control over picture, but comes at a significantly higher price. This is a move by Sony to a digital camera that maintains the position its SP Betacam held in the analogue world.

Properly used, a domestic DV camera will record broadcast-quality pictures that are stable and reliable, with drop-outs being rare except on cheap or damaged tape stock. Its lack of fine technical control, particularly in lenses, limits its usefulness in high-end production. Professional DV cameras bridge this gap (their lenses are superior for a start), while retaining the advantage of lighter weight and cost over Digital Betacam.

Use of DV camera in documentary and current affairs

The DV camera is increasingly being used in observational documentary because the camera's small size is discreet enough for the subject of the shoot to ignore it, and because the camera and tapes are inexpensive. Due to automatic functions, there are no camera setting adjustments to distract the operator (often a cameraman–director) from capturing the action. Current affairs is increasingly a video-journalist operation, where a discreet camera can provide added safety in volatile situations in which the press might be targeted. Having said that, a sole operator doesn't have the second pair of watchful eyes that a professional colleague can provide. Surprisingly, it is seldom used for news, although it is well-suited to that genre, probably because news is produced by the networks who perhaps frown on 'mickey mouse' equipment.

High-definition DV cameras

Most of the cameras noted above will record widescreen as anamorphic 16:9 (i.e. widescreen squeezed to a 4:3 frame), but a secondary issue is whether to take this the further step to HDTV. The advantages are high image quality and market flexibility (many networks in Australia and overseas have some mandated HDTV obligations); the disadvantages can be higher cost and some technical difficulties, particularly at the post-production phase. At the top end, Sony and Panasonic have produced high-definition DV cameras that are a viable alternative to film in drama. HDV cameras, a further development from the domestic DV camera by Sony, are attracting attention from documentary makers because they combine higher image quality with all the advantages of a DV camera (i.e. portability, price). There is debate about whether HDV is a true HDTV format, but there is no doubt that it provides a better quality picture than DV.

14.2   The camera crew

Camera crew size

The make-up of the camera crew will vary according to the nature and needs of the production. The budget is usually framed to accommodate the number of people considered necessary for the style of the production, rather than the crew being the number the budget can afford. The make-up of the crew might be reconsidered only if the production were having difficulty raising the full amount budgeted, or there was some advantage in combining crew roles.

Selection and hiring of camera crew

The principal cameraman, usually called the Director of Photography (DOP), is attached to the production at an early stage, often during development. They will advise on the crew roles needed (including if there needs to be anyone apart from themself) and make recommendations about who to hire for these roles. This may include specialist camera operators, such as Steadicam operators or underwater photographers. The producer has formal approval of engagement of these people.

   Negotiation is managed by the producer or the production manager, but the DOP's advice is generally a key factor. The period of engagement may vary in each case according to when their role is required. It's important that the DOP is familiar with and has confidence in their team, and for this reason they will be central to its selection. They should not be the one making offers of work or a fee to crew members, unless they do that with the authority of the producer. Otherwise, the DOP's role in these matters is advisory only.

Field crew in factual programs

Sometimes there is only one cameraman without the need for a support team. This is mostly the case in news, current affairs, documentary and segments for

Figure 14.1: Camera and sound (field) crews: relationships in documentary production.

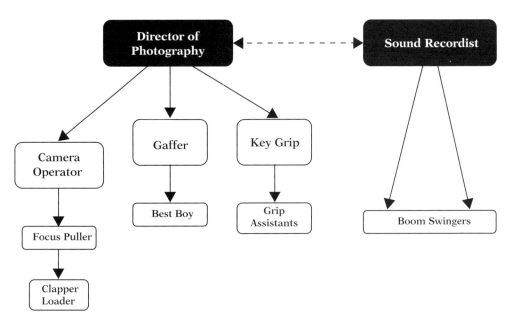

Figure 14.2: Camera and sound crews: relationships in a drama production.

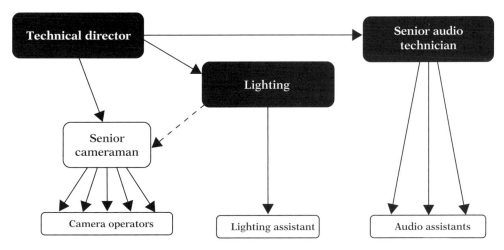

Figure 14.3: Camera and sound crews: relationships in studio or outside broadcast production.

magazine programs. Here, the term camera crew isn't used and cameraman and sound recordist are referred to as the field crew. These days, even the field crew may be one person, a cameraman–recordist, with audio source alternating between a camera-mounted microphone and a cabled microphone held by the director or journalist. More conventionally, the field crew for these actuality programs will be the two-person team of cameraman and recordist (Fig. 14.1). The days of a camera assistant in a three-person field crew are long gone, ever since loading and unloading film magazines ceased to be part of the duties.

Roles in a drama camera crew

At the other end of the scale is a drama (and sitcom) camera crew, where the classic team is DOP, camera operator, focus puller and clapper/loader (Fig. 14.2). Here, the DOP supervises the team, liaises with the gaffer (electrician) regarding positioning of lights, briefs the grip team regarding camera platforms (see section 14.5), and determines framing of each shot and the camera movements within the shot, in consultation with the director. The DOP in the classic crew doesn't actually operate the camera, although they will look through its eyepiece to check framing. The camera operator is the one who handles the camera while each take is recorded. The focus puller operates the camera's focus ring, to a brief, during the take, and provides general camera assistance. The clapper/loader operates the slate (a board to identify scene and take number, and provide a guide for synchronising picture and audio in post-production), loads and unloads film magazines, and also assists generally. A videotape drama has no great need for a clapper/loader, so this position and that of focus puller will be amalgamated as camera assistant. These days, the DOP may elect to operate the camera themself, especially with greater directorial interest in a hand-held camera style, so the camera operator may be dispensed with. Flexibility is the name of the game, as it is in television production generally. The classic camera crew will be varied according to the circumstances of the production.

Preparation by the camera department for a shoot

Much of the DOP's pre-production time is spent consulting with the director, 1st AD, production designer, and often post-production people as well. There is detailed planning of the camera's coverage of each scene, of specific camera, lighting and grip requirements in each case, and of the days on which these are needed. The camera kit is selected and tested, locations are surveyed and production planning meetings are attended as the production coordinates its component activities. The members of the crew are on board for some of these activities. The operator or assistant will assist in assembling and testing equipment for the shoot. Anyone else in the crew may only join it a day or so before the shoot starts.

Second unit crew

A major drama production may have a second camera crew, called the second unit, which is a scaled-down version of the main crew. This will be used for shooting small (often single-shot) scenes without major performers, establishing shots, relevant actuality footage, and other similar material where it would be more cost-efficient to use the separate crew than to tie up the main crew.

Multi-camera crews

Other production modes may have a different line-up of the camera crew from drama or documentary. Studio and OB are multi-camera productions with a number of camera operators. The senior cameraman is responsible for coordinating the team, and is the point of crew liaison for the director (Fig. 14.3). In these productions, the camera team operates as part of a studio or OB crew without the separate identity that characterises a location drama crew. Multi-camera studio drama is still used for soaps. The lighting technician will light the studio for multi-camera use and is a senior studio technician rather than part of the camera team. Reality programs may be shot with multi-cameras (as was *Big Brother*) or with several field crews, often single-person, following the participants (as was *My Restaurant Rules*).

14.3   Hiring of crew

Terms and conditions of hiring

The general procedure of hiring crew is much the same regardless of where in the production structure they fit. Once a crew member is decided, the job can be offered if the production is funded. A fee or salary is negotiated, along with all the other matters that should be agreed before work on the production commences. These include:

- ensuring that they understand the nature and demands of the shoot and what will be required of them
- whether they will be hired as an individual or contracted through a company
- whether it will be a five- or six-day week and arrangements regarding entitlements such as overtime
- whether the production will hire their vehicle or pay for their use of it on production business by a rate per kilometre ('kilometrage'), and the basis of payment for that
- whether they will hire equipment to the production, and the specific details and rates
- arrangements regarding travel, if any is envisaged
- method of payment of the fee or salary
- superannuation fund details if they are eligible (see Chapter 26).

The crew deal memo

Agreed conditions are filled out in a Crew Deal Memo (available from the production manager or as pro formas in the AFC/AFTRS handbook *The Production, Budgeting and Film Management Satchel*), which is used to draw up an employment contract for that crew member. Casual crew can be hired on an order form or simple casual crew contract. The awards covering the production crew are detailed in Chapter 18.

14.4   Audio crew and equipment

When to have a dedicated sound recordist

Although there are opportunities with the development of flexible field recording equipment to make some programs without a sound recordist, it is in the production's interest to make sure it doesn't pay too high a program price for the budget saving. Low-quality audio recording where necessary dialogue (e.g. in an interview) is indistinct or distorted is distracting for viewers and, when it continues, they are likely to give up on the program. It won't even get to that stage if the broadcaster rejects the program for failing to meet technical standards. General chatter and background audio doesn't need the technical attention that location voice and music requires. The single-person field crew may be an option for observational documentary or current affairs if the camera operator has sufficient technical skill to ensure acceptable audio quality. Otherwise a sound recordist should be part of the production crew.

Microphone selection

A dedicated audio person is necessary on any documentary location where audio recording may be problematic, such as where there is noisy ambient sound, a need to ride audio levels, or for recording multiple voices. Live performance and music recording requires specialist skill for the placement of microphones ('mics') for direct recording, or for taking a split from a public address (PA) system or the 'front of house' desk. In a documentary shoot, the recordist might consider radio microphones on the key talent, a directional 'gun' microphone (the Sennheiser ME66 is the industry standard) to chase the general action, and use a small mixer (perhaps four-channel) on location. A solo operator might use a camera-mounted directional microphone, with a radio microphone recording to a second audio track on the videotape. Production scheduling should allow time to set up radio microphones if they are to be used, as it takes a while to get them operating satisfactorily.

Recording interview questions

A director will sometimes say they are not interested in recording the questions for an interview as they intend to use the answers only. This is an unnecessary risk. It is prudent to record the questions off a separate microphone balanced to the interviewee's microphone. Although a program may often set out to drop questions in editing, sometimes a question is necessary to make sense of a good answer. At other times, the interviewee will talk over the question. Muffled questions or contrasting quality is distracting if it cannot be corrected (and generally it can't). Producers and directors should train themselves to be immune to the claim that 'it can be fixed in post'. Post-production can correct some problems but not all. It is much better to not need fixing at all.

Sound recording for drama

A drama production, and most other contrived (i.e. non-actuality) programs, wouldn't contemplate shooting without a dedicated sound recordist. A specialist drama recordist will have a trolley-mounted kit set up for drama, including boom poles to attach directional microphones. The sound crew will probably include one or two boom swingers who target performers with their boomed microphones and ensure dialogue can be recorded with minimum noise interference.

Back-up recording of sound

Video drama will be recorded 'double-head' as a safety measure. It is recorded simultaneously on to a videotape audio track and a separate recorder, as either digital audio tape (DAT) or mini-disc (MD). Audio quality on video formats is as good as on DAT or MD, so the double recording is not for quality reasons, but simply insurance against drop-out or other recording glitches. If the audio source cannot be cabled to the camera for some reason, such as camera mobility, the DAT/MD option provides the assurance that sound can still be recorded.

Film drama cannot be shot double-head as there is no facility for recording audio on film (there once was, but it was restricted mostly to news shooting anyway). Documentary will often shoot double-head for safety, unless the requirement for mobility is sufficiently high that this is a disadvantage.

14.5   Lighting and grips

Lighting crew and grip crew

Two additional crews are included under the DOP's supervision in a drama shoot: a lighting crew and a grip crew. Each is generally hired as a team with its own equipment truck. Lighting and grips are also likely to have a major part to play in a live performance OB. Pre-rigs for both electrics and grips can take some time and will tie up much of the crew. The schedule in a drama shoot will need to accommodate this. Scenes that don't require these crews may be scheduled immediately before a large lighting or grip set-up so that pre-rig can take place at the same time. If this cannot be scheduled, the production may hire a casual pre-rig crew.

The gaffer's equipment

In drama, it is customary for a specialist electrician (the gaffer) to be hired, to set up lights to the DOP's specifications and to attend to other electrical requirements of the shoot. A lighting truck carries a range of lights, stands, transformers, and cutters and gels. The gaffer may bring a small generator or the production might hire a generator truck, depending on the scale of the lighting requirements of the shoot and the production's budget. Some gaffers will charge burn time (replacement value) for high performance lights, whereas others will include burn time in the quote. This should be clarified when negotiating hiring of a gaffer's equipment. A documentary cameraman will more commonly set their own lightweight lights from a four-light kit. However, a gaffer might be hired to assist with a large lighting set-up.

Grip equipment

Grip equipment covers a range of moving and stationary platforms for mounting the camera. These may include:

* dollies (moving camera platforms on wheels) and tracks on which to run them, although dollies can also operate on smooth floors
* cranes and mini-jib arms for elevating and lowering the camera in mid-shot
* flying fox mounts to be rigged for aerial moving shots
* scaffold rigging of towers for high-angle (HA) shooting
* cherry pickers and scissor lifts for moving HA shots
* mounts for cameras to shoot from cars (inside and outside), boats and aircraft.

As some grip gear is expensive, there may be gear on the grip truck that is not needed for the shoot. The production should specify what grip equipment it requires, and exclude non-required equipment from the hire price.

14.6   Art department

Role of an art department

Art department crew can be a major part of a drama, comedy or studio production, especially with a period or costume drama, or a lavish studio variety show, although both have gone somewhat out of favour (the former for budgetary as much as fashion reasons). Documentaries, when they need visual embellishment, generally don't set up an art department unless this will be a major part of the production, such as in a dramatised historical reconstruction. Otherwise, the incidental needs of location dressing, props or costume will be coordinated by someone in the production unit, in discussion with the director. The structure and relationships in the art department are shown schematically in Figure 14.4.

The production designer

Where an art department has been established, the production designer has overall responsibility for its creative output as well as management of the department's budget. The trick to all design in this area (principally sets, location dressing, costume, hair and make-up) is to balance imagination and creativity with economic effectiveness. The production designer works closely with the director, providing ideas and drawings of elements that will visually enhance the story and its themes on camera, providing realism, mood and insight into characters. A production designer liaises with their creative overseers in the component units of the art department, providing the brief for the production and soliciting ideas to present to the director on their behalf.

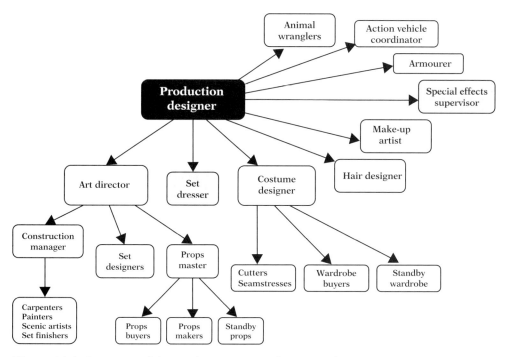

Figure 14.4: Structure of the art department in drama production.

Balance between design and photography

A designer will first make their own breakdown of the script, highlighting items of interest to art department units in each scene. They will swap notes with the DOP, with whom they share responsibility for the visual realisation of the program. Sometimes a mood or effect the director is after can best be achieved in design, sometimes in photography, and sometimes with a combination of the two. A particular colour emphasis can be created with lens filters or by letting the colour predominate in the set; a gloomy mood is created by pools of low light or use of dark wood in the set – or a combination of these. The possibilities are worked through by designer and DOP.

Studio sets and location dressing

The art director oversees set design and construction, and location dressing. Sets may be built for studio shooting, or built on location as a necessary feature added to the actual location structure (e. g. a cellar entrance at the back of a house that doesn't have a cellar). A location may be 'dressed' to give it a particular appearance quite different from its everyday use. Draughtspeople or set designers draw the plans for a set, and the construction manager is responsible for construction of a studio set or building on location, overseeing carpenters, painters, scenic artists and set finishers. The art director also oversees the props (a contraction of 'properties') team, led by a props master who does a props breakdown from the script. The props master is responsible for the scheduling and planning of props making, buying and hiring. The props team includes props buyers, props makers and stand-by props. Stand-by props looks after on-set hand-props that will be used by the cast. They may also make dressing adjustments to the set on the day. Overall responsibility for the dressing of the set (i.e. placing of all portable items such as furniture, drapes) is with a set decorator or set dresser, who works closely with the production designer on the set's 'look'.

The decision to shoot in studio or on location

Early in pre-production, the producer and the director will be consulting with the relevant HODs about which scenes are to be shot on location and which might be shot in a studio. Studio scenes require set construction, so they should generally be sets that will be used in several scenes, or settings for which no suitable location can be found. Building a set costs more, in building time, materials and studio hire, but has performance and camera position advantages, greater control of the shooting environment, and the ability to change or damage structures in ways that aren't acceptable on a location. If the script calls for a door to be kicked in, the owner of a location is unlikely to sacrifice one of their doors for that. For scenes identified as studio sets, the designer will start to sketch out some ideas to present to the director, consulting with the art director. Eventually, the finished design will be passed on to the construction manager to cost and build.

Location art direction

The remaining scenes are passed on to the location manager to search for suitable locations, some of which may require extensive dressing and some very little. Some may require set construction to add some feature to the location that is part of the story, but not part of the raw location. Sometimes a single setting in the story, perhaps a house by a railway line, or a shop, may have to be a composite of two or more locations, say, interior in one suburb and exterior in another, or a kitchen in one house and bedroom in another. Sometimes an interior set is built for the studio to match an exterior location. This relationship in the ABC drama, *Patrol Boat*, is noted in Chapter 12.

Wardrobe

The wardrobe unit is overseen by a costume designer, who designs the look of each character in consultation with production designer and director. Costumes can be bought, hired, or made by the wardrobe unit itself, depending on availability and cost. The wardrobe team has cutters and seamstresses (who make costumes), buyers (who buy or hire), and stand-by wardrobe (who dress the actors for each scene on shooting days).

Determining wardrobe requirements

The costume designer breaks down the wardrobe requirements of each scene, integrating that with discussion about the look of each character with the director, production designer and perhaps DOP as well. Among other things, the script breakdown will establish the number of 'outfits' that will be required for the production. The number of cast, the number of separate story days for each character, and whether the script implies a change of costume over the same day (the overcoat worn to lunch on one day would probably not be appropriate for the bedroom scene late in the same scripted day) are all factored into an estimate of the total number of outfits, a figure used for budget calculations and scheduling of costume preparation. As the list of required outfits consolidates, due consideration should be taken of doubles (for stunt work), scripted damage to clothing (requiring duplication of some clothes), and opportunities to negotiate with cast or their agents for the actors to bring their own clothing (where they would have items appropriate to the character and the story). The producer may see an opportunity to negotiate with fashion companies to supply some characters' clothing as a discounted hire or a contra deal in exchange for an on-screen credit. The contra deal should be agreed in a written contract.

Measuring and fitting actors

Wardrobe needs will place a requirement of several calls on cast for measuring and fitting, whether the costumes are to be acquired or made. The production must make sure these calls are scheduled and budgeted as cast costs. The greater effort and greater allocation of wardrobe resources, including budget, will naturally be on lead cast, where it can have the greatest impact. The smaller the role, the more the production will look for compromises that will help contain wardrobe costs. This is not as easily achieved in period drama, where particular costumes can be hired only if they are available for hire, otherwise they will have to be made by the wardrobe team, a time-consuming and costly alternative. One reason this drama genre is so expensive, often prohibitively so, is that cast have to be dressed fully in period attire. This applies to every actor, no matter how minor, although short cuts can sometimes be taken with extras (but never enough). Fantasy costumes, on the other hand, are generally hard to hire (in that case, the program would be co-opting someone else's fantasy), so these productions can put a heavy load on the costume-makers. Alleviating that problem somewhat might be the possibility that not all characters in a production are fantasy. In fantasy, anything goes so long as it works, opening the way for the imaginative use of low-cost found materials.

Make-up and hair

A production may have a separate make-up artist and hair designer, or the two roles may be combined in one person, depending on the demands of the production. On days on which a large cast is called or where make-up and hair is particularly demanding, such as in period drama with wigs and complex hair design, casual staff will be hired to assist. As with other areas, the make-up artist and hair designer will break down the script to determine the needs of each scene and important changes in hair or appearance over the scripted duration of the story. Adequate time needs to be allowed in the shooting schedule for the long procedure of make-up and hair in ageing an actor. This is often scheduled as overtime prior to the shoot.

Make-up tests and special effects make-up

Make-up and hairdresser should see all key cast before the shoot, ideally initially during rehearsals to form preliminary ideas of the look they will bring to the actor. Tests of this look can be done in the last week of pre-production for director and designer approval, and DOP and costume designer information. Most make-up artists should be capable of special effects make-up (e.g. fantasy and horror looks, wounds, and other physical damage), but prosthetics and animatronics (respectively stationary and movable add-ons to the body, usually to the head) are commonly subcontracted to a specialist.

Make-up facility on location

Although make-up and hair staff generally bring their own materials, for which they charge the production, consideration needs to be given to appropriate facilities for make-up and stand-by wardrobe on set, whether this is a room, a caravan or even a marquee tent in a remote location. Consultation with the make-up artist, hair designer and stand-by wardrobe is necessary to ensure that the facility arranged has all the requirements of space, chairs, lighting and mirrors, hanging space, power for hair dryers, security, and so on. The facility must be a place in which actors will feel comfortable.

Specialist areas

Specialist areas that also come under the production designer's management, and are part of the art department's realisation of visual components of the story, include action vehicle coordinators and mechanics, animal wranglers and trainers, armourers, and special effects (notably explosives, pyrotechnics and bullet hits) technicians. These have safety considerations, which are examined in Chapter 21.

14.7   Advisors and consultants

Performance and subject matter advisors

A range of advisors and consultants might be hired by a production to assist with specialist areas. In performance or dramatised programs, such as drama, comedy or variety, they might provide dialogue coaching, dance and music tuition, choreography, or weapons handling advice. They might provide specialised knowledge or subject matter advice as experts in a field that is the subject of a program. These consultants are more commonly used in actuality productions such as documentary, but may, on occasion, be used in drama. A period drama may also hire a researcher to assist its art department to get an authentic look for the production. Overseas shoots may use local liaison people or 'fixers' who can assist them through the maze of local practices that are too arcane for outsiders to navigate (see Chapter 17). Overseas shoots may also require an interpreter where English is not widely spoken, and will require a translator after the shoot to assist with post-production back at home base.

Contracting advisors and consultants

Apart from the overseas fixers and interpreters, for whom this may not be practical, advisors and consultants should be contracted even if there is some difficulty quantifying their contribution. With technical advisors, this may not be too problematic because they will make their contributions at specified times. With consultants there can often be a general understanding of what they will contribute for which an agreed fee will be paid. Whether they meet expectations will be a matter reflecting the judgement in hiring them. Some flattery or coercion may be necessary to assist the process. Many contribute more than envisaged because they get carried along by the excitement of production; others will have seen it as an opportunity to pick up some easy money. There's always an element of risk. The contract's main purpose will bc to clarify the fee, give the arrangement a sounder business footing, and head off any potential chain of title confusion that might otherwise arise.

Sources and further reading

General reading

Case, D., Gailey, L., Knapman, C., et al., *The Production, Budgeting and Film Management Satchel*, AFC/AFTRS, Sydney.

Specific reading

Browne, Steven E. 2002, *Video Editing: A Postproduction Primer*, 4th edn, Focal Press, Oxford, Chapter 3.
Gillezeau, Marcus 2004, *Hands On*, Currency Press, Sydney, Chapter 5.

Chapter 15

Casting, rehearsal and performance

A key ingredient of television drama and comedy is the cast, the ensemble of actors who will perform for the production, usually from a script. This chapter looks at the process of engaging actors and their preparation for the shoot. The management of cast within a production follows two pathways, which run roughly in parallel: analysis and detailing of cast needs and scheduling by the production office; and selection and hiring of cast for roles in the program, their preparation and rehearsal, and finally their performance on camera.

The interpretation of each character in a program is developed by its actor under the guidance and input of the director, a development that doesn't stop until the program is recorded. Early views about the nature of the character and its role in the narrative and themes of the program are exchanged at casting meetings and may form part of the reason for selecting a particular actor for a particular part. The actor then uses the script to develop their interpretation and understanding of the character, which is developed more fully and translated into actions and modes of dialogue delivery at rehearsal. Finally, there may be finetuning of aspects of presentation of the character in the shooting of a scene. This may even occur between one take and the next, as some mannerism or delivery of a line seems able to be varied to better effect. When the scene is completed and the crew starts setting up for the next scene, there are no more opportunities for the actor to change it further (unless a reshoot is arranged), although the director and editor between them still have that as an option. This is a significant aspect of performance for television – it is not complete until the program is completed. The actor acts, but the final shape of the performance is decided by the editor and director – within the constraints of what has been recorded.

15.1   Types of performers

Lead and support actors

There is a hierarchy of performance in a production that has long been recognised, both within the film and television industry and by the public at large. The actors playing major characters in a program are called lead actors. Their 'star' quality may be as important a reason for casting them in the program as their acting ability. The lesser or minor characters in the script are supporting roles. Casting of support actors (or 'performers') is based on their perceived acting skills. The exception is the 'cameo' role, where a recognisable public figure will play a relatively minor role.

Actors' television award

The terms of employment, including conditions and minimum fees, for all actors come under the Actors Television Programs Agreement (ATPA), an award agreement negotiated between SPAA and MEAA. The ATPA has two sets of minimum rates, for:
1. serial drama or serial comedy
2. programs other than serial drama or comedy.
This does not cover the employment of actors on feature films, who are covered under a separate agreement between SPAA and MEAA. The calculation of the components of cast payments is detailed in Chapter 18.

Classification of lead and support actors under the award

The ATPA doesn't recognise leading and supporting roles, but instead groups all actors with any substantial role as performers. They are divided into two classes according to experience, determined by a formula contained in the award. The cut-off point between Performer Class 1 and Performer Class 2 is a fairly low level of experience, so most actors will qualify as Performer Class 2. In practice, however, actors sort into leads (and indeed, stars) and supporting roles anyway. For a start, award rates are time-based and as a lead actor would be expected to be engaged for more performance days than a support actor, the fee would be higher for that reason. More to the point is that the award provides for minimum rates only. A factor in casting leads is that they often already have an acting reputation, which translates into a market rate for their appearance in a program. Many of the leads will negotiate (or their agents will) a personal margin above the award minimum rate as their fee for appearance. These negotiated rates are nominally confidential, but a producer should always assume the main players may find out the other actors' fees.

Extras

Actors with smaller parts and extras will be paid award minimum rates because they don't have a market presence to negotiate a personal margin, or because the role is too small to exercise their market rate. Extras are actors who are part of crowd or ensemble scenes, and who appear only incidentally or in backgrounds. They don't speak dialogue individually or perform individually under direction, although extras may do these under general direction. An actor who is instructed by the director or assistant director to say a particular line is no longer an extra in that scene. If the instruction is to all extras to talk generally about such-and-such, they are still extras. The actors might be instructed to move in the background as passers-by, and some might be given particular instructions on how to achieve this. In both instances they remain as extras.

Bit players

A bit player is an actor who is not required to speak more than six lines of dialogue or more than fifty words in any program or episode. The agreement between ABC and MEAA for the employment of actors has a similar (but not identical) definition of a category it calls special extra. A character's dialogue may be reduced in the script to avoid a bit player rising to the higher-cost level of performer. A mime is not regarded as a bit player (even though it technically falls within the definition), but a performer.

Doubles

Under some circumstances a double might be used for a cast member, typically for a skill the actor doesn't have, such as horse riding, or in a driving sequence in a remote location where someone of similar build can be disguised as the actor cast. A double is paid at the same rate as an extra unless they are standing in for the actor as a stunt performer, in which case they would be paid at Stunt Performer rates (see section 15.4).

15.2   Script breakdown and cast scheduling

Parallel processes in selecting actors

The selection and hiring of actors for the production begins on two fronts. While the producer and director give thought to who might play crucial roles in the program, the production office determines the administrative aspects of that: how many performers, how many extras, and for how many days in each case; whether the budget can afford all those actors for all those days; and what ancillary requirements and issues there are, such as stunt work, travel requirements and consequent cost.

Script breakdown and cast cross-plot

Script breakdown has already been described in Chapter 12. Each scene in the script is assessed for the production requirements it will generate. These include detailing cast and the circumstances in which they will be used. The script breakdown determines the roles that are performers and bit players, and a preliminary estimate is made of the number of extras needed for each scene. At the same time, the 1st AD will draw up a preliminary schedule from the script breakdown. This is used to draft a cast cross-plot, which is a calendar grid in table format, noting each day each actor is working. Figure 15.1 shows a typical cast cross-plot. Information from the cross-plot is transferred to the Cast Costing spreadsheet, which is tabbed on the AFC budget format.

Other practical issues to be considered

Script breakdown analysis also alerts a production management team to other cost-related issues that will impact on the planning and cost of production. Night shoots create penalty costs and a need to schedule the following day's shoot to avoid insufficient turnaround penalties (see Chapter 19). Some actors may not be available for roles that have a night shoot component if they have pre-existing theatre commitments, unless the night shoot can be scheduled around those commitments. Wet weather cover (see Chapter 19), where alternative scenes will need to be shot if the weather precludes the scheduled scenes, will need to be determined from the script breakdown. Shooting days at out-of-town locations will be noted. Actors under the age of sixteen are also noted. They are not required by the award to be paid more than half the adult rate, but if they are under fifteen, state regulation may restrict their hours of work and place other conditions on the production (see section 15.5).

Efficient scheduling of cast

The cross-plot is a handy overview picture of actor use. It can be used as a reference for assessing the budgetary impact of the initial schedule and any subsequent adjustments to the schedule. Support cast are scheduled, wherever possible, to do all their scenes in one day. Where cast are required for more than one day, the schedule tries to group these days together. Where an actor can be scheduled for four days in a week, consideration might be given to contracting that performer for the full week rather than for the specified days. A weekly contract will give the production more flexibility, although the weekly rate is a bit higher than four times the daily rate. The additional cost of another day at the daily rate would come to more than the weekly rate.

Updating the cross-plot with schedule changes

As the schedule changes, the cross-plot must be updated and referenced across to the budget's Cast spreadsheet to ensure that changes are keeping within budget. Around this time, the 1st AD will clarify with the director the number of extras needed for each scene. This updated information is also entered into the Cast spreadsheet to ensure the Extras line item remains within budget.

Calculation of rights to be acquired

The rights that have to be purchased from performers are also factored into budget calculations. Certain rights will be stipulated in investment, pre-sale and/or distributor agreements, but the production may decide to purchase further rights

'Revenge of the Putty-Eaters' Cast cross-plot as at 12/3/06

Cast ID#	Character	\[March\] 27	28	29	30	31	\[April\] 1	2	3	4	5	6	7	8	9	10	11	12	13	14	15	16	Total shoot days
	Date / Day of week	Mon.	Tues.	Wed.	Thurs.	Fri.	Sat.	Sun.	Mon.	Tues.	Wed.	Thurs.	Fri.	Sat.	Sun.	Mon.	Tues.	Wed.	Thurs.	Fri.	Sat.	Sun.	
	Shoot day no.	1	2	3	4	5			6	7	8	9	10	11		12	13	14	15				
	Week no.	One							Two							Three							
1	Able	1	1						1	1	1	1			1	1	1		1				11
2	Baker		2								2	2	2		2	2							6
3	Charlie			3	3	3					3	3											5
4	Delta				4																		1
5	Echo					5																	1
6	Foxtrot											6				6	6		6				4
7																							
8																							
9	Extras (8 hours)				7																		7
10	Extras (4 hours)				8																		8 × 4 hour
11																							
12																							
13																							
14																							

Figure 15.1: Example of a cast cross-plot.

in anticipation of sales if the level of funding in the budget can accommodate them. The aggregation of these rights requirements will be reflected in a percentage figure that is applied to the fee for all cast, except extras. The performance fee for an extra includes all residuals unless the production has an overseas producer or co-producer.

15.3 Casting

Casting decisions

Casting, the process of weighing up different actors for each role and then making a selection, may be primarily in the hands of the producer (if it is a series), or the director (if it is a one-off program) or both. With major productions, the investors or broadcaster may have final approval of the actors chosen, but are unlikely to participate in the casting process otherwise.

The casting director

A casting director is often hired on a large production to assist in finding the right actor for each role, to liaise with actors' agents, and then to negotiate fees and conditions for the selected actors. A good casting director has a much more detailed knowledge of a wide range of actors than most producers or directors. They know their particular skills and talents, the roles they've played, how they work, and what they are like to work with. They have ongoing relationships with talent agents and managers and they can play a pragmatic insider's role in setting talent fees and negotiating these with the agents.

Casting against stereotype

The casting director may suggest alternative approaches to a character to those that are fixed in the mind of director or producer. Casting against stereotype can often produce interesting results, which bring a freshness and energy to the program. The BBC comedy series, *The Office*, had been looking for a beefy actor to play the ex-commando, Gareth Keenan. With his wiry build and lean face, Mackenzie Crook auditioned for the role of Tim, but it was suggested he could make a different and more interesting Gareth, the role he eventually played in the series. This may not have been a casting director's suggestion, but it is the sort of lateral approach a casting director is often able to make.

The order in which roles are cast

Casting begins with the lead roles. These are central to the program and often determine the way supporting roles will be cast. In a series, the continuing roles may be determined by the producer, with assistance from the casting director, and episode performers and guest roles will be cast by the episode director, with or without the assistance of a casting director. Characters from ethnic groups or with special skills and young children are not always available through the usual channels for actors. Finding the right actors may require some initiative and lateral thinking, as well as take a longer time. Extras and bit players will generally be cast by the 1st AD using a detailed director's brief of some specific requirements. This may even be delegated to the 2nd AD. Scenes that are shot at out-of-town locations will involve casting local extras. It may be advantageous to hire a local person to scout for them.

Interview and audition of actors

The casting process commences with discussions about who to look at as possibilities for each role. It's advisable to not have too long a short list. With a large group of people to compare, it's easy to get confused about which actor has what desirable characteristics. The short-listed actors will meet with the director or producer and chat about the nature of the character under consideration, the story and the themes underlying it in the script. The purpose is to see what insight an actor might be able to bring to their realisation of the character. There may be a reading from a section of the script, ideally with an experienced 'reader' to whom the actor can respond. Potential leads may be called back to be screen-tested, where they will perform a scene from the script on camera. The purpose here is not so much to 'pre-create' the program as to see how an actor looks on screen, how they communicate with other actors, and what body language they might use to create the role. This is also an opportunity to look at a selected lead with different actors to see what chemistry is generated between them. Sexual chemistry is always of particular interest here and has the capacity to create memorable performances. For this reason, the audition should be in an environment that is sympathetic to its purpose. It should be a comfortable place, quiet and spacious, without surrounding distractions. Audition scripts should have lead-ins so the actor can understand the context of the scene. The award allows the first audition to take place without payment of a fee, but subsequent screen tests have a prescribed fee.

Agreement of fees and conditions

Once casting is complete and actors have been chosen, terms are negotiated, usually by the casting director or production manager. Negotiated conditions on major dramas may include the approval of images, trailers and standard of accommodation, publicity obligations, and so on. These conditions can have ramifications for the budget, so that should be checked against before final agreement. The agreed fees and conditions are set out in a deal memo from which the production office will have an engagement contract drawn up. Preliminary dates will be notified for a hold on the actor, which the award stipulates cannot be for more than thirty-six hours. The production office will then start to set up a schedule of calls in preparation for the shoot.

15.4 Stunt performers

The stunt team

Stunt performers are contracted as cast members under the same award. They are graded as Class 1 or Class 2 Performers on the same basis as other actors, but may have a stunt loading on top of the award rate, and they have the same rights and conditions as other cast members. A stunt performer is a professional actor with both training and experience in the difficult actions that would be dangerous if done by an untrained actor. These include falls, vehicle crashes, animal riding and water stunts. Generally hired as a team, the performers set up and carry out their stunts to the director's brief and under the supervision of a stunt coordinator. A qualified safety officer is also hired to oversee all safety aspects of the stunt. The safety officer must not participate in the stunt itself. Safety is a prime consideration and only graded stunt performers should perform a hazardous stunt. To not do so would expose the production company and some of its personnel to prosecution were an accident to happen.

MEAA grading of stunt performers

Members of a stunt team are graded by the MEAA's National Stunt Grading Procedure into:
- Stunt action personnel or stunt trainees, equivalent to apprentice stunt actors, who can only be involved in minor background and group stunt work, not in front-line action. Otherwise they assist with the setting up of stunts.
- Stunt actors, who can be involved in front-line stunt action. Their grading is based on experience, peer recommendation and demonstration of skills.
- Safety consultants or supervisors, who write Safety Reports or work on productions as safety officers (see Chapter 13).
- Stunt coordinators, who supervise the performance of stunts and must have at least eight years experience as an accredited stunt performer.

The production manager should confirm the stunt actors', safety officer's and stunt coordinator's MEAA grading before engaging them. The safety officer's background should also be checked as having been in stunt performance, as the MEAA's grading system allows people with either stunt or special effects with explosives backgrounds to be equally qualified as safety supervisors. An injury on an ABC drama production some years ago emanated from an error in setting up a special effect with explosives. The safety officer was MEAA-qualified, but their background was stunt work, not explosives.

Mixing actor and stunt performer

Many stunts are a single action, where the stunt performer doubles for the actor playing the role. Sometimes, as in a fight scene, director and stunt supervisor can work out a judicious balance of the actor playing the role and the stunt actor doubling for them. Under strict supervision of the stunt coordinator, the actor can participate in some shots without unacceptable risk. This will give the director more options for shots. In other stunt sequences, the actor might be used in close-ups without stunt work. The stunt actor will then double for them in wider shots that include the stunt, but where substitution of the performer will not be noticed by viewers of the program.

15.5 Casting of children

State regulation of the employment of children

The employment of children in production must be properly planned to comply with regulations in the state in which the shoot takes place. Each state has different regulations with widely differing requirements, the most stringent being New South Wales. However, other states are in the process of tightening their regulations, so that the disparity across states may soon be reduced. In some states, children may be employed only with prior permission from the equivalent of a children's employment office in a community services department in that state. This is to ensure children are protected from exploitation, abuse, and inappropriate or unreasonable demands. The welfare of children is paramount when they are on set. Contact details for the responsible body in each state and territory in Australia are listed in Table 15.1.

NSW Office of the Children's Guardian

In New South Wales, the paid employment of children under fifteen in the entertainment industry, still photography and door-to-door sales is regulated under the *Children and Young Persons (Care and Protection) Act 1998* (NSW) and the Children (Care and Protection – Child Employment) Regulations 2001 (NSW). The responsible body for ensuring adherence to the regulations is the NSW Office of the Children's Guardian (OCG). Only producers holding a current Employer Authority, obtainable from the OCG, can employ children in television production. The Authority is not required when the child is over ten and employed outside school hours for no more than ten hours per week. The production must comply with a regulatory Code of Practice for the employment of children, must give the OCG at least seven days' notice of the intention to employ a child and supply a script for relevant scenes, and must keep a record for each child employed. There are restrictions placed on the hours the child may work (summarised in Table 15.2), obligations regarding supply of drinking water, food and toilets, and requirements to protect the health and emotional welfare of the child. There are special provisions and responsibilities placed on the production when it employs a baby under twelve weeks old.

Approval, monitoring and variation of employment of children

Approval for a production to employ a child comes after OCG assessment of the production and OCG staff may be at the shoot where there are stunts, water, large groups of children, highly dramatic portrayals, or any other thing they decide warrants their presence. They are also likely to attend the shoot of a production

Table 15.1: Authority responsible for employment of children in Australia's states and territories.

State/Territory	Responsible authority	Telephone	Website
ACT	Department of Disability, Housing and Community Services, Office for Children, Youth and Family Support	02 6205 7187	www.dhcs.act.gov.au/ocyfs
NSW	NSW Office of the Children's Guardian	02 9025 4200	www.kidsguardian.nsw.gov.au
NT	Dept of Employment, Education & Training	08 8901 4909	www.deet.nt.gov.au
Qld	Commission for Children & Young People & Child Guardian	07 3247 5525	www.ccypcg.qld.gov.au
SA	Office for Youth	08 8463 5552	www.officeforyouth.sa.gov.au
Tas.	Department of Justice	03 6233 3400	www.justice.tas.gov.au
Vic.	Industrial Relations Victoria	03 9651 9200	www.business.vic.gov.au
WA	Department for Community Development	08 9222 2555	www.community.wa.gov.au

Table 15.2: Times of work permitted for children under the NSW Code of Practice.

Age	Hours child may be employed	Number of days of employment over 7 days	Maximum hours of employment per day
Under 6 months	6 am to 6 pm	1	4
6 months and under 3 years	6 am to 6 pm	1	4
3 years and under 8 years	6 am to 11 pm	4	6
8 years and under 15 years	6 am to 11 pm	5	8

company that has recently been authorised. They don't, however, have a history of being overly officious or obstructive in these matters where they are comfortable that the production is taking its responsibilities seriously. Indeed, OCG staff have the discretion to approve variations to the Code if these are raised in advance and the particular child's welfare will not be compromised by them.

The rights and responsibilities of parents

Parents should be consulted and have the right to advocate or intervene on their child's behalf, but they do not have authority to override the Code of Practice. They cannot, for instance, approve the child working extra hours outside those allowed by the Code. A parent or family member is not required to accompany the child at the shoot, although they are encouraged to do so. If they do not, the production must make suitable arrangements for the child's supervision and travel arrangements during the shoot. The employer must ensure that the child can contact their parents or some other responsible person while on the shoot, if the need arises.

Maintenance of the child's educational needs

Another interested government body where children are employed in New South Wales is the Department of Education and Training. It requires a certificate of exemption, issued through the relevant school principal, for children who have missed twelve days of school in the year for employment. The production should check how many days a school-age actor has already missed that year, because after the twelfth day in the year a fully qualified tutor must be hired by the production to teach that child for four hours in each eight-hour shoot day, and a suitable space must be provided to complete school work and study.

15.6 Rehearsals

Calls in preparation for the shoot

There may be several occasions (known as 'calls') when an actor is required by the production in the preparation for their role in the show. The principal preparation event is rehearsal. Other calls will be scheduled on rehearsal days whenever prac-tical, including calls for wardrobe measurement and fitting, hair and make-up tests, and any training that might be required. Training might be for horse rid-ing, singing, dancing, dialogue work or any other aspect of the role that requires additional attention.

Rehearsals

Rehearsal allows the actors to get comfortable with the script and their charac-ter, and to get used to the acting styles of their fellow performers. An actor will finetune their interpretation of their character under the guidance of the director. Every director has their own way of working with actors that has evolved over the productions they have worked on. Some directors give an actor the freedom to interpret their role; others prefer to spell out the role to the actor. Whichever is the starting point, rehearsal then proceeds as a dialogue between actor and director. The director may explore the character's back story with the actor to find moti-vation for their actions. They may work on a specific accent or with mannerisms that will help define the character.

Blocking the scene

With the character determined and the actor's movements in a scene in portraying the character tentatively mapped out, the other main task of rehearsal can be carried out, namely blocking the scene. Blocking means the director looks at each camera position in relation to the actor and the key visual components of the action, and at camera movement in following the action or creating a fluid mood in the coverage. Blocking a scene must take account of all actors in the scene and physical impediments in the set or on the location. In multi-camera coverage, it must also take account of all the cameras on the set.

15.7 Performance on screen

Stage and screen acting

The high tradition of acting is in the theatre and many skilled screen actors have come out of theatre. But equally, many have not and there are signifi-cant differences between screen acting and stage acting. Stage acting involves performing in an artificial setting on a stage, so that whatever interpretation is in the performance can be perceived with the naked eye and ear by all in the theatre. Voice must be heard and actions and mannerisms seen right through to the back row from an unchanging wide perspective. In more intimate the-atre, this requirement can be modified, but in screen acting it is absolutely mod-ified and particularly in a single-camera production. Camera and microphone can pick up the most subtle of nuances and inflections if they are properly directed and the recording equipment properly positioned. The performers don't have to project out to the audience, which isn't physically in front of them any-way. They can be comfortable in the knowledge that the technology is able to reach to them and pick up whatever physical movement they inject into their performance.

Screen naturalism

An experienced actor, knowing how wide a shot is, will know exactly how much they need to put into a movement for it to catch the eye of the viewer. They don't have to find the 'truth' of a character and then find a way of delivering that truth to the back row. Once a screen actor has found the truth of a character, they need do no more than externalise it. The outcome of these different practical requirements is that theatre performance is inherently stylised and screen acting is inherently naturalistic. It is not necessarily realistic, because production will want to accentuate the dramatic aspects of a scene, but it does set out to create the belief that the scene is actually happening in front of the camera in a real setting, even when that setting is a constructed studio set imitating reality. Audiences respond as if the scene were really the result of camera eavesdropping. We are shocked at the sight of blood even when we know it has been put there by the make-up artist.

Performing a segmented script

The other difference between stage and screen is dramatic flow and direct communication with the audience. In theatre, the performance of a play starts at the beginning of the script and doesn't stop until it gets to the end, apart from an intermission that the playwright has written into the play anyway. Screen acting involves constant sampling of short pieces from the screenplay, often repeated several times (called 'takes') for different nuances of performance or to correct a technical problem, and generally with considerable overlap of script between one set-up and another. Breaking the script into pieces like this for shooting puts the onus on actors to understand the place of each piece in the overall story and the point in their character's emotional journey at that place. What's more, the pieces of script are often shot out of screenplay order because scheduling convenience is a greater priority. Although all the shots in any one scene are generally shot in a batch, the scenes themselves are not shot in screenplay order, but for scheduling and camera set-up efficiency. It's amazing, then, that actors can ever find the grain of their character, but they do. They also have post-production to smooth over any bumps in performance. On a shoot, the actor's day is made up of a lot of sitting between shots while technology and other paraphernalia are set up, muted early performance in rehearsing each shot, and trying to produce a concentrated performance to time with the recorded take.

The absentee audience

In addition to coping with the disconnection of the narrative, screen actors also have to perform for an audience that isn't there. Stage actors talk about their sense of communication with the live audience, although it's not clear what exactly this communication is. Perhaps it's just the ability to detect that the audience is appreciating the play, and the use of that feedback to sustain the level of performance. For the screen actor there is no audience, only the promise of one eventually. Instead there is a professional crew, intent on carrying out all the tasks that make a successful shoot, although crew response may sometimes be used by actors in the same way that they use the theatre audience. For the screen actor, the audience will arrive later, long after their performance has finished. If the actor gets feedback it will be from ratings, reviews or the comments of people, but none of this will be in time to feed back into the performance. The die is well and truly cast by then. It may be that this works for screen actors in some way, forcing them to focus their concentration on their fellow actors and the relationships between their characters, perhaps finding a deeper insight into the drama than comes from seeking the appreciation of a paying audience.

Multi-camera production

Multi-camera performance programs allow more of the acting flow that characterises theatre, although with drama production in this mode scenes are still often shot out of script order for scheduling reasons. Unfortunately, multi-camera drama has gone out of favour, but other multi-camera forms, such as sketch comedy, are still popular and, if the program is broadcast live (or recorded 'as live'), it must of necessity be recorded in script order. Performers of sitcoms are in favour of recording a program in a studio in front of a live audience. That way they can know whether the program is achieving the main objective of comedy – to be funny.

15.8 Casting for reality television

Approach to casting

Casting is also an important part of reality television, but it is approached differently. Here the purpose is to put together the right mix of ordinary people based on their actual personalities, not their acting skills. The hope in reality shows is that interesting interactions will develop within the group and that they will be revealed on camera in an unscripted narrative not unlike a 'soap'. Reality TV specialist, Peter Abbott, says it is a mistake to consciously cast for conflict. It's more interesting to watch people who should get along, but who can't because of the natural tensions of the environment. Similarly, it's more interesting to watch sexual tension than to watch a couple of people ostentatiously 'in love'. He doesn't cast for love or sex in *Big Brother*. The likelihood is that these won't eventuate as planned. People are selected for some inherent on-camera interest, aiming for variety and a range of personality types – extroverts and quieter types who will generate their own interactions, whatever they may be. Some sexual tensions will develop; some conflict will develop naturally and more dramatically. Some will be more interesting than others and the program can be tweaked as it progresses to get the greatest play from these.

Process of casting

The process of casting for reality television doesn't need a casting director. It isn't looking for professional actors but for ordinary people over a range of personalities. The casting process is, nonetheless, extensive because getting the selection of these people right is central to the show's success. There is no script as it is created spontaneously by the cast in the environment imposed by the production. A range of interviews and exercises will be conducted, followed by further tests as the numbers are whittled down and short-listed candidates are re-examined. Consideration is given simultaneously to what each person might bring to the show, how they might appeal to an audience, and whether an interesting mix is developing as the participants consolidate. There is no particular science to this. As in much of television production, it's a combination of instinct, judgement and experience. Some producers, however, favour using psychological profiles once it has been decided who's interesting and would make good television. The proposed cast is run past a psychologist to get a reaction to the mix of profiles. This might lead to small variations in casting, but it is only used to confirm or modify instinct. It should not be the basis of selection.

Type of character selected

Casting for reality television is not about looking for archetypes or stereotypes, but about looking for recognisable characters, likeable people and, best of all, polarising people, those people about whom the audience will form a strong divided reaction and about whom many people will change their minds as the layers of the character are revealed. In other words, complex characters. All successful drama is life-affirming with characters with whom the audience identifies or idolises. Reality television is no different. It isn't scripted to that purpose, but it is devised with that intention.

15.9   Casting for documentary

Dramatised documentary

Documentary production is in the business of portraying actuality and for the most part doesn't require actors, but occasionally actors are the only means of portraying some aspects of actuality. A portrayal of historical events, of recent events that have already passed or of events where cameras are not permitted are all subject matter where a documentary might resort to using actors. A dramatised documentary will follow a process that bears some resemblance to a muted version of the drama/comedy process. It is unlikely that such a production will hire a casting director unless it is a program pursuing high production value and with scripted dialogue. More commonly, the performance will involve actions with minimal or adlibbed dialogue that isn't dramatically crucial, placing a lower demand on acting skills of those performers cast – and a consequent lower fee. There may be wardrobe calls, depending on the nature and subject matter of the program, but often there won't be separate rehearsals. Instead, the director will rehearse the action for each shot while the crew sets up for that shot. The scenes are generally vignettes rather than continuing dramatic narrative.

Re-creation sequences

Another format that uses actors is the re-creation sequence. Here, the actors are often cast because they look like the people they are re-creating (of whom there might be photographs or film footage used elsewhere in the program) rather than for high acting skills. The production sets out to duplicate what might be recorded in actuality, so performance is low key and dialogue unimportant. It is improvised more to get synchronous voice than for specific dialogue. It doesn't really matter exactly what is said, as long as it doesn't distract viewer attention by being non-sensical in the circumstances. Often such dialogue is buried under voice-over or narration.

Program presenter

Finally, a performer might be hired as presenter of a documentary program. Again, a casting director would probably not be used because they would not be expected to have much familiarity with the needs of this type of program. Nonetheless, casting might involve screen testing of short-listed candidates. There is an element of performance in presenting a program, although it is of a different nature from that in drama. As in so much of television production, it is a matter of horses for courses, and producers must follow their instincts and exercise judgements for which there is no checklist to guide them.

Sources and further reading

Specific reading

Case, D., Gailey, L., Knapman, C., et al., *The Production, Budgeting and Film Management Satchel*, AFC/AFTRS, Sydney.

NSW Office of the Children's Guardian 2005, *Child Employment Requirements in NSW*, available online at <www.kidsguardian.nsw.gov.au>, viewed 18 December 2006.

Ritchie, Julia 2002, 'How to manage a film', in Case, D., Gailey, L., Knapman, C., et al., *The Production, Budgeting and Film Management Satchel*, AFC/AFTRS, Sydney.

Chapter 16

Locations

In the early days of television, much of production took place in a studio where everything could be kept under reasonable control. Recording on location involved carrying around heavy equipment, dealing with the vagaries of changing light conditions and curious onlookers, and coping with extraneous noise, which made clear audio difficult to obtain. Now cameras are light and portable. One can be embedded in a cricket stump. An acceptable image can be recorded in remarkably low light conditions and ride high contrasts in lighting levels. If the audio recorder cannot exclude unwanted noise on location, there is a second opportunity in post-production. The increasing capacity for effective recording in the real world has driven a change in audience taste over the years. The authenticity of location is generally preferred to the artificiality of studio.

For the most part, locations aren't just there for the taking. Someone or some organisation owns them, or administers or occupies them. When a production finds a location that suits its purposes, it must negotiate permission with the owner, occupant or administrator to enter the location with all the regalia of production, often disrupting whatever activities would normally be going on. For a documentary this isn't such a problem. Documentary moves from location to location much more rapidly than drama and, in any case, there's often a connection between subject matter and location. An agreement to participate in a documentary production will usually embrace agreement to allow access to a relevant location. With drama, it is different. The location generally has no connection to the drama apart from looking right for what the production needs. The occupation by a drama crew is usually longer and more likely to require suspension of the location's usual activities. It can be disruptive. Often, payment of a fee is necessary to offset the inconvenience.

This chapter examines the process of finding locations, negotiating agreements with their custodians, and the surveys that determine what each department will need to do in its use of locations for production. It looks principally at locations for drama production, then the similarities and differences in location use for documentary. Finally, it covers at some length the issues in filming on Indigenous land. This last section is expanded to cover the protocols in portraying Indigenous subjects and dealing with Indigenous communities.

16.1   Locations and sets

Drama locations

In the drama context, a location is a place that will be used for some of the shooting of a program. It may be a building – someone's home, a business premises, a car park – or a football field, or a street in a shopping area. On that location, one or several scenes may be shot. A set is that part of the location that will be on camera for the shot, whether unchanged from its everyday appearance or radically altered by set dressing or a constructed addition. There can be more than one set on a location – there may be scenes in the bedroom, the kitchen and at the front door of the one house – and there may be several scenes from different parts of the script shot on the one set.

Actuality locations

In actuality shooting, the locations are generally not dressed. Where shooting is of a location in its normal activity, any part of that location might be used on camera. The distinction between location and set doesn't have much meaning. Actuality shoots will tend to talk about location and not refer to set at all. An exception might be in re-enactments or stylised shooting, where only part of the location is earmarked for shooting and dressed accordingly. Here the term 'set' might come into use.

Scene and sequence

Dramatised shoots and actuality shoots use the terms 'scene' and 'sequence' respectively to describe the building blocks of the story. Each scene is a continuous part of the story taking place on one set. As soon as the story jumps to another set, a new scene begins. Even if the story later returns to the first set, that will be another scene. In actuality shooting, a sequence is a unit of the narrative, usually shot on the one location, but not always, and covering a succession of actions that embody the one idea or one component of the program's story. A sequence may also be a montage of shots (sometimes called scenes) from several locations. The key issue is that they represent a single idea within the narrative. Unity of idea is more important in defining an actuality sequence than unity of location, although the two often coincide. Nonetheless, actuality programs are scheduled by locations, not ideas.

16.2   The search for locations

The location manager

Drama production often engages a location manager to work with the production designer in finding the right 'look' in a location for each scene that will not be shot in a studio or on a sound stage. The location manager finds locations, negotiates the best price for them, and draws up a location agreement between the production and the location's occupant and/or owner. Sometimes that location is obvious and quickly found, whereas at other times it may require a lot of lateral thinking to arrive at a place or a building that can be fashioned for the production's purpose. Sometimes the obvious location has so many practical difficulties that the production has to consider a range of compromises, or reluctantly look wider for an alternative. A location manager will have built up a database of locations over the years, and developed a repertoire of instincts about where particular locations might be found with some lateral thinking. A building used in a production doesn't need to have the same purpose as in real life.

Location database

Having gone through the list of required sets, drawn from the script breakdown, the location manager makes a list of potential locations using the resources at their disposal. This includes their own database of locations and, if there are some tricky locations to find, may include a location database company such as Sydney's Filmsite or Melbourne's Filmlocations Pty Ltd (see sources below). State film agencies (see contact details in Table 6.2) are usually willing to assist in location search and in dealing with government bodies. The internet is also a valuable tool, using a search engine such as Google or Yahoo, to reach industry or other websites with information leading to the types of location sought.

Initial assessment of location

After first scouting the site from the outside, initial approaches are usually made in person, whether it's a home or business premises. This puts the negotiation on a more personable level and allows an early examination of the location's suitability. The approach should be sufficiently in advance of the production date to allow the authorising person to process the request. It might involve a body corporate, a council, or a board or management meeting. Meanwhile, several things need to be ascertained before the director, producer and production designer look at the site and agree to it as a location. The location must fulfil the brief of the director and production designer for it, but there are also practical considerations, such as:
* access to get equipment on set, via a doorway, elevator, ramp or loading dock
* sufficient space on the location to accommodate crew, talent and equipment
* adequate parking for production vehicles
* no noise interference on the location, such as traffic, flight path, school playgrounds, animals, nearby construction, a noisy air conditioner or PA/piped music.

Factors that will need to be dealt with

Some factors might require additional resources with budgetary implications, including:
- disruption of the occupant's business with compensation for loss of earnings, after checking if there are times when this is minimal
- impracticality of the occupants staying on the premises during shooting, so they are relocated at the production's expense
- a need to rent vans and/or portaloos where there aren't adequate toilets or space for actors, make-up and wardrobe
- a need to hire a generator, where power or other facilities are not available or are inadequate on location
- traffic or crowd control needing supervision by police or production assistants
- the requirement of security guards, overnight or over a weekend, while the location is used for the production.

Light and sound conditions

The need to assess noise interference has already been mentioned. The location manager will also assess the prevailing light conditions on behalf of the DOP. They will work out how light will change through the day for key shooting in the location. The DOP and sound recordist, along with the 1st AD, will also look over the site to confirm the location manager's advice, and make sure that there aren't any problems with the site that might have been overlooked.

16.3 Authorities to approach

Government authorities

Permission must be sought from various government bodies to shoot in areas they own or have responsibility for. The most suitable location for filming a scene in a bushland setting is often a national park, for which the state Parks and Wildlife Services are the approving body. With frequent requests of this kind, the state Parks and Wildlife Services have pro forma location agreements and a standard scale of fees. Their main concern is that filming won't compromise the protection of native plants and animals. Once satisfied regarding this, the state Parks and Wildlife Services process a request fairly quickly. In any city, a range of authorities must approve the use of a location under their administration. In Sydney, for example, the approach might be to the Sydney Opera House Trust, the Centennial and Moore Park Trust, the Royal Botanic Gardens and Domain Trust, or to the Sydney Harbour Foreshore Authority. Every city, large or small, has a number of bodies of these types (and the Sydney list isn't exhaustive) through which access to particular locations is obtained.

Local councils

The body most commonly approached for location permission is a local council. Shooting in a park, on public land, or in a street requires permission from the local council in whose area it is situated. A fee will apply, almost without exception these days, and this fee will vary widely from council to council, even from one council to the council adjacent. Councils are empowered by the Local Government Act in their state to charge a fee for commercial use of public areas under their administration. Some councils see it as an easy way to raise revenue, and some consider all productions to be as cashed up as a feature film. Many states have a department of local government protocol for filming. The NSW Department of Local Government has developed the *Local Government Filming Protocol* to guide councils and production companies, setting out a standard application and approvals process (see sources below). Producers should also be aware that, in New South Wales, the Act excludes current affairs or daily television news from the definition of filming. Shooting a documentary is problematic because it isn't in that exclusion, but many councils don't distinguish between documentary, television drama and feature film, and charge all as if they were a feature film. Many documentary productions, because of their mobility and the difficulty for council officers to check that they have permission before they have moved on to another location, simply don't get council permission unless they want a specific service from the council in addition to the permission to shoot.

Private property in a local government area

The Local Government Act, at least in New South Wales, doesn't give councils the authority to approve or charge a fee to shoot on private property within its municipal area. Some councils are apparently unaware of this. One Sydney council has been known to demand a fee from a production for shooting inside a private house in its area, stating that they had this authority under their council's regulations. However, unless the Act specifically authorises that this as an area for which they can make regulations (and in New South Wales it doesn't), then the regulation is *ultra vires* (outside their authority) and a court would strike it out.

Other authorities to notify

Other bodies that should be notified even if formal permission isn't required of them are, most notably, the local police. Some councils will hold off their approval until the police have been consulted. Police are required to be notified if firearms are to be discharged or traffic diverted, as is the state or territory road and traffic authority for the latter. Shooting on or near water or causing pollution (e.g. smoke, explosions) may need notification to the state waterways, environmental, or land and water conservation authority.

16.4   Geographical spread

Proximity of locations

Among the principles in the search for suitable locations is the aim of trying to group locations near each other. Nearby locations reduce travel time (and therefore cost) spent in relocation during production. Where a major location has been decided, some corner of it might serve the needs of a minor location without much specificity of detail. The fact that the two locations are nowhere near each other in the story doesn't matter. That they are a common location can be disguised with set dressing and camera positioning. Where the minor scene cannot be set in a corner of a major location, it is still preferable to look for the minor location in the vicinity of a location already decided. The shorter the relocation time, the less the pressure on budget and the more the shooting day is spent on production.

Set build on location

Another issue to be thought through is where a location fulfils the director's expectations substantially, but lacks one or two fairly essential features. There are two options here. One is to construct the missing feature on the location, and the other is to split the location. A set build on location saves the cost and lost shooting time of relocation, but there are construction costs in the build. The set will usually be built in a workshop, then taken to location and rigged. Time will need to be allocated for rigging the additional feature, de-rigging after the shoot and restoring the location to its original state. Time taken on the location with these may increase a fee paid for use of the premises.

Split locations

A split location, where one part of ostensibly the same scene is on one location and the other is on another location some distance away, has no additional cost in itself. There will be a relocation cost, however, unless the second location is adjacent to some other location already earmarked for the production. The screenplay might, for instance, call for a particular house alongside a railway line with a scene involving action both in the house and on the railway line. A house that matches the brief perfectly may have been found, but nowhere near a railway line. Rather than pursue the unlikely possibility of a house of this type next to a railway line, the production might piece the two components together from separate locations. Action in the house will be shot on one location, and action on the railway line shot on the other. The two scenes can be merged in post-production by the use of train audio effects over scenes in the house, and connecting an image of the railway through a point of view (POV) shot to one of the actors in the house.

16.5 The location agreement

Location agreement coverage

Once the director approves a particular location, a location agreement is drawn up for signature by the occupant or owner, either an individual or a company, or any person authorised to agree to the production's use of premises or land for filming. As noted above, the state Parks and Wildlife Services have their own location agreement pro forma, but for the most part the location manager will draw up an agreement from a production pro forma. The agreement will cover such items as identifying the location and specifying where the production will operate, the dates and times of access, the fee for use of the location, any other facilities the production might use on the location, and access requirements that are worth specifying in advance. A fee, no matter how small, makes the agreement contractual and therefore makes it difficult for the occupier to change their mind, once the agreement is signed.

Legal implications of location filming

The fee is for access to the location and the consequent inconvenience, not for the right to film there. The purpose of the agreement is not, as is commonly supposed, to get permission to film a building or land owned by someone. The *Copyright Act 1968* allows filming of a building and including it in a television broadcast without infringing copyright. The agreement is to ensure permission to go on the property and film part of a program there, without risk of a trespass action or a verbal agreement being withdrawn on the day. Under the law of trespass, the occupier possesses the property and is legally able to give permission for filming to take place. There is no legal requirement to get permission from the owner, although some producers believe it is good practice to get permission from the owner as well. Others take the view that this is inviting a demand for a second location fee for the same premises. They leave it to the occupiers to notify the owner if they choose. In many cases, the occupier is the owner. It is generally easier to deal with an owner-occupier, but a good location wouldn't be excluded because of this.

Other details for agreement

The occupier will usually want details of the size of the crew, and number and types of vehicles. This information need not be on the agreement (it could have the effect of restricting the production's flexibility) but can be supplied as separate information. The agreement may state that footage shot belongs to the production company. It may also indemnify the owner and warrant that the production has taken out appropriate public liability insurance. Most companies and government bodies will insist on this and many individuals are also aware of its importance. There may be facilities or services from the property that the production would want to use and whose inclusion is part of the fee negotiation. These should be included in the location agreement form.

16.6 Location surveys

Technical survey

As locations are approved, the location manager provides the 1st AD with a preliminary locations list, noting any restrictions on the use of the location or any additional requirements for it. The director and production designer will have already surveyed locations prior to their approval, but when all locations are locked in, the

1st AD makes a schedule for the crew's survey of them, called the technical survey. In addition to director, producer, production designer and location manager, the party would be expected to include the DOP, camera operator, sound recordist, assistant directors, grips, gaffer, stand-by props, stand-by wardrobe, production manager and unit manager. The director will outline briefly what will happen in each scene in each location, and specify the requirements of each department. The crew will use the occasion to start to resolve any difficulties they might see in the location.

Keeping the neighbourhood informed

An assistant director will collate important local information for each location to include on call sheets: the nearest hospital, fire brigade, police (especially traffic police), ambulance and doctor (and vet when animals are on set). Some councils, as a condition of their approval of shooting on public land, will require the production to notify neighbours of the dates of shooting, and any likely disruption to the normal flow of activities in the neighbourhood. Even if not required, a letter-box drop advising the neighbourhood of the filming and its possible disruption is still prudent. It reduces public irritation at any inconvenience. The reality is that if anyone is determined to disrupt the filming, there are limited legal options for the production beyond trying to mollify the irate person.

16.7   Documentary locations

Assessing the location

As a genre dealing with actuality, documentary is mostly shooting on location. Its locations differ from those of drama because they are part of the story, whereas drama locations only illustrate the story. There is generally no need to search specifically for documentary locations. They are an inherent part of the research. Nonetheless, many of the principles in the practical assessment of locations for drama apply also to documentary, except the scouting is done by a researcher rather than a location manager. The sorts of factors to be noted about a documentary location include:

- lighting availability (whether the source is sunlight or fluorescent lights)
- conveniently placed power points in interior locations (for camera lights)
- nearby noise interference (the same concerns as listed in section 16.1)
- access to get equipment on to the location
- room to fit in crew and equipment (less a concern these days with lightweight equipment and smaller crews)
- parking availability.

Visual appeal

The aim is to cover sequences of events that advance the narrative of the documentary. A criterion for these sequences is that they be visually interesting, both in terms of their action and in the visual appeal of their location. This is one of the factors that will favour a sequence in one location over an alternative sequence somewhere else. A sequence of a person sitting and thinking has limited possibilities, as does a sequence in a drab room.

Absence of location agreements

Usually a documentary will not feel the need to draw up a location agreement. There is not such a pressing need to ensure the location's availability because there is less potential for the owners to change their mind about its availability. A location is usually associated with a person who is appearing in the documentary, so if the location becomes unavailable it will probably be because that person has withdrawn from the production. If that's the case, the location is no longer of interest. A person's appearance in a production cannot be contracted as easily as access to a location can. Another reason that documentary locations have less likelihood of falling through is that they don't disrupt the normal activities of the location in the way that drama production does. The documentary is usually intent on filming something that would normally be happening at the location anyway. The worst interference might be to ask people to stop and repeat some action for the camera.

Location survey

Director and cameraman would generally not survey an observational documentary location unless it was going to be a reasonably big sequence or there were known to be technical difficulties that would need to be assessed. Otherwise, the crew would rely on the researcher's notes about the location. However, on a distant location to which the crew travels the day before, it might look at the location on arrival, get familiar with its layout and features, and spot any potential difficulties that might need skirting around in shooting the next day.

16.8   Filming on Indigenous land

Protocols

There are particular conventions when a production wishes to enter Aboriginal or Torres Strait Islander land. The majority of productions wishing to do this are either documentary or current affairs, so they are likely to want to capture Indigenous life on camera and talk to Indigenous people. Many are also likely to be interested in some social issue regarding Indigenous Australians where it might or might not be in a community's interest to have the exposure. Protocols for shooting on Indigenous land have been developed for SBS by Lester Bostock in an attempt to prevent any misunderstandings or conflict. These are the current prevailing guidelines for the industry, although the AFC's Indigenous Unit is in the process of developing its own set of protocols, which are anticipated to be publicly available in 2007.

Principles in the protocols

The guidelines are based on six principles:
1. Program makers should be aware of prejudices and stereotyped beliefs about Indigenous people.
2. An Aboriginal view of Indigenous issues may differ from a non-Aboriginal view.
3. Programs about Indigenous people by non-Indigenous people should be made in consultation with the Indigenous people.
4. Dealings with Indigenous people should be open and honest, fully informing them of the consequences of any agreements.
5. No damage should be done to Indigenous lands, cultural property or the subjects of the program.
6. Information should not be collected for a program to be used against the interests of the people from whom the information comes.

The last principle recognises that there may be a legitimate need to file reports that are detrimental to their subjects. Such reports should examine preconceptions and be balanced by an awareness of cultural norms and the practices of Indigenous people.

Permits to visit designated Aboriginal lands

To visit any designated Aboriginal lands in the Northern Territory, South Australia, Queensland or Western Australia, a visitors' permit from the local Aboriginal Land or Community Council must be obtained. Land Councils act on instruction from traditional Aboriginal owners and custodians who, along with the community, have a right to refuse entry to a production crew or a researcher. Producers can put their case for being allowed into the community, but they should not pressure individuals or communities, or expect a Land Council to intervene on their behalf. Land Councils are not media agents. Their role is to act as a buffer against more predatory journalistic practice.

Liaison with the community

Whether a permit is required or not, the producer (or researcher) should spell out the production's intentions. An Indigenous consultant might be used to liaise between production and community, and to check the authenticity of presentation of cultural activities and rituals in post-production. The types of issues to be worked out prior to shooting include:
- whether interpreters and translators are needed, and where they can be accessed
- arrangements for accommodation while on Indigenous land, if necessary
- whether any funeral or cultural ceremonies are planned that may disrupt the production schedule
- whether there are any prohibitions on the use of landscape
- ownership of dances and song cycles that may be recorded for the program
- gender restrictions that may apply to some crew members at some sites.

Ethical responsibilities

Television coverage of Aboriginals and Torres Strait Islanders should have some reflection of their perspective, especially that of the community that is the subject of the program. Their welfare should be protected, and their dignity and privacy respected. The aims of research and of the program should be clearly communicated, along with the possible consequences of participation. No filming should be done without informed consent, and all people have the right to change their mind about agreeing to be involved.

Key aspects of Indigenous culture

Production crew with permission to go on to Indigenous land should familiarise themselves with crucial aspects of Indigenous culture and social interaction. Many Indigenous Australians live within the bounds of their own cultural structure and languages, with their own religions, political beliefs and history. Program makers need to be aware of the social and cultural integrity of Indigenous Australia and at the same time appreciate its pluralism. Even Indigenous people no longer within their traditional culture may carry out cultural practices and beliefs specific to their group. Aboriginal and Torres Strait Islander societies have traditionally depended on the kinship or tribal group for moral, social and physical support, something still present in today's Indigenous societies. This can be seen in the extended family, which has a complex set of relationships and obligations that impose responsibilities not found in non-Indigenous families. This may affect the way deals are made. It's also seen in the belief in the right to share all things owned communally. Without a concept of personal property, community-owned property can be taken and used without seeking permission.

It should also be noted that Indigenous concepts of time are based on the past and present, and not the future, so conventional time-keeping is not seen as important. With remote communities, time of day is better referred to by progress of the sun (i.e. before sunrise, mid-morning, late evening), and a specific day by the number of days to it (e.g. in five days' time) rather than naming the day as, for example, next Wednesday.

Protocol for deceased persons

In many Indigenous communities, especially in northern and central Australia, it is considered improper for images of an Indigenous person who has subsequently died to be seen by members of that person's clan group. The protocol calls for the image of that person to be edited out or 'blurred' to remove any identifying features. If there is uncertainty about whether someone is now deceased, a warning should be put on the front of the program that it might show images of people who are no longer living.

Presentation of landscape

Another concern relates to how landscape is presented. Certain landscapes might have a 'masculine' association which is linked to a 'feminine' part of the same landscape, and both aspects should be shown together, or shown so that the link between them is maintained.

Indigenous copyright issues

Indigenous concepts of copyright should be kept in mind when making a program with Indigenous communities. Indigenous concepts of private ownership don't exist and a work of art by any Aboriginal is part of the public domain of their clan or group. Whereas in Australian copyright law ownership of a work passes into the public domain seventy years after the death of its creator, Aboriginal artworks are handed down from generation to generation, each becoming the guardian of the work, responsible for its safe-keeping. There can be a complex system of ownership of songs and dances, including custodians of the land that is the subject of the song. An owner of the song and an owner of the associated dance may rehearse the routines and make sure actions and nuances are correct, but they may not perform the song or dance. Producers should be aware of the intricate set of owners, and negotiate an agreement to film with all of them, or with someone representing all of them.

Drama protocols

These protocols also apply to drama presentation of Indigenous culture, even if it is not shot on Indigenous land. It is expected that all Aboriginal roles will be played by Aboriginal actors. It is now unacceptable to use 'blackface', probably as much to television audiences as it is to Indigenous people. Scripts should be authenticated to ensure Aboriginal parts have realistic language, behaviour and motivation, and that portrayal of cultural aspects is accurate. Programs should avoid presenting stereotypes about Indigenous Australians. There is a tendency only to portray them in connection with a racial or social problem.

Casting for Ten Canoes

The telemovie/feature, *Ten Canoes*, shot in Arnhem Land, gives some insight into the complexities of cultural accommodation with remote Indigenous communities. Casting problems were encountered that are not normal in production. The film incorporated a Yolgnu mythical story into a fictional story set in the past, both with substantial contributions from people within the community. Those taking part in the story consultation assumed that they would have claims to a part in the film, but one was overweight to an extent that was not credible for the time in which the story was set. A role was created for him: a comedy character always after honey and always eating too much. The film was based on a 1930s photo of canoeists and the community insisted that those with the closest relationship to the men in the photograph should play canoeists in the film. Thus, casting was taken out of the director's hands. Finally, actors playing other characters in the film had to have the appropriate kinship relationships as the characters they played. There was no screen testing. Casting was mostly on cultural grounds, but there's no evidence that the film suffered for that.

Sources and further reading

Specific reading

Bostock, Lester 1997, *The Greater Perspective: Protocol and Guidelines for the production of Film and Television on Aboriginal and Torres Strait Islander Communities*, 2nd edn, SBS, Sydney.

Ten Canoes press kit, available online at <http://www.tencanoes.com.au/tencanoes/info.htm>, viewed 18 December 2006.

Some internet references

Arts Law Centre of Australia, 'Do I need a film location release?', available online at <http://www.artslaw.com.au/LegalInformation/DoINeedaFilmLocationRelease.asp>, viewed 18 December 2006.

Johnson, Darlene, 'Indigenous protocol', <http://www.sbs.com.au/sbsi/documentary.html?type = 6>, viewed 18 December 2006.

Location database companies, available online at <www.filmlocations.com.au> and <www.filmsite.com.au>, viewed 18 December 2006.

NSW Department of Local Government 2000, 'Local government filming protocol', available online at <http://www.dlg.nsw.gov.au/dlg/dlghome/documents/information/film2.pdf>, viewed 18 December 2006.

Chapter 17

Travel arrangements

Television can bring the world into people's living rooms. It can travel to the remotest corners of the globe, capture images and tell both factual and fictional stories set in exotic locations so that viewers experience vicariously the excitement of being there. As a result, production crews venture to all parts of this country, and any others where a story or setting might be located. Travel arrangements for a production bring in factors that aren't part of shooting in the production's home town, not the least being cost. There are impacts on the production from the procedures of getting people and equipment into and out of countries, and the unfamiliarity with the way everyday things are done in other countries. In Australia these may not be issues, but there is an interest in remote and inaccessible places that can create particular challenges to production. How to get there, how to sustain the crew once it is there, and how to access resources and support for production in an unfamiliar environment become the issues instead. The special needs in dealing with remote Indigenous communities were discussed in Chapter 16.

Arrangements for a production to travel include the means of getting there, accommodation and meals for crew (and cast) when they are there, various documents that are necessary for overseas business travel, and briefing about cultures and customs that will be unfamiliar. Ordinary travel requires research, negotiation and lateral thinking. Travel for the purpose of producing a television program requires all of this on a bigger scale. It involves getting to places by means not designed for transporting production teams, and then making a program in a place that doesn't fully understand what the crew is there for and may not even welcome its presence. On top of the technical, creative and professional demands of constructing a program, travel often demands a greater element of thinking on the run than a home shoot.

17.1   Getting there

Air travel

A production crew is commonly transported to a remote location by air. In the past, production flights have been booked through a travel agent or by a unit's travel officer. These days, it can be done simply and quickly through the internet. Now, only a large-crew production might use a travel agent. A number of discounted fares are always on offer on the internet, although they will generally impose a charge for re-booking to another flight if, for instance, a delay in the shoot necessitates changing travel arrangements. The production needs to decide whether a discounted airfare is worth it by weighing up the likelihood of postponing the flight against the cost of doing so. With a small crew, where the re-booking fee is mostly the increment to an undiscounted fare anyway and the likelihood of re-booking is relatively low, the risk may well be worth it.

Excess baggage charges

Airlines have limits on the allowable weight of accompanied baggage carried on flight as part of the fare, and charge per kilogram over that weight. Documentary and current affairs shoots move quickly through several destinations, so there is no real option to taking equipment as accompanied baggage and incurring excess baggage costs. The weight of equipment taken on a flight can be allocated across a production crew, but a small crew has a limited capacity to reduce its excess weight per person significantly by this method. What's more, there doesn't seem to be any standard industry charge for excess baggage, or consistency in whether there will be a charge at all. Excess baggage has become an unpredictable cost of air travel. The best estimate is to talk to producers or production managers who have dispatched a similar kit in recent times, and add a contingency to their excess baggage cost. Where the shoot is in one location, as a drama may be, the costs of excess baggage can be eliminated by freighting much of the equipment to the destination.

Charter flights

There isn't always a convenient commercial flight between destinations on a shooting itinerary. There may be no flights scheduled on the day, or they may follow a circuitous route in getting to the location. Days spent waiting for a scheduled flight can fritter away production funds, and chartering a light plane can be a viable option if the crew is large enough to warrant it. A two-person crew may not justify the cost, whereas a five-person crew might. If there are no scheduled flights to a location that has an airstrip, the issue becomes whether chartering a light plane is a better option than driving. Chartered flights can also be an option outside Australia although the risk is higher because it is harder to get reliable information about the quality and safety of the service.

Alternatives to air travel

Air travel might be the most common means of getting to location, but it isn't the only option and sometimes isn't even an option at all. An island without an airstrip is best reached by boat, although a helicopter could be a practical option. If there isn't a scheduled ferry service to an island, a chartered boat may get there. Sometimes, especially overseas, travel to the location by bus or train may be considered. In these cases, the crew would be as small as practical and travel as lightly as possible. The production may even make the bus or train journey part of the program and shoot on it while travelling. In situations like this, a lightweight DV camera can be a real asset.

Use of crew vehicles

A small crew might travel to a medium-distance location in a production vehicle, a hired vehicle (see next section) or the vehicle of a member of the crew, usually the cameraman. A crew member's vehicle will be paid for either as an agreed sum for the trip or at a rate per kilometre ('kilometrage'). This rate should cover all running costs, so that there should be no need to reimburse petrol expenses for the vehicle, which don't necessarily relate solely to the production trip anyway. A large production might have specialist trucks travelling to location and these would be paid for in the same fashion as if they are owned by the crew member.

17.2   Getting around on location

Vehicle hire

Usually, a crew will need transport at a remote destination to move itself and its equipment from the airport (if it got there by air) to location, to overnight accommodation and/or back to the airport. The shoot may be in more than one location around that destination. A vehicle or vehicles are hired locally, either from a car hire company or by arrangement with local people involved with the shoot. The car hired needs to be of sufficient size to hold all personnel in the crew, their professional equipment, and personal luggage where overnight stops are involved. The vehicle should also be able to stow this baggage safely, so that heavy equipment cases will not be thrown onto the passengers in a sudden stop or an accident. The upshot of this might be that two vehicles are required rather than one. Depending on the terrain, a four-wheel drive vehicle might be more appropriate. The production should ensure that there is an experienced off-road four-wheel driver on the crew if it is going to be taken onto that sort of surface.

Hire charges and insurance costs

As well as suitability of the vehicle, hire cost will be a consideration in the choice. The assumption that a small or local company will offer the best deal is not one that is always borne out in reality. Often a large international company has better rates and more flexibility than a small company. A decision to hire a four-wheel drive production vehicle should also be made in the knowledge that insurance excess is usually higher for these vehicles. There are also items in the small print of any vehicle hire agreement that limit what is covered by its insurance. Hire companies have a significantly greater number of single vehicle accidents than is the general case. It would seem, not surprisingly perhaps, that people take less care of a hired car than of their own car. Often damage to the roof or undercarriage of a hired vehicle is excluded from insurance, and is instead a charge to the hirer in the event of an accident.

Local transport unavailability

If transport cannot be provided locally, the practicality of flying to the location should be questioned. There are two options. The usual choice is to fly to the nearest destination that has a car-hire base and drive from there to the location. The alternative, driving all the way to location from the home base, has the attractions of eliminating air travel costs and reducing the amount of loading and unloading of the gear, as long as the distance isn't so great that the extra travelling time negates these advantages. With some shoots, some of the transport is so specialised that there is no option but to drive to the location from the home base, regardless of the distance. No vehicle hire company has OB vans, lighting or grips trucks on offer, although consideration could be given to hiring these and their personnel from a major centre nearer to the location than the home base. A shoot in Broome by a Melbourne-based production company, for instance, could look at the possibility of hiring some of its production support from Perth.

Locations without road access

The location may not be accessible by road. Depending on the distance from the nearest road access, carriage by animals or porters may be considered if they are available. Otherwise, the crew must carry the gear. In this case, the equipment should be reduced in size and weight to essentials, and carried in lightweight convenient cases. Wheeled trolleys may help if the terrain isn't prohibitive. As there are limited ways of getting equipment into a cave or up a mountain, the less weight that is carried, the less the task of getting there overwhelms the reason for getting there. An island is another challenge. Tourist centres might have buggies for transporting tourists and their luggage, so an arrangement could be made with a resort even if it isn't part of the shoot. Otherwise, the challenge is the same as the cave or the mountain. These are the conundrums that challenge production and lateral thought is often the best means of finding a solution.

17.3 Documentation for overseas travel

Payments overseas

Like tourists, production crews once had to take large amounts of money as travellers' cheques to pay for production requirements overseas. This meant diverting periodically from the production to look for places to cash cheques. Now, credit cards and automatic teller machines will provide for the production's payment needs in most destinations. There are few cities in the world without automatic teller machines to dispense local currency, and most accommodation can be paid for by credit card. It may be advisable to take some cash – US dollars are usually recommended – to cover the circumstances where an automatic teller machine may not be available. If the crew is out on a risky location, the cash may be left at the temporary production base, in a hotel safe, or with some trusted person (see section 17.6).

Business visas

It is probable that a production crew will need a business visa to enter most countries on an overseas production trip, something that can be checked with the diplomatic representative of each country to be visited. Sufficient time should be allowed for the visa applications to be processed, or an extra fee will need to be paid to expedite the application. While the number of countries for which Australian tourists no longer need a visa or where they can obtain one on entry is increasing, this is not necessarily the case with business visas. Tourists are to be encouraged by reducing red tape, but most governments want to keep an eye on the businesses that are coming into their country. A foreign television crew is no exception to that.

Carnets

When a production shoots overseas, professional equipment is temporarily imported into each country visited. This attracts import duty if the equipment stays in the country, and not if it doesn't. Without an ATA Carnet, a bond would be required by customs at each country visited. A carnet is a temporary importation document issued by chambers of commerce in the sixty-three countries currently in the carnet scheme. It is sponsored by the International Bureau of Chambers of Commerce in Paris. In Australia, carnets are issued by state chambers of commerce, such as the Sydney Chamber of Commerce or the Victorian Employers' Chamber of Commerce and Industry (see sources below). The carnet document includes a comprehensive list of all equipment travelling, with two vouchers for each foreign country to be visited. One voucher is presented to customs on entry, the other on departure. Entry and departure can be from different ports in the country and the goods can be accompanying baggage or sent on ahead. There are vouchers as well for departure from and re-entry to Australia. The cost of a carnet is an application fee and a security bond of the highest assessment of duty for the countries to be visited, plus 10%. The bond is returned after Australian customs forwards the voucher for re-entering Australia to the chamber of commerce that issued it.

Working outside the carnet system

Countries that aren't participants in the scheme will often accept a carnet voucher and list as a temporary importation document without requiring a security deposit, even though they have no formal involvement in the scheme. On the other hand, there is some equipment, such as two-way radios, that is likely to raise suspicion on entry. It might be advisable to take this in separate luggage. Producers should get advice on what might be acceptable in countries to be visited. Single-person crews have found that they can generally take a DV camera through customs without a carnet. This has the attraction of convenience, but it also creates the risk of being taken for a spy when shooting with no entry paperwork to support the claim to be overseas media.

17.4 Accommodation and meals

Booking accommodation

Like air travel, accommodation these days can be found and booked via the internet. The website <www.wotif.com> provides a comprehensive chart of hotels in many countries, including Australia (city and country centres), with prices, availability over the next three or four weeks, and what you get for the price. It also shows some current special deals on offer. Most government tourist bureaus also have a website with comprehensive accommodation listings. A search engine such as Google or Yahoo will locate these and other sites with accommodation listings, although some might have subscriber businesses only. For overnight stays, there is probably no point in doing any more than simply making the booking, but shopping around for the best discount for group bookings over a longer period could be worthwhile. This is especially the case where alternative accommodation is available, or if the shoot is scheduled in the low season. If the production arranges to be invoiced directly for crew accommodation, it should make it clear that it will pay for accommodation only and any extras (e.g. mini-bar, movie hire, room service, telephone calls) are to be paid by the person concerned. The crew should be advised of this as well. A lower-risk alternative is to advance to each crew member the expected cost of accommodation, although this involves more paperwork and may have to be reconciled if there are departures from the planned itinerary.

Type of accommodation

What level of hotel should a production provide for its crew? Hotel or motel accommodation is predictable and therefore more likely to be acceptable. Looking for something out of the ordinary can backfire as some crew members might appreciate it, whereas others, just wanting somewhere to unwind at the end of the day, might not. A heritage building can have inconveniences and a chichi guesthouse may not be to everyone's taste. A hotel that has noisy late-closing bars is not a good idea either. A conventional, well-appointed motel is often the safest option. The crew wants to be able to relax and feel appreciated by the production at the end of a working day, but that doesn't necessarily mean the ostentation and expense of five-star accommodation. This might create an impression that the production is a soft touch, or the shoot is a junket. It is a perception that can become reflected in the quality of the crew's work. The accommodation should be appropriate for a group of professionals there to do a job. No better, no worse.

More austere accommodation

A hotel or motel may not be available at all locations. Shooting in remote parts of Australia or overseas may necessitate staying in accommodation such as shearers' quarters or native huts or even camping in tents. It's part of the profession and, if it is the only option, should be acceptable to production professionals. The production might provide some comforts to offset the austerity of the accommodation, where it can. Few would quibble with this type of accommodation when it was necessary to get program material at that location. Any that do object are probably not working in the right business for them. For most, it's part and parcel of the interest and variety of the job.

Accommodation in home of talent

Sometimes talent will offer to accommodate crew in their home. This sounds like a generous and hospitable offer and it generally is, but a producer should weigh up the consequences before accepting the offer. It runs the risk of the production outstaying its welcome and, in any case, it's sometimes good to be able to get away from the people you've spent the day with, even if they are pleasant people. There is also the possibility that they might want to use the obligation to influence the direction of the program, sometimes without even setting out to do that. If any of these things are an issue, it's generally better to play it safe and diplomatically decline. There can always be a reason that avoids the appearance of a rebuff. There is still a need to work with these people on production. The crew should share a drink with them at the end of the day, if offered, or at least be sociable. It's not in the production's interest for talent to think they are no longer of any consequence once the shooting has finished.

Per diem allowances

Advance per diems (also called travel allowance or TA) provide for meals while on location. These are calculated as the reasonable cost in that location of three meals a day plus incidental costs such as laundry and toiletries. There are minimum per diem rates on location in Australia specified in the awards for crew and cast, although the rates are not the same in the two awards. These rates don't apply to overseas locations where the cost of living might be higher or lower than in Australia. The ATO has ruled on what is a 'reasonable amount' for meals and incidentals as travel allowance. This can be used as a guide to an appropriate per diem in a foreign country. They have been calculated on the cost of a short stay on business in those countries and are updated regularly.

Remote locations without food outlets

If the shoot involves camping or a location well away from where meals can be bought, the production provides the means for reasonable meals. This requires planning each meal on these locations, calculating and buying the ingredients, and packing them along with professional and personal baggage for the trip. If the location has refrigeration and cooking facilities, food can be chosen accordingly. If it doesn't, the wherewithal to cook the food will be packed as well. The crew will include someone responsible for catering and cooking. This person will not have production duties apart from maintaining the camp if the crew is large, as in a drama shoot. With a small crew, as in a documentary shoot, this person may have a production role as well (it is often a production assistant), but it should be scaled back to allow time for preparing meals. In this instance, all crew would be expected to pitch in and accept that as part of the responsibility of a professional team dealing with a remote location.

17.5 Unfamiliar cultures

Working in an overseas location

Production on location can be intrusive on and demanding of people who are not part of the production. It can impose a need to be firm with people sometimes almost to the point of bullying, and there isn't always time to explain fully why the production needs the things it needs. This can be dealt with in Australia where, for the most part, there is an understanding of the sort of persuasive behaviour that is acceptable, and of how to get the facilities and assistance needed. In a foreign country, the production still needs to intrude and demand and still needs assistance, but it is working in a culture of which its insight or experience is limited. The protocols of ordinary life are different there. A production has to tread more carefully through unknown nuances of behaviour – of what is acceptable and what is not. What's more, in Australia there is a pretty good understanding of who can provide support for a production. In other countries, it is so often a matter of finding that they don't do things 'like that' there, and since they don't really understand the need, they have difficulty resolving the issue. Because of all this, shooting in overseas locations can be extremely tiring and extremely testing of everyone's patience. Added to that is the instinctive desire to get as much done as quickly as possible to amortise the expense of shooting at an overseas location. With this pressure, it is easy for a producer to fall prey to an outburst of temper, but this is almost always counterproductive. It will appear that the producer is no longer in control. In fact, they aren't and a fit of temper undermines the producer's command of the situation. An exception is the controlled outburst to achieve an end, but a producer has to know then why they are doing it and manage it accordingly.

'Yes', 'no' and 'maybe'

In dealing with different cultures, production personnel often find that 'yes' means 'no' more than 'I'm polite'. The request may have been misunderstood or the answer was only acknowledging that the question had been noted, or that the person didn't want to disappoint. 'No' often doesn't mean 'no' either. It may be that the wrong question was asked and, reframed, it would get a different response. It may reflect the circumstances at the time of asking, but may be able to be rectified by finding the right connection, perhaps an advisor to the person who makes the decision. There will also be 'maybe', which a producer could keep pushing until the last moment, when a 'yes' might or might not materialise. Peter George, producer of the series *Peking to Paris* for ABC, had Chinese approval to film vintage cars en route to Mongolia. It wasn't till he got there that he found that approvals for the vintage cars and for the production vehicles were on two entirely different routes, 100 km apart. His only practical choice was to follow the vintage cars and argue with officials on the way, but that did get the production vehicles through on the same route as the featured cars.

Researching the cultural climate before departure

With unfamiliar cultures, it can be useful to read up on everyday aspects of that culture and talk to people who have already worked in the country, production people if they can be found, or businesspeople, travel agents or research workers. Any working experience or inside information is helpful. Community newspapers in Australia (if it is known where they sit politically) and embassies (depending on the ambassador's attitude) can also be reliable and useful sources. Local communities in Australia can provide invaluable contacts back in their home country, often local community leaders or relatives, although care needs to be taken that the production doesn't end up being assisted by politically targeted people. Whatever this research unearths should be put in an information sheet and distributed to the crew. The more a production team is able to leave for a foreign assignment properly briefed about the cultural climate it will find there, the less chance of production difficulties through misunderstandings, or even more serious repercussions of cultural ignorance.

17.6 Minders, fixers and drivers

The minder

There are three types of support people that a production might hire locally to assist a shoot in that country. 'Minders' are government-appointed. Their role is to stop the production covering things that government doesn't want covered. They are 'hired' by the production, only in that there is usually a charge for their services, which are ostensibly to assist the production. They generally need to be worked round, but can sometimes be helpful simply because they come with official connections. Sometimes, after a while, they develop an attachment of sorts to the production and provide more useful assistance than their masters intended.

The fixer

Many of the difficulties of overseas shooting can be dealt with effectively with local production support. The production will hire a 'fixer' of its own choice to pursue its real needs, as opposed to the government's, and this person might be in a position to assess a prospective minder, or get a replacement if that becomes desirable.

The right person can often be found through the sources already suggested for other local information: communities in Australia, visiting businesspeople and, particularly, colleagues who have already worked in that country. Embassies are probably less valuable here. The producer must first establish a relationship by email, telephone or fax. The fixer is given a specific focus for the shoot to narrow the things they are to chase up. They are also given broad guidelines at the same time. The contradiction is necessary so that nothing potentially useful is lost through producer unfamiliarity.

'Facility fees'

A fixer who has worked with overseas productions before and has an understanding of the needs of a production crew is best able to expedite the process. Access to locations, permission to shoot, talking to the right people, finding a path around the red tape, bribing a minor official, all are part of their stock in trade. And yes, that does include bribing the right people as a 'facility fee' of sorts. Bribes may be a necessary production expense in some countries to get past petty blockages by petty officials. On a larger scale, such as with border guards, its wisdom is more questionable, except perhaps as a last resort. It is just as likely to expose the production to further demands for facility fees.

The driver

A fixer will also find a driver for the production, a person who must be sharp, smart and reliable. They must be able to use their local understanding to assess the feel of a place and, as a result, get the crew out of potential danger before it's too late. It is important to make the fixer and the driver feel that they are part of the team – and this includes the minder. As well for the production, there is an ethical consideration in what residual perceptions it leaves behind in pursuing its story. The production goes home, but the fixer and the driver stay behind. The production has a responsibility to ensure that they are not left to pay for the 'sins' of its venture in that country.

17.7   Dangerous assignments

Sources of risk

Programs shot overseas often cover some major world event, a civil war or insurgency, a natural disaster or some political crisis. These introduce an element of risk into the production that needs to be considered by the producer and discussed with the production personnel who will be going to the hot spot. It is the nature of news and current affairs to be interested in such things. Often a documentary, in an individual story that appears relatively benign, might find its story touches on undercurrents that carry a risk to the personal safety of those shooting the story. Even a drama shoot might, on occasions, touch a raw nerve in the country where the story is set and shot. The mini-series *A Dangerous Life* is set during the People Power Movement that toppled the Marcos government in the Philippines, and was partly shot on location in Manila. Defence Minister Juan Ponce Enrile, who had made a transition from Marcos to Aquino governments, wasn't convinced that the portrayal of him in the program would be complimentary. Pressure was brought to bear on the production, and it had to leave Manila part-way through the shoot and complete its 'Manila' scenes in Sri Lanka.

Responsibility of the producer

When there is a recognisable risk in a shoot, the producer and the production company have a duty of care to take all necessary steps to minimise the risk. This doesn't mean to abandon the shoot necessarily, although it might if the risk is too great or the crew is unprepared to take that risk. It does mean that the producer must make sure that all crew are fully informed about the inherent risks in the assignment, that they are given a genuine opportunity to withdraw without repercussions, and that steps are taken for their protection in the risky environment if it goes ahead. Many workers in news and current affairs relish the excitement of their genre and would not be interested in withdrawing, but they should welcome any steps to reduce their risk and, even if they don't, the producer has a responsibility to ensure that they don't fall victim to their own foolhardiness, as much as that is possible.

Managing the risk

Risk management is not limited to fully briefing the crew. It also involves steps to be taken on location. Here, the fixer and the driver are crucial. They must be familiar with the volatile circumstances in which the crew is venturing and know the undercurrents. In these situations, the fixer is more usefully someone who knows the political environment than someone who understands production needs. Care needs to be taken to assess how candid they will be. They are often paid good money by local standards and may be reluctant to disappoint with advice that suggests caution. The producer (or journalist if they are the effective producer) must have sufficient lead time on location to assess the situation and find out from others (including other journalists) what level of danger there is. The crew should be able to identify themselves as press in case that becomes an issue, but not so conspicuously that they might make themselves a target. If practical, it should be made known to warring parties that the crew is there and why it is there. Before going to an area of conflict, the right people should be notified that the crew is going there – local people such as the fixer's family, or the production office.

Response when the risk is too high

There are telltale signs of danger to look for: lack of local population (they have fled to safety), demeanour of fighters (if they are nervous, it is time to get out), or fighters looking in the air (a chance of air attack). A helmet and flak jacket may be useful, but may also make the crew feel less vulnerable than it actually is. Perhaps a better view is that if they are needed, the crew shouldn't be there. It should also be impressed on the cameraman that it is safer to get closer to the action with a telephoto lens than by walking up to it. The production might consider physical protection of police or military (unless they are part of the confrontation) or some other bodyguard protection, depending on the circumstances. Failing that, the crew should attach itself to someone in charge and win their confidence as quickly as possible. If one of the crew wants to get out, all should get out even if the fear seems unnecessary. The crew will be a danger to itself regardless. The producer is responsible for their crew, including fixer and driver. They must be able to have the courage to pull out.

Sources and further reading

Specific reading

Bowden, Tim 1987, *One Crowded Hour: Neil Davis, Combat Cameraman, 1934–1985*, Collins Australia, Sydney.
Little, John 2003, *The Man Who Saw Too Much: David Brill, Combat Cameraman*, Hodder Headline, Sydney.

Some internet references

Commerce Queensland, 'The ATA carnet system – some important information', available online at <http://www.commerceqld.com.au/www/index.cfm?pageid=58>, viewed 18 December 2006.
International accommodation directory, available online at <www.wotif.com>, viewed 18 December 2006.
Sydney Chamber of Commerce, available online at <www.thechamber.com.au>, viewed 18 December 2006.
Victorian Employers' Chamber of Commerce and Industry, 'ATA carnet explanatory notes', available online at <http://www.vecci.org.au/professional+services/international+trade/export+documentation/ata+carnet+explanatory+notes.asp>, viewed 18 December 2006.

Chapter 18

Drafting the production budget

The production budget is prepared in two phases. As noted in Chapter 6, a draft budget is calculated on the basis of known components of the production and educated guesses of what the unknown components are likely to be. The purpose of this budget is to get a preliminary indication of the cost of the production so that the appropriate amount of funding can be pursued. When funding has been secured and the decision has been made to commence production, the formal (or 'final') working budget is arrived at by finetuning the draft budget or its successors. By the commencement of pre-production, some of the previously uncertain components of the production will have crystallised and can be costed with greater reliability. However, there will still be components whose cost is uncertain. The pre-production process puts cost estimates on these as they are decided.

The bottom line at this stage of the budget, the total cost of the production, is fixed. It is the total of funds that have been raised for the production, whether that figure is greater than, less than or the same as the total for the draft production budget. This figure cannot rise as the production budget consolidates because there are no funds to support its increase. The decisions that clarify previously uncertain costs are made with the knowledge of the amount earmarked for them in the draft budget. If the cost is going to rise above that amount, achievable offsets have to be found and entered elsewhere in the budget to ensure that the bottom line remains the same.

The process of drawing up a production budget is essentially the same, whether it is the draft budget calculated during development or the final budget that is the outcome of pre-production. The only real difference is the reliability of the figures. Even with a final budget, actual costs will often differ from budgeted costs (the management of this situation is described in Chapter 22), but they are generally closer than the guesswork of the development stage. This chapter describes the processes of calculating a production budget, whether in development or pre-production. The producer is more intimately involved in the first draft (and may even draw it up), whereas subsequent revisions are commonly done by the production manager, albeit for producer approval.

Because a budget is a mix of known costs and educated guesses, there's no such thing as a 'correct' version. It is a series of strategic decisions about what the production might be able to afford, what might be available and at what price (particularly fees for services), and how much leeway the production should allow itself on expenditure. These are matters of judgement, not fact. A budget is constructed within the tension between the knowledge that the lower it is kept, the harder it will be to manage, and that the higher it becomes, the harder it will be to raise the necessary finance.

It should be borne in mind in drafting a budget that all costs are estimated without including the Goods and Services Tax (GST, see Chapter 26). This industry convention will be assumed to be the case by anyone familiar with it. Similarly, contracted investment or pre-sale licence fee amounts are quoted exclusive of GST, although it is wise to ensure the PIA or PLA states this explicitly. The contract will allow for the production to invoice for the contracted amount plus GST if the production entity is registered for GST. It would be extremely unwise (and probably illegal) to embark on production of a television program without GST registration. The budget and contract exclude GST because there will be no net GST cost to the production as it is not an end-user (i.e. consumer). GST payments on production expenses will generally be offset by the GST added to the investment or licence amounts, but even if there was a shortfall here the balance could be recovered from the ATO.

18.1   AFC budget format

The A–Z spreadsheet

The figures for the budget could be entered on a Microsoft Excel spreadsheet, but most producers and production managers use the A–Z formatted budget spread-sheet that is downloadable from the AFC website (see sources below). This is now the industry standard budget format. It is a customised Microsoft Excel spread-sheet, so if any of the formulas drop out they are easily reinstated by anyone with a working knowledge of the software. The AFC provides the following pro forma budgets:
• feature film budget (adaptable for telemovie, drama or sitcom series)
• short film budget
• documentary budget (for one-off or series)
• interactive digital media budget
• animation budget.

The one that best matches the planned production is chosen from the AFC website. As they tend to cover all possible expenses, including the possibility of dramatised sequences in documentary, the first three named are fairly inter-changeable and all could be adapted to most types of production. There are some idiosyncrasies, such as their different assumptions about whether producers and directors will attract superannuation, but none that can't be worked around by an astute production manager.

Deleting and adding budget categories

Each pro forma allows for all the categories in which there might be expenditure for that type of production, but usually not all will be required for any one production. Those categories for which the project will have no cost can be deleted from the spreadsheet, taking care not to dislocate underlying formulas for other active parts of the spreadsheet. It is wise to leave this until late in the budgeting process when zero-cost categories are confirmed. Any expenses that aren't listed in the pro forma can be added to the spreadsheet, checking that the underlying spreadsheet formulas are picking them up. If they don't, it's not difficult for anyone with a working knowledge of the software to insert the appropriate formula.

Above the Line costs

The A–Z budget is divided into five sections, but the two main sections are Above the Line costs and Below the Line costs. The former comprise the elements of the proposal package that is presented to financiers: script, writer, producer, director and principal cast for a drama project; or research and development, producer, director and presenter (if any) for a documentary project. It is assumed that their cost will already be known and for this reason the contingency (generally 10%) applied to the rest of the production at the bottom of the budget spreadsheet is not applied to Above the Line costs. For television, and particularly series television, some of these fees will not have been finalised by the time funding is secured and further expenditure will be likely during pre-production on items included under *A.2 Development*.

Division above and below the line

Below the Line costs are the anticipated or estimated costs of the rest of the production elements in the project. The premise of the Above/Below the Line division is that items above the line are the principal interest of the financiers of a project, who are generally investors. This is a reasonable assumption for cinema, but not for television, where the principal financiers may well be broadcasters who have at least an equal interest in the content of the program as in its marquee names.

The budget format was designed initially for cinema-release projects, and therefore one-off programs. Hence, it doesn't contemplate the production of a series, where some of the items in Above the Line costs aren't known or costed at the time of going to financiers. The distinction between Above the Line and Below the Line costs is something of a budgeting fiction for television. Not all directors of a drama series are known at this stage and research may continue in a documentary (and certainly in a documentary series) after financing at a cost that is not finalised at that stage and therefore should have a contingency applied.

Refining of the budget

The budget is prepared many times, and each preparation is a refinement of the previous version. Its principal phases are in:
- development, as a guide to the level of finance to seek
- pre-production, to determine how to allocate the resources that can be afforded by the level of funding of the project.

The first budget, which is prepared in the development phase, is updated many times over as new information comes to hand and decisions about production detail are made until the budget is locked off for production. A production schedule (see Chapter 19) is drawn up at the outset, no matter how speculative that might be, as a basis for determining the cost of many of the elements. It's not possible to estimate payments to production workers or the cost of hire of equipment or the cost of travel to locations without some idea of the number of days that these might be needed and the places in which the production might take place. In the early stages, the schedule details are educated guesswork, but as the production consolidates key decisions about the detail are made, and speculative figures are replaced with more accurate figures. Indeed, the speculated figures have a role in determining what the production can afford to do. If the confirmed production element will cost more than the current budget figure, a reduction must be found somewhere else in the budget or the production will have a higher total budget. The latter outcome is fine if it is believed that the additional finance can be found but not if the production's funding is already determined.

18.2   Story and script

Story Rights

Category *A.1 Story & Script* of the A–Z budget itemises story and script expenses. Story Rights covers the fees to buy the right to use an existing work as the basis of a program, including any options paid to reserve this right in advance. It usually applies to fiction works only where the plot and characters are converted into a screenplay. A non-fiction work may be a source of information for a documentary (or occasionally a dramatised program) but buying the right to do that would not generally be necessary unless the work had a distinctive approach to its subject, and the production wished to adopt that same approach (see Chapter 5).

Writers' Fees

Writers' Fees generally relate to drama projects. The scriptwriter will often be contracted at the development phase, and some of the scheduled payments for delivery of drafts may have been paid already. All contracted writers' payments, whether already paid or still scheduled, should be costed in this budget category, along with the writers' fees in any anticipated further contracts for the production. The awards that govern minimum writers' fees are between the AWG and the SPAA, except if the producer is the ABC, which has a separate award with the AWG. There is one award covering telemovies and television mini-series, and another covering television series and serials. There is no award covering the writing of documentary narration, which is therefore a matter of negotiation. The award specifies minimum payment, so writers (or their agents) who believe they have a market value higher than the minimum payment will negotiate an above-award fee. The budget should anticipate negotiated fees where this is likely.

Script and story editors

This section also includes fees for script and story editors. These personnel participate in the development phase. In a series they may well continue on through production, working on later episodes of the series as the earlier episodes are being shot and edited. They are, therefore, not strictly above the line, but that is the product of a budget spreadsheet designed initially for cinema production.

Writing for documentary

Writers' fees would not generally be expected to be a budgeted line item in a documentary unless a professional writer has been or will be engaged specifically to write re-enactment scenes or narration. More commonly, a director or researcher will do the writing for documentary or other factual genres as part of their fee for that service. This might be shooting script, narration or any other program component. Alternatively, narration might be written by a presenter or reporter as part of their fee.

Researcher(s)

Conversely, researcher fees are not usual in drama projects, except as background information for a factually based drama. They would, however, be expected to be a major expense in a factual genre. Sometimes, preliminary research will be carried out by the director or a hired researcher during development, and more detailed research will be a component of pre-production. Although the latter is more logically a Below the Line cost, the A–Z format doesn't have a Researcher line item in Below the Line costs. One could be inserted into the format, but it's probably more practical to aggregate all researcher fees in category *A.1*, regardless of the stage of production at which they are incurred.

Limitations of cinema–derived budget spreadsheet

The AFC documentary budget has line items for Location Surveys in categories *M* and *N*. In practice, the documentary researcher will usually assess technical conditions and restraints for shooting, and report the results to the director and DOP. A location survey is a common requirement for a live OB production, but there is no current AFC format for that type of production. The anomaly of location survey expenses in the documentary budget format is no doubt the product of a format designed initially for cinema drama and subsequently refashioned for television and non-drama genres. It's not a major issue, but it is useful to be aware of these idiosyncrasies. The budget format is still useful – and widely used – for non-cinema, non-drama productions despite this. Its users take a flexible approach and, as long as they know how they've defined the categories they use, they will find they are still working with a functional spreadsheet.

18.3   Development costs

Government development assistance

Generally, there will be costs in development prior to the production being funded. These may have been paid out of development funding from a government body or other source, or out of the pockets of some of the production team. Either way, they should be recouped from the production's funding and are therefore to be budgeted as production expenses in category *A.2 Development*. Development assistance from a government agency usually requires repayment of the investment plus a 10% premium at commencement of principal photography. The agency then relinquishes its temporary copyright interest in the program (see Chapter 6). The investment, premium and any interest payment associated with sourced development funds or loans are budgeted. The interest item should not be unrealistically optimistic about the time it will take to secure production funding.

Deferred fees and reimbursements

Other development expenses that have been paid from within the production team should be included and the budget updated as further expenses are incurred. The person who paid for these items will be entitled to reimbursement from the production at some agreed stage on provision of a tax invoice and (preferably) receipts to support the claimed amount. Deferred fees for the development team are likewise paid out of production funds but are not included in category *A.2*. They are included instead as part of the aggregated total fee for each person to whom it applies.

18.4   Producers, directors and principal cast

Lack of market benchmark

Setting fees for producers, directors and principal cast is fraught with uncertainty, especially at the draft budget stage. Fees set for other projects could be used as a guide, but these are often kept confidential, so producers will be familiar with fees on their own past productions, but have limited knowledge of what the people intended to be hired have been paid on other producers' projects. Also to be kept in mind is the view of potential financers of the production of what they would think was a reasonable fee. They might have a clear idea, or an unrealistic idea, or no idea at all. They might give thought to the reasonableness of the fees, or they might not.

Producer fee

As a starting point, a producer fee on a low-budget feature (in 2006) might range between $70 000 and $80 000, and this could equate to a 90-minute telemovie. For the producer of a drama series, this might be extended proportionally to the duration of the production. Another method is to estimate full-time equivalent weeks worked in all phases of the production and apply a weekly rate of between $2000 and $3000 (or more), depending on the nature of the production and the experience of the producer. Because the producer is often, in effect, nominating their own fee, care needs to be taken that financers will not see the figure as unrealistic or even greedy. Other factors may contribute to the producer reducing their fee to get the project up and running. If they have some equity in exploitation of the program, they may reduce their fee to enable the budget to equate to the production's level of funding. Care needs to be exercised that they don't undercut themselves too severely for the sake of getting the production up. There might be other sacrifices that the project could make to enable it to be within its level of funding.

Directors' fees

Directors' fees are usually negotiated by the producer. The Australian Screen Directors' Association (ASDA) provides indicative rates currently being paid in the Australian film and television industry. ASDA also provides guidelines for the minimum fees that directors should expect, but these are not award rates and are therefore not enforceable. The fee is the outcome of negotiation. It will be influenced by the type of production and the experience of the director. A director of a one-hour documentary might expect a fee of between $35 000 and $50 000, whereas a director of a telemovie might expect a fee of $60 000 to $90 000. Where one person fills the role of both producer and director, as is often the case in documentary, the fee is not the sum of the two separate fees, but often the larger of the two with an increment to cover the dual role.

Adjusting the fee to the nature of the production

Experienced producers will have a range of fees for key production personnel that they have set in past productions. These will be used as the benchmark for any current production. Similar productions with directors of similar experience will have a similar fee as a starting point. The budget will provide a context for the director's fee: is it a low-budget production or high-end? The fee might be eased back if it's a project the director will be very keen to work on, but it still must be enough money to show they are respected. By and large, the director works on the project because they are attracted to it rather than for the money, but the allocation of money, nonetheless, has an emotional context. Too high a price raises the possibility that the producer is ingenuous and manipulable; too low a price is resented.

Level of experience

A less experienced producer doesn't have past experience to inform the decision about fee. Until that experience is built, rough arithmetic can be used to arrive at a fee to offer. The director's input is converted to full-time equivalent weeks. A weekly rate of about $2000 for relatively inexperienced directors, or $2200–2500 for more experienced directors, is then applied to this rate. The end result is rounded off, compared with other fees in similar circumstances, and offered as a fee without the calculations that generated it. Another approach is to seek advice from the production manager, using their experience to inform the fee to be offered. A general principle is to balance inexperience in a component of the production team with experience in a connected role, so an inexperienced producer might ensure they hire an experienced production manager to balance, or may offset an inexperienced director with an experienced DOP. All should be paid a fee commensurate with their level of experience.

Deferred fees

Producers and directors will often have worked on the development of the project for deferred fees before the production is funded (see Chapter 6). Deferrals are included in the budget at categories *B.1* and *B.2*, as they are to be paid from the production funding under the arrangement made in the deferral agreement.

Above the Line cast

The inclusion of cast members at category *E(a)* in Above the Line costs relates more to feature film production than television. Principal cast are included here when they are part of the package to secure investor finance and their fee has already been agreed. In television, where this negotiation outcome has often not been reached at the time of financing, it may be more practical to keep all cast together as Below the Line costs in category *E(b)2*, where they will be incorporated into calculation of the contingency. Overseas actors are the more likely candidates to be secured with agreement on fee prior to financing, so they are more appropriately included in category *E(a)1 Offshore Cast*. The agreed fee for overseas actors will usually be in a foreign currency and the exchange rate should be estimated cautiously since, at the time of budgeting, the rate at the time of payment will not be known.

18.5   Below the Line costs

Adjusting to changed costing detail

Below the Line costs are all the remaining production costs of the project and are always estimates at the development stage because many of the specifics of the production are not yet decided, and at pre-production because even when they are decided their cost can vary according to the circumstances on the day. Despite this uncertainty, care is taken to get as much reliability into the figures as is possible. Where a quote is available, it is used instead of an educated guess.

Fees are calculated on the expected production schedule and are updated as the schedule is updated. Where a changed schedule creates increased fees, the budget has to be able to absorb these or accept a higher total budget. Among other things, this enables the production to examine the financial feasibility of the changed schedule. By this general approach, development is a process of constant internal feedback where planning changes are recosted and the new costings determine the capacity of the budget to accommodate them. Where it cannot, the changes are reconsidered.

Budgeting for discounts

Standard costs of items to the general public are used in the budget's calculations, even if there is some prospect of a discount on an item. Unless the discount is already offered in writing and doesn't have conditions that may prevent the production from taking advantage of it, the undiscounted cost should be budgeted. If the discount eventuates, it gives a bit more room for movement in the budget. A budgeted discount that doesn't eventuate creates a need to find offsets after production has started.

18.6   Production fees and salaries

Budgeting for crew

The first category of Below the Line costs, *C. Production Unit Fees & Salaries*, lists the fees and salaries of all the personnel working on the production phase of the project, along with the production office team in support. Calculation of production crew fees will include preparation time in pre-production: consultations and meetings, location surveys, and selection and testing of equipment. The size of the production crew (putting aside post-production for the moment) can vary enormously from the large crew of a major drama (which can be up to fifty people) to the single video-journalist, although even the latter will usually require some production office back-up. The process of determining the components of the crew was dealt with in Chapter 14. As they are decided, their fees and salaries are converted into budget line items. At the very early stages this will have less certainty and the budget in category *C* will be calculated on the usual cost of a crew for this type of production. As the actual crew crystallises, these budget figures are refined with increasing levels of reliability.

Production crew award rates

Working conditions for television crew are covered by the Motion Picture Production Award (MPPA) and wages are covered in the Motion Picture Production Agreement, negotiated between the MEAA and SPAA. Award rates specified in the MPPA are based on a fifty-hour week, which is standard industry practice, and are updated annually. The AFC/AFTRS handbook on production budgeting includes a checklist of technicians' salaries/fees, including award minimums for all technician categories and rates commonly paid on low- and medium-budget features as a guideline. These rates are a guide only, are subject to negotiation and are varied according to the type of production. Like other wages, they increase over time. Personnel with limited experience would be employed at minimum rates. For more experienced personnel, the rate goes up according to their market pull and the nature of the production. It should also be borne in mind that production crew fees will vary from state to state, depending on the demand in that state.

Adjusting crew fees

Production crew fees are based on the most recent production schedule, even though that may not be the final schedule, and amended as the schedule is updated until the budget is locked off. After that point, adjustments can be made to the schedule only when they don't contribute to an increase in the total figure. An increase in a line item can be tolerated as long as it is offset by an equivalent decrease elsewhere in the budget (see Chapter 22). This decrease should be plausible. It's of no benefit to the production to have a budget item that has no realistic possibility of being adhered to. The rates that are applied to the scheduled time of working should not be less than the appropriate award rate. Where the person's usual fee is known, that figure should be budgeted even if there is an intention to try to negotiate a lower fee. Budgets should not assume favourable outcomes of negotiations yet to take place, and which may not be as successful as the production is hoping. Where the person's usual fee is not known and inquiry is not a possibility, the estimate should be the usual fee for someone of that person's skill and experience – or perhaps, a conservative version of it.

18.7 Overtime and loadings

Estimating overtime

The budget of production crew costs includes a calculation of anticipated overtime costs. Overtime will become liable after eight hours working in the one day or after five working days in a week and is specified by the Award as time and a half, double time or triple time (see Table 8.1). Clause 21 of the Award outlines where a six-day week may be scheduled. Where the overtime is scheduled, as in a standard ten-hour day, the two hours of overtime can be incorporated into each crew member's budgeted fee, but some allowance should be made for unscheduled overtime even though the number of hours will be unknown at the time of budgeting. An hourly rate is calculated for the total of all crew members who will attract overtime when the shoot runs over on any day. This is multiplied by an educated guess of the number of hours of production overtime that will be incurred, which is drawn from past experience and scrutiny of the production schedule for the likely number of days that will run into overtime. There are also some crew members whose work inherently involves extra hours due to early starts – make-up, wardrobe and assistant directors are examples in drama – or late finishes – cameramen are an example in documentaries. This overtime should also be budgeted.

Managing penalties

There are some aspects of the schedule that will create penalty loadings. These are increments added to the normal hourly rate for work at times restricted by the Award. A schedule drafted without consideration of these penalty rates can add unnecessarily to the cost of production. The schedule is continually reworked to minimise penalties, the various strategies to achieve this being canvassed in Chapter 19. There must be, for example, a ten-hour break (called 'turnaround') between consecutive working days. Time is calculated from base or location (whichever is specified in the crew call). With a production on location away from its home town, time is calculated from leaving the hotel (or other accommodation) until return to it at the end of the day. When the turnaround is less than ten hours, the crew is paid a loading of single time (i.e. double the wage) until it next gets a ten-hour break. There are other penalty loadings specified in the Award for working late nights, weekends and public holidays (in the state in which the production takes place on that day). These are listed in Table 18.1.

18.8   Fringe calculations

Employees and contractors

Fringes or on-costs are additional costs that are incurred by a production (or by any business) as a result of employing workers. Only crew who are employees

Table 18.1: Overtime and penalty rates in the Motion Picture Production Award.

OVERTIME

Day	Overtime	Pay rate
Monday–Saturday	After 8 hours	Time and a half
	After 10 hours	Double time
	After 12 hours	Triple time
Saturday (as 6th day)		Time and a half
	After 2 hours	Double time
	After 12 hours	Triple time
Sunday		Double time
	After 12 hours	Triple time

PENALTY LOADINGS

Day	Time (hours)	Percentage loading
Monday–Friday	2000–2400	25%
Tuesday–Friday	0000–0600	25%
Saturday	0600–2000	25%
Saturday	2000–2400	50%
Saturday	0000–0600	50%
Monday	0000–0600	100%
After turnaround under 10 hours		100%

are paid fringes. Where a person is contracted as an individual, it can become an issue whether they are a contractor or an employee in law (see Chapter 26). For the most part, individual contractors should be treated as employees by the production for the purposes of fringe calculation even if they provide an ABN and PAYG tax is not withheld (see Chapter 26). This issue requires professional advice from an accountant. Crew whose services are provided through a private (proprietary limited) company are much more straightforward. These workers are not taxed by the production company but by their own company, which in law is their employer. They do not attract fringe payments by the production, although their fee might include a component in recognition of the contracting company's fringe costs.

Calculation of percentage of crew on fringes

The AFC budget starts at a nominal 20% of crew paid fees and not attracting fringe costs and 80% paid wages. This is unlikely these days for most television productions. The advantages of freelancing as a company are less than they used to be. It is safer to calculate fringes on 100% of crew unless it is known that some of the crew will be contracted through a company. The calculation of fringes should be reduced only where it is known workers will be paid by fee to a company. This applies to producers, directors and related personnel as well. They will often not be paid via a company. The AFC budget doesn't feed their fees into the Crew Fringe calculations at category *D*, so the aggregated salary of these people, where they are to be treated as employees for fringe calculations, needs to be added to Above the Line (if taxed) in each Fringe category in category *D*.

The following are the categories in Fringe calculations:
- *Holiday pay* – this is calculated as one-twelfth (8.33%) of the ordinary rate of pay for the period worked and is paid as pro rata annual leave. Industry practice is to pay holiday pay for drama production staff (including cast), but to not pay it to documentary crew on the grounds that their fee is over the Award and that the holiday pay component is already incorporated into the fee. Actors hired for a documentary would be paid holiday pay if they were paid at the Award minimum rate, as would most often be the case.
- *Payroll tax* – this is a state tax levied on wages. It varies from state to state and is frequently changed by legislation. There are different wage level thresholds in each state below which payroll tax is exempt. Often smaller productions such as one-off documentaries will have a wage level below the threshold and will not be liable for payroll tax. This tax is discussed in some detail in Chapter 26 and Table 26.4 lists current tax rates and exemption thresholds.
- *Superannuation* – this must be paid to a complying superannuation fund on behalf of each employee, which is defined very broadly. The current rate is 9% of the earnings base, so this rate is applied to the total salary for this fringe calculation. Chapter 26 provides further detail about the operation of superannuation payments.
- *Workers compensation* – this insurance is payable for both crew and cast (see Chapter 26). Calculation of the actual payment is based on total payroll plus annual leave plus overtime, but excluding superannuation. For purposes of the budget estimate a figure of about 1% is applied to total salaries, varying from

state to state and from insurer to insurer. In New South Wales, the figure usually used is 1.02%.

- *Fringe Benefits Tax* (FBT) – this is payable by employers on fringe benefits provided in place of, or in addition to, salary of employees. Items that commonly attract FBT in production include: entertainment (such as restaurant meals), petrol and hire cars for travel between home and work, social functions held off company premises, provision of a tutor, and car park charges near the production office or a location (see Chapter 26). The rate is currently 46.5%.

18.9 Cast

Personal margins

Drama and comedy productions may have a considerable number of cast to be budgeted. Smaller parts and extras will be paid award minimum rates, but for many of the leads a personal margin will be negotiated as their fee for appearance. At the time of budgeting, the outcome of most or all of these negotiations will be unknown. The budget must make an estimate of the likely outcome, once again as an educated guess. Its basis will be what has been paid in the past to a particular actor if the production already has someone in mind, or what is generally paid for roles of that kind in production, factoring in the marketability of the actor that the production will seek to attract to the program.

Classification of actors

The ATPA sets working conditions and minimum rates for the various categories of actor. The calculation of cast payments starts with a base figure for the performance, called a basic negotiated fee (BNF), the sum of the ATPA minimum rate and the actor's personal margin, if there is one. On top of this are built additional allowances and rights as they become necessary. Bit players, doubles and extras will all be paid a BNF at the appropriate award rates. They have a minimum call of four hours. For performers, the minimum call is eight hours. Performers who are paid at ATPA rates are divided into two classes according to experience (see Chapter 15), but at the time of budgeting it is unlikely that the actors who will be cast in these roles will be known. As most actors will qualify as Performer Class 2, it is prudent to budget all Performers as Class 2, at least until it is confirmed that any are Class 1. Stunt performers are contracted as cast members under the same award, with a stunt loading.

Child actors

An actor under the age of sixteen is paid not less than 50% of the minimum adult rate. Very few child actors have the market power to demand a rate above the 50% minimum, although sometimes it might be a productive gesture to offer a fifteen-year-old actor a somewhat higher rate for a major role. There are various conditions and restrictions on the use of child actors that are set by each state, some quite stringent, some not (see Chapter 15). Under varying circumstances in each state, qualified child care for preschool children, and tutors for school-age children are required. These should be covered in the budget.

Allowances for additional calls

In addition to performance on shooting days, a number of cast payments are budgeted in category *E(b) Cast & Casting*. The production schedule should include rehearsals, and make-up, wardrobe and publicity calls (see Chapter 15 for details). These are entered in the tabbed Cast page in the AFC budget, taking into account the ATPA rates for these activities. Aggregated totals are entered into the main budget spreadsheet. Where screen tests or auditions are planned, both cast costs and the costs of crew and facilities to record the tests should be budgeted. The ATPA has an hourly rate with a minimum payment of one hour, but this does not apply to the initial audition, only to call-backs. Hold-over days are days on location where the actor is not required to work but cannot be returned home for the day. These are paid at the BNF for an eight-hour day. If cast have to travel on a non-working day to a distant location, then they are paid at the ATPA rate for a minimum four-hour call.

As with production crew, the cast attract overtime and penalty loadings, some of which can be inferred from the schedule and some will be generated on the day. The former are factored into budget calculations and an allowance is made for the latter. There may also be payments eventually for postponements and cancellations (from schedule changes or wet weather) and 'post-syncing' (re-recording voice) in post-production, but these generally are not known at the time of budgeting. It is, nonetheless, prudent to make some allowance for their possibility in a big production. Finally, actors generate the same range of fringe payments as other production workers: holiday pay, superannuation, payroll tax and workers' compensation. They aggregate automatically in the AFC budget.

Repeat and residual payments

The ATPA's minimum rates buy the right to the actor's performance for one television screening of the program in Australia. They do not pay for repeat screenings on Australian television or use of the program for video release, pay television, hotel or in-flight entertainment in Australia (ancillary use) or overseas broadcast or ancillary use (residuals). Repeat fees and overseas residual payments for actors are set out in the Australian Television Repeats and Residuals Agreement (ATRRA). It is customary for a production to buy up-front three runs on Australian television plus Australian ancillary rights and overseas residuals. The total fee for all these is calculated from the actor's BNF. To this would be added:
- two repeats on Australian FTA or pay television, the first at 35% of BNF, the second at 25%, for a total of 60% of BNF, plus
- Australian ancillary rights calculated as 2.5% of BNF, and
- overseas residuals (overseas television and ancillary rights, excluding US networks) calculated as 30% of BNF

for a total additional fee of 92.5% of the actor's BNF.

Total cast budget

The estimated fee for each character in a drama is the product of their rate and the time for which they will be engaged. ATPA provides the former, the production schedule the latter. As the schedule is refined, changed details are entered into the spreadsheet, which automatically adjusts the totals. As the total budget consolidates, the market value that has been set for hoped-for lead actors may have to be modified if it creates a production budget that is higher than the funds that the production could be expected to raise – or higher than the funding the production has secured. As the whole budget is a process of refining as a result of production decisions and the reality of what is available to the production, so cast budget is also adjusted to emerging realities. What the production would like to do is balanced against the funds available.

Non-drama production

The above outlines cost implications for the use of actors in drama and comedy production under the ATPA. Performers on other productions – documentaries, variety programs, television commercials, corporate and training videos – are covered by the Actors Etc. (Television) Award, also negotiated between the MEAA and SPAA. In this Award, there are only two categories, performers and extras, with a minimum four-hour call for either. Where documentaries use actors, for example, in dramatised documentaries or re-enactment sequences, this Award will determine minimum rates of pay and other conditions. There are special rates for narration or scripted voice-over in documentary, which is based on studio time or unedited running time, whichever is the greater. A character voice requires a higher fee.

Actors in features and ABC productions

Producers and production managers should be aware that the two Awards referred to in this section do not apply to actors in feature films or ABC productions, both of which have their own actors' award.

18.10 Materials costs

Costume costs

Costs in category *F.1 Costume* are calculated from:
- breakdown of the script (see Chapter 12), particularly the number of cast and the number of 'days' involving the cast member (from which is inferred the number of different costumes)
- the estimated cost per costume, taking into account whether they are contemporary, period or fantasy.
  Preliminary decisions are made about whether costumes are more likely to be purchased, made by the wardrobe department or hired. In many instances, extras and minor roles bring their own costumes, which is also possible sometimes with major parts although the budget should not assume that. Fantasy costumes may

be subcontracted to a specialist, in which case a quote is obtained for budgeting purposes. The budget should reflect any need for duplicate outfits (or part of them) for stunt players and doubles. The wardrobe budget should also allow for washing machines (purchased or hired, depending on the size of the production) and expendables (e.g. washing powder, safety pins and bleach). Advice from an experienced wardrobe designer (preferably the intended designer for the production) can ensure a more reliable estimate.

Make-up and hairdressing materials

Costs for category *F.2 Make-up & Hairdressing* will be relatively small unless there are special requirements such as wigs, or special effects make-up (e.g. wounds, monster faces, prosthetics). The make-up artist and hairdresser each have a kit for which they are usually paid a weekly allowance for stock replenishment. There will also be an allowance for additional expendables bought as one-off items. Rental of a make-up van or room, as well as a wardrobe workroom and storage space, is included in category *L. Rentals & Storage*.

Other art department materials

Category *H. Sets & Properties* is best estimated by a production designer or art director who is involved with the project from the outset. The necessary props are inferred and costed from analysis of the script, taking account of whether the director intends to cover a particular scene in wide perspective or treat it intimately. Equally important is the decision about what will be shot on location and what, if anything, in studio. A construction manager is used to advise on the cost of set construction, anticipating reuse of flattage elements where feasible to keep material and labour costs down. Action vehicles are costed per vehicle per shooting day. The production will look at the relative merits of per-day hire and long-term hire when a car is required on several shooting days. Apart from the cost of hire or purchase, there may be costs for storage, mechanical work, exterior signage, or cost of transport to location (if the vehicle is not registered to travel on a public road). Special effects and armoury are specialist areas where the material costs are usually based on quotes using detailed descriptions of the effect required. In the early stages of budgeting, where details of the effect may not be available, a guesstimate figure is used, but this should be updated as soon as details of the effect are known.

18.11 Location costs

Location fees are paid to owners or occupiers for the right to shoot in or around a location. Time for which the fee is paid should include dressing and wrap time. Councils will charge fees to set up a shoot on public land in their administrative area, and other government bodies (e.g. state Parks and Wildlife Services) may charge for access to property they administer. Council fees vary widely and often for different types of productions, so a quote for anticipated public locations should be sought. Productions should shop around for more favourable council fees where they have some flexibility on locations. There may also be costs for adjacent parking, overnight security, and police crowd and traffic control. Factors affecting location choice and costs are covered in Chapter 16.

18.12   Equipment and stores

Camera team equipment

The choice of camera type will be determined early in the production by director and DOP. The script (or in the case of a documentary, the director) will indicate whether an underwater camera or other specialised equipment will be required. Category *K. Equipment & Stores* budgets at facility hire card rates, unless a written quote for a discounted deal has been provided by a supplier. Discounted card rates might be sought, but the budget should not assume these until confirmed in writing. The director and DOP will advise on the needs for mountings (of camera on cars or in aircraft) and the range of grips equipment that is planned. In the early stages of production, many of these decisions will not have been made, and the producer and production manager will infer an estimate for category *K.4* from the script. A drama production is likely to hire a fully equipped grip truck by the day or week if it has a range of shots requiring moving or rigged camera platforms. It may hire a lighting truck, and possibly a generator truck as well, for the entire shoot. Productions with limited grip requirements, including documentaries, are more likely to hire equipment individually at a daily rate. A documentary cameraman will often hire their own camera kit plus a kit of three or four lightweight lights to the production. Additional lighting would be hired on days where the cameraman's kit is insufficient. Expendables, such as gels, batteries, light bulbs and gaffer tape, should be budgeted on the basis of past experience.

Sound equipment

The sound recordist will usually hire a range of sound equipment to the production, the size of the kit relating to the type of production. In addition, the production may have to hire additional or specialist microphones, or playback equipment. A noisy interior location may require hire of baffling for temporary soundproofing, which is something that can be hard to anticipate for budgeting purposes because its need is generated by the location, not the script.

Field communication

Walkie-talkies will be hired for communication with roving crew members, particularly assistant directors and unit personnel, on location shoots. The number required will depend on budget level (i.e. affordability), logistics and the size of the production. Documentaries may sometimes need a walkie-talkie if the shoot will involve crew separating to different points, although these days a mobile phone may sometimes serve the purpose.

Rental, storage and office expenses

A large production is likely to impose rental and storage costs on the budget (category *L*). Rental of a drama production office, if the production company doesn't already have one, will include space for the component departments. A documentary's production office is likely to be on a smaller scale. If it is a lean production working out of someone's home, it would be reasonable for that person to recover a market-rate rental for the use of the premises. Furniture, computers, telephones, stationery and other fittings and incidentals within the production office are costed under category *P. Office Expenses*. There may need to be temporary office space on location for a major drama production, or access otherwise to make-up and dressing areas for cast. Where toilet facilities are insufficient at location, portable toilets will be hired. Storage space may be needed for props and action vehicles, as well as rehearsal space, although this need not be purpose-built. A church hall will often suffice.

18.13 Travel and transport

Travel expenses

Travel costs can account for a substantial part of the total production budget in many types of production. Documentary may involve extensive travel, although generally with a small crew. Drama, on the other hand, may not involve much moving about, but any travel will be with a considerably larger crew with living expenses while away from home. Detailed estimates of travel, transport, accommodation and meals may take time to research. They should be calculated on the Travel breakdown page attached to the AFC budget file and tabbed on the bottom of the file. Aggregated figures are transferred to the main production budget.

Airfare discounts

Airfares are widely discounted, but these discounts come and go. A production budget should not assume that they will be available on days that are useful to the production, and should instead work from the full fare rate, or at least one that is routinely available. In any case, discounted airfares are generally not particularly flexible. The price will rise if the production needs to re-book to a different flight because of shoot overrun. When the time to fly comes, the production might decide to take advantage of discounted fares, especially if it is a small-crew documentary and fees for re-booking are not prohibitive.

Vehicle hire

A range of vehicles may be necessary to transport crew, cast, equipment and materials. These will be hired, or people will be paid an allowance for using their own vehicles. For drama, there will be several hired cars to accommodate the needs of the different departments. All are budgeted in category *M. Travel & Transport*, as are camera trucks, art department vehicles and stand-by props trucks. Grip and lighting trucks, however, are budgeted in category *K* and make-up and wardrobe vans in category *L*. Documentaries may budget for a production vehicle and a camera vehicle. The latter might actually be hired from the cameraman, and may be sufficient to hold the field team and its equipment; this will be included in the invoice to the production for their services. A documentary crew moving considerable distances between locations is more likely to move from location to location by air and rent a camera vehicle at each destination.

Private vehicle allowance

Production workers who use their own car will be paid either an agreed weekly rate or an agreed rate for kilometres travelled on production business (as kept in a log book or on a spreadsheet). This private vehicle allowance will include petrol and other costs of running the car. There will be petrol costs for rental vehicles, however, and parking costs and tolls that will have to be estimated for all vehicles. Once again, past experience is a useful guide.

Overseas travel costs

Overseas travel follows most of the principles above, although a greater degree of research is necessary to arrive at practical budget figures. Travel is likely to be by a combination of air, rail, bus and more exotic forms of transport, with rental cars to service the production in each location area. There will also be costs of visas (business, not tourist visas), departure tax and carnets (customs documents for taking professional equipment overseas temporarily – see Chapter 17). A budget allowance should be made for excess baggage charges even though they are quite unpredictable, unless steps have been taken to keep baggage to a level that is below excess weight. Excess baggage charges vary enormously without any apparent logic or consistency.

Documentary location survey

Budgeting of accommodation and meals (category *N*) includes location surveys, generally likely in drama production only. For documentary, the crew seldom surveys a location away from the home town for cost reasons, unless there is a particular need to do so (see Chapter 16). Most commonly, the researcher will do that as part of their research brief, or the director will travel to the location a day or so earlier than the crew. Research travel costs are budgeted under category *A.2 Development*, although a late research trip might be costed under category *N* if the production elects to do so. The guiding principle is that anticipated costs are included in the budget estimate somewhere that is logical, under categories that could be anticipated by people who need to refer to the budget.

Accommodation

Accommodation costs, like travel costs, can be detailed in the Travel back-up spreadsheet. Accommodation is estimated at published hotel rates after researching the options, which are usually conveniently found on the internet these days, even though the production might seek discounts when it comes to booking. The producer must decide what level of accommodation the production will provide.

Meals and per diem allowances

Meals are provided to cast and crew during the shooting period of a drama production. The awards for cast and crew specify which meals are to be provided and when this will include a second meal. The size, nature and location of the production will determine whether to hire caterers (in which case, quotes are sought) or to get runners to purchase food on each occasion. On the other hand, meals are generally not provided to a documentary crew working locally unless they are nowhere near a place to buy food or there is insufficient time in the break to go and get food. Where the documentary is shooting away from home and not using a local crew, the production will either buy all meals for the days away (regardless of the hours worked) or, more commonly, provide per diems (see Chapter 17). The ATO publishes 'reasonable' rates that vary across different countries and, in Australia, different cities and rural areas. Where a crew is camping or living in ad-hoc quarters, the production will supply food for the days away, and the budget will anticipate this cost.

18.14   Insurance

A television production may take out a range of insurance policies to protect itself against risks with economic consequences. A judgement has to be made in each instance about what insurance is desirable for a production and, where it is considered appropriate, the extent of coverage necessary. Chapter 13 covers in more detail the range of insurances that might be considered. At the initial stages of budgeting, these judgements might be fairly tentative, but as pre-production progresses they consolidate and the budgeting of insurance becomes more reliable. Budget estimates of insurance items from quotes are entered in category *O. Insurances* of the AFC budget, with some exceptions. The main insurance items to be considered are listed below:

- Workers compensation insurance is a statutory requirement regulated by each state and territory in Australia. It is calculated at category *D. Fringes & Workers Compensation*, which is separate from the other insurance items, as was noted in section 18.8, and is discussed further in Chapter 26.
- Film producers' indemnity (FPI) covers postponing or abandoning the shoot through death or disability of nominated personnel, mostly in major drama production. The cost is included in the budget estimate under category *O. Insurances*.
- Negative film risk covers accidental loss or destruction of recording stock.
- Multi-risk insurance covers props, sets, wardrobe or production equipment.
- Public liability insurance covers liability for damage to property of others while under the production's care, and indemnifies the production for death or injury of non-employees.

- Motor vehicle insurance is for hired vehicles that are not otherwise insured.
- Travel insurance is prudent if the production is shooting overseas.
- Errors and omissions (E&O) insurance, where required by a broadcaster, is for indemnity against defamation, or breach of copyright or contract.

18.15   Post-production

Film costs

The post-production budget implications of a film shoot are extensive and complex, but as film is seldom used in television production these days it will not be covered in this book. The items to be considered would include film stock, laboratory processing and printing, sound transfers and post-production pathways.

Digital tape costs

Post-production of a digital tape shoot is much more straightforward. Category *J. Tape – Shooting + Rushes* (in the documentary spreadsheet) or *Digital Video Production* (in the feature film and short film spreadsheets) is used instead of category *I. Film & Lab – Shooting + Rushes* and the items to be estimated are video and sound stock, and transfer costs for viewing tapes or DVDs. Quotes from likely suppliers combined with an estimate of the amount of footage that will be shot will provide the necessary estimates for this section. Categories *R*, *S* and *T* are used for post-production, whether the program originates on film or tape, since in either case it is likely to be digitised and edited on a non-linear edit suite such as Avid or Final Cut Pro. There may be a cost to hire a replay deck for digitising if the edit suite doesn't have a replay machine for the format in which the program is shot. Post-production crew cost is estimated by the same process as other crew (see section 18.6), and facility costs are based on quotes or card rates of expected suppliers. Sound editors are included under category *R* if they are part of the program's post-production crew, but more commonly audio post-production is taken to a specialist facility and its costs will be budgeted under category *V. Sound – Post-Production*. Sound post-production will include track lay, mix and layback time as well as stock costs. Often an audio post-production facility quotes a rate inclusive of the crew costs.

Archive costs

The costs of obtaining archive and stock footage, most commonly in documentary, are budgeted under category *U.1 Lab. Costs – Editing*. In practice, most archive is accessed from tape copies where the original was on film, so there is unlikely to be any laboratory costs per se. Instead, there will be costs for search and handling time, supply of audition tapes (these two items may be combined as one fee) and duplication of footage selected (time and stock costs). The rights acquired to use selected footage are also costed here. A conservative estimate is made of the likely duration of archive footage in the program, and the fee of the principal supplier is applied to this. If a small amount of expensively licensed footage is expected from another source, this is factored into the estimate. Calculation is at the rate for rights that the production must obtain at this stage, and those required by broadcasters or other end-users (e.g. theatrical release, publishers) already committed to the program. Quotes should be obtained for rights that are not yet required, but may be required in the future. Sales requiring extension of the program's archive licence can then be made knowing the marginal cost of the sale. A conservative estimate of archive costs provides some leeway if the project cannot raise the full budget estimate. It might be possible to reduce the cost of archive materials by dispensing with the more expensive sources or reducing the amount used.

Titles, graphics and special effects

The cost of titles and graphics, of onlining the program from an edit decision list (EDL) produced in the off-line edit, and of grading the picture, are also included in category *U.1*, regardless of the logic of this. Any special digital effects or CGI costs are budgeted under category *U.2*.

Music

Music costs are principally a negotiated fee if the music is commissioned (the most flexible way of obtaining it). Otherwise, an estimate is made of the cost of the predicted use of production library music for the rights that need to be obtained. Extension of the rights for later sales will require payment of an additional fee to the music source, whereas commissioned music should be contracted with such wide-ranging rights that future sales will not create an additional music licensing cost.

Post-production script

A post-production script, prepared from the completed program, is often required by a distributor or licensee. It is a timed dialogue script (for either drama or documentary) and is typed by a specialist from whom a quote is obtained for the budget estimate. It is an item that is often overlooked and costs more than is generally anticipated.

18.16   Finance and legal

Audits, loan interest and company establishment costs

A number of costs are incurred by a major production from the financing of that project, and these should be budgeted. An investment agreement might require a final audit of the project when it is completed, at a cost to the production. The project may have a completion guarantor, a person with contractual powers to take the steps necessary to ensure for the investors that a completed program is delivered within the budget (see Chapter 8). If it does, they would require a final audit to complete their responsibilities. If the production is part-funded with bor-rowings, the interest on these loans is a budgeted cost. If a company is formed as the production entity, the costs of setting up that company are legitimate produc-tion expenses.

Legal costs

A production will be funded through licence and/or investment agreements for which the producer should always seek legal advice before signing, so there will almost certainly be legal costs regardless of the scale of the production. The cost will vary widely depending on lawyer and law firm, and on the nature of the production. Large firms tend to charge more, and less experienced lawyers tend to charge less to build up a client base. It would be inadvisable to use a lawyer who didn't specialise in media law. A rule of thumb, often used in the absence of more specific estimates, is to budget legal costs at 2% of the production budget.

18.17   Contingency

No production budget will predict with absolute accuracy the cost of all bud-geted items. There are too many opportunities for the unexpected for that to be a realistic possibility. A contingency, usually 10% of Below the Line costs, is con-ventionally added to the budget to give some capacity to cover unexpected costs. However, the main means of dealing with variations in actual costs from the bud-geted figure is through offsets. Contingency is a means of more breathing space, especially when offsets are no longer easy to find, late in the production. Producers should resist the temptation to allocate the contingency early in production, and often production agreements prohibit this. The process of budget management by offsets and contingency is examined in greater detail in Chapter 22.

Sources and further reading

General reading

Case, D., Gailey, L., Knapman, C., et al., *The Production, Budgeting and Film Management Satchel*, AFC/AFTRS, Sydney.

Some internet references

Australian Film Commission, 'A–Z budgets', available online at <http://afc.gov.au/ filminginaustralia/azbudget/fiapage_1.aspx>, viewed 18 December 2006.

Chapter 19

Scheduling the shoot

While pre-production is developing and planning what will be carried out in the production phase by the groups involved – the camera crew and the art department (where there is one) – the production office is collating information as it emerges from this planning. The groups consult with each other, coordinated under the producer so that, as their plans consolidate, they remain integrated as the one project, and their various needs can be accommodated across the production. This accumulating information is gathered into a schedule of the daily shooting order of the scenes or sequences that are earmarked for production. Its extent is determined by the budget. A production cannot shoot any more material in any more different places than the budget permits. There are, however, tricks of the trade that allow some costs to be reined in by compromises in the shooting, and by so doing this allows the shoot to extend further in other areas. It's a matter of balancing priorities of what should be shot to maximise the material that is provided for post-production.

The time allocated to each scene indicates to the director how much time the budget can afford to be spent on that scene. There are different ways any scene can be shot, with some of them able to be completed faster than others. Directors will have to determine an approach to shooting a scene so that it can be completed in the time allocated. Their first choice would be the approach that is aesthetically and creatively the most appropriate. If that can be achieved within the time allocated, that's the way it will be done. But if that's not possible within the time, they will have to resort to the best option of those that are, or else look with the 1st AD at a different way of shooting another scene to enable the time to be extended on this one.

The order in which the components of the program are shot is also determined by budget. Ideally, the shooting schedule would cover the scenes in script order, but that is almost invariably not the case – with the exception of observational documentaries that will be constructed chronologically. The ruling dictum is to place scenes in the schedule to the greatest budgetary advantage. How this is achieved to best effect varies from genre to genre, with schedules being drawn up by differing people in the different genres. In drama and sitcom, it is a detailed process that the 1st AD will carry out. Documentary and current affairs, which don't usually have a 1st AD, are more flexibly scheduled by the production manager or the producer. Sketch comedy scheduling may be done by the 1st AD, but this is just as likely to be the job of the production manager or an associate producer. For magazine format, it is often drawn up by the series producer. The differing people responsible reflects the differing requirements of scheduling across the genres, but nonetheless the general principles are common to all genres.

19.1 General principles of scheduling

Clustering high-cost elements

The driving principle in scheduling a shoot is to contain costs by clustering or blocking the high-cost components. Most production resources (including people) can be hired by the hour, day or week. Mostly the daily rate is significantly lower than the hourly rate for a whole day, and the weekly rate correspondingly lower than the daily rate. The aim then is to schedule expensive resources as a block so that they are used throughout each day rather than spread over a few part days, to maximise their use while they are being paid for and to minimise the total time for which they need to be hired. This is achieved by scheduling the scenes in which they are involved into a full day as much as is feasible. It might be a high-cost actor, scenes with an animal, the use of expensive equipment such as cranes or Steadicam, or the use of stunt performers. Alternatively, scenes at one remote location that involves travel costs will be shot as a block. All scenes at that location are shot together so that the cost of getting to the location and back will be incurred just once.

Shooting in blocks

The first cluster is to generate the shortest duration of the shoot. This will be set up so that all shooting days will be full days and consecutive days, allowing for days off that are necessary to keep within the budgeted level of penalty payments. By keeping the number of shooting days down, the cost of the ongoing crew for the shoot is kept to a minimum. Each day will have scheduled a full day's shooting (usually ten hours) with as many scenes or sequences that can be practically and realistically fitted in. This grouping of consecutive working days of the whole shoot is also called a block. It's positioning on the calendar will be determined by the timing of one or more of its time-critical elements, such as the availability of lead actor, availability of crucial location, timing of key event, timing of the availability of funding, or scheduled broadcast date. A one-off program will have its entire shoot scheduled in one block, apart from pick-up shots. A series may shoot each episode in a separate block or may shoot two or three episodes back-to-back in a block, then break before another block of two or three episodes begins shooting. Pick-up shots are those with timing issues that prevent them from being scheduled within the block, or shots from the block that need to be reshot for whatever reason.

Mutually exclusive clusters

Within a shoot there will be clustering of budget-critical resources to get the most value out of them while they are hired and to reduce the duration of hiring. Sometimes these clusters will be mutually exclusive. Scheduling Steadicam scenes together may force scheduling of performers or locations to be spread over a larger number of days, or vice versa. When this occurs, the 1st AD and production manager will look at the cost implications of each alternative and opt for the one with greatest savings. In practice, a 1st AD will generally know from experience where greater savings are generated and probably won't need the comparative costing exercise.

19.2   Minimising travelling costs

Relocation as unproductive expenditure

As noted in Chapter 16, a major consideration is often the cost of moving from location to location, either from one locality (be it town, city or countryside) to another, or relocating within the same locality. The simple economic fact is that crew time spent moving is not time spent shooting. Costs while moving (e. g. salaries, equipment hire and travel costs) are not costs generated in shooting the program itself, but merely the expense of getting to a place to do that. The more these costs can be kept down, the more the production budget can be spent directly on recording the program. Time in transit is unproductive expenditure so that the more time spent relocating and the more frequently the crew moves, the greater the component of production cost spent just on moving.

Proximity of locations

There are several strategies in location selection that can keep travel time to a minimum. The overriding principle is to shoot the location out. This means that once the crew is on location, all scenes set there are shot before moving on to another location. While on that location there cannot be any budget wasted on relocation. Proximity is another important principle. The closer together appropriate locations are found, the less time is spent getting from one to the next where any of them don't have sufficient scenes to fill a day. As well, the closer they are to the production base, the less time is spent getting to them in the first place. As is so often the case, it's a question of balancing priorities. The most suitable location is not necessarily the nearest. A production decision must be made on how much better the best location is, and whether it warrants a greater cost in non-productive schedule time in the shoot.

Travel for actuality shoots

In actuality shooting – documentary and magazine programs – travel tends to be further and more widespread than in dramatised programs, and with a significantly smaller crew. Here the cost of moving is not so much in crew and equipment hire as in the costs inherent in the travel itself – transport, accommodation, and meals and incidentals (called per diems). Where there are viable options, the production will choose the nearer locality over the more distant one. It will also schedule a round trip of the destinations so that the least total distance is travelled, rather than going to each one in turn from the production centre. This will keep transport expenses to a minimum, although it won't affect the accommodation and per diem expenses. Their cost is contained the more efficiently the shoot is scheduled in each destination.

19.3 Use of a location

Multiple sets on a location

Some locations have more dramatic and unique features than others. Where a location has been found with particularly desirable features, the production looks at maximising its value with other sets that can be contrived, if necessary with art department input, in some corner of the location, even if that set is unrelated in story terms to other story settings of the location. The more parts of one location that can be commandeered as sets for the production, the less time spent relocating to other locations. Once on location, the principle of shooting out a location is applied also to sets. If there are several scenes in the kitchen and in the bathroom of the one location, all scenes are shot in the kitchen regardless of place in the script before moving on to the bathroom set and shooting all the scenes there – or vice versa. Not only does shuffling backwards and forwards between two sets make no economic sense when a single move would be feasible, but unnecessarily moving crew and gear is an irritating waste of their time.

Exterior and interior sets

Where a location provides both interior and exterior sets in a building, they too will each be shot out in turn, rather than the crew traipsing in and out of the building for successive scenes. Exteriors often serve more to establish the story location, in which case they will be dramatically less demanding and better used first for that reason. However, they will also generally be shot first so that the interiors can stand by as wet weather cover (see section 19.4), unless there is a time-of-day preference for the exterior (such as the director and DOP favouring a late afternoon look, or the story requiring it). In that case, it will be shot first or last depending what that preference is. If there are time-of-day preferences at each end of the day, exteriors may be shot first and last with interiors in the middle – if it can be managed within the budget – or if the shoot on that location is over more than one day, the exteriors may be scheduled on two different days. Interiors are not so susceptible to time of day because that can be created by lighting.

Optimum availability of locations

Many locations, especially businesses, have optimum times of their availability. There may be particular times of the day or particular days of the week where they can be used with less disruption to their business. For instance, business offices are more likely to be available at nights or on weekends, restaurants on Mondays or Tuesdays, supermarkets these days in the morning, and schools on weekends or school holidays. Domestic locations are generally more flexible, but there may be considerations of adjacent noise interference, such as schoolyards or construction sites. Shoots should be scheduled to avoid the noisy time of the day.

Day and night

Shoots are usually scheduled on ten-hour days, which may incur overtime on some days where things haven't gone as smoothly as they might. The various awards require a ten-hour turnaround between one day and the next, and this has to be factored into the schedule. A failure to have the ten-hour break will result in penalty payments until a ten-hour break is possible. This can have serious budgetary implications with a large crew. It also means that the crew and cast will be getting tired and not be able to give their best to the production. To get around this, night scenes are shot as a cluster or block if possible, and day scenes shot as a separate block. The transition from night shoots to day shoot has to be planned carefully because if a shoot finishes at 2 am, say, the next day cannot start before midday. Sometimes half-day, half-night blocks (or day/night shoots) can be scheduled in the middle or to enable the shoot to stay on the one location, but include some night scenes.

An example of the transition from night to day is given in Table 19.1. Here, an hour more than the award turnaround requirement is scheduled to allow for the possibility of the shoot running up to an hour over on any day. Sometimes day or night shooting can be 'cheated' by blacking out windows or shooting in the shade with an underexposing camera. This is called 'day for night'. Its reverse, 'night for day' (or 'available lighting') is also possible by lighting an interior at night to look as if it has natural sources of light.

19.4   Wet weather cover

Rainy day scenes

Where a script requires rain, it would be unusual to wait for a rainy day. That's too unpredictable and rain tends to come and go, so it's hard to get a consistent rainy

Table 19.1: Scheduling a shoot for turnaround requirements.

Day	Start	End	Turnaround
1 (night)	5 pm	3 am	11 hours
2 (day/night)	2 pm	Midnight	11 hours
2 (day/night)	11 am	9 pm	11 hours
4 (day)	8 am	6 pm	11 hours

look across the shots in the scene. Filming in rain can be dangerous with slippery roads and the risks of mixing water and electrics. Rainy day scenes are shot instead with controllable special effects rain machines. When it rains, a director might sometimes take advantage of the wet look, but in practice the production nearly always moves to wet weather cover. This is an alternative schedule of interior scenes that can be shot even though it's raining. It will often be the interior scenes for the exterior scenes that have been interrupted by rain.

Deciding on wet weather cover scenes

Any day whose exterior scenes would have to be postponed if it rained will have wet weather cover scheduled. The wet weather cover will be selected to ensure that there will be no more additional cost than is necessary. As much as possible, the scenes should be with actors called for the original schedule. There will be no more additional cost for them. It should also use a lower costing location unless all scenes in that location will be cleared by the revised shoot. In that case, the production cost of the location is what it was always going to be. If there is a studio set in the production, it is often suitable for wet weather cover. The studio scenes are then scheduled late in the shoot so that they can serve as wet weather cover in the earlier part of the shoot.

19.5   Cast considerations

Cast with availability limitations

We have already noted that cast is scheduled, as much as possible, so that the more expensive actors have their working days minimised. Sometimes cast are contracted with some limitations on their availability. They may be working in a stage show at nights or already be engaged on another production halfway through this one. The schedule will have to work around this limited availability, but it is an arrangement that can come unstuck because of its inherent inflexibility. It is better to avoid putting this restriction on the schedule and cast someone more generally available, unless there are overriding reasons to cast this performer despite the risk.

Children

Chapter 15 covered the restrictions placed by state regulations on the hours of work for children in production. The younger the child, the more limited the hours it can work, as summarised in Table 15.2 with the example of the NSW Code of Practice. The regulations are different in each state or territory and will need to be researched so that the schedule can be devised to accommodate them.

Extras

Extras can become a significant expense where scenes need a large number of them. However, extras can be engaged on a minimum four-hour call so that scenes with many extras should be blocked together to maximise the number that can be released after four hours.

Period dramas

The schedule will need to accommodate the extra time in period dramas for preparing wardrobe and make-up for performers and extras. Lead performers will have detailed preparation, which should be scheduled to start sufficiently early so that crew won't be standing around waiting for the actor to come on set. Although extras don't have so much care lavished on their period appearance, the number of them may require careful scheduling (and hiring casual wardrobe and make-up staff) to ensure that there is no production hold-up there either.

19.6   Timing of the shoot

Schedule overruns

It was mentioned at the beginning of this chapter that the time allocated to each scene indicates the budget's limits. In scheduling a drama shoot, the 1st AD takes account of the various factors that will influence the time a scene will take. If a realistic assessment suggests the budget-determined timing of the scene's shoot is not feasible, the production must take steps to rectify that. A scene that cannot be shot in the time allocated, given the intended time-determining inputs, will have a knock-on effect that will eventually put the shoot into overtime or mean that a scene scheduled for that day is unable to be shot. The ramifications can be serious at the end of the shoot if there are scenes still unrecorded, as a required actor may not be available for extension of contract. An anecdotal example of how to overcome this was provided in Chapter 9.

Factors that slow a shoot

A scheduler will consult with the director about their directing style and how they will shoot each scene. This gives an indication of how long it will take to complete each scene. Action scenes (and especially fight scenes) may or may not take a long time, depending on whether they are to be broken down into many short shots or covered fluidly with a hand-held camera. Similarly, the 1st AD will need to find out from the DOP how long it will take to light each scene to the director's expectations. There are various components that can be more time-consuming than others. Interior and night exterior scenes require more lighting time than day exterior. Public areas will often require crowd control and dealing with drunks and disgruntled residents, which can delay the scene. Vehicles of all sorts, stunts and special effects, and machine-generated rain and wind all have a capacity to slow down production as set-ups are adjusted to achieve a desired result. Children and animals don't take direction as well as professional adult actors. They can get distracted, lose interest or get tired. Difficult terrain, extreme climatic conditions, and locations that are not easily accessed are circumstances that will slow down the production process. Where these factors are expected to conspire to prevent the shoot keeping to its schedule, either the shoot must be extended (and the subsequent cost increase offset) or the script modified.

19.7   Updating the schedule

Costing a preliminary schedule

A preliminary schedule is drawn up early in the pre-production process to set a framework for the shoot. This will determine some of the cost elements that will make up early production budget estimates. The preliminary schedule might produce a budget well in excess of the level of funding that could be expected to be raised. In this case, the schedule will need to be trimmed and adjusted to bring its cost down to the expected funding. On the other hand, the preliminary schedule might produce a budget under the level of expected funding. This will give the producer some options. Additional elements could be brought into the shoot to increase the program's production values, elements that might have been considered earlier but abandoned because they were thought to be beyond the means of the production. Alternatively, additional money could be allocated to other aspects of the production, such as more sophisticated CGI work or lead performers with higher cost (and greater market power). Or the production could take advantage of the lower-than-expected cost of the shoot and pursue a lower level of financing for the project.

Adjusting the schedule

This process continues in one form or another through to production. The shooting schedule is constantly being revised and updated as decisions about the production are finalised by the director and producer, in consultation with HODs. Each department's requirements are notified and factored into the schedule. When conflicts arise or departmental choices push the schedule over budget, they can be discussed at regular production meetings, and varied to resolve the conflict or reduce the budget. A new schedule will be circulated.

The stripboard

Traditionally a drama schedule is set out manually on a stripboard, a board on which is fitted long strips of coloured card. Each strip represents a scene from the script, and the colours allow some key variables to be seen at a glance. Each strip will have scene number, day or night (D or N), interior or exterior (Int. or Ext.), location and set, and each cast character required in the scene indicated by a number. Spacers separate each shooting day. Day and night, as interiors and exteriors, can be coded with four colours. The pattern of day, night and day/night shooting can be seen at a glance, and any trouble areas that might create unnecessary penalties can be quickly spotted. As the schedule is changed through the consultation and consolidation process, the strips will be moved around on the board to reflect the updated schedule. From the order of scenes on the stripboard, a full schedule is drawn up with further detail such as props, special requirements and a one-line synopsis of the scene.

Scheduling software

These days the shooting schedule is laid out and updated in a computer program, which is modelled on the stripboard. It would be possible to do this on an application like Microsoft Excel, but productions more commonly use customised software such as Entertainment Partners' Movie Magic Scheduling. Breakdowns, schedules and reports can be generated with Movie Magic Screenwriter and Movie Magic Budgeting. The Screenwriter software program provides script information to the Scheduling software program to create breakdown sheets with information such as set, scene number, page count, cast members, props and costumes. This can be viewed as scheduling strips that are electronically moved, sorted and grouped. Other reports, such as props list and cast cross-plot, can be produced, and the schedule can be exported to the Budgeting software program to update the cost implications of the schedule.

19.8   Scheduling actuality shoots

Blocking the shoot

Scheduling of documentary, current affairs and magazine programs has its own distinctive features, although the principle of blocking expensive components to manage costs still applies. These productions usually don't have big crews so there are not the detailed logistics to be dealt with. However, crews and equipment are still more cheaply hired by the week than the day (equipment is often charged for a seven-day week at four times the daily rate), so a shoot will be scheduled as a block to take advantage of that. If preferred crew are booked as a block problems of unavailability are also reduced, which is more likely with hire on disparate days. Events that happen on a specified day may have to be left out of the block and then only if it is impractical to schedule the block around the day of that event. A documentary series might be scheduled as more than one block, with a fixed-date event from an episode in an early block being scheduled in a later block.

Travel schedule

Where programs involve considerable travel, this is scheduled in blocks within the shoot. The production would not go to any destination more than once unless the nature of the shoot made it unavoidable. Nor would it make a number of return trips to each destination. The production will, instead, schedule a round trip of destinations where they are in the same general direction, even if they involve different modes of transport. A Sydney production might schedule Brisbane, Cairns (both by air) and the Atherton Tablelands (by road) in the one trip, wouldn't necessarily include Adelaide or Perth in that trip because there is no particular saving in not going through Sydney, but would add Alice Springs, Darwin or surrounding localities to the itinerary if they arose as locations. The same production would cover Melbourne and Hobart on the one trip, but it could be done as a separate block within the shoot. There is no need to run trips consecutively in the shoot once there is no saving in doing so. Where there is a crew member or on-camera talent who is only required for some of the destinations (sometimes a local sound recordist might be used), the schedule will attempt to cluster those destinations together so that the person can return to base earlier, with consequent savings on accommodations and per diems.

Magazine programs

Scheduling of magazine programs has its own characteristics. They are always in series format, often long-running, with pre-production, production and post-production of different segments for different episodes taking place at any one time. A segment may only take one or a few days to shoot, so scheduling of its shoot is not complicated, but the art is in scheduling the ongoing production to enable the most efficient use of resources, including time. There may be more than one crew, more than one editor, and more than one segment producer. A schedule is devised so that all of these people are working on a succession of segments, and all are working on one of the segments at any one time. The schedule will seek to devise a block of shooting with costly resources. Where travel is involved, the production will seek to amortise the cost of getting there by setting up a few segments to be shot on that trip. In all probability, they will not be segments for the same episode, but will be stockpiled for different episodes across the series.

Revising the magazine program schedule

The particular skill with scheduling magazine programs is flexibility and the capacity to respond readily to changes in the line-up of segments. New segments might be substituted for those already in the line-up because they have just been unearthed and are too good to let go, or because the earlier segment has fallen through. As new segments arise and are slotted into the production schedule, the whole schedule is adjusted and updated, all the time maintaining the principle of keeping key production people – crew, editor and segment producer – with a continuing succession of segments to work on. This can be achieved effectively by scheduling as a flow chart with the graphics facility of a Microsoft Excel spreadsheet. Adjustments are made quickly by cut-and-paste, and an updated schedule is circulated regularly to the production unit. The schedule will include delivery dates for all segments currently on the schedule. The line-up of each episode can be built from the segments expected from the production schedule to be available at the time of compilation of the episode.

Sources and further reading

General reading

Turnbull, Mark 2002, 'Scheduling', in Case, D., Gailey, L., Knapman, C., et al., *The Production, Budgeting and Film Management Satchel*, AFC/AFTRS, Sydney.

Chapter 20

Preparing studio and outside broadcast productions

Television began making its programs using multiple cameras in a television studio. It saw a golden era in the 1960s with studio-based variety and sitcom, but with the development of lightweight field recording equipment and sophisticated post-production, most program-making activity is now on location in single-camera production. The ease of operation of modern cameras and editing has negated much of the cost and efficiency advantage of multi-camera production. However, live programs, apart from live news crosses, still require multi-camera coverage. The mobility of television's recording equipment has enabled it to cover live events, particularly sporting events, on location at a high level of technical and production sophistication. Central to its production is an outside broadcast (OB) van, basically a studio on wheels. This is not an innovation in itself, since OB production has been with television from the start, but it has progressed considerably from the early clunky units.

The approaches to development and pre-production already covered will apply in one form or another to studio and OB production. The concept still has to be developed into a fleshed-out proposal, but most studio and OB programs are produced by the network that will broadcast them, even if they contract out the production. Funding may not be outsourced from other broadcasters, distributors or investors, but found from within the network's budgeting, although it may be offset by an interest group underwriting some of the cost. For commercial broadcasters, the estimated advertising revenue that a program might attract determines its funding viability.

Like any other production, pre-production is a process of consulting, detailing and consolidating a production plan. Crews and facilities are booked, budgets and schedules are drawn up, and sometimes performers are cast. As well, there is office back-up and a succession of production meetings. But multi-camera production also has its own way of doing things and there are distinctive aspects to its preparation.

The roles and techniques of studio and OB production are similar, but differ from single-camera shoots in two important respects. First, a multi-camera shoot has a large crew, requiring a considerable degree of planning, coordination and communication. Second, it is shot live, or 'as live', where it is recorded as if it is a live transmission, and replayed to air later unedited or with minimal post-production. The program is edited as it happens, cutting online between shots from different cameras or other sources, and mixing sound at the same time. This type of production requires instant decisions and fast reflexes. If a multi-camera production goes into post-production, it is usually to make corrections and finesse the recording.

A multi-camera producer doesn't need to be able to direct in that mode, but does need to understand the process their director is using, and what skills are drawn on. Multi-camera direction is the simultaneous coordination of a variety of production elements through a control room or an OB van. The output from studio is as near to a finished program as possible. If the program is a live telecast, it *is* the finished program. The coordination is of both technical operations and the actions of 'talent' (the industry term for any person on camera). Once the challenge of mustering the complex machinery of production has been met and is in place, the task turns to dealing with people, both in front of and behind the camera. The director is simultaneously concerned with the visualisation of each shot and the sequencing of those shots. Crucial to the reliability of this coordinated process is a communications system connecting the director with control room personnel and the studio floor.

20.1   Layout of the studio

The studio floor

The basic television studio has two main areas, the studio floor and the control room (or rooms), sometimes called the gallery. A studio will normally have a permanent lighting rig in the ceiling, a curved fabric cyclorama along at least two of the walls, and an even floor that allows pedestal-mounted cameras to move smoothly and freely. The output signal of cameras and microphones is transmitted via cables to connections on the back wall of the studio, and up to the control room. Microphones will sometimes connect by radio instead of cable. The studio should be acoustically 'dead' with no reverberation (it can be added by the sound mixing desk, but not taken out). Camera operators, sound and lighting assistants, autocue operator and cable pullers work on the floor, as does the floor manager, who may have assistants. The floor manager's role is to coordinate all activities on the floor, and relay cues and other information from director to talent. There will be areas nearby for make-up, dressing rooms and a 'green room', where guests can relax until the studio is ready for them. Scenery (or flats), set dressings and props are nearby also, stored in a scenery bay (or scenic runway).

The control room

The control room has three main desks with operating consoles for production, lighting and sound. A typical layout of a studio control room is shown in Figure 20.1. Director, director's assistant (DA) and vision mixer (or vision switcher), and sometimes technical producer and character generator operator, sit at the production desk. The producer usually sits at the back of the control room behind them. Sound and vision supervisors sit at their own desks. A bank of monitors in front of the production desk shows the output of each of the various sources (cameras, videotape replay, graphics, character generator, and remote sources such as satellite, OB or another studio), the transmission (Tx) picture (a line monitor, showing the output of the studio), and a preview picture (the anticipated next picture, or a rehearsal of a coming edit). The vision mixer cuts between sources, or may use an effects bank on their console to select a transition from one source to the next. It may be a dissolve or a wipe, or a more complex movement from the range of available visual effects. Videotape operators will replay tapes into studio, and record studio output in a machine room that might be attached to the control room or might be elsewhere in the station complex.

Communication between control room and studio floor

In most studios, the people in the control room have no view of the studio floor. All they can see is the studio's output via cameras. The control room does, however, have an extensive communication system with the studio floor, which is called talkback or intercom. A microphone on the production desk enables communication with the floor manager, camera operators, autocue operator and sound boom operator, all of whom wear headphones ('cans'). The floor manager will pass on information or instructions to anyone else on the floor by voice or hand signals. People on the floor can talk back by a switchable microphone to a speaker in the control room. Individual teams can communicate with each other by talkback independently of the production desk. With the interruptible foldback (or feedback, IFB) system, the director or producer can talk to talent while the show is on air. Camera operators will also use visual signals to communicate with the director, zooming in and out to attract their attention, and tilting for 'yes' and panning for 'no', in imitation of a nod or shake of the head.

20.2 The planning stage

Elements available to the production

At an early stage, the producer discusses with their director what the content of the show will be in order to meet its editorial brief. In other words, what is available to the production that relates to the program's subject matter and themes? These may be segments in studio, at some remote source, or pre-produced for replay in the production. The discussion will determine which of those elements

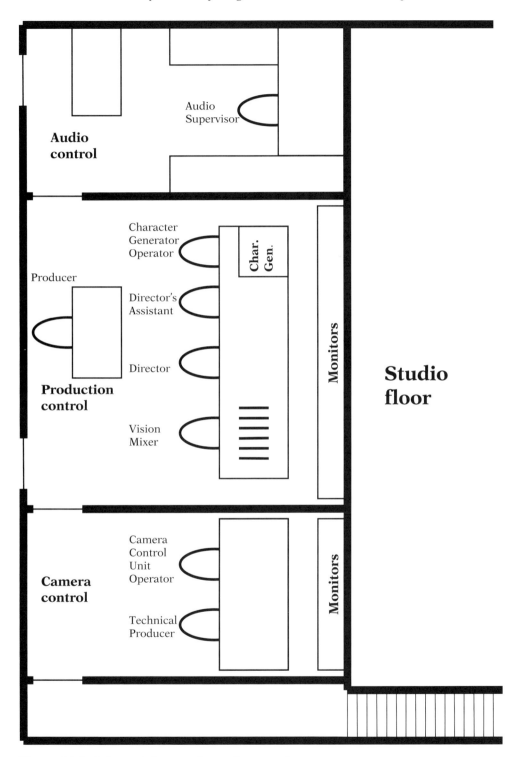

Figure 20.1: Schematic layout of a studio control room.

integrate best into the program. These discussions might even take place in the development phase and be incorporated into a proposal, but as studio production is often network-initiated, it is not unusual for this discussion to be the start of pre-production.

Briefing meetings

Once the production elements have been decided, key personnel are briefed so that they can begin planning their input to the production. Director and producer will discuss the look of the program with the set designer, so they can draw up some concepts and then preliminary sketches and designs for the production set. The director will brief the technical producer, the lighting supervisor and the sound supervisor about the intentions and requirements of the production. While these people are assembling initial thoughts about their contribution to the production, the production manager will consult with various personnel and draw up a preliminary budget. This will evolve, in consultation with the producer, as pre-production proceeds. As with any other production, the components that are proposed for the production must be achievable within its allocated budget, or else modified (or some other component modified) so that the budget can be brought back to the allocated figure.

The creative director

A director needs to have the experience and technical knowledge to operate live and faultlessly in a multi-camera environment. These skills are essential to their role, but there can be a tendency to let the mechanics of production push style to one side. A good studio director has a creative touch that can bring additional flair to live production and lift it out of the ordinary, to make it more than a journeyman coverage. It comes from ideas for framing shots, for placement of talent in the studio, and for movement of cameras while they are on air. It will also be reflected in the director's brief for design and lighting, and in their choice of music to use in the program. However, there's a need for caution that a director's style doesn't so overwhelm the program that its audience loses track of the narrative driving the program. It's a matter of editorial judgement, and it's important that the producer both encourages directorial style and offers a critical and pragmatic appraisal of what is proposed.

Little margin for error in recording

The planning of a multi-camera production has added pressure, since the adage 'it can be fixed up in post-production' cannot apply to a live program and is limited for as-live recording. Whether live or recorded, online production leaves little time for fixing elements that are absent or not functioning. The recording is not paused until a problem is sorted out, but continues online with whatever is available. If the problem is discovered as it's required on air, the program will show whatever ad hoc adjustment has been possible. If it is discovered before it's required, there is not much time to find a replacement or think of an alternative. Planning must cover all production detail, no matter how trivial, because this mode is all the more vulnerable to loose preparation.

Confirmation, not assumption

The key to pre-production then is the accumulation and confirmation of all relevant information. A good producer makes a database of all production personnel, so they can be contacted readily. They should do this for any production, but it is critical for live programs. They will also ensure that everyone knows how to contact them. They will not rely on secondhand information or assumptions about what should happen, or anything else they guess about what is in place for the production. Nothing is confirmed until they have been told it by the person who is directly responsible for it. Robbie Weekes, with long experience in studio and live production, oversaw the SBS coverage of *Corroboree 2000*, the Reconciliation conference and march at Sydney's Opera House and Harbour Bridge. His aphorism for the production team: 'Assumption is the mother of all foul-ups.' 'Don't assume', he says, 'find out!'

Running order

One of the early pieces of paperwork for studio or OB production is a running order, which is put together by the director after discussion with the producer. This is a sequentially numbered list of the elements that will make up the program, along with the estimated duration, source and initial technical information for each sequence. An initial running order might look like that shown in Table 20.1. This document is distributed to all production personnel so that they know from the outset the intended shape of the production, and can see the places where they will have specific input. It will be updated from time to time as the intended program is finetuned, and further detail of each production element is confirmed. The updated running order is circulated so that the production crew can work with and contribute to a current plan for production.

The Facilities Request

Key production personnel confer with the director about equipment that will best provide for the production's needs. This is passed on to the production manager, who draws up a Facilities Request, listing all items identified. It may include props and costumes. The Facilities Request is as essential to communicating about the program as is the script. It might be online (as read-only access) on customised software, or on a spreadsheet or database application. The Facilities Request details each item of equipment, including model, source (in-house, hired or purchased), dates and times required, pick-up times arranged, date of booking and status of booking. With a computer-based request, there is less chance of people working off an out-of-date version. It is the only version available at any one time, and is updated as details come to hand, or are confirmed or varied. The request will also include general information about the production: program title, names of producer and director (and often presenter), date and time of rehearsal and recording bookings, and on-air transmission time. It will

Table 20.1: Sample running order for studio production.

	'Living in the Fast Lane' Producer: Jane White Record date: 1 April 2007 Record venue: Studio 5, Acme TV Centre	Director: Robert Black	
	Segment	Source	Duration
1	Opening titles	VT	00.20
2	Host welcome and intro	Studio	00.45
3	Montage of episode topic	VT	01.00
	Host V/O	Studio	
4	Live report from location 1	Remote	02.00
5	Host introduces guests	Studio	00.20
6	Guest discussion	Studio	03.00
7	Field story 1	VT	03.30
8	Live report from location 2	Remote	01.30
9	Guest discussion	Studio	05.00
etc., etc.			

include equipment booked for pre-produced segments that are to be replayed into the studio recording, and editing bookings for those segments. Equipment permanently installed in the studio does not need to be listed separately on the request, but it is wise to detail it with the studio, which should itself be a facility item.

Floor plan

A studio floor plan has the position of all its fixtures laid out on a scaled grid. On it, the set designer marks accurately all the production's set elements: scenic flats, desks or other furniture, staging elements such as rostrums or audience seating, chroma-key or back projection screens, and so on. The director uses it to plan their positioning and movement of cameras. Cameras are numbered so that their place on the control room monitors represents their position on the studio floor, which the director cannot see. Camera 1 will be on the left end of the line of monitors and on the left hand side of the studio floor, and so on. The director will decide the principal coverage to allocate to each camera, and then movements of the cameras on the studio floor as the production proceeds. They will need to make sure that cameras won't get in each other's shots, and that their cables won't tangle as they move around. They will also need to check how the cameras are positioned so that they don't 'cross the line' in cutting from one camera to another. This is a convention of directing that requires cameras in successive shots to stay on the same side of an imaginary line along which the action takes place. The classic example is between two people in conversation, where cameras either side of the line make them appear to be standing shoulder to shoulder, instead of facing each other when talking.

20.3   Consolidation of pre-production

Final running order

The initial running order of the program is consolidated during pre-production. The final version incorporates any changes to the initial run-down, along with detail that has come to hand. It includes the breakdown of studio segments into shots with shot description and anticipated camera covering, transitions between segments, camera movements in shot, graphics and stills that might be used, and music that will be played in. It won't include that degree of detail for prerecorded segments. They are already completed when played into the program. The only detail that might be included is a component to be added through studio, such as voice-over, a graphic or music, and an 'out cue' (dialogue or action to cue the cut from the segment to the next item).

Scripting studio programs

Studio productions generally run in part or fully from a script. Presentation pieces and links are pre-scripted, but interviews and panel discussions are not. A newscast is fully scripted, a panel show has sections scripted and the bulk unscripted, but with predetermined camera positions. A snooker match has only 'openers' and 'closers' (opening and closing pieces to camera) scripted, and the rest unscripted with adlibbed camera coverage. The coverage will follow a general formula that has been developed over the years. Although interviews and panel discussions are unscripted, the producer and interviewer will have mapped out a structure for the discussion and earmarked some key questions. Many of the answers can be reasonably guessed, but not the exact wording, and there can be surprises in the answers that trigger unscheduled questions.

Layout of studio script

The scripted part of the program is laid out in a two-column format not unlike a shooting or editing script for documentary (see Chapter 23), with vision on the left and audio on the right. 'Vision' lists each planned shot by running order number, indicating which camera will take it and the framing of the shot (close-up [CU], mid-shot [MS], two-shot [2S], etc.). An image to be inserted from a framestore will be indicated, as will text from a character generator to be superimposed ('supered') over the picture, which identifies a speaker, for instance. 'Audio' mainly details spoken word, but will also indicate in and out points for music, or where sound will come off replayed videotape, which is known as sound off tape (SOT).

Studio camera cards

The script will be, among other things, a running order of the shots for each studio camera. This information, from the vision side of the script only, is transferred to camera cards that the cameraman clips onto the camera, one for each camera, listing all the shots in order for that camera, and the shot number in the script's running sequence. It won't show scripted words. The cameraman is not concerned about them, only in setting up the shots in order, although they will have a copy of the script for reference anyway. Cutting in and out of words is the province of the vision mixer. The camera card might include a camera movement such as zoom in (Z/I) or pan right (PAN R), which will be cued from the control room, or the cameraman will be given script wording from which to take their own cue.

Production time line

Because of the complexity and coordination involved in multi-camera production, time is particularly crucial. Time is always a finite resource, but some preparation shouldn't be glossed over. Scheduling needs to find a balance between the competing needs of thoroughness and time limitation. The pursuit of specific issues can get bogged down if the production's overseers aren't careful, and time can slip away, with serious repercussions for later preparation. A detailed production time line is drawn up to enable efficient management of the two most crucial days: rehearsal and recording. The detail must be such that it is clear what every person will be expected to be doing. All aspects of the final preparation are covered, from the arrival of guests to each stage of rehearsal, and key points in the recording schedule. If the day's activities are slipping behind schedule, adjustments to it must be made so that some key activity later in the day isn't left unattended.

20.4   Rehearsal

What can and can't be rehearsed

Rehearsal is an opportunity to see if the director's camera coverage, worked out on paper, will work in actuality, or whether it creates unforeseen problems. Not every aspect of the program can be rehearsed and this will vary according to the type of program. Guests are generally not at rehearsal. They are most likely unavailable. They are most likely unavailable, but even if they were available, rehearsal could diminish the spontaneity of their contribution. Guest performers might be rehearsed since they usually have a predetermined performance. It is advantageous for the production to see it, and plan and preview its coverage. Where and how the production is rehearsed will depend on the nature of the show.

Studio drama

Studio drama is rehearsed away from the studio, on an open floor with tape markings indicating where in the studio scenic flats and other restrictions to actor movement will be. The marked up floor will duplicate the measurements on the studio floor plan. Boxes and chairs will be placed in positions indicating where furniture will stand in the set. The purpose of this rehearsal is principally to rehearse performance, although the studio crew is likely to attend late in the process to preview planned shots and discuss their feasibility with the director. Ideally, camera coverage is determined by the movement and performance of the actors, so the drama rehearsal is an opportunity for the director to adjust their shots to take advantage of what an actor brings to the character. A director should be cautious about dictating actions to an actor to suit camera placement, but often a discussion can arrive at a compromise that suits both camera and actor.

Major studio productions

A major studio production of a variety or event show is likely to rehearse over a full session, generally the day before recording. It will take place in the studio with most, if not all, of the set in place. Presentation talent is likely to be present, as well as some guest performers, but other guests are not. This rehearsal is principally for the benefit of coverage, not performance. Here, the presenter can expect to have their movements determined for the benefit of the cameras. The rehearsal starts with a walk-through of each segment of the program. These are stop–start exercises where salient features of the coverage are pointed out and trialled, steps and actions are repeated and adjusted, and possible obstacles to camera and microphone movement are spotted and rectified.

The walk-through prepares the presenter for the detail of their required performance, and allows subtle adjustment for camera benefit. It is also an opportunity to anticipate what the absent guests might do, and formulate some directions to be given to guests on the day. A production assistant or the floor manager might sit in for the guest at the rehearsal. Later, a full rehearsal will go through the whole production in schedule order. Initially it will be a stop–start rehearsal to make any last-minute adjustments, and then an uninterrupted run-through (or a few of them) to make sure that the whole crew is familiar with every aspect of the recording session, so that the production can flow smoothly on the day.

Routine studio productions

A more straightforward production, such as a panel discussion or a routine studio booking, might have a scaled-back version of the above procedure. The shift might be used to rehearse, and then record. The first part of this shift would be used for a walk-through of the segments that make up the program, followed by full rehearsals as stop–start exercises, and then uninterrupted. At the scheduled time, guests are brought on to the studio floor and the recording (or live transmission) can commence.

20.5 Studio guests and live audiences

The comfort of guests

Many studio productions will have guests participating in the program. They could be performers, such as musicians or comedians, academics for a panel discussion, or a movie actor for a celebrity interview. In most cases, they will not have been in that studio before. Some may never before have been in a television studio of any sort. Few will be intimately familiar with studio procedure, and some might find the studio atmosphere quite daunting. It is crucially important that their passage through the studio environment is made as comfortable and as non-threatening as possible. They should be assured by a perception that they are in the hands of seasoned professionals, and that everything is under control. This is the principal task of minders or 'guest wranglers', ensuring that studio guests are relaxed and properly informed of what is going on and when.

Getting to studio

The producer may not work directly on every aspect of getting guests to the studio, making sure that they are relaxed while they are there and, just as importantly, making sure that they go on to wherever they are going after the production. However, the producer must make sure that those who have been delegated this task are pedantic in their attention to its detail. Little is more disastrous for a production than a guest who hasn't turned up because the person responsible for getting them there 'thought' someone else was attending to it. Assumptions again! If guests insist that they will get to the studio under their own steam, the minder should make themself aware of how they intend to get there, and probably check at some key stage that they are on their way.

The green room

When guests arrive, they don't go straight on to the studio floor. Until the production is ready for them, they relax in a studio lounge, called the 'green room' after the theatre convention. There, they can drink something non-alcoholic or nibble on a savoury. A production assistant should act as host and ease any apprehension the guest might have. If there is more than one guest, they might share each other's company and, at the same time, relax one another – as long as the guests are compatible. If they are there because they represent diametrically opposed points of view, it is probably better they wait in different rooms. Another room is made up as a temporary green room with another production assistant hosting. The guests should not feel that they are in a railway waiting room.

Alcohol in the green room

Providing alcoholic refreshment to guests while they wait in the green room is not a good idea. There's no better illustration of the wisdom of this statement than the appearance of Mark 'Chopper' Read on ABC's *McFeast Live* after he had taken full advantage of a slab of beer left in the green room for him. He had drunk enough to be mischievously dangerous, but not so much that it was obvious from the outset. It's a credit to host Libbi Gore's professionalism that she dealt with this potentially explosive situation as well as she did.

The studio audience

A live studio audience is a special type of bulk guest. An audience can bring a distinctive atmosphere to a program, both in the studio and for viewers at home, but managing an audience in a studio is a fine art, fraught with traps for the unwary. The audience must be called in sufficient time that they can be in the studio and relaxed well before the production is scheduled to start, but not so early that the need to keep them occupied takes up resources that are better devoted elsewhere at this key time. The studio audience will assemble in dribs and drabs, some well before the announced time, some late. The early arrivals are easy enough as they can wait in the channel foyer. Dealing with the inevitable latecomers needs to be worked out in advance. Some will have excuses and insist that they be allowed in, having gone to the trouble of coming. It is seldom in the production's interest to let latecomers in, but they need to be dealt with tactfully and firmly.

Procedure on the day

Usually the audience is chaperoned first to a room near the studio, where they are briefed about requirements and safety procedures, and wait until the production is ready for them. In good time before the scheduled start of recording, they file in and take their places in seating tiers on the studio floor. A crowd of people in a confined space such as a studio is a safety risk. The safety briefing will be recapitulated to the audience, and they will be shown the exits in case of fire. While the crew makes final preparations and stands by to record, the floor manager will tell the audience any specific activities required of them in the production and entertain them (usually with a variation of a bad music hall routine) until the recording is ready to start. From that point, the audience is part of the production, the enjoyment, excitement and magic of live television.

20.6   Outside broadcast production

Components of an OB production

The OB van is a compact studio control room on wheels, but with much the same functions as a studio. A typical layout of the OB van is shown in Figure 20.2. Audio, vision and production control desks are sectioned off in the van, and there is a videotape record/reply facility. OB production may need, in addition to the components of a studio, a generator truck to power the OB van, and an electrics truck providing cabling for communications, cameras, monitors and lights. There will also be riggers for camera platforms, engineers and drivers. If mains power is available at the venue, it might be used instead of the generator, which will then function as power back-up. Other personnel are much the same, although the director sometimes does their own mixing. At the other end of the scale, there may be one or two small OB vans in addition to the large van. The small vans are downstream units, with mixers responsible for compiling insert components, such as instant replay segments or DVE composites (with pictures from several sources combined on the screen), as the program is recorded. The output of the small vans is fed as a source to the main van.

Planning of camera placement

Early in pre-production, the director will look over ('recce') the venue for the event, deciding where cameras should be positioned, how many should be fixed, and how many should be roving. Conventionally, one camera is positioned for a high-angle perspective of the event, as well as an establishing shot the director can

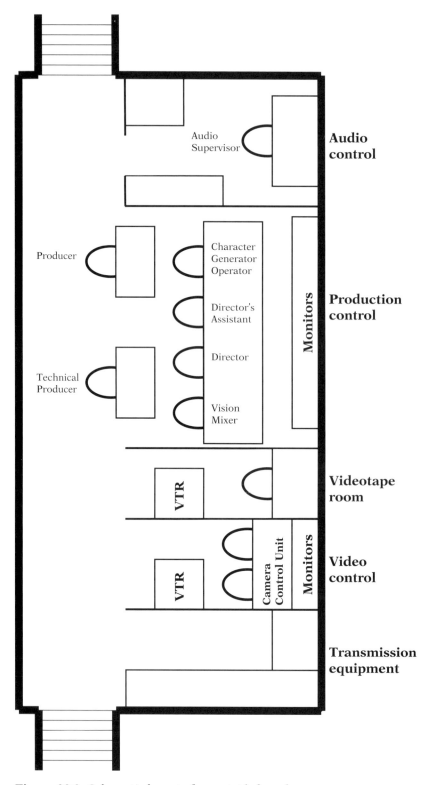

Figure 20.2: Schematic layout of an outside broadcast van.

cut to if they run into difficulty with shot selection while making the program. An OB is often covering a one-off event, so there may not be any rehearsal to determine exactly where cameras should be placed. They are placed, instead, knowing where the main action is expected to take place, and ensuring all active parts of the venue have at least some coverage. This is particularly the case with a sports event. The outcome isn't known in advance, or how events in the game will produce that result. On the other hand, a publicly staged extravaganza may have a rehearsal for its performers, providing an opportunity for the director to be more judiciously selective with camera placement.

A location survey will also enable the 1st AD and the TP to review practical and technical issues, such as access to the venue for personnel, mains power sources, the need for lighting, PA availability and additional audio needs, and parking availability for trucks. The OB van needs to be reasonably accessible to power and the cameras. Consideration is also given to microwave or satellite uplinks to the broadcasting station, if the program is to be broadcast live or transmitted to the station for recording, and to where the links van could be placed.

Preparation and recording

Preparation otherwise follows much the same pattern as studio production, with detailed planning and rehearsal. Differences stem from the fact that the production is among the public, and of an event that is generally outside the producers' control. As with any production, key personnel make themselves familiar with the event in advance, to prepare for as much as can be anticipated. At public events, the public are also present and there to enjoy the event. Camera cabling should be rigged, using ties, poles and mats, so it isn't a hazard to the public, and camera positions should not obstruct their view.

An OB production rehearses like a studio production, starting with a technical walk-through, to ensure all crew are familiar with their role in the operation. Communications are checked for proper functioning. It's harder than in studio to contact crew if it breaks down. If things do go wrong during the recording of the program, such as a spectator standing in front of an on-air camera, the only solution is to cut to another camera. The broadcast won't stop for anyone or anything. Keeping calm is the key to live broadcast – and keeping alert. A director will have one eye on the monitors to scan the shot options at any time. Often a camera will offer a telling shot to one side of the main action, something on the arena that the director, cocooned in the OB van, would not be aware of.

Iso recoding

A feature of live broadcast these days is the capacity for instant replay of some action that has just taken place. Instant-replay operations use 'iso' recorders (usually hard disks or read/write optical disks) with fast search-and-retrieve speeds. The iso recorders will be constantly recording the signal from preselected cameras, regardless of whether they are on air. A replay can be from the program recording, and will repeat the coverage just seen, or it will be from an iso recorder giving a different view of the action from that just seen. Iso records can also be used in as-live recording where some post-production is envisaged. Here it will provide cutaways and optional shots that could be dropped into the main OB recording.

Microwave links

Because OB production is remote from its television station and is often broadcast live, the means of transporting the video and audio of the broadcast signal to the station must be decided. Most commonly, the signal is carried via microwave from the OB van or a separate links van. Signals can be sent directly from location to station only if there is an unobstructed line of sight between them. Microwave signals travel in a straight line and may suffer interference if tall buildings or hills block the direct line to the television station. In these cases, one or several intermediary links, called mini-links, are set up, usually on top of buildings or a hill or even on a helicopter. They relay the signal to the station through a series of straight lines. In metropolitan areas, various television stations have permanent microwave relays installed in strategic locations so that live signals can be sent back on short notice.

Satellite links

When microwave links are particularly problematic, or the event is too distant from the station for microwave linking to be practical, a communications satellite may relay the signal instead. These satellites are positioned in geosynchronous orbit, staying in the same relative position to the ground below. Specialised vans can provide mobile uplinks to transport the broadcast signal to a satellite. A receiver–transmitter, called a transponder, in the satellite re-broadcasts the signal in a downlink to the television station's receiver. The passage of the broadcast signal from the OB van via satellite (or microwave relays) to the television station happens so instantaneously that the station is able to broadcast the program live by these links.

Sources and further reading

General reading

Zettl, Herbert 2006, *Television Production Handbook*, 9th edn, Thomson Wadsworth, Belmont, CA, chapters 1, 19, 20.

Chapter 21

Management of the shoot

The production phase, or the shoot, is for many of the production personnel the time of most intense activity during the whole production process. Ironically, it's a time when, in many ways, the producer can take a step back and keep an overseeing eye on things rather than concentrating on the detail. Because it is a time of intense activity, it is also a time of intense spending, so budget is a major management concern. This will be examined in Chapter 22. The production phase itself is the culmination of the preparation that has preceded it, and is in the hands of all the specialists and their support crews who have been hired to carry it out. The producer's main role here is to make sure that the train of production stays on the tracks during this phase.

21.1 Monitor progress, deal with the problems

Oversight with limited hands-on

It might seem anomalous that the producer is least closely engaged with the stage of production that many regard as the most crucial stage of the process, but in fact the more hands-on they have to be at this stage the more it probably reflects flaws in pre-production. The purpose of the preparation for the shoot is to hire the people who are believed to be best able to provide for the needs of the production. If that judgement has been correct, the problems in the shoot should be limited, and anyway best dealt with by those hired for their professional and creative expertise. The producer's role is more one of ensuring that is how they are being handled, rather than rolling up their sleeves and grappling with the nuts and bolts of the problem themself.

Leaving it to the experts

The producer has been with the project from inception or very early in its life, guiding it along its pathway as various components are brought into the production machinery. They should be familiar with all the cogs that are driving the machine. Their role during the shoot is to keep in touch with the component groups, monitor their readiness for the input when it's needed, and encourage them to keep them informed about how their preparation is going. If a problem develops in an area, their role is to make sure that area is aware of the problem and rectifying it, offering a few pointers if necessary, but primarily leaving the solution to people with relevant expertise. That's what delegation is about. If you have a dog, you don't do your own barking.

The symbol

The producer is also something of a figurehead at this stage of production, a reassurance that the project has leadership and confidence in its crew. Their role is to be seen to be interested in how production is proceeding, and relaxed in the knowledge that the people who are working on the project know what they are doing as part of a team that will produce the desired result. Even when an issue arises that needs to be resolved, their role is to show they are confident that the people hired are able to work it out.

Juggling the production stages in a series

This production equivalent of an admiral's role is more in the nature of one-off programs, but in fact the majority of television programs are series. When some part of a series is in production, other parts are in various stages of pre-production and yet other parts in post-production. The producer's priority will be in making sure the preparation for later shoots is not stumbling, and that decisions are being made about aspects of those shoots that have become problematic – locations or talent becoming unavailable, costs going out of budget range, whatever. They will also be looking at elements of the series that are emerging from post-production to see if they measure up to expectations or still need further work.

Keeping a finger on the pulse of the shoot

Even though pre- and post-production warrant more of their attention, it is still in the interests of the production that they be seen to be keeping an eye on and a keen interest in the shoot. They will be seen on set a few times to reinforce that impression. It's not pretence though, because they will be in frequent, generally daily contact with the two key figures on the set, the director and the 1st AD. They will also keep in close touch with what's happening with the budget through the production manager. They will be studying the Daily Progress Reports (see Chapter 13) to look for a quantitative assessment of the shoot's progress, as well as any warning signs of looming problems. The producer's role is to monitor the battle from the grassy knoll.

21.2 Review of footage shot

Timely editorial and technical review

Footage from the shoot might come to post-production daily if it is shot locally, or in batches if it is shot away from home base, particularly if it is an overseas shoot. It will come via the laboratory if shot on film, or directly for digitising if shot on videotape. The producer will want to review footage shot on some sort of timely schedule to ensure that it appears to be heading in the right direction editorially and creatively, and to review the technical quality of the footage. If technical problems have emerged, the director and DOP or sound recordist need to know of them and their nature and extent as soon as possible, so whatever remedial action that is necessary can take place. For this reason, the sooner the producer can see the footage, the better.

Daily rushes and batch review

Drama production will usually have daily 'rushes' (synced but unedited camera footage) that are screened the day after they are shot. If shot on film, laboratory reports will forewarn the production of technical problems, and they can be investigated as a matter of urgency. If there are editorial issues, they need to be dealt with sooner rather than later. Drama is a costly entity to have to reschedule substantially to recover lost editorial direction. On the other hand, the output of a documentary shoot, nearly always shot on videotape, usually arrives in batches from different legs of the shoot. As it is digitised, it may be copied onto VHS or DVD for the producer to view and for the director to plan the edit. If this is able to be done in stages throughout the shoot, it gives the producer an opportunity to review its editorial direction and ensure it is adhering to its brief or, if it has diverged from that, it has done so in a productive way that should produce a better program. Videotape's playback capacity allows cameraman and director to check technical quality in the field, so the producer's role in viewing documentary footage will be editorial rather than technical.

21.3 Production safety

Duty of care

In common law, every employer owes their employees a 'duty of care'. This duty includes the provision of:
* competent, appropriately trained staff
* adequate plant and equipment
* a safe system of work.

Employers must weigh up the risk and seriousness of a workplace injury against the means, including cost, that are necessary to control or remove the risk. In deciding if an accident is possible, the employer must be aware that hazards can arise from the inadvertence, carelessness or even disobedience of an employee. No single event ever causes an accident. In any chain of events which results in an accident, there usually exists at least one and frequently a number of hazards that were previously considered insignificant and were not rectified. In a chain they can maintain a momentum towards a mishap. On behalf of the production company, the producer has responsibility for OH&S throughout the production, and particularly during the shoot when the risk of workplace injury is greatest.

Occupational health and safety legislation

Each state and territory in Australia has its own OH&S legislation, but each spells out the same principles of the duty of care of employers to take all reasonable practical steps to ensure a safe and healthy work environment. This applies to clear and obvious hazards and to the accumulated risk of a number of minor hazards. Employees, manufacturers, suppliers, installers and contractors also have responsibilities under these statutes, and may be found to have contributed to workplace injury, and be held to be jointly liable.

Liability for breaches of duty of care

The Film Industry Safety Code, compiled by the MEAA (and currently in process of being updated), and the industry's Safety Guidance Notes provide practical guidance on how best to meet the duty of care in specific areas of production activity. They have no legal force and there are no penalties for not observing them, but they may be used as evidence in legal action under an OH&S act or regulation. The law applies a test of foreseeability to breaches of duty of care. Employers are not held liable in common law for events they cannot possibly have anticipated, but a breach of the duty occurs if a reasonable person would have foreseen the possibility of injury, even if the risk is very low. If the Code was not observed, a breach may be taken as proven unless the court is satisfied that the act or regulation was complied with in some other way.

Hazardous action

A program's producer determines, in the first instance, whether a production has any hazardous action and will designate which scenes are hazardous. A hazardous action in production is any component or activity that, without proper precautions and supervision, carries an unacceptable risk of injury to any crew or cast member, or any member of the general public. The producer commissions a Safety Report (see Chapter 13) to specify the safety precautions that are necessary in each case. All recommendations in the report should be followed. To not do so would expose, at minimum, the production company and producer to liability if an accident were to occur.

Permits and licences

The areas where hazardous action is most common are special effects with explosives or pyrotechnics, use of firearms or weapons, and stunt work. The producer, through their production manager, should ensure that a special effects coordinator has all the necessary permits and licences covering products and equipment used, together with literature on all relevant chemical compositions, and safety guidelines for the use of smoke and flammable materials. The relevant permits can be found on the internet, generally through websites for the various Work-Cover and WorkSafe authorities in each state and territory, the same bodies that are responsible for workers compensation listed in Table 13.2. There are different permits for special effects with explosives and with pyrotechnics. A producer should ensure that the special effects person has the appropriate permit. Similarly, with firearms and weapons, an armourer must hold a Theatrical Armourer Permit in New South Wales, or one of a range of licences and permits in other states and territories. Specific detail can be obtained from the state police website. Stunt performers are graded by the MEAA's National Stunt Grading Procedure, which was described in Chapter 15. Other areas of safety concern are with the use of animals and action props, and with electrical equipment and cables.

Managing non-hazardous elements

In production, there will also be activities that are not, of themselves, hazardous. Without due care, however, they may contribute to a chain of events that results in an accident. Such non-hazardous action need not be the subject of a Safety Report, but it is the responsibility of the producer, the 1st AD and the safety officer (if one is present) to ensure non-hazardous elements don't become a threat to safety through inadvertence or carelessness. The producer should ensure that aesthetic or dramatic requirements of production do not take priority over safety requirements. Where an approximation of the aesthetic or dramatic effect can be achieved with a variation of the configuration of cameras, cast, position, and so on, and that reduces considerably the degree of risk, that compromise option should be taken.

General need for alertness

Safety issues can be as mundane as a hot water urn on an unstable table, or as uncertain as the dangerous assignments discussed in Chapter 17. Much of the needs of safety involve common sense and keeping alert to the possibilities of workplace injury. The University of Technology Sydney's Faculty of Humanities and Social Sciences has produced a location safety checklist which, while pedantic perhaps in some of its items, provides a very useful and thorough list of potential safety issues (see sources below).

21.4 Impact on the budget

This chapter is necessarily short because there are a limited number of specific things that a producer does during the shoot that aren't dealt with elsewhere in this book. It is principally a time of keeping an eye on how the shoot is progressing, and making sure that any difficulties or impediments are being attended to. With a series, the producer may focus more on pre- and post-production of other components of the program. The greatest area of scrutiny during the production phase will probably be on management of the budget. It is during this phase that the greatest part of the budget is committed. This is the subject of Chapter 22.

Sources and further reading

Specific reading

AFTRS 2004, 'Film and television safety guidance notes', AFTRS, Sydney.

MEAA 2004, 'Occupational risk management in the Australian film and television industry – draft national safety guidelines', available online at <http://ohs.alliance.org.au>, viewed 11 December 2006.

MEAA 2005, 'Occupational health and safety for news media workers', available online at <http://ohs.alliance.org.au>, viewed 11 December 2006.

Some internet references

UTS Faculty of Humanities and Social Sciences, 'Film and TV production: location checklist and safety report', available online at <http://www.hss.uts.edu.au/student_info/forms_documents_bookings/location_survey.pdf>, viewed 11 December 2006.

Chapter 22

Management of the production budget

Chapter 18 described the preparation of the production budget, beginning in the development phase (see Chapter 6). When funding is fully secured, a final production budget is arrived at by adjusting the then-current version so its total does not exceed the funds available. The final budget is the blueprint for expenditure on the production, a process whose description began in Chapter 5 and will continue through to Chapter 23.

The final budget anticipates a cost for every expense category in the production, but for a variety of reasons not every category will see expenditure exactly as predicted in the budget. Some categories will end up costing less than was budgeted (e.g. a discount may have become available) and that's not a problem, but some will cost more. If the additional cost over budget (called an overage) is ignored, it could create a total production cost in excess of the production's budget. If the production does not have the funding to cover this project overage, and that is likely to be the case, an invoice that comes late in the production will be unable to be paid. The budget is managed within its bottom line (the total budget figure) by identifying offsets where costs can be managed down so that the production can stay on target to come in within budget. To do this, the offsets must be timely. There is no useful purpose in identifying an offset where funds have already been spent, or the work has already been done, so that the payment cannot be avoided. Management of the budget must be ongoing and current. Solutions must be achievable.

This chapter describes the strategies employed by producers, generally in conjunction with their production manager, to keep the production's total expenditure on budgeted target, so that it can be completed without having to pursue further funds, which, in all probability, are not available anyway. Periodic financial reports are the producer's means of tracking the financial position of the production. While they don't need to be prepared by an accountant, it is useful for producers to be able to read financial reports and recognise the implications for the production in what they read. This chapter first covers some of the basic principles of accounting that are useful for producers to know, and then it looks at applying those principles to the specifics of production budget management.

22.1   Some basic accounting principles

Debit and credit

In accounting, the ledger is a collection of accounts. Whatever the form of the account, it will contain at least two columns. The left-hand column is called the debit side and the right-hand column is the credit side. The debit and credit columns are so named simply because of tradition. Debit means 'left' and credit means 'right', and the words have no other meaning in accounting. The layperson's notion that debits are bad and credits are good should be discarded, as these interpretations are not meaningful in accounting. Often, there is a third column, called the balance, which is the difference between the total debits and credits. Figure 22.1 shows the layout of these accounts.

Double-entry accounting

In industry, the convention is for assets to be recorded as debits and liabilities as credits. The balance of credit (i.e. the amount needed to make the two columns equal) is the owner's (or shareholder's) equity, the excess of assets over liabilities. Table 22.1 shows a typical company balance sheet. Every transaction in both columns must be accompanied by a balancing entry in the financial system, either the same amount posted in the other column or a negative entry somewhere else in the same column. For example, if, in the balance sheet shown in Table 22.1, an Accounts Payable of $5000 was paid in cash by the company, Accounts Payable would reduce by that amount to $40 000 and Cash by the same amount to $2000. Both totals of the balance sheet would reduce by the same amount, so they would remain in balance. Similarly, if $10 000 of goods was sold but the invoice was awaiting payment, Inventory would reduce by that amount to $55 000 and Accounts Receivable would increase by the same amount to $100 000. Totals on the balance sheet are unchanged as the double-entered transaction balances itself out in the Assets column. This is the principle of double-entry accounting. In every transaction, money must go *from* somewhere *to* somewhere. Double-entry accounting reflects this, as well as allowing a means of checking the arithmetic by keeping the account in balance.

Cash accounting

The simplest accounting system is one where transactions are recorded as cash paid or received, whether as currency, cheque or electronic funds transfer (EFT). This is called cash accounting and was an early form of accounting. It is payment-based and has traps for the unwary. It might record what has been spent, but it

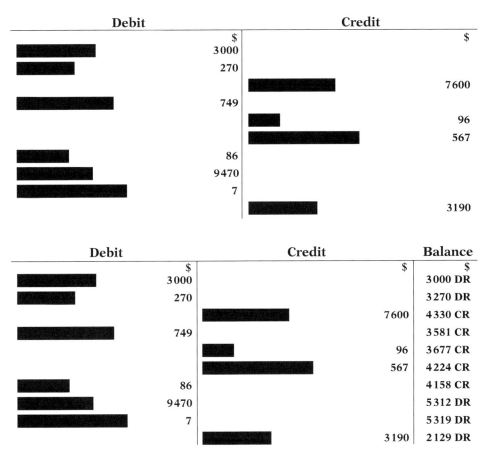

Debit		Credit	
	$		$
	3 000		
	270		
			7 600
	749		
			96
			567
	86		
	9 470		
	7		
			3 190

Debit		Credit		Balance
	$		$	$
	3 000			3 000 DR
	270			3 270 DR
			7 600	4 330 CR
	749			3 581 CR
			96	3 677 CR
			567	4 224 CR
	86			4 158 CR
	9 470			5 312 DR
	7			5 319 DR
			3 190	2 129 DR

Figure 22.1: Layout of ledgers.

doesn't record what is irrevocably committed to spending. For instance, it doesn't take account of a service received but not yet paid for, the remaining payments of a contract, or accumulated leave entitlements. The NSW government operated on a cash accounting system until the 1980s, when it was potentially near bankruptcy from its accumulation of superannuation and other unfunded liabilities. At that time, the state had $5 billion of unfunded liabilities.

Accrual accounting

These days, industry and government generally operate an accrual accounting system. It takes account not only of transactions involving cash, but also transactions that will involve a cash transfer some time in the future, sometimes in several years. Thus, all property of the company, accounts owing to the company, or investments made by the company are recorded at the redeemable value to the company. They are accrued assets. All financial obligations of the company – unpaid accounts, loans received, bonds bought, regular commitments, unpaid

Table 22.1: Typical company balance sheet.

AUSTRALIAN BAKING COMPANY – TAMAR VALLEY (ABC-TV)
Balance Sheet as at 30 June 2006

ASSETS	$	$
Current assets		
Cash	7 000	
Accounts receivable	90 000	
Inventory	65 000	
Prepayments	4 000	
Total current assets		166 000
Fixed assets		
Equipment, furniture, fittings	40 000	
less Accumulated depreciation	17 000	
Net equipment, etc.	23 000	
Land and buildings	227 000	
less Accumulated depreciation	32 000	
Net land and buildings	195 000	
Leased vehicles (net)	26 000	
Total fixed assets		244 000
Other assets		
Investments	7 000	
Goodwill	28 000	
Total other assets		35 000
Total assets		**445 000**

LIABILITIES	$	$
Current liabilities		
Bank overdraft	10 000	
Accounts payable	45 000	
Tax payable	4 000	
Dividend payable	6 000	
Accrued expenses	7 000	
Total current liabilities		72 000
Non-current liabilities		
Capitalised lease payments	12 000	
Mortgage	145 000	
Total non-current liabilities		157 000
Provisions		
Long-service leave	12 000	
Total liabilities		241 000
		12 000
OWNERS' EQUITY		
Issued and paid-up capital	100 000	
Share premium reserve	20 000	
Asset revaluation reserve	68 000	
Retained profits	16 000	
Total owners' equity		204 000
Total liabilities and owners' equity		**445 000**

contracts – are recorded at the expected payment by the company. They are accrued liabilities. Accounting in this way gives a much more accurate and timely picture of the company's financial position than simply recording the cash transactions when they eventually occur.

Production accounting

There are two major applications of these principles to macro-management of a television production budget. In production accounting, all expenses (credit side of the ledger) are offset against a budget funded by the periodic payments of a cash-flow schedule (debit). For the most part, the production's accounting concerns itself with the credit side only, although it must ensure it is not spending faster than the cash-flow feeding onto the debit side, as illustrated in Table 13.1. That is the first aspect of budget macro-management. The other is that the total expenditure cannot exceed the total funds available in the budget (i.e. the bottom line). Any expense that threatens to put its line item (cost category) into overage will need to be offset by reduced future spending in that or another category, so the total expenditure of the production doesn't go into overage as a consequence. The sooner the potential overage is detected, the greater the choice of offsets that will still be available. For this reason, management of a production budget will be more effective as accrual accounting than cash accounting. Timely detection of the need for expense offsets is the principal concern of budget management and of this chapter.

22.2   Cost Reports

Expense categories on the Cost Report spreadsheet

The production manager and the producer work from a Cost Report that has every line laid out as in the AFC budget format (see Chapter 18), ignoring those lines for which there is no budget and no expenditure. The categories may be modified to reflect more practically the nature of a particular production. It should best serve the needs of the production rather than conform to a generic format. If, for instance, the production will involve some travel by air on scheduled flights, some on chartered flights and some by train, the Cost Report may have separate categories for Airfares (Scheduled), Airfares (Charter) and Train Fares, even though the AFC format doesn't have these. If there are to be additional editors who will pre-cut some segments, they may be budgeted as a separate line item from the principal editor. It should not be difficult to see where the new categories are slotted into the spreadsheet. Where, for one reason or another, expenses are incurred on unbudgeted items, the cost category should be inserted as a new row in the spreadsheet against a zero budget for that category. This will be a category that is immediately in overage. As we will see in the next section, it will have to be offset somewhere in the system along with other categories that are projecting an overage.

Transactions entered in the production ledger

The financial information in the Cost Report comes from a link to the production's ledger where every expense (exclusive of GST) is recorded as a separate transaction. It is initially entered as a commitment, if the ledger is operated on the basis of accrual accounting, and eventually as an actual payment from the production's bank account. The transaction is posted (i.e. entered in the ledger), along with its budget category code, as soon as the expense is known to have been incurred, when the goods were supplied, the service provided, or the work done. Each line item in the budget and on the Cost Report has a separate numerical code to identify it. The expected cost is entered for the item, but a column in the ledger, with a character code (it might be 'I' for 'invoice paid') that indicates the expense has been paid, is left blank. When the invoice arrives for this item, the amount of the transaction is checked and corrected if necessary, but the 'invoice paid' column remains blank. Finally, when the invoice is paid, by cheque, EFT or any other means, the 'invoice paid' column is coded to indicate that. The sequence of events in entering transactions in the production ledger is shown in Figure 22.2.

Costs for the period and costs to date

Transaction information in the ledger aggregates automatically into the Cost Report format. It is published periodically, usually weekly or fortnightly depending on the scale of the production and its level of activity, for circulation to producer, executive producer, production company executives, investors, completion guarantor and anyone else with a legitimate interest in the current financial performance of the production. All paid invoices will aggregate by expense category into the first of a series of columns on the spreadsheet of a Cost Report, as illustrated in Table 22.2. It is headed Actual Costs To Date. Transactions in the ledger that are indicated as not yet paid (commitments) are aggregated, along with the actual costs, in column 2, Actual and Committed Costs.

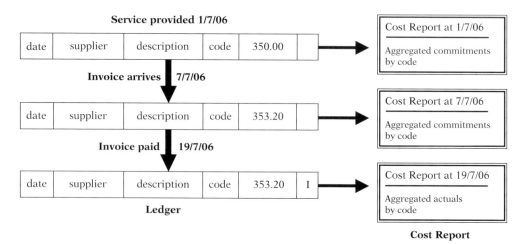

Figure 22.2: Sequence of events in entering a transaction in the production ledger.

Estimated cost to complete

Actual and Committed Costs are inevitable production expenses that will soon draw from the production's funds if they haven't done so already. They may be higher or lower than the budgeted figure for those expenses at this particular stage of the production, but they are irrevocable. The item has been supplied or the work has been done. There will still be budgeted expenses for which the production is not yet committed to payment because the goods or services have not yet been used. The production, in theory at least, could choose not to proceed with these. These are projected costs which are earmarked to fund the remaining activities of the production, as long as they don't create an overage for the final cost of the production. The total costs of the remaining production activities are calculated for each cost category, either at the rate at which the budget was calculated, or at an amended rate if more accurate cost information has come to hand since. Category totals of these uncommitted costs (updated, where appropriate) are tabulated in a third column, Estimated Cost to Complete.

Comparison of budget and current projection

Actual and Committed Costs for each category and Estimated Cost to Complete are combined in the next column as the Estimated Final Cost, which is the current projection of what the cost of the production would be if there was no change in the activities planned for the remainder of the production process through to delivery. The column after that has the budgeted figure for each category and, like the other columns, its total figure for the production. A producer can look at a draft Cost Report at this stage and see if the production is projecting an overage or underage by simply comparing the bottom line for Estimated Final Cost with the bottom line for Budget. If the Estimated Final Cost is lower, the production is currently projecting an underage. A decision will be made on where to allocate the funds freed up. But if the Estimated Final Cost is higher, the production is projecting an overage. If it continues on its current path without change, it will eventually commit itself to expenditure for which it has no funds. That is the crux of budget management and is dealt with in the next section.

Variance

The final column, or columns, in the Cost Report is the Variance. This is the difference between the projected cost and budgeted cost in the two preceding columns, either as underage or overage (conventionally shown as negative or in brackets) for each category. In each report, the production manager provides a short commentary (the narration) to explain each underage and overage. People who read the reports are not so interested in variances that arose in previous periods and that have already been explained. Their interest is in recently arisen variances. In addition to the current variance, a Cost Report may have two further columns: Variance Last Period and Variance This Period (the difference between the two preceding columns). With these columns, a Cost Report will only comment on variances in the final column. Any underages in the current Cost Report have

Table 22.2: Draft Cost Report in summary form.

'Wandering with the Ancients'
Cost report for the period ending 27 July 2006

	Actual costs to date	Actual and committed costs	Estimated cost to complete	Estimated final cost	Budget	Variance
Development	0	1 539	0	1 539	1 540	−1
Producers/directors						
Executive producer	6 000	8 000	8 000	16 000	16 000	0
Producer/director	20 000	25 000	15 000	40 000	40 000	0
Production unit fees and salaries						
Production manager	4 100	4 850	3 150	8 000	7 500	500
Associate producer	4 750	5 010	4 500	9 510	9 600	−90
Director of photography	3 250	6 500	4 000	10 500	10 000	500
Consultant	0	0	2 000	2 000	2 000	0
Fringe benefits and workers compensation	4 903	6 353	4 460	10 813	10 700	113
Cast	0	0	500	500	500	0
Locations	227	327	150	477	600	−123
Tape stock	437	437	140	577	600	−23
Equipment and stores						
Camera	1 195	2 385	1 190	3 575	3 540	35
Sound	350	1 600	800	2 400	2 400	0
Lighting	0	700	400	1 100	1 300	−200
Rentals and storage	375	375	1 000	1 375	1 500	−125
Travel and transport						
Airfares	0	1 270	3 300	4 570	4 400	170
Vehicle hire	115	620	580	1 200	1 150	50
Vehicle costs	376	420	1 200	1 620	2 200	−580

	1	2	3	4	5	6
Taxis	127	127	173	300	300	0
Miscellaneous				0	450	−450
Accommodation, living, catering						
Accommodation	520	654	500	1 154	800	354
Per diems	1 196	1 196	880	2 076	1 840	236
Office, entertaining, miscellaneous	186	214	436	650	650	0
Insurances	2 185	2 968	0	2 968	2 500	468
Office expenses	383	420	530	950	950	0
Post-production						
Editor	0	560	13 600	14 160	13 600	560
Editor's fringe benefits		74	1 721	1 795	1 800	−5
Editing suite	0	0	7 200	7 200	7 200	0
Graphics	0	0	500	500	500	0
On-line	0	0	4 500	4 500	4 500	0
CGI animation	12 500	12 500	167 500	180 000	180 000	0
Sound post-production	0	0	4 100	4 100	4 100	0
Music	0	0	2 000	2 000	2 000	0
Publicity	0	0	360	360	500	−140
Legal and business	1 300	3 750	2 150	5 900	5 000	900
Contingency				0	14 000	−14 000
Total	**64 038**	**87 849**	**256 520**	**344 369**	**356 220**	**−11 851**

already absorbed some of the overages. This column identifies the source of a projected overage, but not its solution. Either the cause of overspend is already committed, or it is anticipated in a future activity. The unspent component of the category with an overage could be cut back to bring that category back on budget, but that may not be in the production's best interests. Offsets are determined on production priorities, not to punish cost categories.

22.3 Offsets

Identifying the low-priority remaining activities

If a production is projecting an overage in its draft Cost Report, some adjustment has to be made in the remaining expenditure to bring the project variance back to zero. This adjustment is called an offset. Some activity in the remaining production activity has to be curtailed in order to lower its cost, and lower its contribution to the Estimated Cost to Complete. The question producers must ask themselves can be characterised as: 'Of the remaining production activities, which would have the least impact on the program if cut back?'. When that activity has been identified, and it has been decided how it will be cut back, the production schedule is adjusted accordingly. It might be a sequence that was regarded as a luxury, which is able to be abandoned if the money gets tight. It might be reducing the number of extras in a scene yet to be shot. If, after reducing that activity and recalculating the Estimated Cost to Complete, the production is still projecting an overage, albeit a smaller one, the question is asked again and a further activity is curtailed – and so on until the Estimated Final Cost is no longer greater than the Budget. Clearly, some judgement has to be exercised about whether the reduced activities are proportional to the overage to be eliminated. A series of minor, small cost reductions is not the best way to deal with a large overage. Some harder, more drastic decisions would have to be made.

Timing of projected overages

The earlier the production becomes aware of an overage projection, the wider the range of activities from which to choose an offset. This is a reason for the production to not wait until invoices are actually paid, before they are calculated as a cost. It has the information available from which a potential overage can be projected from the moment a cost is committed. If the production takes corrective action immediately, it can curtail a lower priority activity than the smaller selection of activities that will remain available when the invoice is paid, some time later. In practice, an overage can often be predicted before the production is irrevocably committed to it. If the price of the airfare to a location has gone up since the production budget was framed, then this will be known to be causing potential overage before air bookings are confirmed. The producer must decide whether it is in the production's interest to offset the cost increment of the airfare by reducing activity elsewhere in the production, or whether it should look for a nearer location that could serve the production's purpose nearly as well, or get by with a smaller crew going to that location.

Protecting post-production from cost overruns

Accrual accounting allows this timeliness of deciding offsets. It minimises the impact of offsets on the final product. If decisions about offsets are held off, post-production will bear the brunt of category overspending, whether that is in the production's interest or not, simply because there is little other choice by then. A budget preference might be to reduce expenditure by reducing the costs of extras, but waiting till the end of the shoot removes that as an option. A crafty producer might even look at padding their post-production budget slightly with more activity (and therefore cost) than would occur in a tightly funded production. This might be the purchase of more archive footage or further CGI work. The additional post-production could be seen as a bonus of extra production value for the project if the shoot has been cost-effective, and not if it hasn't. It's an additional contingency that is convertible to production value at the post-production stage if not required to offset earlier costs. This strategy requires sufficient production funding to sustain it. It is counterproductive to deny an important or crucial aspect of the shoot so as to enable a possible post-production embellishment. This is a matter of producer judgement. There is, after all, the official contingency to be factored into the costs management equation.

Contingency

The discussion so far in this section has ignored an important aspect of offsetting cost overruns, the Contingency. Calculated on the AFC budget spreadsheet as 10% (usually) of Below the Line costs, its purpose is to provide an alternative offset to reducing production activity. The offsets for cost overruns are looked for in Contingency as well as in other categories, and this is the source of initial offsets. Reducing Contingency requires no curtailing of production activity. In theory, the production need not look elsewhere for offsets until the contingency has been fully absorbed, but this strategy can limit the range of offsets when they are eventually required. Post-production will again bear the brunt of production overruns. Restricting post-production has a direct impact on the final product. Curtailing some aspect of pre-production, while it is important, doesn't impact as directly on the look of the program. Experience indicates the rate at which Contingency can be expected to be absorbed into the production cost. If, early in the piece, this rate seems to be higher than usual, that's a sign to start looking to offsets elsewhere, while there are still reasonable options.

Applying offsets to the Cost Report

In the example in Table 22.2, the projected underage of $11 851 includes $2149 of Contingency, which would otherwise be overage. Projected costs are $2149 more than the non-Contingency part of the budget, but the Contingency (which can never be an expenditure item, only a repository of uncommitted funds) is significantly greater than that non-Contingency overage. If this is a Cost Report part way through the shoot, that is probably an acceptable call on contingency. Any smaller underage would further reduce contingency. In that case, offsets would be sought. These might be modification of travel in the remainder of the shoot, or reduction of consultant use – whatever would have the least impact on the finished program.

Expenditure concentration

The producer, production manager and accountant periodically go through the process of drafting a Cost Report, identifying offsets and finalising the Report to ensure the production is projecting an on-budget outcome. It's not as mammoth a task as it might appear. Most costs are concentrated in one phase of the production. At any one time in the production process, many categories have not yet started to spend, or else they have completed their spending (as commitment, at least, even if invoices are still to come). Their Estimated Cost to Complete, or their Actual Costs to Date, will be unchanged from the previous Cost Report. Only those categories that have had activity during the preceding week require detailed attention and, if they have conformed to budget expectations, no further work is required after columns are adjusted for the week's expenditure.

22.4   Reporting to investors and others

Changes to the production schedule

The Cost Report is distributed to those with an interest in and responsibility for the production's financial wellbeing. One copy goes to the producer, but as they have been involved with its redrafting, it is not so much reporting to them as providing a record of decisions made. Offset decisions have to be passed on to those who will be affected by them – director, 1st AD and HODs. These people may well have been involved in some discussion when the offset strategy was formulated, so it will quite possibly only confirm what they already know. It will specify necessary changes to the production schedule and to production activities. This information is passed on to all affected production personnel so the production can proceed under the amended schedule.

Reporting to production company executives, investors and completion guarantor

Cost Reports are also distributed to production company executives, investors and a completion guarantor. The production will attach the Cost Report to a Statement of Investors' Funds. Drawn up by the production accountant, this is a summary of the accounting of these funds at the time of the Cost Report. It will include: current balance in the production bank account; recoverables such as floats, deposits and debtors; provisions for group tax and the like; and production cost to date as per the attached Cost Report. Attached will also be notes for the Cost Report. They will explain each overage that has appeared in the current period, and each underage, whether they are the result of offset decisions or from actual expenditure being under budget. It will also report on the balance of Contingency remaining.

Investor comfort

If the production's finances are properly managed, these reports will give comfort to investors and others. It will also give them sufficient information for further discussion if they feel the need, but a production that appears to be under control is a production for which little further discussion is necessary.

Sources and further reading

General reading

Case, D., Gailey, L., Knapman, C., et al. 2002, *The Production, Budgeting and Film Management Satchel*, AFC/AFTRS, Sydney.

McKinlay, Gill 2002, 'The role of the production accountant', in Case, D., Gailey, L., Knapman, C., et al., *The Production, Budgeting and Film Management Satchel*, AFC/AFTRS, Sydney.

Chapter 23

Post-production through to delivery

The final phase of the production cycle is post-production, where the material shot or gathered during the production phase is either polished, if shot as-live in studio or on OB, or shaped into a completed program. The latter has been increasingly the case over the last two decades, as the impact of digital technology within post-production has grown. Digital editing has opened up a range of new approaches to the craft and, as a result, triggered dramatic changes in editing styles.

Post-production involves expensive and sophisticated equipment, which might create the impression it is principally a technological phase, but it is not. It is as creative as any other phase of the production cycle. All the elements that have been gathered to tell the program's story are brought together in this phase, to construct a cohesive narrative progressing logically to an end point, or otherwise build through steps or segments that have a unity and generate some sort of enjoyment for the audience. The craft of getting that progression to flow smoothly and entertainingly is the craft of editing. It is the art of putting shots in order so that they make sense and tell a story.

The cost of the technology that carries out this craft has the capacity to seriously damage the program's budget, at a time when there are few offsets for the production to recover its position. Planning and scheduling of post-production should begin in pre-productions, so that the budget allocated to it can be realistic and achievable. The time it will take to edit a program is somewhat speculative. It can't be estimated as an aggregate of its components, such as with a shooting schedule. It is based on experience, and allows for the time it might take to resolve difficult problems that will inevitably arise and slow the process. Among other things, the post-production schedule must be a realistic assessment of the time editing will take, not an optimistic one.

Post-production is the culmination of the process that began in Chapter 5 with the concept. It is the final step in the realisation of that concept as a program, or of a program that has evolved from the concept. It is the final opportunity for the producer to see that the program is shaped to meet its editorial objectives, and to work as a program for its audience. Editorial oversight is one of the producer's main roles in post-production. Another is to ensure that this phase, like all the others, is properly facilitated.

23.1 Role of the producer

The proper resourcing of editing

As with many aspects of the production process, producers don't necessarily need to know how to operate the technology of post-production or to perform the craft. They do need, however, to have a general knowledge of what these people do, what resources they will need in what sort of time frame, and what sorts of results are reasonable to expect from their efforts. They need to stay abreast of new developments and what they provide, so that they can be considered for inclusion in the production from the outset. While they will have advice from the editor and director, this should mainly be to provide specifics of a general approach they have already formulated.

Editorial oversight

The technical resources are the means of delivering the finished program and, while they are important, what the program will say to its audience – the editorial issues – are ultimately the crux of its success or failure to communicate. These issues should have been discussed and fleshed out at the development stage, so the production has worked to a clear editorial brief. They should be revisited from time to time along the production pathway. Post-production is a time to confirm the editorial brief, and ensure that it is still underpinning the finished product.

Review of the editing script

A review of the footage shot (called 'rushes', from the film convention of processing them for speedy review of technical and artistic quality) and footage sourced is an opportunity to make sure the brief is still in the sights of the director. Sourced footage, such as archive or home movies, is predetermined, but there is still a selection process involved. It should be used because it can contribute to telling the program's story, not just because it is there. Footage shot for the production, on the other hand, should have been purpose-shot for the narrative that stems from the program's brief and was the spine of its shooting script. Shot or sourced footage, that is earmarked for incorporation into the program, is indicated in an editing script (or 'paper edit') drawn up by the director. Before going into editing, producer and director will discuss the script to make sure it looks as if it will fulfill the editorial intention of the program.

Producer's role during the editing process

It's generally prudent for the producer to leave the editor and director to shape the program from its script, at least until 'rough-cut' stage. Here, the program's sequences are in order and cut roughly to length, all key shots are in place, transitions and bridges are an approximation of their finished form, and graphics, animation and other inserted material are either in the cut, or indicated in their place in the cut that they are coming. A producer can cast a fresh eye on the program at this stage, something no longer possible for the editor (particularly) and director, who have been immersed in the editing process. The producer, with a freshness of view, is more able to identify aspects of the cut that may not say to the audience what the director thinks they are saying. With feedback, the program can be finetuned to avoid any ambiguities or lack of clarity. A producer seldom has the final say, however, on when a program's edit is accepted. Other parties with an editorial interest, such as production executives or broadcasters, may view the program at a late stage of editing. When all interests are happy, a fine cut can be presented to those who will authorise it as 'locked off' (the agreement that the picture edit is complete).

23.2   The three historical phases of post-production

First phase of editing

Video editing has moved through three broad historical phases: physical film cutting, electronic transfer editing and non-linear editing. At the beginning of television, programs were either edited live by vision switching through studio or OB, or recorded on film and physically cut by a film editor in the same way as movies. In the first change to this pattern, two developments enabled studio output to be recorded for transmission at a later date: videotape and telerecord. Telerecord (or kinescope) allowed the electronic signal to be played onto unexposed film stock, which was then processed and could be cut if required. It could be projected through telecine, which was used to deliver film-sourced programs to the electronic broadcast system. Telerecord was useful for program syndication because it enabled a studio-produced program to be scheduled in different time zones at different times, but it was cumbersome as an editing medium.

Videotape

Videotape is a magnetically based recording medium that can record an electronic signal, then replay that signal into the transmission system some time later. Telerecord didn't have the quick turnaround capability of videotape. What's more, its technical quality rapidly fell behind improvements in videotape quality, and eventually it was consigned to the television museum. Videotape developed beyond its record–replay role through editing by electronic transfer, with videotape recorders controlled by computers, and edit points cued with audible tones. The editing function was standardised with 'time code' giving each video frame a digital 'address', thus allowing editors to manage shot lists, and permitting frame-accurate cutting.

Decline of film

As videotape's technical characteristics began to bridge the gap between it and film, and shooting with videotape cameras became more flexible and the cameras more lightweight, the format gradually replaced film as the prime medium on which television was shot. Today, only a few high-end dramas and commercials are shot on film and, except where both television and cinema release is expected, this is decreasingly so. Television is currently a medium of videotape. Already digital tape has replaced analogue tape, but it may not be long before digital videotape is superseded by disk or hard drive.

Non-linear editing

Editing has followed a similar progression. No-one edits on film any more, even when the program is shot on film. Analogue tape-to-tape (linear) edit systems have been replaced by their digital equivalents, but most editing is carried out now on non-linear systems. These convert the footage, whatever medium it has been recorded on, into digital information. This is manipulated into the data of an edited program and output, directly or indirectly, back to the original medium – or any other medium the production may choose. Videotape editing had an aura of engineering about it, but non-linear editing has brought post-production back to the 'desktop' level reminiscent of the Steenbeck flat-top film editing machine. The ability to make editing less of a technical accomplishment and more a film editor's intuitive work sold non-linear systems to the industry. Avid introduced non-linear editing with computers in 1988, based on the Apple Macintosh platform. Prevailing over its main competitor, Lightworks, Avid has held its market leading position, but the release in 2000 of Final Cut Pro (FCP), another Macintosh-based system, has also introduced Avid's main competitor.

Future prospects

Non-linear editing has potential connections to the future with the multi-platform demand for 'digital interactivity', the capacity to move digital content about from platform to platform. Non-linear systems are already being networked as news program servers. The storage facility, which is remote from the digital editor and widely accessible, offers a possible prototype of future interactive editing by the public, as well as an indication of how video on demand might operate.

23.3   Linear editing

The process of linear editing

Traditionally, videotape editing for television was edited on a linear system, although it wasn't described as linear until non-linear systems were developed. In a linear system, shots are selected from a source tape (usually the camera-record tape) and copied in a specific order on to another tape where the edited program is being compiled. The editor must roll through the source tape until they get to the shot to be used, hence the description 'linear'. 'In' and 'out' points on the replay tape are cued and that section is recorded on the edit master tape, cued from the end of the last assembled shot, or cued somewhere within the assembly (the 'edit point') if it is an overlay or cutaway shot to be dropped in. This system will transfer vision with synchronous ('sync') sound from the camera tape unless the sound is switched off. Alternatively, sound only, for voice-over for instance, may be transferred on to a second audio track on the edit master tape.

Generations of editing

Once the process of transferring shots is complete, the edit master tape has a potentially finished segment, or program that could be put to air. However, watching the segment may reveal changes that could be made to improve the story. With few exceptions, this would involve repeating the process onto a new edit master tape, possibly several times over. The record tape may be able to have limited shots insert-edited into it, but if the segment needs to be changed by shortening shots, changing their order or the sequence order, or editing in different material, the edit master tape becomes the source tape and a new edit master tape is created with the newly edited version of the story. In the analogue system, each new edit master tape is a generation further removed from camera tape quality, each with picture quality further downgraded. With digital tape, there is no significant generational loss (see Chapter 2). This technical shortcoming of linear editing has been negated and, as a result, it retains a niche role in television production.

Editing fast-turnaround items

Linear editing is used principally where the program requires only cutting between shots. Dissolves between shots or more complex transitions are possible using multiple tape sources, but these are not usually required in the genres that still use this mode of editing, such as news stories and other fast-turnaround short items. Non-linear editing, as we will see in the next section, involves digitising the source footage before editing can commence. As this requires replay at normal speed, the total duration of all source footage is spent getting the footage to the point that it can be edited. In a program that will be in editing for some weeks, that is neither here nor there. In a program that must be edited that afternoon, it is not good time management to digitise footage for editing when the time could be better used getting started on the editing itself. For this reason, non-linear editing, for all its technical and operational sophistication, is not the more efficient method of cutting stories simply and quickly. For any other editing project, it has radically changed the face of post-production.

23.4   Non-linear editing

Technical basis of non-linear editing

In non-linear editing systems, video and audio information is stored in digital form on computer hard drives or optical disks. Available in both PC and Macintosh platforms, these systems allow instant random access to shots and sequences, and enable easy rearrangement of these shots and sequences. Linear editing copies selected shots, but non-linear editing selects them from an image file and makes the computer play them back as a programmed sequence. It is a system that revolves around file management, where the editor can try a variety of combinations and save the data for those editing decisions that seem for the moment to work. What is created and saved is a variety of edit decision lists (EDLs). The computer will draw on EDL data to present a sequence of video images (and audio) on the screen. It makes it easy to change cuts and undo previous decisions by editing the list. These editing systems also have software available to deliver a vast range of transitions and special effects with speedy real-time rendering. The pathway of non-linear editing in post-production is illustrated in Figure 23.1.

Digitising the media

The operational process of non-linear editing begins with downloading source material into the computer, a process called digitising or capture. The footage can originate on analogue or digital videotape, film or DVD, and is replayed from a compatible system that is connected to the computer. Digitising is generally a time-consuming process, even with fast-speed download systems, but refinements of the basic operation keep appearing. The advent of DV-based video formats was accompanied by Firewire interface cabling, which is a simple, inexpensive means of getting video in and out of computers. Modern internet-based editing systems can take video directly from a camera phone or 3G mobile connection.

Storage capacity issues

Most non-linear systems will compress the data as it is digitised, so the system can operate with relatively small computer storage. A decision is made whether to digitise at high or low resolution ('res'). This will depend on the storage capacity of the system and how much material is to be digitised. More material needs lower resolution to fit it on the drive. Not all footage that has been shot for a program need necessarily be digitised. The director, in reviewing the footage to prepare an editing script, may decide that some of the sequences shot no longer have a place in the story. They won't be digitised, so that the program won't generate a storage capacity problem.

Logging of clips

Digitised rushes are broken into separate clips, which are named and filed in folders called bins. Each clip would correspond to a single take on the camera tape unless there was some reason to break the footage down differently. Bins might correspond to sequences for which the clips were shot, but the exact nature of this logging is at the discretion of the editor. As with any computer-based system, housekeeping is important. The logging system must be comprehensive and unambiguous, so that files can be easily found.

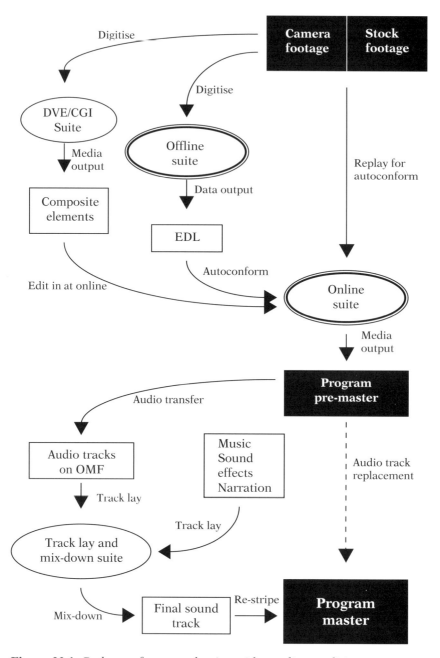

Figure 23.1: Pathway of post-production with non-linear editing.

The non-linear edit process

In the editing process, precise 'in' and 'out' points are marked on selected clips, and they are dropped into the program. The editor is not creating a physical program here, but a timeline which tells the computer what media (image and sound) it needs to play off the hard disk at any time. Through a repetition of this process, an edit of the program is built up as an EDL. At any time, the computer can use the EDL to display the media that it describes. Like any computer also, the non-linear editor has the potential to crash, malfunction or be stolen. The project file should be backed up at the end of each day and saved onto a portable disk.

Autoconform

When the picture edit is locked off, its EDL is downloaded on disk and used to make a high-resolution online copy of the program. The process up to this point is called offline because it is not working with the camera tapes, but with a data-captured compressed copy of them. The EDL is autoconformed by the computer, prompting for each source tape in turn to be put up on a connected replay machine. Each shot is copied with the exact timing that the EDL data specifies. The procedure is repeated for every shot in the edited program, until a new version of the program has been assembled in high resolution. Where animation, graphics, main titles or visual effects (VFX) have been constructed separately from the off-line, they are imported into the online from tape. Most offline suites are also capable of onlining, if the footage has been digitised at high resolution. However, a dedicated online suite can produce a far greater range of effects without a need for rendering time, as well as colour grading, mattes and keys. It is now possible to export video sequences between different non-linear editing systems (Final Cut Pro and Avid) using an Open Media Framework (OMF) interface. Examples are the transfer of a multilayered visual effects sequence created in Adobe After Effects to either Final Cut Pro or Avid, or a Final Cut Pro offline to Avid Symphony for onlining.

Online edit

The next stage is online editing, where graphic supers and any visual effects that are still required are added. Most offline suites will generate simple titles as a guide, but the online edit can replace them with broadcast-quality titles with a far greater range of fonts and layouts. Titles may be: supers (or captions) identifying people or places at the bottom or top of a frame; subtitles as translation of foreign language or some other text purpose; or credits, listing the people who worked on the program. The main title of the program is usually more elaborate and may be immersed in a short vision-and-music sequence. Autoconforming a non-linear EDL could include 2D vision effects such as mixes (or dissolves) and wipes, or 3D effects if the software was in the offline edit system. More complicated effects are better constructed with the greater flexibility of the online edit machinery.

Checking for dropout

Online editing is also an opportunity to check that there are no errors in the autoconform or 'dropouts', which are frames with recording errors that show up on the screen. Dropouts on individual frames are usually repairable, whether they emanate from the autoconform or the rushes, but where they derive from the rushes and run over continuous frames the repair work is much more difficult and may entail choosing another shot.

Colour grading

Picture quality is also checked at this stage, making adjustments to colour and lighting levels where required, within the limits of tolerance of the system. If a high level of colour grading is required, and the budget can afford it, that may be done in a separate grading suite with high-end equipment and a specialist grader (or 'colourist'). The director should attend the online edit, particularly for any colour grading.

Online costs

An online suite is a complex technical facility and comes at a quite high hourly rate, so any problems in the online process can prove costly if they take time to solve. As Marcus Gillezeau points out in *Hands On*, which provides operational detail of the editing process, an online facility may make mistakes, or pass off technical problems as 'normal' or blame the absent offline editor. The producer should be in a position of understanding the processes of online editing, and of having access to expert advice about what is and isn't normal, if they are to dispute a bill that seems to involve excessive time in online editing.

23.5   Archive and other sourced footage

Sourced footage on a common format

Sourced footage could be on any format: film, analogue tape or digital tape. It is advisable to consolidate it on the same format as the program's camera-original tapes, for partly technical and partly logistic reasons. Old analogue videotape formats, such as U-matic, S-VHS and Hi8, can be unstable and using this material off a digital tape ensures their stability for the program. Replaying other formats for digitisation or onlining requires hiring a number of replay machines. This is neither cost-efficient nor time-efficient. It is much better to be able to replay them all from the same machine.

   This applies to original footage as well. If it was shot on more than one format, which may be the case if shot over a long period with different cameramen, it is best to consolidate all camera footage on the format of the major part of the program's shot footage.

Dealing with archive footage

Archival material, whether originally shot on film or tape, is usually made available for editing on SP Betacam or VHS, with timecode displayed in the vision (called 'burnt-in timecode', BITC). This will be digitised, and incorporated into the program during the offline edit. When the picture is locked off, archive material in the final edit is transferred from its original source format, using timecode display as a guide, to the format that the program is mastered from (i.e. the major camera-original format). This may be dropped into the offline edit in place of the timecoded scenes, but this may not be necessary if the online software can recognise identical timecode on both archive copies. The editing of non-broadcastable archive footage has advantages for both parties. For the production, it allows a considerable amount of archive footage to be considered without high copying costs by using a low-cost format. For the archive, it limits the amount of usable footage that is at large and potentially able to be pirated.

Dealing with aspect ratio

Another consideration with sourced footage is aspect ratio (see Chapters 2 and 14). Increasingly, programs are shot on a 16:9 format because that is what broadcasters want, but sourced footage and particularly the older archival footage is likely to have been shot on a 4:3 format. When they are different, sourced footage is converted to the same aspect ratio as camera original and these copies will be source tapes for the program. Prior to digitisation, a decision is made whether the 4:3 source should be converted to 16:9 in pillar-box format or cropped top and bottom. Temporary archive on VHS need not be converted, although it may appear horizontally stretched in the off-line display as a result. The selected shots will be converted to 16:9 format before replacing the temporary archive footage and onlining.

23.6   Computer-generated effects and animation

Composite imaging

Computer-generated imagery (CGI), producing visual effects or animation, is produced in a separate suite from the offline edit, and often by a separate company. It is specialised work, requiring particular skills and software. The software will be in a suite dedicated to high-end visual effects, or in a post-production house that has built up the expertise and technology. It can be labour-intensive, expensive, and requiring powerful computers and software. The lower end is the composite image, a moving collage layering into a single picture a number of visual sources, including text. The impact is of an animated graphic design, with elements of vision positioned in the frame, and either changing or moving. It is a dynamic upgrading of the static graphic design of early television. The design can be anything from a number of boxes inset into a background to overlapping layers resembling layered clothing.

Computer-generated animation

At the higher end is the re-created object or living thing, placed in a re-created environment or an actuality-shot scene. Each solid object to be created is first shaped in the computer, with lines joining the key points of the shape to create a 'wire-frame' model. The lines are defined in three sets of coordinates, so the shape can be rotated in three dimensions. If the object is capable of motion, such as an animal, a human or a vehicle, it is animated to move in 3D. Whether it moves or not, the 'camera' can move around it in 3D.

Creating photorealism in the computer

If the CGI object is to be combined with live-action footage, the wire-frame model is given a simple surface and tested with the live-action vision. When the designers are happy with the way they integrate, the surface of the wire frame is rendered with complex surfaces and textures to create a photorealistic effect. Fine detail, such as dust on surfaces and animated movement of animal hair, is added after the prime surface textures are in place. Lighting on the object is created with CGI software to match that in the live-action scenes in which it will be keyed or matted. Finally, when all the layers and elements of a shot are completed, they are combined to form the final shot, a process called 'compositing'.

Incorporation into the edited program

Test runs of the composite shot, such as the basic-rendered wire-frame model, can be saved and imported into the offline edit. The editor can then work with the right timing for the shot while editing the program. The final version can be imported into the offline edit as well if it is completed in CGI, or it can be added at the online edit, with or without further image manipulation by the online's visual effects software. Layering of the elements in a composite image can often be done with online software.

23.7 The art of editing

The art of storytelling

The art of editing is the art of storytelling. A good editor has an intuitive feel for pace, timing and the flow of events that drives the story. Experience – storytelling techniques that have been found to work over the years – extends this instinct. Stories also need to have a logic to their progression, so the editor must have insight into the logic that can be perceived by an audience, which must grasp the story as it unfolds. If the logic is there but not obvious, then for all practical purposes it is not there. This part of the craft is the skill of selection: selection of the most telling shots that will maintain audience interest while advancing the narrative. It requires an eye for a fresh visual point of view, but not one that places freshness above meaning. Form should make content engrossing, not replace it.

The craft of problem-solving

A second aspect of the craft of editing is problem-solving. With dramatised footage, there may be mistakes where for one reason or another the shots don't cut together as effectively as planned. There may be continuity problems across the cut, some visual feature in a different place in successive shots, such as a hat on in one shot and off in the next. The shots may 'cross the line', breaking the convention that the camera's view must stay on the same side of an imaginary line of dramatic action in successive shots (see Chapter 20). Movement may not flow naturally through the shots. Lines may be delivered unconvincingly. Something may be happening that the logic of the story says shouldn't. All these audience distractions need to be masked in some way with judicious shot selection and editing, so the viewer doesn't notice them.

With actuality footage, it can be an interviewee getting a fit of coughing or losing track of their thoughts, or it could be someone on camera talking to the director, or it could be some action that's irrelevant to the program's story. These also are solved by the editor's skill in cutting around the problem, without losing the flow of the story.

Common to both dramatised and actuality shoots is footage that slows down the story through inaction or irrelevance, or just plain dullness. The stock approach is to shorten the sequence by cutting the middle out of it and masking the cut with a cutaway, or else starting the sequence later or ending it earlier.

Further aspects

There are two main approaches to the construction of sequences in editing:
1. Narrative or continuity editing – where the succession of shots tells a continuous story, often skirting around irrelevant action to stay focused on the main dramatic points in the sequence.
2. Montage editing – where the succession of shots conveys an impression with underlying emotion about an aspect of the story or a character or a place. There is seldom a narrative to advance such a sequence, but usually music and/or action will give it unity and flow.

There is much more that can be said in the analysis of the art of editing. It is a complex and creative skill through which all the preparation that precedes it is crafted into a finished product. A dissertation on the art of editing could fill a whole book (and has done so), but that is not the role of a book on the business of producing television. Producers don't do the editing (or seldom do), but commission it. They need to know what editors are capable of, but can leave to them the nuances and craft of doing it.

23.8 Music

Sources of program music

There are three principal sources of music for a television program:
1. Commercial recordings – these are an expensive option whose cost escalates if there is a need to extend the rights to enable the program to be exploited more widely. Sometimes a record company may agree to do a deal on the grounds that exposure of the music in a program will promote sales, but the argument would need to be persuasive.
2. Production (mood) music – this has been composed especially as a low-cost option for film and television, and is a less expensive alternative to the above. Its price also rises considerably if there is a need to extend the rights.

3. Commissioned music – this is where a composer writes and produces music specifically for a program for a contracted fee and with contracted rights.

Commercially recorded music

There are several implications in using well-known music from commercial recordings. Viewers who are familiar with the music may associate it with something in their lives that has nothing to do with the program. They will attach to it a different mood from the one intended with its use in the program. Often music that is designed to stand alone has a powerful presence and risks overwhelming the vision it is designed to complement. Music should underscore or highlight, or otherwise complement the picture it accompanies, so any choice of music should be considered in its context in the program, and not separate from it. Quite often, a piece of music that sounds just right in a program, sounds bland and characterless by itself. This is because it is designed to go with the picture, not to stand on its own.

Production and commissioned music

Production and commissioned music are written with this in mind. Quite often, production music will create just the right mood in a program that more nuanced music would not. Where the music is required quickly, such as in magazine or current affairs programs, this is a good option. The advantage of commissioned music, though, is that it can be written specifically to match the pictures and their timing in the program, whereas production music can only provide the appropriate mood. Commissioned music can also be contracted for a package of rights, rather than having to pay further fees each time the rights need to be extended. In Australia there are a considerable number of good screen composers, so the producer is in a good negotiating position. A composer trying to build a client base is not in a position to hold out on rights, and will often agree to a fee that covers all media throughout the world. Alternatively, the fee may cover Australian rights with a second contracted fee to extend the rights to the rest of the world.

23.9 Audio post-production

Sound editing in a non-linear edit

Sound can be edited in the non-linear offline suite, using up to six audio tracks. For short items, such as magazine segments and fast-turnaround stories, this will produce an acceptable result. Sound effects, atmosphere tracks and music will need to be imported into the system, which will mix the tracks down. However, a much more polished soundtrack is obtainable with a more sophisticated dedicated sound editing system, such as Digidesign's Pro Tools, and a mixing theatre.

Sound editing

Picture editors will do some track laying and initial sound editing in the offline edit, adding sound effects where they are crucial to the story. With picture lock-off, sound is exported to a sound editing system by EDL or as an OMF. With EDL, the sound editor reconforms the audio from camera tapes or digital audio tapes (DATs). The OMF exports directly all sound that is on the offline timeline for the edited program without the need to re-digitise from source tapes. As it only transfers sound that is on the offline timeline, the picture editor must make sure all sound for all included shots is on the timeline, and that there are sound extensions to allow cross fades at the mix. The sound editor will lay in all sound components that are needed to mix down a completed soundtrack for the program. This might include sound effects (from an effects library, or recorded on a Foley stage with a variety of surfaces, on which sounds are physically produced), atmosphere tracks (e.g. traffic, crowd, air conditioners) or music. A drama program might also have automatic dialogue replacement (ADR). Dialogue is re-recorded in synchronisation with the original, to replace that original where there were issues of technical or performance quality. When all tracks are in place, they are exported to the mixing suite as audio files or laid back to digital eight-track tapes.

Audio mixing

The first stage of the audio mix is the pre-mix, where all dialogue, effects and music tracks are mixed down to three stereo pairs of tracks. Any equalisation, or audio effects such as reverberation ('reverb'), are done at this stage. The three pre-mixed pairs are then mixed against each other, with the levels lifting and falling depending on their relative importance at any given time, to achieve the right balance between them. This final mix is laid back to stereo DAT or an eight-track digital tape, or mastered directly on to the program tape. If the program is intended for international release, or even as a matter of course to ensure flexibility for subsequent versioning of the program, an international or music and effects (M&E) mix is made without the dialogue tracks. A high-end mixing option is a surround-sound mix for Dolby Digital 5.1. It must be done in a suite equipped and licensed by Dolby Laboratories, and this program will also need to be licensed by them.

23.10 Sound aesthetics

The soundscape

At one time sound editing was a process of laying in all the sounds that logically matched what could be seen on screen. Sound was edited for documentaries by the picture editor and called track laying. Drama might have had a separate editor, but it still worked largely on the principle of matching sound to vision. However, while the camera might not have a view of much more than 100 degrees at best at any one time, sound always has a 360-degree perspective. It can indicate dramatic interest outside the camera's visual range. It can add to the viewer's understanding of the setting of the story. We don't need to see a cutaway of a children's playground to know there's one next door. It can be in the soundtrack. Sound can be used to evoke all sorts of feelings about the place and the story in the same way as music. These days the sound editor is often called a 'sound designer', and their work a 'soundscape'. Sometimes the soundtrack will serve the utilitarian purpose of complementing the picture we see, whereas sometimes it will be akin to a music score and serve the same purpose as music.

Some important features of sound aesthetics

As with picture editing, there is now an art in sound aesthetics, whose detail is beyond the scope of this book, but there are some points about these aesthetics that a producer should keep in mind. Sounds from the key dramatic figures on screen should predominate over others in the mix, such as the voice of a main character in a crowd that is singing. At the same time, sound should have a perspective to match the placement of things in the shot. Things near to camera should have a presence that objects in the background don't give to their sounds. As noted above, sound can create an ambience for a sequence. Sirens, shouting voices and grinding machinery can add to the picture even if their sources are not on screen. The sounds need not be literal. They can be artificial but evocative, neither effects nor music, but occupying the netherworld between.

Continuous audio quality

As a final point, there should be a continuity to sound. Voice sounds different on different microphones and in different locations because acoustic qualities change in both. It may not be noticeable at the recording, but it is when the two pieces are edited together, so much so that they are sometimes perceived as different people talking. Where possible, reporter narration should be recorded on location with the same microphone, if it is to flow on from reporting on camera. In the same way, background atmosphere may change imperceptibly during the shooting of a sequence, but when two parts of the scene are cut together the background change becomes a jump. An atmosphere track allows this change to be balanced up in the mix. These are just some of the aesthetic issues to be considered in putting together a cohesive soundtrack. The important principle is to respond as a viewer, get an understanding of where problems have come from, and learn to make sure as much as possible that they are headed off before they happen.

23.11   Editing factual programs

Different approaches of drama and actuality in post-production

The post-production of a drama will follow closely the scenario outlined in this chapter. It has a prescriptive script, which has been adhered to with minor changes in the shoot, and followed, again with minor changes, in post-production. The edit of an actuality program will use the technology of post-production in the same way, but its methodology is somewhat different because it has a different way of working with its script.

The shooting script

Ideally, a documentary or current affairs shoot should have a shooting script to guide it. Unlike a drama script, this is not a prescriptive document. For a one-hour program, it might run for four or five pages. Each page is split into two columns, image on the left side and sound on the right. The script detail indicates the planned structure and sequence order of the intended program, so that shooting can bear that intention in mind. The script will include a general description of sequences to be shot, and indicate their main role in advancing the script's narrative. It will paraphrase expected statements by interviewees that might be used to drive the narrative, and have indicative grabs of narration. It will indicate where montages, music bridges and other stylistic elements will sit, and what sort of vision will carry them. It will indicate important overlay vision, and where the story will be told with archive and other sourced footage.

The reality of shooting

The shoot will work on the assumption that some sequences will not work out as well as envisaged (or may not even eventuate), some will be stronger than expected, and some material that will have an important role in the program will not have been apparent until during the shoot. The shoot must therefore have an in-built flexibility that recognises that the program that is put together in editing will have evolved from the one the production set out to shoot, and provides the wherewithal to do this. With the shooting script as a starting point, and as material available on the day becomes apparent, the director (who may often be the producer as well) can adjust the planned program in their mind to accommodate looming changes in the way the story will be told. They can shoot for them to be incorporated into the story.

The editing script

In preparation for post-production, the director reviews footage that has been shot and rewrites the shooting script as an editing script, still in the two-column format. Tape numbers and timecodes will indicate specific shots or groups of shots to be used. The description of sequences will derive from material actually available, instead of material hoped to be shot. Any interviews should be transcribed, so that sections can be marked up on a paper copy. Grabs of talking head ('sync' interview) and voice-over will be indicated in the 'Sound' column of the editing script, with opening and closing words and timecodes. Vision overlay will be specified, as will any archive or file sources of footage. Places where music is to be used will be indicated, either as a specific work or, more commonly, with some note about the musical style, for the editor to make a choice or to guide a commissioned composer. Any graphic or animation sequences that have become apparent will appear in the editing script. A draft narration will be written and inserted in the places it seems necessary. All the material that will be sourced to put together the program in editing will be indicated in some way, while allowing the editor the flexibility to mould the story from that material for the director's approval (in the first instance).

Building towards the finished program

The editor will assemble the program according to the script, then the director and editor will view that and restructure it, if needed, generally restructuring more than once. When the structure is right, the editor moves on to the rough-cut stage, firming, moulding and pacing the assembled structure. If director and producer are different people, the producer may have discussed the scripts with the director, but it's often advisable for them to stay away from the early stages of editing. When it is close to taking shape they can view it with a fresh eye, an option that is no longer available to either director or editor. For a program with a producer–director, the executive producer could take on this role of providing a review of editing progress. Other parties with an editorial interest, such as production executives or broadcasters, may also view the program at rough-cut stage. When all interests are happy with the near-finished program, it can be fine-cut – the final finesses and flourishes of the picture edit stage – and presented to those who will authorise it as a program for lock-off. It is then ready to go to online editing and into audio post-production.

23.12   Delivery materials

Tape delivery requirements

A licence agreement with a broadcaster will specify a number of materials to be delivered as part of that contract. First and foremost, of course, will be a broadcaster master copy of the program. The contract will stipulate the format for delivery of the program, including aspect ratio and technical specifications. There will often be a requirement for at least two VHS copies of the program for preview screening. If the contract includes a distribution agreement, the producer will also be required to deliver textless backgrounds for supers and titles, or a textless master, as well as an M&E soundtrack mix. Delivery of the program on DVD may be required as well.

Paperwork requirements

There will also be paperwork and publicity delivery requirements. Paperwork includes a post-production script (professionally typed and laid out to industry format), a full list of credits for cast and crew for each episode, and completed music cue sheets for reporting to the Australasian Performing Rights Association (APRA, see Chapter 25). There will be a requirement for rights and clearances documentation for music, archival and stock footage, and any other copyright material used in the program. The broadcaster may require a solicitor's written opinion confirming that all rights in the contract have been acquired, including chain of title, and that the program will not give rise to any legal action, in particular in defamation, contempt or copyright.

Publicity materials required

Although the broadcaster will almost certainly want to take charge of publicity for its broadcast of the program, it will require from the production a range of materials in order to do this. These might include:
- one-line, one-paragraph and one-page synopses
- technical information, such as gauge, format and duration
- a director's (or producer's) statement
- biographies of key production personnel
- production anecdotes.

   The production would also be required to provide a number of publicity stills in JPEG and/or TIFF formats, each accompanied by a caption and a short description (see Chapter 11).

After delivery

Delivery of the required materials brings to a conclusion the production process that began in Chapter 5 with the concept. It doesn't, however, bring to an end the producer's role in the project. Decisions must be made about which production materials and paperwork need to be archived, and particularly what will need to be accessed in the process of back-end exploitation of the program and its production materials. The marketing of programs was outlined in Chapter 11. This process will continue until the producer and the program's distributors run out of ideas for exploiting the program. While sales are being made, there will be requirements to make further copies of the program, or perhaps to version it to the requirements of a licensing broadcaster. There may have been decisions made in the development phase to import program content to a number of other delivery platforms, as discussed in Chapter 10, or such a decision may have been made as a marketing option after the production is finished. This process also can continue long after delivery of the program to its initial broadcaster. The project never has a finishing point if it has gone into production. Its activities get more and more infrequent, until to all intents and purposes it is effectively completed.

Sources and further reading

General reading

Browne, Steven E. 2002, *Video Editing: A Postproduction Primer*, 4th edn, Focal Press, Oxford.

Gillezeau, Marcus 2004, *Hands On*, Currency Press, Sydney, Chapter 6.

Zettl, Herbert 2006, *Television Production Handbook*, 9th edn, Thomson Wadsworth, Belmont, CA, chapters 13, 14.

Specific reading

Fairservice, Don 2001, *Film Editing*: *History, Theory and Practice*, Manchester University Press, Manchester.
Patmore, Chris 2003, *The Complete Animation Course: the Principles, Practice and Techniques of Successful Animation*, Thames & Hudson, London.

Some internet references

Caldwell, John Thornton, 'Video editing', The Museum of Broadcast Communications, available online at <www.museum.tv/archives>.

Part D

A nod to the gatekeepers: the environment of television

Chapter 24

Building the television schedule

Programs are acquired by a broadcaster to be placed somewhere in their transmission schedule. This means that the person within the network who commissions a program does so, in effect, for an internal client, namely the person who schedules the broadcaster's programs. This person is often called the network programmer, and is usually one of the executives consulted in a broadcaster's commissioning process. They might even be the person who ultimately says 'yes' or 'no' to a proposed program purchase. If a network programmer is a key person in program commissioning, it's useful for producers submitting a program proposal to have an understanding of the principles that drive television scheduling, so they can have some insight into the programs a particular network might be looking for.

Every network tries to maximise the audience for each program it has commissioned, whether it is a commercial or public broadcaster, whether its programs are to attract advertisers or to fulfil a public charter. This doesn't mean that the network's objective is necessarily to attract the largest possible audience across the board, although in a broad sense that's the object of commercial television. Public television has other reasons for commissioning programs, but having identified the sorts of programs that fit with network policy, the preference is for a larger rather than smaller audience for that program, although not by abandoning the reasons for choosing it in the first place. A program chosen for the loftiest reasons will serve no useful purpose for a network if no-one watches it. Pay television, as noted in Chapter 3, is in the business of attracting subscribers rather than viewers. Because subscribers have already paid for a schedule they might or might not watch, a pay television channel doesn't in theory need viewers. However, subscribers who find nothing of interest to watch on a channel are unlikely to renew their subscription to it. Pay television, like FTA television, prefers a larger to a smaller audience and, as advertising grows as a significant part of its business plan, this will be increasingly so.

Scheduling is about attracting and retaining audience for the programs the channel has chosen to broadcast. This chapter reviews the strategies used in television scheduling to achieve this, and the art of laying out a transmission master plan. It will focus primarily on the scheduling process for FTA television because its determining factors are more established, but the same principles are at play in scheduling a pay television channel. The different environment of pay television means that the principles will be applied for different outcomes.

24.1 Schedule layout

Programmer and scheduler

There are two principal roles involved in scheduling a channel's programs for transmission. The network programmer is the more senior and draws up a layout for the weekly pattern of the channel's schedule – a master plan as a framework into which specific programs can be slotted. Supplementing this, the role of the television scheduler is to place programs from the network's inventory into those slots, consistent with the layout pattern. The programmer's master plan is determined by weighing up the various influences determining who will or could be watching television at any particular time. Research can assist with this, but much of it is programmer intuition and experience. The scheduler fills the layout's spaces with what is available to the network in the short term, and what can be commissioned in the longer term.

Familiarity and habit

A schedule layout has a blueprint for each day of the week, broken into half-hour blocks, some of which are combined for program slots of one hour or more. The broad objective is to juggle the various genres into a user-friendly format. A good outcome is a layout that is so comprehensible and familiar that viewers will know where they can expect to find a program that interests them. Figure 24.1 shows how the schedule master plan is laid out, in this case for prime time on ABC. It is assumed that people won't necessarily scrutinise a TV guide each day to see what they might watch, but will watch at certain times of the week out of habit and because they know what type of program will be there generally. In the case of a long-running favourite program, they will know specifically what program will be there, and watching it will be a regular habit which the programmer will try to work with to the network's advantage. Where there's no particular logic to the placement of a program in the schedule, viewers may spot it in the guide, but the broadcast time won't be strongly imprinted. There is a strong possibility that they will only realise later that the program they had earmarked to watch has come and gone.

The main news bulletin

In building a weekly pattern for the schedule, most programmers will start with the daily news programs as the cornerstone of the layout. A network position on

Time	Monday	Tuesday	Wednesday	Thursday	Friday	Saturday	Sunday
6.00 pm	**CHILDREN'S** **DOCO SERIES (DOCUSOAP)**	**CHILDREN'S** **FACTUAL**	**CHILDREN'S** **FACTUAL**	**CHILDREN'S** **FACTUAL**	**CHILDREN'S** **FACTUAL** Message Stick	**SPORT** **ENTERTAINM'T** Head 2 Head	**ARTS** **ENTERTAINM'T** At The Movies (rpt)
6.30	**FACTUAL** Talking Heads	**FACTUAL**	**FACTUAL (FOOD)**	**FACTUAL**	**FACTUAL** Can We Help?	**FACTUAL** Gardening Australia	**ENTERTAINM'T** The Einstein Factor
7.00	**NEWS**	**NEWS**	**NEWS**	**NEWS**	**NEWS**	**NEWS**	**NEWS**
7.30	**C. AFFAIRS** 7.30 Report	**C. AFFAIRS** 7.30 Report	**C. AFFAIRS** 7.30 Report	**C. AFFAIRS** 7.30 Report	**C. AFFAIRS** Stateline	**DRAMA**	**DOCO**
8.00	**C. AFFAIRS** Australian Story	**DOCO SERIES**	**ENTERTAINM'T** The New Inventors	**FACTUAL (SCIENCE)** Catalyst	**ENTERTAINM'T** Collectors		
8.30	**C. AFFAIRS** Four Corners	**DRAMA** The Bill	**ENTERTAINM'T** Spicks & Specks	**DRAMA** The West Wing	**DRAMA**	**DRAMA** The Bill	**DRAMA**
9.00	Media Watch	**C. AFFAIRS**	**COMEDY** Absolute Power				
9.30	**ENTERTAINM'T** Enough Rope	Foreign Correspondent	**COMEDY** The Glass House		**COMEDY** The Chasers' War on Everyth.	**DRAMA**	**SPECIAL**
10.00		**ARTS/MUSIC**	**ENTERTAINM'T** At The Movies	**COMEDY** Kath & Kim (rpt)	**COMEDY**		
10.30	**C. AFFAIRS** Lateline	**C. AFFAIRS** Lateline	**C. AFFAIRS** Lateline	**C. AFFAIRS** Lateline	**C. AFFAIRS** Lateline	**DRAMA**	**FACTUAL (RELIGIOUS)** Compass
11.00							

Figure 24.1: Prime time television schedule layout for the ABC (2006).

where to place its nightly news will have been established well before a new lay-out is devised. This would be moved only if there was some compelling reason to do so, such as poor performance which is believed to be the result of sched-ule placement rather than journalistic and production shortcomings in the pro-gram. However, the scheduling of other broadcasters' news is also a factor in determining where each channel will place its main news bulletin. This intro-duces another factor that might cause a move in the time of a daily newscast: a response to another channel moving its news bulletin. For a long time, the main news bulletins on Australian FTA television started at either 6.30 pm or 7 pm. In the 1980s, news on Seven and Nine was moved earlier to 6 pm, joining the Ten network, which had started up scheduling its main newscast at that time. In 1991, Ten subsequently moved earlier to 5 pm, but the other commercial sta-tions remained where they were. ABC's news has always been at 7 pm, so SBS (it was Channel 0/28 then) scheduled its internationally oriented news in the space between commercial television and the ABC. The main news bulletin has always been a half-hour program on all networks except Ten, apart from the ABC's ill-fated attempt to combine nightly news and current affairs as *The National* in 1985.

Scheduling 'fixtures'

With scheduling of the evening news settled from the outset, a programmer will build around that, beginning with the 'fixtures'. If the network intends to have a nightly current affairs program, it will follow the news as a matter of habit, or because that's where viewers will expect to find it. It would be a bold move to put it somewhere else. The other likely 'fixture' is a long-established and success-ful program. Again, it would be a bold move to put it somewhere in the sched-ule other than where the viewer expects to find it. Occasionally, these programs will be moved to try to deliver audiences to other parts of the channel's sched-ule, but that is a risky venture. Succeed with that and everyone will be saying that the programmer is a genius (until they get something wrong), but if it fails the network is likely to get a new programmer. Usually the fixtures go where everyone would be expecting them to go, and the programmer then fills in the spaces.

Classification zones

Filling out the balance of the schedule is built on the desire to create a poten-tial for audience flow, dealing with prime time and working around classification restrictions. As discussed in detail in Chapter 25, programs are classified accord-ing to their suitability for different audiences, particularly children. Commercial and public broadcasters are governed by classification zones restricting the hours in which certain classifications can be shown. Figure 25.1 shows the zones for FTA broadcasters in Australia. Scheduling in the 6–8.30 am and 4–7 pm periods is limited to programs suitable for general viewing. Apart from a period in the middle of the day, programs for mature audiences cannot be scheduled before 8.30 pm. These are the parameters in which FTA programmers operate. Although pay television uses the same classification guidelines, it is not restricted in the times it can screen programs.

The schedule day

Thus, the schedule day can be broken down to pre-news, where the focus is usually on game shows and children's programs, prime time, and late evening. Late evening doesn't have classification issues and, because audiences are smaller, it is not a time when advertisers exert much influence (see next section). It is a place to schedule movies, programs that have limited value but were bought in a package that included other desired programs, and programs for a niche audience. Some programs in this last group have generated strong cult followings: *The Sopranos*, *Six Feet Under*, *Arrested Development*, and *Scrubs*, for example. They are often made for pay television, without commercial breaks, so are more suited to the time when advertiser interest is lower. The ABC and SBS will also schedule marginal or special interest programs at this time to appeal to niche audiences or to fulfil charter obligations.

Prime time

Prime time, the period of largest audience, is generally considered to start with the channel's main news bulletin and continue through to about 10 pm. The 8.30 pm opening of the schedule for broader classification is regarded as the start of more mature evening programming, including harder-edged drama. This is the period of largest audiences and of greatest advertiser interest. The most popular programs are scheduled here, even on a non-commercial channel. Friday and Saturday prime time have the prized slots, as these are usually the most watched times of the week. Prime time requires a disciplined schedule, where everything is geared to half-hour junctions. Programs must be multiples of a half-hour, or an interstitial program (short filler) will need to be found to take the schedule through to the half hour. What the networks want in practice is multiples of a 'commercial half hour' , between twenty-two and twenty-six minutes duration (and between forty-four and fifty-two minutes for the commercial hour), allowing time to schedule advertisements and program promotions before the half-hour junction. Even the ABC, without formal advertising, wants non-program time within the hour to promote its programs and merchandising.

Audience flow

In recent times, despite the fixation in the schedule with half-hour breaks, commercial channels habitually hold the finish of their most successful programs over the half hour break. This strategy is to hold the large audience for a popular program until it is too late to switch to another channel, where a program has already started. The hope is that the audience will then stay with the channel it is on. The creation of audience flow – the delivery of audience from one program through to the next, and preferably to those that follow later – is a key objective of the television programmer. The art works around barriers to flow such as regulatory restrictions, and tries to work observed viewer behaviour to the network's advantage.

Genre scheduling

A prime-time schedule might feature a succession of programs that target a similar audience. In theory, the audience will stay from one program to the next. This is the thinking behind ABC's Monday night line-up, where *Australian Story* is followed by *Four Corners*, and then through *Media Watch* to *Enough Rope*, all information-based, with the last having an element of entertainment as well. Care needs to be taken that successive programs aren't too similar, particularly with dramas, so the audience doesn't sense a sameness in the night's line-up. With the ABC example, are *Australian Story* and *Four Corners* too much current affairs, or is the more personal and intimate *Australian Story* sufficiently differentiated from the harder-hitting *Four Corners* in viewers' minds? These are the types of issues a programmer weighs up. Another tactic is scheduling genre nights. Networks will often schedule a well-promoted comedy night on a particular day. Again, there should be different types of comedy to avoid a viewer perception of repetition.

24.2   Scheduling influences

Network identity and charter responsibility

A starting point in shaping the schedule framework is network policy and station identity. Each network decides on (and from time to time, evolves) an image or brand identity that it will project to the viewing public. It will naturally seek to program its output in a manner that is consistent with its network identity. Nine has long built its schedule around sport, current affairs and network personalities – very male skewed. Much of the advertising it attracts reflects this. Seven has had a less clear identity, and may have paid a price for that in the past. The Ten network, on the other hand, took a bold step in the 1990s when new owners, CanWest, mandated as policy that the network would target the under-45 demographic (a term derived from 'demography', the study of human populations). Over a long career, Bob Donoghue has been programmer for Ten, ABC, Screentime and Ovation. 'At that time,' he says, 'it was unthinkable that a free-to-air network would forget about overall ratings and concentrate on a particular demographic.' It was a masterstroke, enabling Ten to be the most profitable of the networks without having the largest total numbers of viewers.

Public broadcaster charters

The two public broadcasters have their own network identities, forged in part out of their statutory responsibilities. They both have charters to guide their broad programming policies. The ABC and SBS have charter obligations to 'comprehensive' programming, and SBS also has a responsibility to reflect the cultural diversity of the Australian community. There are obligations on both to entertain and inform. They look to service audiences that are significant, but not in such numbers that would be attractive to commercial television. They will program in science and the arts, and provide for interests in rural, Indigenous and religious matters. Slots for these specialist areas are part of the ABC's schedule master plan and, to a somewhat narrowed degree, SBS's as well. Both broadcasters will therefore be in the business of acquiring, by commissioning or purchase, program material to schedule in slots identified for this material.

Audience

Implicit in the pursuit of audience flow is the question of who is watching and what are they watching. Audience research provides many of the answers. Its methodology is dealt with in the next section. A programmer wants to know, not so much how many people were watching each program, but how these audiences break down by gender, age, socioeconomic group, education, size of household, and any other demographic detail of assortive viewing (i.e. viewing by groups of like individuals). Research can show how much of one program's audience continued to watch the next program, confirming the expectation of audience flow, or it will show how many switched off at the end of a program, refuting the expectation. Demographic information indicates which groups prefer which programs, and what times of the day they favour.

Targeted demographics

Programmers set out to maximise their audience. They put popular genres where the audiences are naturally highest, and demographically targeted programs at times that those audiences prefer. If there is a demographic that is targeted as a network priority, programs will be commissioned or bought to appeal to that audience. They will be scheduled with its known viewing habits in mind. The Ten network's courting of the under-forty-five demographic over the years has been remarkably successful, and its purchasing and scheduling reflects this. Its programming is dominated by entertainment programs, and drama and comedy aimed at the under forty-fives. *The Simpsons* and *Seinfeld* are old stalwarts of the Ten schedule, and more recently they have enjoyed a following with reality programs such as *Big Brother* and *Australian Idol*.

Neglected audience

Audience research might also reveal groups of the potential viewing audience that are poorly served. This can be a network opportunity to pick up a neglected audience. It will program genres that appeal to that audience, especially if there is advertiser interest in them. From time to time, networks may find that their programming is skewed towards, say, male audiences and set out to correct that. Medical dramas and medical reality programs, costume drama and family sagas have been shown to appeal to female viewers. This information might be used by programmers looking to build up that particular demographic.

Advertisers

Thus, we come to another influence on the schedule's structure – advertisers. The network's sales department will have a major input into a commercial television station's schedule. Commercial television is in the business of selling advertising. Television programs are the means of attracting them, so programs that draw the audiences that advertisers are looking for are of particular interest. A small audience of niche consumers is more valuable than a large audience of paupers. In general, broadcaster and advertiser are both looking to maximise the audience, so there is a comfortable synergy there. However, advertisers have particular consumers in their sights, so broadcasters will focus their programming on those groups. This is behind Ten's commercial success, in spite of its third ranking in total viewing numbers.

Scheduling against competitors

Another consideration for any channel is what its competitors have scheduled and where. Commercial television's program schedule will often be a response to what the other channels are doing, or what they think the others will do. It's a cat-and-mouse game as each channel wants to keeps its intentions hidden while trying to second-guess its competitors. There is an element of this rivalry between the ABC and SBS as well, even if the public interest is best served by them programming to complement each other. Sometimes television networks will risk public irritation by scheduling like against like. When it comes to considering the programs that are already known to be performing well, the competitive tactical options are problematic. Does a network schedule to take on a rival's 'big guns', especially if it can be detected that a popular show may have peaked? Or does it schedule a program with low audience expectation, but with some public kudos? The ABC delayed the start of its East Timor drama, *Answered By Fire*, to avoid clashing with *The Great Escape*, the Nine special about rescued Tasmanian miners. It was expected to draw a huge audience to the exclusion of other channels – and it did.

Program options

The other influence is what is available and how much money there is to obtain it. Networks are quite passive in their relationships with the production industry. They wait to see what's on offer more often than they actively generate program ideas. Like the country grocer waiting to see who comes into the shop, they will wait for proposals to come to them, preferably from production houses with a solid track record. When they have heard the sales pitch, they will decide whether to commit or not. Even safer is to wait for the program to be made with someone else's money and then consider it for acquisition, although in Australia this is more likely to result in acquiring imported rather than local product.

Purchasing on program potential

It is hard to get a production up in this country without local broadcaster attachment. How much of what types of program a network is able to purchase depends on the network's financial means, especially the public broadcasters with the majority of their funding from the annual federal appropriation. A commercial broadcaster can offset a program's cost with an estimate of advertiser revenue it will draw, but it will not find out until after it has bought the program whether this was an astute purchase. The tighter the funding environment, the greater the proportion of overseas programs purchased, with their double advantage of generally lower price and pretesting of performance in other markets.

Programming from success

Past performance influences a current schedule. A network and its programmer will be constantly monitoring and evaluating the performance of its existing programs, as reflected in the audience figures. By extension, they are also looking at the performance of genres, and will adjust the presence of both genres and specific programs in the schedule accordingly. Ten increased its scheduling of *The Simpsons* with its continuing large following, and was prepared to schedule the range of programs in the *Big Brother* franchise to near saturation point, a factor in Endemol Southern Star licensing the program to it. This is not unique to the Ten network, even though they might be more aggressive in its pursuit than others. Nine has extended the *CSI* brand considerably following its ratings success, and the ABC has done similarly with *The Bill*. When you're on to a good thing, it seems, the programming response is not to stick to it, but to flood it!

Struggling programs

On the other hand, a program that is struggling to find its audience often produces a scheduling panic. Commercial television, particularly, is littered with the corpses of programs that were axed within a few weeks because they weren't performing up to expectations. Sometimes slow starters will be moved to a different, less favourable timeslot, although this might do no more than ensure their demise. A program that is struggling in prime time won't do better out of prime time, but then low audience out of prime time doesn't worry network executives so much. Often the move is only to see out the contract with the program's producers. Occasionally, a slow starter builds its audience over time for long-term success. *Sixty Minutes* and *Neighbours* are notable examples, although the latter had to switch networks to achieve it. The question for the network is: how long can it pour money into a struggling program in the hope that it will come good? The answer for most is: not very long at all.

24.3   Audience research

Gathering audience data

The main vehicle of measuring program performance, particularly in the commercial sector, is audience research. Audience size and demographic breakdown is estimated from viewing statistics of a sample, calculated as a cross-section of the community, and extrapolated to the community as a whole. OzTAM, owned by Seven, Nine and Ten, gathers television ratings data for all metropolitan FTA and pay television channels in Australia. A 'people meter' records detail of television activity in selected homes, minute by minute, and people in the house register their television usage with a remote control. Every night the data is downloaded automatically by modem to OzTAM, who package a variety of statistical reports for their subscribers.

Ratings

The principal figure is the rating, which is the estimated audience tuned to a particular station at a particular time. It may be calculated with households (as HUTs, households using television) or people (as PUTs, people using television) and expressed in thousands, or as a percentage (called a rating point) of all households or people, whether a television set is in use or not. A program that appeals to a whole family or household is likely to have a higher HUT than PUT. A program that is more specialised in its appeal would be expected to have a higher PUT. Ratings points can provide a measure of the overall popularity of a program, and ratings averaged over an evening is a measure of the performance of a station for that evening. A target audience rating point (TARP) is similar to a rating but applies to a specific demographic, such as 'women 18+', and is expressed as a percentage of total people in that group.

Share and reach

These are the figures that are of prime interest in audience analysis. The other two statistics that are often of interest to broadcasters are share and reach. Share is the audience for a specified program, and is expressed as a percentage of the total number of people watching television at that time. It is the share each station has of television sets turned on. Reach is the number or percentage of people who have seen a specified amount (usually five minutes) of a program or time band. It's a statistic of limited use, but is attractive to broadcasters because it will be higher than ratings, but it will include people who didn't like a program and switched off after five minutes.

What do audience figures tell us?

Audience flow can be measured from the tracking of audience figures by the minute, and its breakdown by groups. When a popular show finishes over the half-hour junction, a jump in audience numbers can often be seen on other channels the minute that show finished. But audience figures don't necessarily measure the viewers' assessment of a program. People that tune into a one-off program, or the first episode of a series, don't have an opinion of the program because they haven't yet seen it. Numbers at this stage are a measure of the audience expectation of a program, as generated by its publicity. Audience figures for subsequent episodes of a series will be a measure of viewer opinion of the series, although they would still not reflect an opinion of the episode they are watching. Audience drift away from a program while it is broadcast is the only statistical measure of viewer opinion of it. If audience numbers fall off more than the usual low rate of attrition, it is reasonable to conclude that the program has failed to meet expectations.

Focus groups

Audience data is quantitative research. There is an option of qualitative research with focus groups, with freewheeling discussions of a program after a private screening to representative groups. This will produce individual insights and opinions, but broadcasters are wary at present about whether they reflect broad views. An attempt has been made to quantify this information with 'Q scores', but opinions vary on whether this is pseudo-science, and whether the environment of focus groups is too artificial to represent the opinions that viewers will come to in their homes. Focus groups are, however, often used to assess pilot programs, since they are about the only means of getting some independent audience response at that stage.

24.4   Commissioning for the schedule

Regardless of what audience research is actually measuring, commercial broadcasters take audience figures seriously because advertisers take them seriously. So do the public broadcasters for their own purposes. As long as this remains the case, audience research will continue to be a significant influence on television scheduling. A broadcaster will commission programs bearing in mind its schedule layout, and particularly where it is short of material to fill certain timeslots. In Chapter 5, it was suggested that examination of a channel's schedule in the TV guide is a good way to get an insight into that network's programming interests and priorities. The schedule informs broadcaster commissioning decisions. An understanding of the factors that influence the design of the schedule and network assessment of program performance allows producers to operate with some knowledge of the market in which their product is engaging. They should also keep in consideration restraints, both legal and regulatory, that might be imposed on the content of programs.

Sources and further reading

Some internet references

(Anon) 2005, 'Pay television in Australia', Get the Picture, Australian Film Commission, available online at <http://www.afc.gov.au/gtp/wptvanalysis.html>, viewed 15 December 2006.

Australian Film Commission, Australian TV ratings, available online at <http://www.afc.gov.au/faqs/aust_tv_ratings/faq_128.aspx> and <http://www.afc.gov.au/industrylinks/distbcast/tv_ratings.aspx>, viewed 20 December 2006.

Nielsen Media Research, available online at <www.nielsenmedia.com.au>, viewed 20 December 2006.

OzTAM, Australian Television Audience Measurement, available online at <www.oztam.com.au>, viewed 20 December 2006.

Peters, Bob 2005, 'Free-to-air television: trends and issues', in Get the Picture, Australian Film Commission, available online at <http://www.afc.gov.au/gtp/wftvanalysis.html>, viewed 15 December 2006.

Peters, Bob 2005, 'Trends in audience share', in Get the Picture, Australian Film Commission, available online at <http://www.afc.gov.au/gtp/wftvratingstrends.html>, viewed 15 December 2006.

Chapter 25

Legal constraints on content

Like all sectors of the contemporary world of business, the television industry is guided and constrained in its activities by regulation and the law. We have already seen the regulation of Australian content in Chapter 3, and the regulation of the employment of children in Chapter 15, and we will see in Chapter 26 the laws and regulations governing the establishment and running of a business, as well as the law's requirement of it regarding employment, taxation and insurance. This chapter examines the ways in which the law restrains some content from being shown on television, either because it belongs to someone else (copyright law), or because it would unjustifiably sully someone's reputation (defamation law), or it would undermine the legal process (law of contempt and sub judice), or it is not fit to be presented to the public (law of offensive material), or it provides misleading information about goods or services (trade practices and consumer law), or it offends any of the other myriad laws and regulations that are part of 'civilised' society. Interestingly, there is little law in Australia to constrain the media imposing on people's privacy, as long as it isn't defamatory at the same time.

25.1 What is copyright?

An early film copyright case

In 1907, the Kalem Company produced a one-reel film version of *Ben Hur* from Lew Wallace's novel. Wallace's publishers sued, as did the producers of a play based on the book. Kalem's defence was that neither publisher nor author suffered damage, and the film was a good advertisement for the book and the play. After four years of wrangling, Kalem settled out of court for US$25 000, a considerable sum in a fledgling industry at that time. It had found out the hard way that permission must be sought from a copyright work's owner(s) before the work can be used, regardless of any benefit the owner might get from that use.

Copyright aspects in a TV program

Copyright law is the law that enables people to control use of their own original created works, and prevent unauthorised copying of them by others. This means that in television production all program content must either belong to its producers, or have permission from its copyright owners, whether domestic or professional, to be used in the program. Thus, home movies and snapshots from someone's family album must be cleared for use in a program, just as much as footage from an archive or from another program. Not only that, but other works incorporated into the program in some way – poetry readings, music, filmed paintings – also have to be cleared with the copyright owners for use in the program. Copyright in works incorporated into a program, whose copyright owners may be its producers and investors, is known as its underlying rights.

The Copyright Act 1968 (Cth)

The source of all copyright law in Australia is a piece of federal legislation, the *Copyright Act 1968*, which is obtainable from the Australian Government Printer or, more conveniently, on the internet from the Australasian Legal Information Institute, a joint operation of the University of NSW and the University of Technology, Sydney (see sources below). Copyright law does not exist in this country outside the Act, and the Act does not determine the law of copyright in any other country. The ultimate arbiters of precisely what the words in the Act mean in law are the Australian courts and, particularly, the High Court of Australia. Copyright is a branch of property law, called intellectual property. It is not necessarily the same as owning a work. An artist who keeps their painting owns both the painting and its copyright, but a person who buys a CD owns the CD only, not copyright in the music on it.

Registration of copyright

Copyright belongs to the author or creator of a work from the moment it is created. There is no need for authors to register their ownership of copyright, and there is nowhere in Australia that can be done anyway. Nor does writing the copyright symbol © on a work establish legal ownership any more than not having the symbol, although it does generally serve notice of who claims to be the copyright owner. This can be useful for someone seeking permission to copy the work. In law, a work without the copyright symbol requires clearance just as much as one with the symbol.

Requirements for copyright

A copyright work must be original and must not be copied from another work. 'Original' in this sense means no more than the product of its creator's own skill and labour. The work doesn't necessarily need to have any artistic merit, or be unique or aesthetically pleasing in any way. It must be created, but need not be creative. It does, however, need to be in some material form, such as on paper, canvas, film, or recording tape or disk. Thus, an original whistled tune or jazz improvisation is not copyright until it is recorded on audiotape, or written down as music notation. If a known tune (recorded elsewhere) is whistled or improvised on, then its composer will have underlying rights in the performance.

No copyright in ideas, opinions or facts

Protection is afforded only to the form in which something is expressed. There is no copyright in ideas, opinions, information or facts. In a 1960 case, *John Fairfax & Sons Ltd v Consolidated Press Ltd* [1960] SR (NSW) 413, the court ruled that the *Daily Telegraph* could not reproduce the style and sequence of birth and death notices in *The Sydney Morning Herald*, but could publish the same information in an altered form. The facts of birth and death were not copyright, but the form in which *The Sydney Morning Herald* presented those facts was. The idea that is the basis of a program is similarly not subject to copyright law. In the landmark Privy Council case, *Green v Broadcasting Corporation of New Zealand* (1988) 2 NZLR 490 (the *Green Case*), the Broadcasting Corporation of New Zealand had broadcast a show that was similar to the UK talent quest, *Opportunity Knocks*, of which Hughie Green was compere. The New Zealand version of the show was also called *Opportunity Knocks* and had catchphrases and a 'clapometer' that had featured in the original. Green's lawyers claimed that the scripts and dramatic format of the NZ show infringed his copyright, but no scripts were produced as evidence, and the court found that nothing was shown 'in which copyright could subsist'. Scripts, as inferred from the evidence, only expressed a general idea or concept for a talent quest, and were not subject to copyright. Although there were features common to the two shows, the court had difficulty isolating them from the rest of a changing show, and still calling it an 'original dramatic work'. A dramatic work, the court said, must have unity to be capable of performance, but features of a 'format' are only accessories to a show.

Implications of the Green Case

There are two important implications of the *Green Case* for television producers. First, the idea embodied in a proposal document is not copyright, only the specific words in the document are; but this would not protect the same idea expressed in different words. There is no point in writing 'copyright' on the document, but in most circumstances it would be protected by the law of confidential information (see section 25.6). There may be some point, therefore, in writing 'confidential' on the document. The second consideration to come out of the *Green Case* is the question that it raises about the validity of 'format rights'. This is dealt with at more length in section 25.5.

Categories of protected works

Protection of copyright is afforded to two groups of created works called, somewhat unimaginatively, 'works' and 'subject matter other than works'. Works are the traditional material of copyright protection, where copyright initially belongs to the author. The five categories of works that have copyright are:
1. literary works, printed or in writing, and including tables and lists, and computer programs
2. dramatic works, including film scripts, and dance or mime (recorded or notated)
3. musical works, when recorded or notated
4. artistic works, such as paintings, sculpture, photographs or craft works
5. adaptations and arrangements of literary, dramatic and musical works.

Subject matter other than works is a new group, largely derived from twentieth century technological developments. Here, the copyright owner is initially the producer or manufacturer. The four categories are:
1. films, including videotape recordings and soundtracks
2. sound recordings
3. television and radio broadcasts in the form of radio waves, but not when transmitted through cable or optical fibre – in this instance, no material form is required, but they must be broadcast to the public
4. published editions.

Copyright law regards recorded television programs (which it calls 'films' regardless of the medium on which they are recorded) and television programs in transmission separately, enabling live television transmission to be protected even if it is not in a material form. Copyright in television programs exists independently of any underlying rights there might be within the program. Where news footage has been incorporated into a program, the producer has copyright in the completed program, and the news agency retains underlying rights in that particular footage. A similar relationship exists, for example, in a published edition of artworks, where the publisher has copyright in the edition, and the artist has underlying rights in the artwork.

Performance rights

Although not strictly copyright, the Act provides protection against the unauthorised use of someone's performance of a dramatic or musical work, a reading or recitation of a literary work, dance, a circus or variety act, or a folkloric act. Presentation of news, documentary, education or sporting programs, teaching, or playing sport are not performances under the Act, nor are people playing themselves in an actuality program, or being interviewed. Where performers are covered by the Act, permission must be obtained from them to:
• make an audio or film recording of the performance
• broadcast or re-broadcast the live performance
• distribute and use the recording.

Once permission has been given, the performer has no further rights to the recording, and cannot prevent its use unless there was an express limitation made at the time, or there are contract or award restrictions. An exception is the use of the recording as a soundtrack for a film or television program, for which the performers' permission is required. As a result of the Australia–US Free Trade Agreement, the Act now stipulates that the maker of a sound recording after 1 January 2005 is the record company or producer, and the performer(s), who have an equal share of rights in the recording. This does not apply, however, to film or video recordings. A performer may have copyright in an underlying right of the performance, such as its composition, and these rights will be exercised in the usual manner.

25.2   Rights of copyright owners

Ownership of copyright

The author or creator of a work is the person who turns it into a tangible form, so this will be a ghost writer rather than the source of the information, a subeditor of a rewritten story rather than the journalist, and a translator rather than the original author, although the others may have underlying rights. Once a work is in a material form, copyright is automatic and the creator of the work is generally the copyright owner. However, the Act specifies circumstances that will create exceptions to this rule of thumb, such as:

- a film or television production, which is owned by the person arranging the production, usually the producer or production company
- where the work is created in the course of employment (here the employer is the copyright owner), but not if created by a contractor, unless copyright is assigned in the contract
- where a film or television production has an investor contracted as a first copyright owner
- a broadcast signal, where the broadcaster is the owner
- where rights have been assigned or licensed to a publisher or agent, as is often the case in music composition, or
- records, tapes or disks, where the record manufacturer is the copyright owner if it owns the master recording, although a composer or their agent may own underlying rights in musical works on the record, and performers may own rights in the performance.

What the copyright owner can do

The copyright owners of a work have the right to make copies of the work, publish the work, broadcast the work or transmit it to subscribers of a diffusion service (e.g. cable/pay television), and to perform the work in public. Others cannot do any of these things without permission of the copyright owner. Any use of material in a production, with a few exceptions that are noted in the next section, must be cleared with the copyright owner before the program is delivered to a broadcaster. The clearance will be a written agreement specifying the rights that have been granted for use of that material in the program. In most instances, the clearance will require payment of a licence fee. Licence is one of two ways the owner can deal in their copyright, the other being assignment.

Licence of rights

Licence allows others to exercise some of the owner's rights in the work listed above, but this does not pass copyright ownership to the licensee. The rights in the licence are specified in the licence agreement. With a television program this is typically the territory (i.e. country) or territories in which the licensee may broadcast the program, the media on which it may be shown (e.g. FTA, pay television, online), the duration of the licence, and the number of broadcasts allowed within that time (e.g. three runs over five years). A licence may be exclusive, in which no other party can be licensed to exercise any of the rights in the exclusive licence, or it may be non-exclusive, where others can also acquire a licence (also non-exclusive) for the same rights. The non-exclusive licence would be expected to have a significantly lower fee. Most library footage is licensed non-exclusively. An exclusive licensee can take legal action for breach of copyright against anyone except the copyright owner. For any program they produce, television producers could be both a licensee (of footage owned by others that is included in the program) and a licensor (of the program to a broadcaster).

Assignment of rights

A copyright owner can also assign their rights in the work, either partly, where some rights are retained by the owner, or fully, where none are. This is, in effect, a sale of the copyright to the assignee. The new owner can take legal action for breach of copyright against anyone, including the former owner. Assignment or exclusive licence must be in writing and, since it is contracted, cannot be terminated at will. A non-exclusive licence need not be in writing. It can be oral, or implied from the conduct of the parties. This licence can be withdrawn by the licensee under certain circumstances.

Unequal bargaining power

Producers should tread carefully in getting material from people with no experience of business negotiation, and ensure that they do not appear to have been coerced into assigning or licensing their material to the program. Courts may negate the agreement if there was unequal bargaining power between the parties, and the terms of the agreement are harsh or unfair. Gilbert O'Sullivan was a postal clerk and part-time songwriter who assigned copyright in all his songs to an agent for five years, with no independent legal advice before signing the contract. *O'Sullivan v Management Agency & Music* (1984) 2 WLR 448 held the contract to be void through unfair restraint of trade, obtained by undue influence through MAM's exercise of its superior bargaining power.

Duration of copyright in works

Real and personal property remains the property of the owner in perpetuity until they dispose of it, but ownership of intellectual property has a finite lifetime. Protection of copyright in literary, dramatic, musical or artistic works generally lasts for seventy years after the end of the year in which the author dies, if the work is published, performed or broadcast. Unpublished literary, dramatic or musical works will remain protected in perpetuity or until they are published, in which case they are protected for the next seventy years. Where there is joint authorship, protection lasts until seventy years after the death of the last surviving author. Photographs are protected for seventy years after they were taken (if that was before 1969) or after they were first published (if they were taken after 1969).

Duration of copyright in subject matter other than works

A work is published when copies are offered to the public by sale or otherwise, but performance, exhibition or screening is not publication. Copyright protection of sound recordings, film and broadcasts generally lasts until seventy years after first publication. Films are not protected in Australia at all if they were made before 1969, although underlying rights (such as music or script) in the film might still be protected. Films are protected for seventy years after first publication, if made after 1969, and protected in perpetuity if unpublished (i.e. did not get released). Broadcasts are not protected if they were made before 1969, even if they are re-broadcast, but are protected for fifty years after first broadcast if that was after 1969.

Duration of protection of performance rights

The protection of performance rights has a different activating date because the legislation was enacted at a later date. Performances after 1989 are protected for twenty years after the performance, except for sound recordings of a performance, where the protection continues for fifty years after the performance.

Public domain

When works pass out of copyright, they come into the public domain and may be used freely. There is an obvious budgetary attraction to producers for material that is in the public domain, but care should be taken that all rights are public domain, and not just the obvious ones. As already noted, films that are out of copyright might have components whose underlying rights are still protected. Editions and adaptations will create a new copyright in that version of the work, but if the unadapted version was in the public domain, it remains so and is available to be used freely, even if the adapted version is not.

25.3   Infringement of copyright

What constitutes copying

Copyright in a work is infringed by any use of the work without permission of the copyright owner. Liability will be with the person using the work, anyone instructing or allowing use of the work, or anyone dealing in an illegal copy of the work. In the context of television production, this could include the person who makes the copy, the production company that instructed the copy to be made, or the network that broadcast a program with the infringing material. It is not necessary for the whole work to be copied, only a substantial part, and generally enough to be recognisable. The copied parts must themselves be an original part of the plaintiff's work, and not sourced from elsewhere.

In *Warwick Films v Eisinger* (1969) 1 Ch 593, there was held to be no infringement in copying extracts from transcriptions of Oscar Wilde's trial from another book. The transcriptions were out of copyright, and none of the original author's editing or commentary appeared in the later book. Proof of copying usually comes down to the degree of similarity between works, and whether the copying was conscious or unconscious. In *Harmon Pictures NV v Osborne* (1967) 1 WLR 723, a film script about the Charge of the Light Brigade was held to infringe copyright through similarities of detail and choice of incidents, even though it was an historical account. In *Francis Day & Hunter Ltd v Bron* [1963] Ch 587, the composer of a 1959 song persuaded the court that he did not consciously copy a 1926 song despite considerable similarity between the two songs.

Exemptions

The Act allows some uses of copyright works without permission to be exempt from action for infringement. Copying for bona fide educational institutions is permitted. Filming public sculptures and works of artistic craftsmanship in public places is not an infringement of any copyright, nor is filming of a building or a model of a building. A public reading or recitation of a literary or dramatic work is not an infringement of its copyright, nor is the reading on a television broadcast, if sufficient acknowledgement of the work is made. But the most common exemption is when a work is copied for fair dealing. This covers research or study, criticism or review, and reporting the news. Use of the work must be directly associated with the news item, and not to illustrate a story. Similarly, a clip from a film must be used in a review of that film, not in a program about the themes of the film. A clip from the film *Once Were Warriors*, for instance, could be used in a review of that film, but not in a documentary about domestic violence without permission of the copyright owner.

Incidental use of artistic works in a program

The other exemption is that copyright of an artistic work is not infringed if its use is 'only incidental' to a film. We don't know what incidental means in the Act because it has never been tested in court, at least not in this country, although it has been interpreted very conservatively by an English court. Some media lawyers will advise extreme caution in this and say that if the work is recognisable it should be cleared. The wording in section 67 of the Act is: 'only incidental to the principal matters represented in the film or broadcast'. It would seem that the artistic work would have to be featured in the shot in which it appears in order to risk infringement. If it is seen in the background, no matter how recognisably, it is incidental as long as there isn't a reference to it and the camera hasn't singled it out. However, producers will have to make their own judgement. It should be noted that the Act applies this exemption to artistic works only. There is no equivalent exemption for musical works.

Penalties for infringement

The legal remedies awarded for infringement are compensation through damages, or an account of profits. Damages are assessed as loss of value of the copyright by its infringement; in other words, an estimate of sales lost, or a reasonable licence fee. In account of profits, the infringer pays the copyright owner the amount of all gains made from the breach, proportionally if the infringement was incorporated into a larger work. The court may award additional damages for flagrant breach, such as when the infringer was put on notice of a potential breach. The court may also impose an injunction to restrain broadcast of a program that would infringe someone's copyright. An interim injunction might be placed on the broadcast until a hearing can take place to determine whether permanent restraint is justified. The courts will balance the case for an injunction against the public interest in free speech. The founder of the Scientology movement, L. Ron Hubbard, sought to restrain publication of a book criticising the church with selections from Hubbard's writings. In *Hubbard v Vosper* [1972] 2 WLR 389, Lord Denning was unwilling to grant the injunction, as exposure of quack scientific beliefs would be in the public interest.

25.4   Copyright collecting societies

Agents for copyright owners

Copyright collecting societies collect licence fees for the use of works when licensing individually is impractical, and distribute the fees to their copyright owner members. The societies act as agents for copyright owners in negotiating, collecting and distributing royalties, either from individual users of their members' works, or through blanket agreements with organisations such as broadcasters.

Collection of rights for music

Copyright collecting societies for music are the:
*   Australasian Mechanical Copyright Owners Society Ltd (AMCOS) – established by Australian music publishers to collect royalties for most published music where it is dubbed on records (mechanical rights), dubbed on film (synchronisation rights), or kept as a copy after twelve months from broadcast (retention rights); this includes the use of production (mood) music, that is, prerecorded music specifically written and recorded for dubbing into film or television programs
*   Australasian Performing Rights Association Ltd (APRA) – administers public performance of music (composition and lyrics, but not the sound recording) on behalf of authors, composers and publishers; since 1997, APRA and AMCOS have been amalgamated and share the same offices and staff, but they operate as separate companies and manage separate rights

• Phonographic Performance Company of Australia (PPCA) – issues licences on behalf of record companies and Australian recording artists for broadcast of commercial recordings and music videos.

Collection of rights for other works

Copyright collecting societies for other works are the:
• Copyright Agency Ltd (CAL) – collects licence fees for copying of print material by educational institutions, the public, governments and corporations
• Visual Arts Copyright Collecting Society (VI$COPY) – licenses copyright in artistic works, and collects royalties on behalf of its members, including many Aboriginal and Torres Strait Islander artists; this includes where an artistic work has been shown in a film or television program.
• Screenrights – administers statutory licences allowing education institutions and governments to copy material from radio or television, and collects fees on behalf of the rights owners (broadcasters, producers and distributors)
• Australian Screen Directors Authorship Collecting Society (ASDACS) – established by the Australian Screen Directors Association (ASDA) to collect royalty income for film and television directors from 'secondary' use (blank videotapes, re-transmission of broadcasts, and video rental) of rights under legislation in some European countries; Australian copyright law doesn't allow secondary rights to be protected; in Europe, the director is the author and first copyright owner of film and television programs
• Australian Writers' Guild Authorship Collecting Society Ltd (AWGACS) – distributes statutory authorship monies collected by European societies for Australian and NZ scriptwriters of film and television.

25.5   Other aspects of copyright

Moral rights

Moral rights protection has long been a facet of European copyright law. Australian creative workers lobbied for similar rights in Australian legislation, and the Copyright Act was amended in 2000 with three moral rights provisions. The Act now prohibits false attribution of authorship (i.e. claiming to be the author or that someone is the author, when they are not). In such a case, the court can award damages, or an injunction to restrain the false attribution or offering, or showing the work to the public. An altered work is prohibited from being offered for sale or exhibition as an unaltered work. The third provision is the right of integrity, where the work cannot be treated in a way that is prejudicial to the honour or reputation of the author. Probably the moral rights provisions were already largely covered in other law, such as trade practices, but when they came in many workers thought they had sweeping new powers to stop changes to their work in programs. Producers and broadcasters reacted as if this was correct. As a result, production companies and broadcasters will seek consents in production contracts for specified changes to the work contracted – to edit to meet timeslot, legal or classification requirements, to use excerpts for promotion, to consult regarding other changes – and require consents to be obtained from contributors.

New media

Many people have expressed concern that the Copyright Act does not adequately protect use of work by new media, because it was drafted before the technology became available and hadn't anticipated it. That is probably not the case, but there can be difficulties in pursuing breaches because of problems of jurisdiction. Material obtained from the internet is not placed there in the same legal jurisdiction as it is accessible. Indeed, it can be difficult sometimes to locate the geographical source of material on the internet, and difficult therefore to know who to pursue and in which legal system.

Format rights

The Privy Council ruling in the *Green Case* (section 25.1) suggests that there are no such rights as format rights recognised in law. Ideas do not attract copyright, and the format for them would not either until the idea was expressed in considerable detail. The detail can generally be varied without much difficulty while retaining the idea, to avoid copyright problems, but nonetheless format rights are often sold. Becker Entertainment and the Seven Network licensed the format of the UK show *Ground Force* about the same time as CTC Productions produced a similar backyard makeover program, *Backyard Blitz*, for Nine. The makers of *Ground Force* threatened legal action for breach of their format rights, but the matter never got into the court. In reality, parties buying 'format rights' are probably buying the production 'bible' for the program. This is a worthwhile purchase when the production approach is complex and not obvious from watching the program, if it is already in the public domain. Purchase of these 'format rights' can save a lot of time and expense on production research, but the purchase is of information, not the licensing of rights. Where it is quite clear how a program was made, it's hard to see the point in buying format rights.

Unjustifiable threat of action

A party who is threatened unjustifiably by another party with legal action for infringement of copyright can bring an action against the party making threats. The action will succeed if it can be shown that the party threatening knew there was no basis to the claim.

25.6   Confidential information

Presumption of confidentiality

The law of confidential information impacts on television production in two principal ways: protection of program ideas while the producer tries to attract broadcaster and investor interest, and restraint of the use of certain private material on air. This law prevents unauthorised use or disclosure of confidential information that the recipient knows or ought to know is communicated in trust and confidence. It can be stated explicitly that information is confidential, but the law will presume that confidentiality was intended under certain circumstances, even when this has not been stated. Information that is not public about a business is shared in confidence with employees of that company, and they are not permitted to divulge its content outside the company, even if they cease to be employed by it. Most professional relationships, such as doctor and patient, lawyer and client, and banker and customer, have communications between the parties that are protected by confidentiality. Information, such as a program concept, that is presented in a business context is presumed by the law to be confidential, although if the same information is disclosed in a social context it probably is not.

Public knowledge

The information that is protected cannot be self-evident or trivial, nor can it be public knowledge. Once it has entered the public domain, it is no longer protected, although entering the public domain is not always clear-cut. The information might have been shared with a number of people, but provided they have kept it confidential, it hasn't entered the public domain. If there has been a minor public revealing of the information, the court might still rule it is not in the public domain. In *G v Day* [1982] 1 NSWLR 24, a journalist threatened to publish the name of a witness who gave evidence on condition of anonymity. Even though Channel Ten news had mentioned his name twice, the court regarded this as transitory, and unlikely to be remembered by anyone who didn't know him. The journalist was prevented from publishing the name.

Media leaks

A producer or a broadcaster is not liable for a breach of confidentiality of which it was unaware, but it may be prevented from broadcasting information from the time it knows that the information is confidential. Usually a producer will have at least grounds for suspecting a leak is confidential. Confidential information may be revealed where it is in the public interest, although where public interest overrides confidentiality has not been tested in Australian courts. Private personal information will also be protected by the law, if it fulfils the criteria of confidentiality. In 1978, the UK court would not prevent John Lennon's ex-wife publishing material about her marriage break-up because of earlier revelation by the Lennons (*Lennon v News Group Newspapers Ltd* [1978] FSR 573). The application of the law to government documents is different because these are public rather than private interests. The material is protected only if the public interest in the material being restrained outweighs the public interest in its disclosure.

Protection of a program concept

The law has been used to protect information about Aboriginal cultural and religious ceremonies (*Foster and others v Mountford and Rigby Ltd* (1977) 14 ALR

71), and a scenario for a television series. In *Talbot v GTV* [1980] VR 224, an independent producer presented a written proposal and pilot script to GTV9 for a television series on life stories of self-made millionaires. GTV declined the series, but some time later promoted a series of interviews with millionaires in *A Current Affair*. GTV argued in court that a program about millionaires was so commonplace it was public property, but the court held that Talbot had taken the concept out of the public domain by showing how millionaires made their money. GTV was prevented from broadcasting its interviews.

Determining confidentiality

In assessing whether information in a creative work is confidential, the law will look at: the value of the idea to its creator; the extent to which it has been disclosed to others and if it was disclosed confidentially; the difficulty of the ideas being duplicated independently; and measures taken to keep it confidential. The third criterion can be important in determining if a breach of producer confidence has occurred. There is no requirement for the material in a program proposal to be unknown to the rest of the world, but it has to be sufficiently unique for an unlikelihood of someone else devising a program with it. It is still open to the defending party to show that the information was arrived at independently, from another source.

25.7 Defamation

Defamation laws in Australia

Defamation law in Australia was different in each of the states and territories until 2006. Now it is uniform across the six states and the Northern Territory. The ACT's defamation laws are slightly different. Defamation is a communication that lowers or harms a person's reputation, holds them to ridicule, or leads others to shun and avoid them, without a legal defence. The news media are the main targets for defamation actions, but they can arise from other publications as well, such as television drama and documentary, novels, cartoons and songs. It is a law that aims to balance free speech against the right to a reputation without indefensible attack, but it can be misused. Queensland premier, Joh Bjelke-Petersen, was notorious for threatening defamation action to stifle critics of him or his government.

Defamation actions

An action in defamation must now commence within one year of publication of the material under question, although the court does have discretion to extend this time. Court actions for defamation take place in two stages: determining whether the plaintiff has been defamed, then determining if the defamation has an allowable defence. Defamation actions can be costly, difficult to defend, and are often characterised by a plaintiff so consumed with outrage that an out-of-court settlement is not an option.

What must be proven

For a defamation action to succeed, the plaintiff must prove three things:

1. The communication has been *made to a person other than the plaintiff*, by any means, written, spoken or pictorial. Everyone involved in a television program is potentially liable – the person who makes the statement on camera, the producer, the director and the broadcaster. All can be sued. Repeating a comment made by someone else is not a defence.
2. The communication is *about and identifies the plaintiff*. The plaintiff must prove this. It is not hard if they are named, but the use of a false name will not defeat this requirement if the plaintiff can be identified by other means. A reference to address, occupation or social habits may be sufficient to identify them. A dead person cannot be defamed, although living relatives may be, if the communication defames them by association. A class of people cannot be defamed, although a member of a group may be if the group is small enough for the statement to be imputed to each person in the group. Companies and their organisations cannot be defamed, apart from a few specific exceptions relating to their purpose and number of employees.
3. The communication *defames the plaintiff*. This is judged from the viewpoint of 'ordinary reasonable people in the community in general'. What was meant to be said (or what the plaintiff thinks was meant) is not as important as what the ordinary viewer or reader will understand to have been said or implied. This will take account of the viewer's capacity to read between the lines, and to suspect that reported allegations are fact. A statement or picture must be considered in its context in a publication and not taken out of context to find an imputation, and a reader or viewer must infer a statement of fact from the publication. Words intended as a joke may be safe, if the audience is unlikely to understand them as factual. It's not necessary to prove the imputation is false or actually caused the plaintiff harm, but it is also insufficient that it upset them. Their reputation must be adversely affected in some way.

Defences for defamation

If in a defamation hearing it has been found that an imputation is defamatory, defences are raised to justify the defamatory statement. Before the uniform defamation laws of 2006, there were variations in the allowable defences from state to state. As a result, a plaintiff might have looked for the state that gave the least opportunity for defence as the jurisdiction to take their case, a procedure known as jurisdiction shopping. Now the defences are the same in all jurisdictions (except ACT). The three principal defences are outlined below:

1. *Justification or truth*. If the material is proven to be substantially true, this provides a complete defence. The law presumes the material is false, so the defence must prove it is true, requiring evidence that is admissible in court (i.e. documents, and witnesses who are credible and willing to testify) but not hearsay evidence. Public benefit is no longer a requirement for this defence.
2. *Qualified privilege*, where there is a legal, social or moral duty to communicate something and a corresponding duty to receive it, as long as it isn't motivated by malice or revenge. This defence protects references given by employers, or

complaints to the police. Generally, material published in the media will not be able to use this defence because of the difficulty in showing a media duty to its audience, but there are two exceptions. A person who has been attacked publicly is entitled to a public response. The other exception is the interest of the Australian public to receive information about government and political matters, recognised by the High Court in *Lange v ABC* (1997) 145 ALR 96.

3. *Honest opinion* (fair comment), in which the material is an expression of an honestly held opinion rather than a statement of fact. The defence must prove that: it is an opinion, criticism, judgement, remark or conclusion; it was based on facts that were stated or widely known, and were clearly distinguishable from the comment; and it was a matter of public interest. The opinion can be extreme, as long as it is honestly held. The defence of honest opinion is important to critics, satirists, comedians and anyone else working in social commentary.

Other defences

Other defences include triviality, consent by the plaintiff, protected reports of court and parliamentary proceedings (absolute privilege), and innocent publication (where a newsagent, bookshop or internet service provider could not be expected to be aware of the defamatory nature of something it had on offer). The new law allows a publisher to make an offer of amends within twenty-eight days of receiving a complaint that a person has been defamed. The offer must include publishing a correction and apology, and cover financial losses incurred as a result. If the offer is rejected and it is subsequently held that the offer was reasonable, that can be used as a full defence.

Remedy of damages

Compensation is provided by an award of damages, taking account of: the nature of the defamation and the circumstances in which it was published; injury to personal feelings; financial loss suffered; position and standing of the plaintiff; and mitigating factors such as apology or retraction. General damages are now capped at $250 000 under legislation, although aggravated damages, where the publisher failed to make proper inquiries or failed to apologise, are unlimited.

25.8   The law of contempt

Sub judice cases

The law of contempt includes control by the courts over publications that prejudice court proceedings while they are in process or are pending (i.e. they are sub judice). This starts when a person is arrested or charged with an offence, or a warrant or summons has been issued, but not when a suspect is sought by police or their arrest is imminent. The case remains sub judice until judgment in any appeal, or the time for appeal runs out. The media may report the bare facts of a crime, but it may not print material that could influence the outcome of a trial, such as refer to the past record of the accused, or make statements from which a reader or viewer might infer the accused was guilty (or conversely, was innocent). The courts are more lenient towards comment about a civil case than a criminal case. The prejudice could be alleviated if there was a long time between publication and the start of the trial. The court did not accept that *Four Corners* had prejudiced the Fine Cotton racing substitution trial, in *Waterhouse v ABC* [1986] 6 NSWLR 733, because the trial didn't start for twelve months after the program was aired. Furthermore, the law takes the view that judges are not expected to be influenced by media comment, but juries are. Thus, the media have considerably more leeway in commenting on a case after the verdict, even if an appeal is pending.

Pressure on participants in court actions

It is contempt to pressure a litigant with strong negative comment or abuse for exercising the constitutional right to have rights and obligations determined in court. The NSW court held, in *Commercial Bank v Preston* [1981] 2 NSWLR 554, that a pamphlet was contemptuous because it vilified a witness. Preston handed out a pamphlet outside the bank saying it was paying thousands of dollars to sue him, and that one of the bank's managers, a likely witness in the case, had been found by a court to be a deliberate liar. It is also contemptuous to publish material that may influence witnesses called to give evidence in trials, but the courts are likely to be quite liberal in applying this. A High Court judge has said that the tendency of material to influence witnesses would have to be demonstrated, and not merely speculated. An exception is the identification of accused persons by eyewitnesses, where photographs or film of the accused can prejudice the unaided identification. After Paul Mason was charged with three brutal murders in 1989, television news ran pictures of the handcuffed accused showing police where he had committed the alleged murders, and one interviewed him on the aeroplane taking him to the murder scene. Even though Mason committed suicide before his trial began, the television channels were fined heavily for contempt on the facts when the material was published.

Balancing contempt and matters of public concern

The courts will balance the law of contempt against freedom of speech, and are prepared to make concessions on the competing public need. A 1937 formulation in the NSW Supreme Court continues to be applied: 'The discussion of public affairs and the denunciation of public abuses cannot be required to be suspended merely because (it) may, as an incidental but not intended by-product, cause some likelihood of prejudice to a person who happens at the time to be a litigant.' Where the matter is of public concern and the published material addresses that concern principally, the courts are reluctant to find contempt. Some subsequent cases are indicative of the extent to which the courts will make concession.

Three illustrative cases

The Sydney Morning Herald ran allegations of police violence to a man after his arrest as part of a series of articles about police misconduct. Although the man's trial had not then commenced, the matter was held to be of public concern, and the article primarily addressed that concern. The allegations were of violence after the arrest, and the trial would concern events before the arrest. There was ruled in *John Fairfax & Sons v McRae* (1955) 93 CLR 351 to be no contempt. A later case involved an item on a Willesee television program implying that James Anderson, who had made allegations of corruption, had a criminal background and little credibility. Unknown to the program, Anderson was on trial at the time for stealing a necklace. The trial was aborted because of the danger of the item prejudicing its outcome. The judge was critical of the channel for not having a system to check if cases were pending, but in *Registrar of the Court of Appeal v Willesee* (1985) 3 NSWLR 650, Willesee was found not guilty of contempt. The outcome was different in *Hinch v Attorney-General (Victoria)* (1987) 164 CLR 15, when Derryn Hinch broadcast on radio material about the record of offences regarding children of a person awaiting trial on similar offences. Here the material related principally to the accused, rather than a general issue of public concern, and was clearly prejudicial to the court outcome.

Misuse of defamation

The courts will not allow a defamation writ to use the law of contempt to stifle criticism. Milan Brych's cancer clinic had been attacked in the press, and he started a defamation action against the Melbourne *Herald*. When *The Herald* published two further articles about setbacks in his work, Brych claimed they were prejudicial to his defamation action, but the court ruled against him in *Brych v The Herald & Weekly Times Ltd* [1978] VR 727. The articles didn't relate to the defamation proceedings, appeared to report factual events, and the defamation action would not be heard for several months.

25.9 Offensive material

Blasphemy and sedition

Prosecutions for obscenity, blasphemy and sedition have become increasingly rare in Australia. Classification systems, advising the public of the nature of material and leaving it to decide whether to read or watch it, are replacing the old common law offences of obscenity. There has been no prosecution for blasphemy in Australia, although it is still a statutory offence in two states (NSW and Tasmania) and the Australian Capital Territory, while other states have repealed their blasphemy legislation. The sedition laws were last used in 1960 to successfully prosecute a Department of Native Affairs officer for urging 'natives' of Papua New Guinea to demand independence from Australia. Section 24D of the *Crimes Act 1914* (Cth) has been repealed, but new sedition laws in the *Criminal Code Act 1995* (Cth) (s 80.2) have controversially shifted the law to what people say, rather than the outcome of their actions.

Obscenity

It is an offence under common law to publish obscene material. Several states also have a statutory offence of publishing obscene or indecent material. The classic (English) judicial definition of obscenity is 'the tendency to deprave and corrupt those whose minds are open to such immoral influences'. In Australia, the focus has been on whether the material offends public standards of decency, the formulation pronounced in the last High Court obscenity case in 1968. Whether material should be judged against the standards of the community as a whole, or the standards of the community to which it is targeted, is not resolved, but there is a requirement for the material to be considered in context.

TV licence compliance with OFLC classification

The *Broadcasting Services Act 1992* prevents the broadcast of material that has been refused classification or given an X or R rating by the Office of Film and Literature Classification (OFLC), by making that a condition of commercial, community or pay television licences. An exception is pay television, which is allowed conditionally to show R-rated programs on its Adults Only channels. The license also requires the licensee to not broadcast material that offends another federal Act, or a state or territory law. The public broadcasters are not subject to these licence conditions, but voluntarily comply with them.

Vilification law

Instead of pursuing obscenity, blasphemy and sedition, there has been an increased focus on material that is offensive or discriminatory. In recent years, the states and territories have made it an offence to incite racial hatred or violence, or to vilify a person or group because of race. The states have extended their vilification laws to prohibit religious hatred and homosexual vilification. An exception permitting fair reporting of acts of racial vilification gives some protection to the media. Legitimate publications and discussions for academic, artistic or research purposes are also permitted.

25.10 Classification of television programs

Commercial TV Code of Practice

The commercial television industry, through Free TV Australia (formerly Commercial Television Australia [CTVA], and Federation of Australian Commercial Television Stations [FACTS] before that), has a self-regulating Code of Practice. It is accessible on the Free TV Australia website (see sources below), and operates in conjunction with the Australian Communications and Media Authority (ACMA) standards for children and Australian content (see Chapter 3) and the ACCC codes for advertising. Under the Code, program material must be readily distinguished from commercials, community announcements, and program or station promotions. Commercial arrangements for content of factual programs must be disclosed to viewers. Under the Code, commercial FTA cannot broadcast a program that:
- simulates news or events, misleading or alarming viewers
- depicts hypnosis

- contains subliminal images or messages
- is culturally offensive to Aboriginals and Torres Strait Islanders, or ethnic or racial groups in Australia
- provokes intense dislike or ridicule of persons because of age, colour, gender, national or ethnic origins, disability, race, religion or sexual preference, unless it is an artistic work (including comedy or satire), discussion or debate in good faith, or a fair report on an event or matter of public interest.
  Under the Code, news and current affairs programs must:
- be factually accurate and present viewpoints fairly
- not create public panic
- consider relatives and viewers when showing images of dead or seriously injured people
- not invade the privacy of a person (especially a child) without an identifiable public interest
- be sensitive to the feelings of bereaved relatives, and survivors and witnesses of traumatic events
- not identify victims before the family is notified
- not report suicide unless there is an identifiable public reason, and then without graphic detail or glamorisation
- avoid unfairly identifying individuals when commenting on behaviour of a group
- correct significant errors as soon as possible.

Classification of programs

The Code also provides guidelines for the classification of programs by a network's classification officer, and time zones in which the various classification categories can be shown (Fig. 25.1). ACMA's Children's Television Standards classifies some programs as C or P, where they meet criteria for children (under 14 years) or preschool children. This document can be accessed on their website (see sources below). Other programs are classified under Code guidelines derived from those published by the OFLC, except where the programs have already come under them. Both public broadcasters have their own classification system, which also uses the OFLC guidelines and adheres to the same classification time zones as commercial television. A film, documentary or short film with first release in Australia through cinema or video sale/hire is classified by the OFLC according to its guidelines. All other programs (except news, current affairs and sportscasts) are classified according to the Code's Television Classification Guidelines, or the ABC or SBS Code of Practice. Overall, the bulk of programs come under these guidelines, which provide the following classification codes:

- G (general) – not necessarily intended for children, but mild in impact and with nothing unsuitable for unsupervised children
- PG (parental guidance recommended) – careful presentation of adult themes and concepts, mild in impact, and suitable for children with adult supervision
- M (mature) – recommended for viewing only by persons aged 15 or over

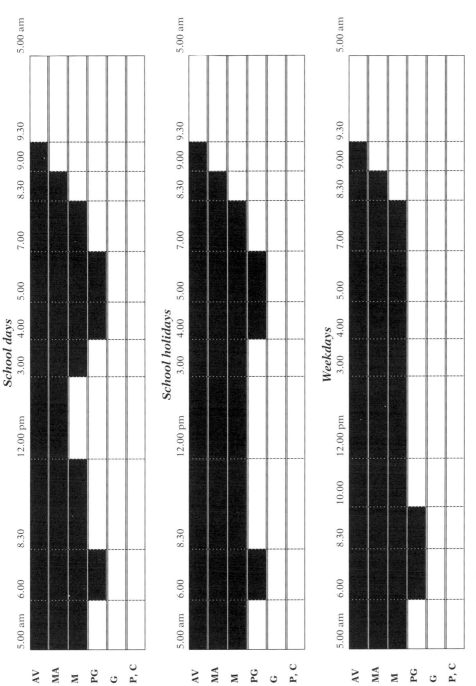

Figure 25.1: Classification zones on Australian FTA television.

- MA (mature audience) – suitable for viewing only by persons aged 15 or over, because of intensity or frequency of sexual depiction, coarse language, adult themes or drug use
- AV (adult violence) – suitable for viewing only by persons aged 15 or over, because violence is intense, frequent or central to the program.

Classification of pay TV programs

Pay television has a somewhat different approach to classification, outlined in the Australian Subscription Television and Radio Association's (ASTRA) Code of Practice for the sector (see sources below). Pay television involves a direct contract between the service provider and the subscriber. It is voluntary and therefore gives the subscriber freedom of choice, and the capability and responsibility to select programs. ASTRA describes pay television as 'an invited guest, brought into the home in the full and prior knowledge of the guest's behaviour'. Its Code recognises a difference between the mass market of FTA television and the niche market of pay television. Pay television's code for programs is much the same as FTA television's code, and it classifies programs using the OFLC guidelines as an advisory service to subscribers, but its members are not required to operate within classification zones as FTA broadcasters do. A program can be run on pay television at any time of the day, regardless of its classification. Pay television channels cannot broadcast R- or X-rated material (restricted to people eighteen years old and over), nor can they run R-rated material currently, although there is an expectation that the Commonwealth Parliament will soon approve pay television broadcast of R-rated programs, where they can be restricted by a disabling device.

25.11   Privacy and trespass

Limited common law right to privacy

Apart from the narrow provisions of the *Privacy Act 1988* (Cth), which limits the collection of private information by some organisations, but specifically exempts media organisations in the practice of journalism, there is no general right to privacy in Australia. There are no individual rights embodied in the Australian Constitution as there is in the US constitution, nor is there a Human Rights Act as there is in the United Kingdom. However, there has emerged in Australia a common law right to privacy under circumstances founded on human dignity. Police executing a search warrant took video pictures of a suspect in his underpants, and the video came into the hands of television broadcasters. It was held in *Donnelly v Amalgamated Television Services Pty Ltd* [1998] 45 NSWLR 570 that film that is gratuitously humiliating could be constrained from being shown by applying the law of breach of confidence (see section 25.6). The High Court confirmed the Donnelly decision, but didn't apply it, in *ABC v Lenah Game Meats* [2001] HCA 63, which involved secret filming of possum slaughtering at a meat processing plant. The court took the view that not every act observed on private land is a private act, and while activities at the plant might be distressing to some people, they are not confidential and don't involve an affront to human dignity.

Trespass

Privacy can, however, be protected to some degree by the law regarding trespass. The Nine Network was ordered to pay $310 000 after *A Current Affair* reporter didn't leave a builder's home when told to, but instead shouted through the closed door that the builder should answer questions. The judge held that intrusion was part of the value of the story to the broadcaster, and it could not be obtained without trespass. Reporters can legally approach a homeowner to request an interview, but not if cameras are rolling at the same time. Damages were also awarded for false and misleading conduct from the reporter and his researcher, who were pretending to be a young couple looking to build a home. This case illustrates how closely this type of current affairs story treads at the edge of the law. Trespass is a civil wrong. It is not a police matter, but one where the individual concerned must take court action, and requires first a reasonable request to leave. Some people, such as meter readers and delivery people, are allowed to enter property without permission, but this doesn't include media. It's doubtful that public interest could be raised successfully as a mitigating issue in trespass.

Sources and further reading

General reading

Armstrong, Mark, Lindsay, David, Watterson, Ray 1995, *Media Law in Australia*, 3rd edn, Oxford University Press, Melbourne.

Pearson, Mark 2004, *The Journalist's Guide to Media Law*, 2nd edn, Allen & Unwin, Sydney.

Some internet references

Arts Law Centre of Australia, 'Legal information', with information papers on 'Performers' rights', 'Confidential information – protecting your ideas', 'Defamation', 'Privacy and the private sector', and 'Sedition law in Australia', available online at <www.artslaw.com.au/LegalInformation>, viewed 14 December 2006.

Australasian Legal Information Institute, *Copyright Act 1968* (Cth), available online at <http://www.austlii.edu.au/au/legis/cth/consol_act/ca1968133>, viewed 13 December 2006.

Australian Communications and Media Authority, 'Children's television standards', available online at <http://www.acma.gov.au/ACMAINTER.1507598:STANDARD::pc=PC_90095>, viewed 14 December 2006.

Australian Subscription Television and Radio Association, 'ASTRA's Codes of Practice', available online at <http://www.astra.org.au/article.asp?section=4&option=3&content=15>, viewed 14 December 2006.

Free TV Australia, 'Commercial television industry Code of Practice', available online at <http://www.freetvaust.com.au/Content_Common/pg-Code-of-Practice.seo>, viewed 14 December 2006.

Victorian Peace Network, 'Be alarmed about Australia's new sedition laws', available online at <www.vicpeace.org/sedition>, viewed 14 December 2006.

Chapter 26

Business structure and operation

One of the first decisions to be made by anyone moving into independent production is what sort of business structure to operate under. The tendency is to want to set up a company, not least because this shows you are a serious player. A company is a more costly structure than some of the alternatives and, while it may offer many advantages, there may be reasons to consider other options in the early stages. The choice of business structure needs to be an informed decision that is made after weighing up the pros and cons (see Table 26.1), not a decision made on a whim, or for reasons of self-image.

Sole trader is a simple low-cost structure. While it does not provide personal protection from liability for the business operation, there may be advantages in being taxed at personal income rates rather than company tax rates in the early stages of operation, where set-up costs outweigh returns. On the other hand, the bigger the operation becomes, the more unwieldy it is as a sole trader and the more personally exposed the individual becomes to its trading liabilities. A partnership involves similar cost and tax considerations, but has the advantage of pooling resources and skills. A private company may be a more practical approach as the operation gets bigger, even though it brings responsibilities with it as the courts keep closer scrutiny on company principals and their corporate duties. The offsets are tax advantages, and limited liability for failure of the business's operation. Although it is not a decision to be taken lightly, it can be the right decision after getting informed and practical advice.

This chapter looks analytically at the business structure options available in Australia, and what they entail. It examines some of the significant legal and administrative responsibilities imposed on those businesses, particularly in the areas of employment, taxation and insurance.

Table 26.1: Advantages and disadvantages of business structures.

	Sole trader	Partnership	Private company
Advantages	• Easy to set up • Inexpensive to establish and operate • Few government regulations • Independence • All profits to sole trader • Losses may be offset against other income or future earnings • Total business privacy	• Relatively easy to set up • Inexpensive to establish and operate • Few government regulations • Shared responsibility and risk • Additional expertise from partners • Additional capital from partners • More options to raise finance • Possible tax advantages from income splitting • Capital losses can be offset by non-business capital gains of partners • Non-disclosure of profits to public	• Liability limited to share capital and any personal guarantees • Separate legal entity (enter into agreements, sue and be sued) • Additional capital • Profits taxed at company income tax rate • Structured control • Company continues to exist (not dependent on owners) • Transfer of ownership simple • Authority of shareholders controlled through type of shares issued
Disadvantages	• Unlimited liability • Pay tax at personal income rates • Fewer options to raise finance • Business will only operate if you work	• Unlimited liability • Each partner equally and jointly responsible • Limited flexibility in distributing profits from business • Difficult to operate if personal differences arise • Only lasts as long as partners agree to or are able to trade together	• Expensive to set up and maintain • Personal guarantees often required (nullify limited liability) • Greater regulations and more statutory requirements • Revenue and capital losses must be retained by company; cannot offset owners' incomes • Responsibilities of directors • Public disclosure

26.1   Sole traders

Definition

The simplest business structure is sole trader, where a person sets up and operates a business in his or her own name. The business is run as an extension of that person, without partners or co-owners. A sole trader has full control of the business, including ownership of all profits, but also responsibility for all debts and liabilities. Creditors may recover debts by seizing personal assets, such as a car or house.

Few requirements

The only formal requirement is registration for an Australian Business Number (ABN) (see section 26.7). There is no requirement or mechanism to register as a sole trader if a person trades under their own name, but they may elect to register a business name that is not their own name. The cost of registering the business name, if this is done, is the only establishment cost for this business structure.

Taxation

There aren't special tax rules for sole traders, as there are for companies. A sole trader is taxed as an individual, and income tax after deductions is calculated from personal income tax rates. Legitimate business expenses in the course of trading are tax deductible. This can provide an advantage over a company structure for a person with other sources of income that are taxed. If the business is anticipated to trade at a loss for the first few years, and income is received from somewhere else, the losses of the business may be offset immediately against that other income. For this reason, sole trader is more attractive as a start-up structure for a business that is forecast to make losses initially, and the trader has income from other sources. When that business grows and is expected to make a profit, a company structure would be more beneficial than conducting business as a sole trader.

26.2   Private companies

Definition

A private company is the most common business structure used in Australia. In this situation, you have your own company with your own shareholders and directors, rather than being listed on the Australian Stock Exchange. Funding sources for a television production project may insist on funding a company only as the production entity. A sole-trader producer would either have to form a company, or attach the production to an existing company which will contract them as producer.

Limited liability

The most important benefit of a company is that it has limited liability. A company or corporation is a separate legal entity, and enters into contracts under its own name. If a company is sued, generally only the company is liable, not any of the individuals in it. Shareholders are protected from liability for the company's debts, except where there is misrepresentation, misleading or deceptive conduct by the directors or officers of the company, someone has given a personal guarantee (banks often require a personal guarantee from a director for loans to a company) or it can be proven that someone was negligent in causing the liability. It should be noted, however, that with small companies with few or no assets, personal guarantees can put the liability of the company on a similar footing to the unlimited liability of the sole trader.

Incorporation

The process of setting up a company is called incorporation. It involves registering a company name, lodging prescribed documents and paying prescribed fees. The cost of incorporation is about $1500, and there are various reporting requirements under the *Corporations Act 2001*, even for small companies. Advice from a solicitor and an accountant when setting up a company will add to the set-up cost. Nonetheless, this is generally money well spent.

Company name

A company name must indicate the company's legal status and the liability of its members. A proprietary company (privately owned and controlled) must include 'Proprietary' or the abbreviation 'Pty' in its name, and if liability is limited the company name must end with 'Limited' or 'Ltd'. Only a company name that is not already registered can be chosen. The National Names Index on the Australian Securities and Investments Commission (ASIC) website lists all Australian company and business names (see sources below). Even if ASIC registers a name, a person or corporation with a similar registered name may still take action against the owners. It is the owners' responsibility to ensure that no problems could arise from already registered names, which might be confused with the new company's name. Checking and registering the name, say, of Pacific Wildfire Pty Ltd as a production company, for instance, may not reveal the existence already of a production company called Wildfire Pty Ltd, but the latter may well be able to argue a case to deregister the newer registration on the grounds that the public might not distinguish between them.

Internal management

Before lodging an application to register a company, the owners must decide how the company will be internally managed: by the 'replaceable rules' in the Corporations Act, or the company's own constitution, or a combination of these. A table under section 141 of the Act sets out the provisions that apply as replaceable rules. If a company uses these to govern its internal management, it doesn't need to have a written constitution of its own. The Act allows for a proprietary company with a single shareholder who is also the sole director. In this case, there is no requirement for formal rules governing internal relationships, only rules sufficient to conduct business and deal with contingencies, but the company may, nonetheless, elect to have a constitution. If an additional director is appointed, or an additional person takes up shares in the company, the replaceable rules will automatically apply to the company, except to the extent that the company already has a constitution.

Consent of officeholders

A proprietary company must be limited by shares, with no other shareholder liability for the company's debts, and have no more than fifty non-employee shareholders. A public company, on the other hand, is able to raise funds from the public through a prospectus, and is limited by guarantee. Many of the provisions of the Corporations Act which apply to public companies do not apply to a proprietary company, but it must have written consents from the people who will fill the roles of director(s) (there must be at least one, and over eighteen years old), secretary (not mandatory, but must be over eighteen) and shareholder member(s) (there must be at least one). The consents do not need to be lodged with the registration application. They are kept with the company records.

Bankruptcy

A person who is a declared bankrupt, or within five years of a conviction or release from prison for fraud or under company law, or who has been banned by ASIC from doing so, cannot become a company director. Such persons are not allowed to manage a company either. It is a serious offence for someone to set up dummy directors while they effectively manage a company.

Registration application form

Application for registration of a company is on ASIC's form 201, which is obtainable from its website. It requires details of the proposed company name, class and type of company, and details of registered office, principal business office, director(s) and secretary, share structure and members' shares. ASIC gives the company an Australian Company Number (ACN), registers it, and issues a Certificate of Registration. The company applies separately for an ABN from the Australian Business Register (see section 26.7), which will add two additional digits to the ACN. An ABN can be used in lieu of the ACN on company documents.

Fiduciary duty of directors

By law, directors owe a fiduciary duty to the company, requiring them to act honestly, with diligence and in the company's best interest. Directors are also required to not make improper use of inside information or of their position. Company law requires them to be aware of what their company is doing, ensuring it keeps proper financial records, regardless of the size of the company, and can pay its debts when they are due. A director may be personally liable for a company that is trading while insolvent, and may also face criminal charges. A director of a company that is having difficulty paying its debts should get immediate professional advice.

Taxation

Companies are required to pay state and federal taxes under separate company tax systems, including income tax on its profits (currently at a flat rate of 30%), payroll tax, and stamp duty and GST on transactions. A benefit of a company structure is that it can help minimise personal income tax by spreading it across financial years, or by splitting the tax burden between shareholders. The company tax rate is a particular advantage of the company structure over the sole trader, once the business is earning substantial income. Above a net income of $63 000 per annum (p.a.), individuals continue to pay a 30% tax rate instead of the 42% they would be paying as a sole trader. The situation is reversed in a low-earning company, however, where the company still pays 30% even though the personal income rates of the sole trader may be lower.

Accounting records

Accounting costs are much greater for companies than they are for sole traders, and this should be weighed up in any decision to form a company. Company law requires companies to keep accounting records, accurately recording all their transactions, and holding them for a minimum of seven years. However, if a company is classified as a 'small proprietary company' (with two of the following: gross operating revenue under $10 million p.a.; gross assets under $5 million; fewer than fifty employees), it will generally not have to prepare formal annual reports for ASIC or appoint an auditor, as do large proprietary companies and public companies.

Registration of company and business names

When a company is registered under the Corporations Act, it is automatically registered as an Australian company, and can conduct business throughout Australia without needing to register in individual states and territories. Sole traders and partnerships are required to register their business name with the relevant state or territory authority (see section 26.7), but this does not create a legal entity or allow the use of the privileges to which a company is entitled, such as a corporate tax rate or limited liability. A business name has no legal status. If a company carries on a business in a name that is different from its company name, it must register the business name with the appropriate state or territory authority. In this case, the business has the same legal status as the company, and is often indicated in legal documents by the construction: 'Company Pty Ltd trading as Business'.

Shelf companies

In the past, when it took a number of months to incorporate a company, solicitors and accountants would pre-incorporate companies, called shelf companies, for their clients to buy. It would involve transferring shares in the shelf company to the purchaser, resignation of the shelf company's directors and appointment of new directors, and often a change of company name. Now, when a company can be formed in a few minutes through an online service such as Cleardocs, there is little point in involving these transfer processes. However, the name shelf company has remained, although providers of 'shelf company services' actually provide company registration services.

26.3   Trust companies

Definitions

In recent years, trading trusts have been commonly used as a structure for carrying on a business with the main objective of tax minimisation. A trust is a relationship or association between two or more people, whereby one party holds property on trust for the other. The first party, vested with the property, is called the trustee; the other, for whom the property is held, is the beneficiary. A company may trade as trustee of a trust, and where a trustee carries on a business for the benefit of beneficiaries it is called a trading trust.

Trust deed

A document called the trust deed usually sets out the trustees and beneficiaries, the property held in trust, and other duties and obligations of the trustee. In addition to any powers given under the trust deed, legislation in Australia gives trustees powers to:
- invest proceeds of the trust
- sell, mortgage or lease trust property
- take out insurance
- give advances to beneficiaries out of trust property.

Tax on trusts is determined by 'present entitlement'. If beneficiaries are entitled to receive income that is in the trust, they will be taxed on it; if they are not, the trustee is taxed. Losses in a trust cannot be distributed and cannot be offset against other income of the beneficiaries. Further tax rules apply to incorporated trusts.

Trust company in production

There are no obvious advantages in a production company operating as a trust company, but freelance workers might consider setting up as trust companies into which fee payments are made. Payments from the trust will be taxed at the marginal rates that apply to them and their family as individuals, taking account of all income each receives. The trust company may also pay some family expenses directly without subjecting the payments first to personal income tax rates. Professional advice should be sought to ensure such a structure will work to their benefit as intended, and will operate within the law.

26.4   Partnerships

Definition and advantages

A partnership is an agreement between two or more persons and/or companies to contribute time, money and talent to make a profit from a continuing venture.

Large legal firms, for instance, may have twenty or thirty partners, all working together. One of the main benefits of a partnership is a greater skill base. Partners bring in additional expertise, resources and capital to the business, which is usually most successful where that expertise is complementary. Unlike a company, a partnership is not incorporated. It is not a legal entity in its own right, and has no separate legal existence apart from the members of the partnership. It does, however, need to register a business name and apply for a partnership Tax File Number (TFN) and ABN as it's not enough that each partner has their own TFN.

Partnership agreement

The rights of partners are governed by a partnership agreement, which may be made in writing, verbally or by implication from the partners' actions. However, it is unwise to enter into a partnership with family or friends on a 'gentleman's agreement', handshake or verbal understanding. Misunderstandings can occur and, as in any contract, an agreement in writing minimises arguments about terms of the agreement. In setting out the relationship, the agreement should include:
• what the partnership assets are and shares will be
• how the profits will be distributed
• how liability will be allocated among the partners
• the degree to which each partner can act on behalf of other partners
• how partners can join, resign or transfer their partnership share to another person
• how disputes and deadlocks will be handled.
  In the absence of a formal written agreement, the law will assume each partner has equal share in the business, and the partnership will be governed by the Partnership Act in its state or territory.

Liabilities of partners

A partnership enters into any business contract in the name of its partners. Unless agreed otherwise, they are jointly liable for obligations under the contract. Unlike companies, partnerships have unlimited liability. If one or more of the partners is found to be liable for doing or failing to do something, then all the partners are personally liable without limit, even when those other partners were unaware that a partner had created the liability. However, it is possible to create a limited partnership with two classes of partner:
1. general partners, with the same rights and liabilities as an ordinary partnership
2. limited partners, who contribute to partnership capital and share in its profits, but have no right to participate in its management, nor any responsibility for its liabilities beyond their capital contribution.

Accounting records and taxation

Partnerships don't have any accounting or recording requirements in law, but should keep proper accounting records for taxation purposes. They are not separate legal entities, and therefore cannot be taxpayers. Each partner pays taxes separately, the income and losses of the partnership being apportioned according to each partner's shareholding in the partnership. Partners must include their share of the partnership income and/or losses in their own tax returns. Capital gains and losses on partnership assets and GST are also apportioned among the partners. A major benefit of a partnership is that losses can be distributed to partners, who can then offset the losses against their other income. Foxtel is a partnership between entities owned by Telstra Corporation Ltd, News Corporation Ltd and Publishing and Broadcasting Ltd (PBL), where the partners were able to offset the large initial trading losses.

Personality clashes

Partnerships formed among people already having difficulties with their personal or business relationships are often doomed to acrimonious failure. Business partnerships tend to magnify any residual conflict or personality clashes. When the business arrangement fails, it tends to exacerbate the personal animosity. Partnerships are best formed among people with a common business interest, often with complementary skills, and without strong personal relationships to distract their judgement about the business viability of the arrangement.

26.5   Joint ventures

Definition

A joint venture can take a variety of forms with varying complexity and similar characteristics to a partnership. It has no strict legal meaning, but is an association of persons or companies for a particular trading, commercial or financial purpose for mutual profit. Each participant usually contributes money, property or skill. Joint ventures work best when they are equal in substance and capabilities, and the people understand clearly each other's objectives. A joint venture may be incorporated as a company or unit trust (more usually), or unincorporated as a partnership.

Joint venture company

In a joint venture company, the joint venturers become shareholders in the company, which conducts the venture on their behalf, owning and developing the project, and raising capital. A board will generally be appointed by the venture parties to manage the affairs of the company. Its directors will represent the interests of the company, as well as those of the venture parties. The advantages of a joint venture company are those generally of a company structure – limited liability (unless directors have been required to give personal guarantees), easily transferable interests, flat tax rate and unlimited retention of profits – as are the disadvantages, such as directors' duties, and losses retained in the company.

Unit trust

Where the joint venture is a unit trust, the joint venturers purchase units in the trust proportionate to their interest in the venture. A trustee company, appointed by the joint venture parties, will own the assets of the venture. It will be managed by directors appointed by each venture party. The main reason to structure a joint venture as a unit trust, rather than as a company, is tax benefits.

Risks

A joint venture is a reasonably complicated and sophisticated business structure. It shouldn't be set up without appropriate legal and accounting advice, or without the appropriate corporate backing. For this reason, the merits and risks of an unincorporated joint venture, as a partnership, should be weighed before going down this path. The partnership agreement should ensure no venture party can impose liability on co-venturers, and that each party will be taxed just on the proceeds of selling its share of the product, not as a member of a partnership. Probably, the term 'joint venture' for, say, a producer and director making a documentary, doesn't add anything to the term 'partnership'. The concept of a joint venture is best kept for incorporated ventures, or ventures by incorporated bodies (i.e. companies).

26.6   Setting up an office

Home office

An important decision that may have to be made about a business is whether to work out of home or rent office space. If the operation is impractical to run from the home, for space reasons or whatever, there is no decision needed, but if a home office is an option, there are points to consider. Whether it will work for any individual will depend on that person's nature and family lifestyle. The upside is that there is no rent to pay, no commuting, and the comforts of home can be enjoyed more. On the other hand, there are likely to be interruptions, sidetracking by domestic matters or lack of privacy. It may also be hard to separate work from leisure. There might be no clear cut-off to mark the end of the working day, or there could be too many things during the day that distract from the business operation. From the family's point of view, it may be unattractive to have the home invaded by business, and the telephone always engaged.

Alternating between home and premises

A compromise option is working out of home at the development stage, and taking out a short-term lease on premises when production commences. It's an industry where it's acceptable to have meetings in a coffee shop, and to use a copying business such as Officeworks or Kinko's, and a more up-market supplier for printing and other promotional needs. Once leases are being taken up with reasonable frequency, it's time to consider a longer lease and offset the cost of downtime with the lower rent in a long-term lease.

Features of rented premises

If a home office is not feasible, then a producer will need to rent premises and give some thought to where to set up office. Which suburb? Where in the suburb? Where in the building? It is often practical to be in a suburb where a range of media businesses are located, particularly suppliers of services the business might use. There is also an advantage in being in a building with other related businesses. This may present opportunities of synergy and mutual service from time to time or, at least, the possibility of social interaction, networking and an occasional professional sounding board. Premises at street level often have higher rent than those above and below street level, because they are prime retail space. As the business is not in retail, it is questionable what advantage it will get for the more expensive rent.

Size of rental space

Another issue is how much space is needed. It is a judgement between allowing some capacity for periodic expansion and paying for space that might never be called on. If the business grows significantly, it might be better to move premises than rent space at the outset for staffing peaks that may be infrequent, or may not even eventuate. If the expansion is only temporary, an option could be short-term rental of additional premises nearby.

26.7   The ABN and business name

Application for ABN

Every business in Australia, whatever its structure and no matter how large or small an operation, must have an ABN and may operate under a business name if it so chooses. The simplest way to apply for an ABN is to go to the Australian Business Register website (see sources below) and follow the prompts to register. If you intend to register for GST, or are required to, that can be done at the same time.

Registration of business name

A business name is the name under which your business operates if you don't use your own name. If you operate under your own name, you don't need to notify any government body, unless you use it in conjunction with someone else's name in a partnership. However, a business name must be registered with the relevant department in each state or territory in which you will conduct the business. Business names are administered under state law by state authorities.

Ensure name not already owned

Check that no-one is already using the name you choose for your business. The National Names Index on the ASIC website (see sources below) lists all current Australian company and business names, but it won't tell you if your business name or part of it is a registered trade mark. You will need to search the Australian Trade Marks Online Search System (ATMOSS) trade marks database at IP Australia (see sources below) to determine that. A name that is deceptively similar to another business name will not be registered as a business name, nor will names that are misleading about the business, or rude words, insults, racist names or words that promote drugs.

Reserve and register name

If your chosen business name is available, you can reserve it with the business names office in your state or territory, while you apply to register that name. The application will include the nature of your business and its proposed date of commencement. A fee may be payable, and in 2006 was $137 in New South Wales. Offices to reserve and register business names in Australia are listed in Table 26.2.

Transfer and cancellation

Business names may be transferred by their owner, generally when a business is sold. Cancellation of a business name may occur when the proposed business

Table 26.2: Offices in Australia for registration of a business name.

State/ Territory	Name of office	Telephone	Website
ACT	Business ACT	1800 244 650	www.business.act.gov.au
NSW	NSW Office of Fair Trading	13 32 20	www.fairtrading.nsw.gov.au
NT	Department of Justice	(08) 8935 7777	www.nt.gov.au/justice
Qld	Office of Fair Trading	13 13 04	www.fairtrading.qld.gov.au
SA	Office of Consumer and Business Affairs	1300 138 918	www.ocba.sa.gov.au
Tas.	Department of Justice	(03) 6233 3400	www.justice.tas.gov.au
Vic.	Consumer Affairs Victoria	1300 55 81 81	www.consumer.vic.gov.au
WA	Department of Consumer and Employment Protection	(08) 9282 0777	www.docep.wa.gov.au

does not commence, the business ceases, or the name is found to be similar or the same as an existing name or is otherwise unacceptable.

Trade mark, company and website names

Registration of a business name gives you no ownership of that name. It is not the same as a trade mark, company name or website domain name. If you want to protect your name, beyond the protection afforded simply by using it, by buying exclusive legal rights to it throughout Australia, you must register a trade mark with IP Australia, and details of how to go about this can be found on their website (see sources below). If you incorporate as a company, you have to register a company name with ASIC, although your company name need not be the same as your trading name. If you want to have your business name as part of your website address, you need to register a domain name. For names ending in 'au', visit the AusRegistry website, and for global domain names, visit the Internet Corporation For Assigned Names and Numbers (ICANN) website (see sources below).

26.8   Goods and services tax

Operation of GST

The GST is a broad-based federal tax of 10% on most goods, services and other items sold or consumed in Australia. Generally, GST-registered businesses add GST to the price of sales to customers, and use that to offset GST included in their business expenses. While GST is paid at each step of the supply chain, businesses don't actually bear the economic cost of the tax, because the GST included in the price of goods and services they buy is recovered in the GST on the price of goods and services they sell. In a television production, the GST included in production expenses is reimbursed from GST added to investor payments and sale of the program. The production business pays the Australian Taxation Office (ATO) only the excess of GST received over GST paid, or recovers the shortfall of GST received over GST paid.

Conditions for registration

If you are in business, you must register for GST when your annual turnover is $50 000 or more. Under $50 000, it is your choice whether to register for GST. Generally, if you have a significant number of business expenses, as do most production businesses, you will have a reasonable GST cost, and registering for GST will allow you to recover this cost. You need to have an ABN to register for GST, and can use the same application to register for both.

Goods and services that attract GST

Registered traders must include GST in the price of most or, more commonly, all goods and services they sell. An activity statement is completed every month, quarter or year to report GST on sales, claim credit for GST in purchases, and pay or be paid by the ATO for the difference. There are some GST-free goods and services, but these are not greatly relevant to the television industry. They include basic food items, some education and health services. Overseas expenses do not have GST, and therefore provide no offset for GST received from sales. If you are not registered for GST, you cannot add GST to the price of your sales, but you will still pay GST on your purchases.

Tax invoices

You must issue a tax invoice for all taxable sales, so your customer can recover the GST cost. The words 'tax invoice' must appear prominently, and the invoice must include the name of the seller/supplier (and for sales over $1000, name and address or ABN of buyer), ABN, GST-inclusive price and amount of GST. To claim a GST credit, you must have a tax invoice for purchases over $55 (including GST). For purchases under $55, cash register dockets, receipts or invoices are sufficient. You are not entitled to claim a GST credit for any portion of your purchase that is used for private purposes.

26.9   PAYG withholding

Registration

You must register for pay as you go (PAYG) withholding when you know you'll need to withhold tax, such as when you take on employees, or receive an invoice from a business that doesn't quote an ABN. You register online through the Australian Business Register (see sources below), or by completing an 'Add a new business account' (NAT 2954) form from the ATO. You can register for PAYG on the same form as for an ABN.

Operation

PAYG is withheld from employees' wages and company directors' fees, but not from contractors' fees, unless they don't quote an ABN or have a voluntary agreement with you. However, the fact that a worker quotes an ABN doesn't necessarily mean they are a contractor. This is determined from the circumstances of their engagement (see section 26.10). If you operate as a sole trader or in a partnership, and draw money from the business to live on, you don't withhold from these drawings, but it would be advisable to make provision for your income tax liability through the PAYG instalments system, or open a specific account to hold your accumulating income tax liability.

Withholding rates

To work out how much to withhold from payments to employees, use the PAYG withholding tax tables published by the ATO on its website (see sources below) and information employees give you in a 'Tax file number declaration' form and a 'Withholders declaration' form. Withholding rates provided in the tax tables approximate a payee's final end-of-year tax liability, taking account of some of their personal circumstances. If the employee doesn't quote a tax file number, you complete a 'Tax file number declaration' form with what information you have about them, and withhold 46.5% from all payments made to that employee. PAYG is not withheld from employees under eighteen who are paid no more than $112 weekly or $489 monthly.

Voluntary agreements

PAYG voluntary agreements enable businesses to withhold an amount from payments they make to contractors to help them pay their income tax. You can use the ATO form 'A voluntary agreement for PAYG withholding' (NAT 2772), or any written agreement that includes all the information specified on the form. The amount withheld is at either the contractor's instalment rate notified by the ATO, or a flat rate of 20%.

Withheld amounts

You should withhold 46.5% from payment to a supplier who doesn't quote an ABN, unless:
- the total payment to the supplier is $50 or less, excluding GST
- the supplier is under eighteen and payments are not more than $120 per week
- goods or services are supplied through an agent who has quoted its ABN
- the supply is wholly private and domestic, or made as part of a hobby
- the supplier is exempt from income tax.

Any withheld amounts are reported and paid to the ATO, using an activity statement it supplies. Withholders of $25 000 or less a year pay withheld amounts quarterly; withholders of $25 001 to $1 million a year pay monthly.

Payment summaries

Payment summaries show the total payments made and the amount withheld for each worker during the financial year. You must give each worker a payment summary (two copies) by 14 July each year, so they can fill out their income tax returns. Where a business hasn't quoted an ABN, you must give them a payment summary on the ATO form 'Payment summary – withholding where ABN not quoted' (NAT 3283) when you make the payment. Under tax law, you must keep all records that explain your PAYG withholding transactions for at least five years.

26.10   The status of workers

Terms of employment

Many (probably most) of the staff of a production company are hired project by project, contracted for a specified role on a specified production. This was covered in Chapters 13 and 19. There may be a core group of employees (they are more likely to be employees than contractors in law, no matter how they have been formally engaged – see below) covering ongoing office and financial needs. These people should have letters of engagement at the least. This helps to resolve any later disputes that might arise about exactly what the terms of engagement were. Terms of agreement in an engagement letter should include the period of engagement, whether it is fixed term or to continue indefinitely until terminated, whether employment is offered on a probationary basis, salary and frequency of payment, ordinary hours of work, entitlements (including superannuation, holidays, leave and provisions for overtime) and the grounds and process of termination (including period of notice).

Status of workers

It is important to know the status of production workers for tax purposes. They could be employees, from whose wages you generally have to withhold PAYG, or contract workers, self-employed and having a contract to provide services. You don't have to withhold tax from payments to contract workers, who provide for their own income tax liability. Whether a worker is an employee or a contractor depends on the circumstances under which that person works.

Employees and contractors

Employees are engaged under a contract *of* service, which assumes they are agents of their employer. The employer is legally responsible for their actions in the course of work. Contract workers are engaged under a contract *for* services. They act independently, so the employer generally has no vicarious liability for their actions. Contractors are engaged to perform a particular task, or produce a specified result, and are usually available to provide similar services to the general public. Payment is based on completion of these tasks or results.

Legal tests of status of workers

The ATO, and ultimately the courts if it gets to that stage, will apply a number of tests to determine the status of workers. These are summarised in Table 26.3.

Changing an employee's status

An employer cannot change an employee's status from employee to contract worker. However, an employer may be able to terminate a worker's job and contract that work out, and the ex-employee can tender for it. The employer would need to ensure the termination was lawful. You cannot avoid award obligations by creating a sham contractual relationship.

Labour hire

If a labour hire firm supplies some of your production staff, you pay the labour hire firm, not the workers. You are not required to withhold PAYG from payments made to labour hire firms, unless they don't quote an ABN.

Table 26.3: Factors differentiating employees and contract workers.

Factors	Employee	Contract worker
Control over work	Employer directs and controls employee's work; employer free to manage the business as seen fit.	Contract specifies contracted services to be carried out; contractor free to exercise own discretion in doing this.
Independence	Work performed according to the generality of an employment contract.	Contractor performs only specified services; additional services only by agreement.
Payment	Usually based on time worked, but can work on commission.	Dependent on performance of contracted services.
Commercial risks	Generally bears no legal risk regarding work; employer legally responsible for work carried out.	Bears legal risk regarding work; can make profit or loss, and must remedy defective work at own expense.
Ability to delegate	Performs work personally and cannot subcontract to another person.	Can subcontract or delegate work unless contract specifies otherwise.
Tools and equipment	Employer usually provides tools and equipment.	Generally provides own tools and equipment.

26.11   Payroll tax

Payroll tax obligation

Payroll tax is a state tax on the wages paid by employers, calculated on the amount of wages the business pays per month or year. The wages taken into account are those paid throughout Australia, not just in the state or territory of the business's office, but not those paid to workers overseas. A business must pay tax if its total Australian wages exceed the exemption threshold in its state or territory. In New South Wales, for example, businesses whose total Australian wages exceed $50 000 per month are required to pay NSW payroll tax of 6.0%. You must register with the Office of State Revenue (OSR) within seven days of the month in which wages first exceed $50 000. The OSR will advise whether payroll tax needs to be paid monthly or annually.

Working in other states

Payroll is not taxed where all the worker's services for the month were provided in other states, but wages paid in another state for services provided in New South Wales for the whole calendar month are subject to NSW payroll tax. Nor is payroll taxed for services that were provided in other countries for at least six months. Wages paid outside Australia for services provided mainly in New South Wales are taxed, regardless of how, where and when they are paid. Payment need not be made directly to an employee, or directly by an employer to incur payroll tax. They can be by or to a third party, such as an agent, or payment through a company or trust.

Payroll tax across the states

Payroll tax operates similarly in other states and territories to that outlined above for New South Wales. The main differences are in the exemption thresholds and tax rates, which are summarised in Table 26.4.

26.12   Other taxes

Fringe Benefits Tax (FBT) is a tax payable by employers for benefits paid to an employee or the employee's associate in place of salary or wages. It is separate from income tax, and is based on the taxable value of the various benefits provided. The most common fringe benefit is a car made available for the private use of an employee. Other benefits include cheap loans, expense payments, and meals and entertainment. Laptop computers, mobile phones and in-house health care are exempt from FBT.

Federal income tax is levied on the taxable income of a business, calculated on assessable income less any allowable deductions, the same formula that applies to personal income tax. The current rate is 30%.

Rates are property taxes, which are charged by local governments on properties in their municipal area.

The Simplified Tax System (STS) is an alternative method of determining taxable income for eligible small businesses with straightforward financial affairs. To be eligible, you must have an average turnover of less that $1 million p.a., and hold less than $3 million in depreciating assets. The benefits of the STS can include:
• an immediate write-off for assets costing less than $1000
• more generous, simpler depreciation for many assets
• no annual stocktake requirement
• an immediate deduction for business expenses, paid up to twelve months in advance.

If you are in the STS, and have an annual turnover of $50 000 or less, then you are eligible for the entrepreneurs' tax discount of 25% on your business income

Table 26.4: Payroll tax exemption thresholds and tax rates in Australia (2005–06).

State/Territory	Collection agency	Exemption threshold	Tax rate
ACT	ACT Revenue Office	$1 250 000 p.a.	6.85%
NSW	Office of State Revenue	$50 000 p.m.	6.00%
NT	Territory Revenue Management	$1 000 000 p.a.	6.20%
Qld	Office of State Revenue	$850 000 p.a.	4.75%
SA	RevenueSA	$42 000 p.m.	5.50%
Tas.	State Revenue Office	$1 010 000 p.a.	6.10%
Vic.	State Revenue Office	$550 000 p.a.	5.25%
WA	Office of State Revenue	$750 000 p.a.	5.50%

tax liability. The discount phases out when turnover is greater than $50 000 and ceases at turnover of $75 000.

26.13   Superannuation

Requirements

Most employees, whether full-time, part-time or casual, will be covered by the superannuation guarantee legislation. Employers are required to make superannuation contributions on behalf of their eligible employees (generally those paid $450 or more a month), at least once each quarter. The superannuation rate is currently 9% of the earnings base, which is salary for ordinary hours of work (not including overtime) and includes over-award payments, shift allowances and commissions. There is a maximum limit on any employee's earning base for each quarter, which for the 2006–07 financial year is $35 240 (i.e. $140 960 pa). Under federal superannuation law, the *Superannuation Guarantee (Administration) Act 1992* (Cth), section 12(3), you are considered to be an employee if you are a sole trader and work under a contract where labour is the principal component of the contract, and similarly under section 12(8)(c) if you are paid in connection with making a film or a television broadcast. Employers can claim tax deductions up to certain limits for superannuation contributions made for their employees.

Relevance of awards

Award conditions cannot override superannuation law. Award superannuation was introduced in the 1986 National Wage Case, but now lags behind most legislated requirements. Awards that provide for superannuation payments under a prescribed rate (often as low as 3%), or a qualifying period before superannuation payments become due, or exclude part-time or casual employees from superannuation, are overridden by the *Superannuation Act 1990* (Cth). There is, however, no superannuation obligation for employees under eighteen who work no more than thirty hours a week. Such a worker – a young actor, for instance – need receive superannuation only if an award requires it, and only to the extent required by the award.

26.14   Insurance

Workers compensation is compulsory for all businesses in Australia employing staff, and is covered by separate state and territory legislation in a system administered by a state or territory authority. Details of the authorities, their websites and principal legislation is provided in Table 13.2. Employees must be insured through an approved insurer against injury or death caused in the workplace. In New South Wales, seven insurers are licensed as Agents of the NSW WorkCover Scheme, the regulating authority. As noted in Chapter 13, 'employees' is defined quite broadly in legislation, and includes most workers contracted as individuals, as well as trainees and casual employees. A company contracted to supply a worker is responsible for their workers compensation insurance, although the principal contractor is generally required to ensure the subcontractor has done so. Through workers compensation, injured workers receive weekly payments to cover loss of earning capacity, payment of medical expenses, and vocational rehabilitation expenses, where necessary, to assist them to return to work.

Someone who is self-employed won't be covered by workers compensation, so they will need to cover themselves for accident and sickness insurance through a private insurer. Life insurance can be in the form of investment-type funds, where contributions over time are returned with interest at a maturity date, or as a more conventional insurance policy designed to cover risk.

Public liability insurance protects the individual and their business against the financial risk of being found liable to a third party for death or injury, loss or damage of property, or economic loss resulting from negligence. Its importance in television production lies in the fact that a production generally won't get access to locations without evidence that it has sufficient public liability cover, generally at least $10 million.

26.15   The list goes on

The above is not an exhaustive list of the taxes for which a business might be liable, or the insurances a prudent business might take out, but it does indicate the principal items that should be considered. Further responsibilities will depend on the specific operation of the business, and its particular requirements. No two businesses have exactly the same needs, but similar businesses have similar needs.

Sources and further reading

Some internet references

AusRegistry, available online at <www.ausregistry.com.au>, viewed 14 December 2006.

Australian Business Register, available online at <www.abr.gov.au>, viewed 14 December 2006.

Australian Securities and Investments Commission, available online at <www.asic.gov.au>, viewed 14 December 2006.

Australian Taxation Office, available online at <www.ato.gov.au>, viewed 14 December 2006.

business.gov.au, available online at <www.business.gov.au>, viewed 14 December 2006.

Cleardocs, available online at <www.cleardocs.com>, viewed 14 December 2006.

Internet Corporation For Assigned Names and Numbers (ICANN), available online at <www.icann.org>, viewed 14 December 2006.

IP Australia, 'Australian Trade Marks Online Search System', available online at <www.ipaustralia.gov.au>, viewed 14 December 2006.

NSW Office of State Revenue, available online at <www.osr.nsw.gov.au>, viewed 14 December 2006.

Index